2nd Edition

# dBASE III® Plus Handbook

# dBASE III® Plus

# Handbook

## 2nd Edition

### George Tsu-der Chou

Que™ Corporation
Carmel, Indiana

Dedicated to

my wife, Jane-Wen
and our children
Doris, Tina, and Tom

*Product Director*
David Paul Ewing, M.A.

*Editorial Director*
David F. Noble, Ph.D.

*Acquisitions Editor*
Pegg Kennedy

*Production Editor*
Bill Nolan

*Editors*
Gail S. Burlakoff
Katherine Murray

*Technical Editor*
Doug Ferris

# About the Author

George Tsu-der Chou, of Vancouver, Washington, is a consultant in the field of database design and development. He has developed database management systems for a large number of clients, such as Gregory Government Securities, Morley Capital Management, Hi-Tech Electronics, West Coast Lumber Inspection Bureau, NERCO, Inc., and others. These systems include analytical managerial database systems and administrative database management programs that deal with inventory and accounting functions.

The author earned his Ph.D. in Quantitative Methods, with supporting studies in Computer Science, Economics, and Econometrics, from the University of Washington. He is currently a full professor at the University of Portland in Oregon, where he teaches courses in business data processing and data management, quantitative methods, operations research, business forecasting, and other subjects. He has taught computer programming in FORTRAN, COBOL, BASIC, and IBM Assembler.

Dr. Chou wrote the popular *dBASE III Handbook* and *Using Paradox*, both published by Que Corporation. He is also the author of *Microcomputer Programming in BASIC* and *Computer Programming in BASIC*, both published by Harper & Row. The former has been translated into Spanish and published in Mexico; reprints of that book have also been distributed in the Philippines.

Dr. Chou has also written a financial analytical modeling program, COMPASS (Computer Assisted Portfolio Planning Management System). Combining database and analytical tools, this software represents the first major effort in the computerization of portfolio management. COMPASS, marketed by Morley & Associates, has now been adopted by many major banks and financial institutions in the United States and Canada.

# Contents

## 483 Appendix E: Built-In Functions

| PLUS |

# Trademark
# Acknowledgments

Que Corporation has made every attempt to supply trademark information about company names, products, and services mentioned in this book. Trademarks indicated below were derived from various sources. Que Corporation cannot attest to the accuracy of this information.

Apple is a registered trademark of Apple Computer, Inc.

Ashton-Tate, dBASE, dBASE II, dBASE III, and dBASE III Plus are registered trademarks of Ashton-Tate Company.

COMPAQ is a registered trademark of COMPAQ Computer Corporation.

CP/M-80 is a trademark of Digital Research Inc.

IBM is a registered trademark of International Business Machines Corporation.; IBM PC XT and Personal System/2 are trademarks of International Business Machines Corporation.

Kaypro is a registered trademark of Kaypro Corporation.

MS-DOS and Microsoft are registered trademarks of Microsoft Corporation.

Osborne is a trademark of Osborne Computer Corporation.

TRS-80 is a registered trademark of Radio Shack.

*Composed in Wiedeman, Megaron, and Que Digital*
by Que Corporation

*Cover designed by*
Listenberger Design Associates

*Book designed by*
Positive Identification, Inc.
Indianapolis, Indiana


Screen reproductions in this book were created by means of the
PRINT SCREEN program from DOMUS Software, Ltd, Ottawa,
Ontario, Canada.

# Introduction

Welcome to the wonderful world of dBASE III® Plus. Just a few years ago, the power of database management could be enjoyed only by users of large, expensive computer systems. However, the introduction of dBASE II® changed the way data was organized and manipulated on small and cost-effective but powerful microcomputers. As a result, individuals and small businesses could benefit from these types of database management programs.

Although many different database management programs are now available and new products are being added to the market almost weekly, dBASE II has maintained its leading share of the market. But because dBASE II was designed for the early generations of microcomputers and has limited memory capacity and computational power, the size of the database and the processing speed of the program were compromised. In addition, dBASE II was not considered user-friendly because its effective use required programming. However, the introduction of dBASE III® has effectively solved these problems.

Even though dBASE III evolved from dBASE II, dBASE III is a drastically different computer program designed to take advantage of the greater power of present-day microcomputers. The program's data-storage capacity and computational speed have been greatly increased; and dBASE III is easy to use, without sacrificing dBASE II's programming capability. Certain other database management programs that may be more user-friendly than dBASE III are adequate for many simple, small-scale database applications. But larger and more complex database applications need the strong, flexible programming features offered by dBASE III—features that have been matched by no other program.

Ashton-Tate, Inc., the developer of dBASE III, responded to the demand for a friendlier, more powerful program by introducing dBASE III Plus in late 1985. This new version of the program provides not only additional data-processing commands but also a pull-down menu interface; to perform many dBASE III commands, the user simply selects dBASE III Plus menu items.

## PLUS How Do You Use dBASE III Plus?

As a database management tool, dBASE III Plus has two processing modes: *interactive mode* and *batch-processing mode*. In interactive mode, you can create and manipulate data files by typing easy-to-use, English-like commands directly from the keyboard or by selecting the appropriate menu options. Because the computer responds instantly, you can monitor the input and output processes.

The other mode, batch-processing mode, is one of the most important capabilities provided by dBASE III Plus. Batch processing offers all the power and flexibility necessary for designing an integrated menu-driven database management system.

A primary objective of the *dBASE III Plus Handbook*, Second Edition, is to demonstrate how dBASE III Plus commands can be used for effective database management. For purposes of clarity, the examples in this book have been kept simple and concise. To maintain continuity among the examples, the same database is used to illustrate as many different commands as possible. Because of all the features incorporated, simple examples give you a better understanding of the underlying principles. Once you fully understand the principles of database management and the correct uses of the dBASE III Plus commands, you can easily design a more sophisticated database system of your own.

The *dBASE III Plus Handbook* is intended not as a substitute for the dBASE III Plus manual but rather as a user's guide that goes beyond the basics presented in the manual. The book shows you how the commands can be integrated to perform useful tasks. Furthermore, because the dBASE III Plus commands are grouped by functions, the *dBASE III Plus Handbook* may be used as a comprehensive reference manual.

# Who Should Use This Book?

If you own dBASE III Plus, you should use this book. If you compare database management with writing, you can think of the dBASE III Plus manual as a dictionary that lists and describes the commands and vocabulary, whereas the *dBASE III Plus Handbook* shows you how to compose with these commands and vocabulary items. From the easy-to-follow examples, you can learn how to design and create a database for your own data management needs. By duplicating the examples, you can learn firsthand how those commands are used for various functions. When it comes to mastering the dBASE III Plus commands, no approach is better than doing it yourself.

This book is also for you if you do not own dBASE III Plus but are considering purchasing the program. Chapter 1 introduces the concept of a database and gives you a general understanding of how a database can answer your data management needs. Chapter 2, "Introduction to dBASE III Plus," provides an overview of dBASE III Plus and of ways you can use the program to perform database management functions. Examples in subsequent chapters demonstrate the powerful utilities offered by dBASE III Plus.

If you own dBASE III, this book will be useful: You can learn about the new features of dBASE III Plus before you decide whether to switch from dBASE III to dBASE III Plus. All dBASE III commands are valid and acceptable in dBASE III Plus; those commands can be used for the examples in this book. Using dBASE III's interactive mode, you enter the commands at the "dot prompt." You can use the same method with dBASE III Plus; furthermore, you can also select appropriate Assistant menu options for many of the commands. The menu interface may seem more "friendly" to first-time users of the program; but after you have learned how to type in a command at the dot prompt, you may find this method more efficient than using the menu interface.

If you are a dBASE II user, the *dBASE III Plus Handbook* is for you. In addition to the comparison of dBASE II, dBASE III, and dBASE III Plus that appears in Appendix B of this book, the *dBASE III Plus*

*Handbook* provides in-depth discussions of new commands and programming features offered by dBASE III and dBASE III Plus. From this information you may see that you can significantly increase your programming productivity by switching from dBASE II to dBASE III Plus.

One of the significant new features offered by dBASE III Plus is its networking capability. Because of the complexity of setting up dBASE III Plus in a network environment, a complete discussion of that topic is beyond the scope of this book.

## What Is in This Book?

Chapter 1, "An Introduction to the Database Concept," discusses the basic concept of database management. The chapter introduces some commonly used models for data organization and explains the differences between hierarchical databases and relational databases. In this chapter, you will see the simplicity of the relational database model, which is the model chosen by Ashton-Tate for dBASE III Plus.

Chapter 2, "Introduction to dBASE III Plus," covers the specific features of dBASE III Plus and the development of the program from dBASE II and dBASE III. In addition, this chapter explains the design philosophy that makes dBASE III Plus a more powerful computer program than many programs currently on the market.

Chapter 3, "Getting Started," introduces the basic steps involved in configuring your system for using the dBASE III Plus program. The chapter begins with a brief discussion of the basic components of an IBM® Personal Computer and then explains how to initialize a disk with the disk operating system (DOS). In addition to describing how to install dBASE III Plus on your computer system, this chapter explains how to prepare the system disk and specify the necessary number of files and data buffers.

Chapter 4, "Creating and Displaying Data," begins a discussion of the dBASE III Plus commands and Assistant menu options that can be used in interactive mode to perform basic database management functions. This chapter explains the initial steps for defining a data structure and creating a database file. The chapter also discusses the menu options and dot-prompt commands used for displaying the information stored in a database file. Menu options and dBASE III Plus commands for managing disk files also are discussed in this chapter.

Chapter 5, "Querying the Database and Editing Data," discusses the steps for modifying the structure and contents of an existing database file. This chapter shows you how to use dBASE III Plus query operations to filter the records in an existing database file. Furthermore, this chapter illustrates the procedures involved in adding new records to, removing records from, and changing the existing contents of a database file.

Chapter 6, "Sorting, Indexing, and Summarizing Data," explains the procedure for rearranging the data records of a database file. The text describes the methods for sorting data records and indexing files and explains why one method is better than the other. Examples illustrate these operations in detail. In addition, this chapter introduces the dBASE III Plus menu options and commands you can use to generate such summary statistics as sums, totals, and averages.

Chapter 7, "Memory Variables, Expressions, and Functions," discusses storing data in temporary memory locations called *variables*. The chapter demonstrates the usefulness of expressions in data manipulation and shows how you can perform sophisticated mathematical operations and convert data from one type to another by taking advantage of dBASE III's built-in functions.

Chapter 8, "Generating Reports," introduces the methods for generating custom reports. In addition to explaining the dBASE III Plus menu option for designing and producing reports, this chapter discusses the program's powerful built-in label and report generators. You can avoid tedious, laborious steps by using these label and report generators to design custom labels and reports.

Chapter 9, "Fundamentals of Command-File Programming," introduces the use of batch-processing mode. The text explains how a set of dBASE III Plus commands can be assembled as a program file, which is then processed as a batch of instructions to be carried out by the computer. Through the use of numerous examples, this chapter shows the power and flexibility of batch mode. Most important, this chapter shows how easily you can use batch mode in complicated data management applications.

Chapter 10, "Input and Output Commands," discusses the ways in which input and output operations can be performed by commands in a program file. The chapter introduces program segments you can use to edit or append the data records in a database file and shows how you can use command-file programming to produce custom reports on a monitor or a printer.

Chapter 11, "Conditional Branching and Program Loops," covers the use of the DO WHILE command to perform database management functions that require repetitive operations. This command is one of the vital links between interactive command processing and command-file programming. The power of command-file programming lies in the DO WHILE command.

Chapter 12, "Modular Programming," discusses the concept of structured programming. In this chapter, you learn how to divide a database management system into several smaller easy-to-manage subsystems that you then link through a multilevel menu. You also learn how to design a database management program that uses several different database files.

Chapter 13, "An Integrated Database System," presents a model illustrating a complete database management system for a small business. In this chapter, you see how to design and integrate various data management functions such as billing, inventory, and account maintenance in a menu-driven dBASE® program.

# The Appendixes

The *dBASE III Plus Handbook* contains six useful appendixes. Appendix A presents the standard ASCII character codes. The differences between dBASE II, dBASE III, and dBASE III Plus are summarized in Appendix B. Appendix C is a summary of the function and control keys used in dBASE III Plus, and Appendix D is a summary of dBASE III Plus commands with many examples. The program's built-in functions are listed in Appendix E. Appendix F presents a summary structure of the Assistant menu options. These handy reference sections should prove valuable to both beginning and experienced dBASE users.

# PLUS Conventions Used in This Book

For purposes of clarity, different typefaces are used in this book to distinguish entries made from the keyboard, messages displayed by dBASE III Plus, and dBASE III Plus menu options from the surrounding text. Keyboard entries, when they appear in running text, are in *italic type.* Messages appearing on-screen appear as follows: End of file encountered. Menu options, such as **Setup** and **Create**, are also in a contrasting typeface.

Series of menu options and keyboard entries appear as follows:

Create/Database File/B:/*EXAMPLE.DBF*

The slash (/) serves only to delimit menu selections and keyboard entries; it is not entered from the keyboard.

In explanations of the "dot-prompt" commands, the dBASE III Plus dot prompt (.) is shown for illustrative purposes. The dot prompt is displayed by the dBASE III Plus program and should not be entered from the keyboard.

In illustrations of the dot-prompt commands and dBASE III Plus functions, angle brackets (< >) are used to indicate variable command elements, as in

. SORT TO <sorted file> ON <key field> FOR <a qualifier>

The angle brackets should not be entered; a file name, without angle brackets, should be entered in place of <sorted file>.

Because of space limitations, many of the command lines are shown on two lines in this book, even though the commands are actually entered on a single line at the dot prompt or in a program file. For example,

. SORT TO ROSTER ON ANNUAL_PAY/D, LAST_NAME FOR MALE

should be entered on a single line at the dBASE III Plus dot prompt or in a program file.

The [PLUS] symbol in the margin indicates that a paragraph or section discusses commands, operations, or program features that have changed or are new with dBASE III Plus.

# Introduction to
# the Database Concept

## An Overview

Database management systems have long been used to organize and manipulate large collections of business data. These systems are powerful computer programs that can effectively manage a huge number of data elements. Such systems are expensive, however, and they run only on large, sophisticated computers.

These difficulties were remedied by the introduction of dBASE II, the first database management program for microcomputers. With dBASE II, users of smaller computers could begin to enjoy computerized data management at an affordable price. With the advent of dBASE III and a new generation of microcomputers, new programs had capabilities approaching those of earlier programs that were designed only for large computer systems and that cost tens of thousands of dollars. The introduction of dBASE III Plus has further increased the power of the program.

dBASE III Plus performs most database management functions. The program is actually a set of tools with which you can organize and manipulate data in a simple yet effective manner. However, the effectiveness of these tools can be fully realized only by the user who has a clear understanding of the underlying concepts of database management. This chapter introduces the database management concepts that are necessary for the effective use of the dBASE III Plus commands discussed in the following chapters.

The basic topics covered in this chapter are

Database management system (DBMS)
Organization of data in a database
Types of commonly used databases
Fundamentals of a relational database
Basic components of a relational database
Functions of a database
A computerized relational database program, dBASE III Plus

The following special terms are introduced in the chapter:

Database
Hierarchical database
Relational database
Alphanumeric data
Numeric data
Relational database file
Database structure
Data record
Data field

# Definition of a Database

The term *database management system* (DBMS) has long been used to refer to the systematic organization and management of a large collection of information in a large computer system. Although used for some time by data-processing personnel, the term has become more generally known since the introduction of such microcomputer programs as dBASE II.

In the past, only computers with large memory capacities and high processing speeds could effectively handle the tasks of practical database management. Because of the introduction of such powerful machines as the IBM Personal Computers (IBM PC, IBM PC XT™, and Personal Computer AT) and the availability of low-cost, high-capacity storage devices, a reasonably large database management system can be implemented with only a limited investment. As a result, more database management systems are being developed for personal and business applications.

A *database* is a collection of useful information organized in a specific manner. For instance, you can view a personal telephone directory as a database:

| | |
|---|---|
| James C. Smith | (206) 123-4567 |
| Albert K. Zeller | (212) 457-9801 |
| Doris A. Gregory | (503) 204-8567 |
| Harry M. Nelson | (315) 576-0235 |
| Tina B. Baker | (415) 787-3154 |
| Kirk D. Chapman | (618) 625-7843 |
| Barry W. Thompson | (213) 432-6782 |
| Charles N. Duff | (206) 456-9873 |
| Winston E. Lee | (503) 365-8512 |
| Thomas T. Hanson | (206) 573-5085 |

This telephone directory is a listing of names and telephone numbers arranged randomly—arranged, that is, in the order in which they were entered. However, you can organize these telephone numbers in a specific order or form according to your preference. For example, you can group the entries by area codes and alphabetically by last name within each area-code group:

| | |
|---|---|
| Charles N. Duff | (206) 456-9873 |
| Thomas T. Hanson | (206) 573-5085 |
| James C. Smith | (206) 123-4567 |
| Albert K. Zeller | (212) 457-9801 |
| Barry W. Thompson | (213) 432-6782 |
| Harry M. Nelson | (315) 476-0235 |
| Tina B. Baker | (415) 787-3154 |
| Doris A. Gregory | (503) 204-8567 |
| Winston E. Lee | (503) 365-8512 |
| Kirk D. Chapman | (618) 625-7845 |

# Types of Data

Data can be classified into two main categories, *alphanumeric* and *numeric*, depending on the nature of the information and how it will be used.

# Alphanumeric Data

*Alphanumeric data* consists of alphabetic characters (letters A through Z), numerals (0 through 9), and some special symbols (such as # and $). For instance, the model number of a television set, RCA-XA100, is alphanumeric data. Names, account numbers, and employee identification numbers are other examples of alphanumeric data.

# Numeric Data

*Numeric data* can be quantified and is represented by the set of numeric digits. In a payroll database, the number of hours worked by an employee (for example, 38.5 hours) is an example of numeric data. The number of students in a class, the credit limit for a customer, and the level of inventory for a given item are other examples of numeric data.

Although both alphanumeric and numeric data are stored in a database, the two data types play different roles in their applications. Numeric data is used computations. Alphanumeric data, on the other hand, can be used only as text for identification or labeling purposes; alphanumeric data cannot be used in a formula. For instance, if you use the set of digits 83024 as an alphanumeric string that represents the identification number of an employee, the string is treated only as a label. The string may resemble a numeric value, but it cannot be used in a formula.

# Types of Databases

Information stored in a database can be organized or viewed in a number of ways. You can therefore define many different kinds of databases according to how the information is organized. The two most popular models of organization are the *hierarchical* model and the *relational* model.

# Hierarchical Databases

A *hierarchical database* organizes its contents in a hierarchical model resembling a tree. The hierarchical "tree" not only identifies the data elements in the database but also defines the relationships among these data elements.

Several types of hierarchical models are available. The simplest is the model that organizes all data elements in the database in one-to-one relationships. Other hierarchical database models define the relationships among data elements as one-to-many or many-to-many. Figure 1.1, a tree model of a classroom database, illustrates the hierarchical structure.

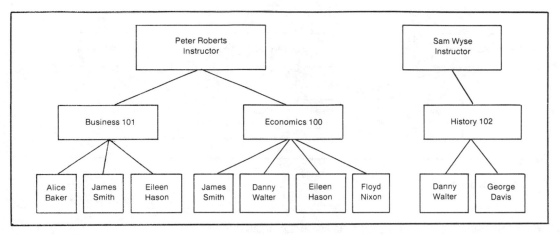

*Fig. 1.1. Hierarchical tree model.*

The data elements in this database include names of instructors, of classes, and of students in these classes. When the tree is viewed from bottom to top, the link between a student and a class is a one-to-one relationship; that is, any one student belongs to only one class. When James Smith takes more than one class, his name appears twice in the hierarchical database as two separate data elements. (One element belongs to Business 101; the other, to Economics 100.) A one-to-one relationship between two data elements is shown by a single line. A similar one-to-one relationship exists between the name of a class and the instructor.

However, when this hierarchical database is viewed from top to bottom, the relationships between an instructor and the classes taught and between a class and its students are one-to-many. For instance, instructor Peter Roberts "owns" two classes: Business 101 and Economics 100. Each class, in turn, has several students.

The classroom database can also be organized in another version of a hierarchical model. The network tree model shown in figure 1.2, for instance, gives a different view of the relationships among the same data elements.

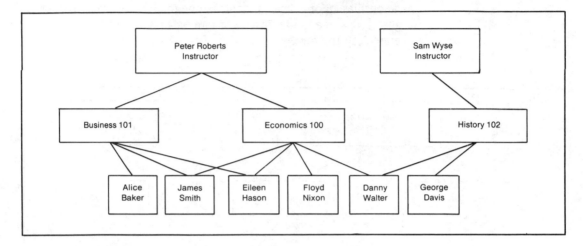

*Fig. 1.2. Network tree model.*

When the elements of the classroom database are organized as in figure 1.2, for some students the relationships with classes taken are many-to-many. For example, student James Smith belongs to more than one class, and each class has more than one student. Multiple lines connect James Smith and the classes he takes: Business 101 and Economics 100.

In such a network model, each data element is unique. The name of a student appears as only one data element in the model, even though the student belongs to several classes. For this reason, fewer data elements are contained in the network model than in the previous model; however, the relationships among the data elements in a network model are more complex. There are trade-offs between the number of data elements and the complexity of the relationships between them.

# Relational Databases

A database can also be organized on a relational model. The *relational database* structure was originally developed for use on large computer systems. Relational databases have recently become popular applications for microcomputers because of the simple structure that defines the relationships among data elements. With this structure, nonprogrammers can set up and manipulate interactively a large amount of information.

A relational model organizes data elements in a two-dimensional table consisting of rows and columns. Each row contains information belonging to one entry in the database. Data within a row is divided into several items, each occupying one column in the table. The classroom database is organized in a relational model in figure 1.3.

| Row # | Column #1<br>Instructor | Column #2<br>Class | Column #3<br>Student |
|---|---|---|---|
| 1 | Peter Roberts | Business 101 | Alice Baker |
| 2 | Peter Roberts | Business 101 | James Smith |
| 3 | Peter Roberts | Business 101 | Eileen Hason |
| 4 | Peter Roberts | Economics 100 | James Smith |
| 5 | Peter Roberts | Economics 100 | Danny Walter |
| 6 | Peter Roberts | Economics 100 | Eileen Hason |
| 7 | Peter Roberts | Economics 100 | Floyd Nixon |
| 8 | Sam Wyse | History 101 | Danny Walter |
| 9 | San Wyse | History 101 | George Davis |

*Fig. 1.3. Relational model.*

## Organization of a Relational Database

As shown in figure 1.3, elements in the classroom database are organized in a table of nine rows and three columns. Each row is a *data record*, and each column is a *data field*. A data field can be assigned a field name, which is an alphanumeric string serving as a label (such as INSTRUCTOR, CLASS, STUDENT). As each data record is entered, it is given a number similar to a row number in a table. This number represents the order in which the data record is stored in the database. The different parts of the record are stored in different columns, or fields. As a result, any data element in the database can be identified by its record number and field name.

The telephone directory presented earlier in this chapter can also be organized as a relational database. The data fields are defined as follows:

| Field Number | Field Name |
|---|---|
| 1 | FIRST NAME |
| 2 | INITIAL |
| 3 | LAST NAME |
| 4 | AREA CODE |
| 5 | PHONE |

The data elements in the relational database can be viewed as the table shown in figure 1.4, which has 10 rows and 5 columns. Each column, or data field, contains one item of the directory listing for one person. Each row represents a data record containing a person's name and telephone number.

| | | Data Field | | | |
|---|---|---|---|---|---|
| RECORD NO. | FIRST NAME | INITIAL | LAST NAME | AREA CODE | PHONE |
| 1 | James | C | Smith | 206 | 123-4567 |
| 2 | Albert | K | Zeller | 212 | 457-9801 |
| 3 | Doris | A | Gregory | 503 | 204-9801 |
| 4 | Harry | M | Nelson | 315 | 576-0235 |
| 5 | Tina | B | Baker | 415 | 787-3154 |
| 6 | Kirk | D | Chapman | 618 | 625-7843 |
| 7 | Barry | W | Thompson | 213 | 432-6782 |
| 8 | Charles | N | Duff | 206 | 456-9873 |
| 9 | Winston | E | Lee | 503 | 365-8512 |
| 10 | Thomas | T | Hanson | 206 | 573-5085 |

Fig. 1.4. Telephone directory as a relational database.

## Components of a Relational Database File

A *relational database file* consists of two main parts. One part defines the structure of the data records, and the other part contains the data itself.

### Data Records

The preceding examples have shown that the contents of a relational database are organized into data records and fields. A *data record* holds the data items for a single entry. In the telephone directory database, for example, a person's full name and telephone number make up a data record.

Data records in a database are usually arranged in the order in which they are entered. Each data record is assigned a sequential record number when the record is added to the database. Users can subsequently identify these data records by their record numbers.

### Data Fields

A *data field* is a storage unit holding a single data item within a data record. Each data field is given a name by which it is identified in the database. A field name contains a fixed number of characters, which may be a combination of letters, numbers, and certain symbols.

The contents of a data field may be an alphanumeric string or a numeric value. An alphanumeric string may be as short as a single letter or as long as a paragraph. A numeric value can be either an integer or a number with a decimal point. The number of characters reserved for alphanumeric strings and the number of digits reserved for numeric values must be clearly defined in the database structure before the data field is used.

In some database management systems, including dBASE III Plus, other types of data fields can also be defined. These field types are *date, memo,* and *logical* fields. Some of these fields are special kinds of alphanumeric fields, and others are reserved for holding data in special formats.

# Database Structure

A database structure contains detailed descriptions of each field in a data record. These details include:

*Field name:* name or identification of the data field

*Field type:* kind of data field

*Field width:* dimension of the data field

Defining the structure serves several purposes. When you manipulate data, you can use the field names specified in the structure to recall and refer to data stored in those fields. For instance, you can use the field name LAST NAME throughout a database application to locate all the information associated with a particular last name.

Specification of the data type dictates how the information is to be used. If you define a data field as numeric, items stored in the field can be included in formulas. But data stored in fields defined as alphanumeric can be used only as a label or as the object in a search operation; an alphanumeric string can never be included in a formula.

Because most database management systems assume that data fields are of a fixed length, the dimension of a data field is defined as the number of characters to be used by the largest data item that will be entered in the field. By declaring the dimension of a data field, you reserve the necessary storage space for anticipated data items. If the longest last name in your database has 10 characters, you must declare the dimension of the field LAST NAME as 10 even though some last names require fewer than 10 letters.

# Applications of a Relational Database

As the preceding examples illustrate, a relational database provides an effective means for maintaining and manipulating a large amount of information. Some useful functions you can perform on a relational database include:

Maintaining and updating the contents of the database

Locating and retrieving data that meet a given set of specifications

Sorting or rearranging a set of data items into a predetermined sequence or order

Linking data items in different database files to have indirect indexing on the data items

Data maintenance operations include adding data to the database, changing part or all of its contents, and deleting items from it. New data records can be inserted in a relational database, and any part of an item can be modified or deleted. In the telephone database, for example, a new telephone number can be added to the database by appending a new record to the end of the file. Any item in the database, such as an area code or a local number, can be modified or replaced. This data-maintenance capability is a useful tool for inventory management, as well.

Another important function in database management is being able to locate and retrieve data in the database by referring to the item's record number and field name. In a relational database, finding a record that contains a specific item in one field is a fairly simple task.

The ability to sort, or rearrange, the data records in a database is another valuable feature in a relational database management system. For instance, in a mailing-label application, having all the names and addresses in descending or ascending order by ZIP code is often desirable; and telephone numbers are usually sorted alphabetically by the person's last name.

Linking data elements in different database files is yet another powerful feature in a data management system. For instance, by using the account number as a data field in several files, you can link all the records containing a given account number in those files.

These functions are discussed more fully in later chapters of this book.

# A Relational Database Program: dBASE III Plus

dBASE III Plus is a relational database management system. The program runs on IBM Personal Computers and compatible machines, and is designed for creating, maintaining, and manipulating relational databases.

dBASE III Plus stores data in a relational data table. Information in the database can be processed in two ways. One way is *interactive command processing*. In that method, information in the database is manipulated by means of commands entered interactively from the keyboard. After each command is entered, results are displayed on an output device such as a monitor or a printer.

Another method for processing information with dBASE III Plus is *batch command processing*. Processing tasks are defined in a set of command procedures. The collection of commands is stored in a command file, which can be considered a computer program. These commands are then executed in a batch. With a batch-command file, a processing menu can be designed so that users can select specific tasks while the program is running.

The main objective of this book is to introduce the dBASE III Plus tools used in those two processing methods. You need these tools in order to handle effectively the information stored in a relational database.

# Chapter Summary

A database is a collection of useful information organized in a specific manner. The types of information stored in a database include alphanumeric text and numerical values. Alphanumeric text consists of information in the form of letters, numbers, and special symbols.

Information stored in a database can be organized in several ways. A database can be organized in either a hierarchical or a relational model. Data in a hierarchical database is organized in a tree structure with one-to-one, one-to-many, or many-to-many relationships. A relational database organizes the data in the form of a table that has rows and columns. Each column of a relational database is called a data field, and each row is called a data record.

A database consists of a set of data records, each of which contains data elements for a single entry. Each data record is given a record number and is divided into data fields. Data fields are identified by a name, or label. Names of data fields and the type of data to be stored in each field are specified in the structure of the database.

A relational database provides an effective means for maintaining and manipulating a large amount of information. Important functions of a database system include the ability to locate and access any item in the database, to sort data records into a desired order, and to link database files. These procedures are essential tools for managing business databases.

The term *database management system* (DBMS) has long been used to define a systematic way to organize and manage databases in a large computer system. Because of the introduction of powerful microcomputers and computer programs like dBASE III Plus, database management on microcomputers is now possible. The main objective of this book is to introduce the dBASE III Plus tools that can be used effectively to manage a database.

# 2

# Introduction to
# dBASE III Plus

## An Overview

The preceding chapter introduced the basic concepts of database
management systems and discussed their organizational models.
The material in this chapter concentrates on a versatile computer
program with which you can easily perform database management
functions. That computer program is dBASE III Plus.

dBASE III Plus is a relational database management system that
organizes data in data tables, which are logical and easy to read.
With no other special knowledge of computer programming, you
should be able to create a useful database after reading this book and
learning the simple, English-like dBASE III Plus commands.

dBASE III Plus can be used in two processing modes. By entering
your commands directly from the keyboard in *interactive mode,*

you can monitor all the input and output operations. Once you understand the dBASE III Plus commands, you will be ready to enjoy the powerful features of command-file programming in *batch mode,* which is the other mode in which dBASE III Plus can be used.

To provide a better understanding of the strengths and limitations of dBASE III Plus, this chapter presents the program's design philosophy in historical perspective. The basic structure and technical specifications of a dBASE III Plus database file also are introduced.

The following special terms related to a dBASE III Plus database file are discussed in this chapter:

> File name
> Character fields
> Date fields
> Numeric fields
> Logical fields
> Memo fields
> Memory variables

# A Brief History

dBASE III Plus evolved from an earlier database management program. This program, dBASE II, was developed several years ago; it originally ran on 8-bit microcomputers using the CP/M-80™ disk operating system. That version of dBASE II was used on various microcomputers, such as the TRS-80®, the Osborne™, the Kaypro® portable, and the Apple® II (with a CP/M® card installed). dBASE II later was rewritten for the IBM Personal Computer and compatible machines. Version 2.4 was released in September, 1983, for IBM PCs running under PC DOS V1.1, 2.0, or 2.1.

Before the introduction of dBASE II, database management systems were used mainly on large computers because the systems then available required powerful processors and huge amounts of computer memory. The processing languages for these database management systems were foreign to most nonprogrammers; processing data with those systems required programs written by professionally trained programmers. Because of the high costs of purchasing and operating database management systems, the power of database management could be enjoyed only by users of larger computer systems.

The release of dBASE II represented a bold attempt to tap the power of recently developed microcomputers for database management applications. Since its release, the program has become the best-known microcomputer software for database management. Although the limited processing power and memory capacity of the early microcomputers often compromised the power of dBASE II, that program revolutionized the way information was handled on microcomputers.

Early criticism of dBASE II was directed toward its slow processing speed and the small size of the databases it supported. These problems were due partly to the restricted processing power of microcomputers.

Nonprogrammers, furthermore, often complained that the programming language was difficult and time-consuming to master. dBASE II was not user friendly because its design philosophy was largely adapted from that of systems for large computers; database management applications for those systems were written by professional programmers. In addition, the computer language in which dBASE II was developed was not designed for performing the kinds of processing tasks required by a large database management system. As a result, the computational power of dBASE II was not satisfactory for some database management applications.

Since the introduction of dBASE II, computer technology has advanced rapidly. Most microcomputers now use powerful 16-bit microprocessors, which process data much faster than the 8-bit processors of earlier microcomputers. Large memory capacity also is now readily available at low cost. New and more powerful computer languages, such as the C language, have been developed and perfected.

In response to the technical advances in hardware and software, dBASE III was introduced in 1984. Although evolved from dBASE II, dBASE III is drastically different from its predecessor; dBASE III therefore cannot be considered simply an upgraded version of dBASE II. dBASE III is designed for the 16-bit microprocessor. Because the program is written in the efficient C language, the processing speed of dBASE III has been greatly increased. dBASE III also has a much larger memory capacity than dBASE II. The major differences between dBASE II, dBASE III, and dBASE III Plus are summarized in Appendix B at the end of this book.

The strength of dBASE II lies in its programming features, which provide powerful tools for creating database management applications. However, dBASE II is not designed to support menus, which simplify database management for nonprogrammers. dBASE III has corrected most of the deficiencies of dBASE II. With the help screens (detailed helpful hints accessed by a single keystroke) and the ASSIST command, microcomputer users can start manipulating data in a relatively short time. However, because of the program's tremendous power and flexibility, considerable time and effort are required to master dBASE III before serious business applications can be developed.

PLUS  Responding to the demand for an even friendlier and more powerful program, Ashton-Tate introduced dBASE III Plus late in 1985. Networking capabilities and a menu system distinguish dBASE III Plus from dBASE III. The networking features, which are beyond the scope of this book, include password protection and encryption of files, file locking, and record locking. The menu system is by far the more important improvement for the average user. Now, many operations can be performed by selecting options from the menus rather than typing commands at the "dot prompt." The menus therefore eliminate, in many cases, the necessity of remembering command syntax. Furthermore, the menus serve as a teaching aid for the user who wants eventually to learn to use the dot-prompt commands. As options are selected from the menus, the equivalent dot-prompt commands appear at the bottom of the screen.

# Design Philosophy

As mentioned earlier, the creators of dBASE III Plus adopted most of its design philosophy from database management systems used on large computers. The predominant mode of processing on large computers is *batch processing*. In this mode, tasks of data processing and computation are first laid out in a series of detailed steps. Each step is coded into a command, or instruction, in accordance with a set of clearly defined rules. This collection of commands, which constitutes a computer program, is fed into the computer. With no further human intervention, the computer processes the batch of commands. In batch processing, a complex application can be handled by a large set of commands that were coded and assembled before processing.

Batch processing is an effective method for data management; dBASE II, dBASE III, and dBASE III Plus all support that processing mode. In this respect, dBASE III Plus can be considered a computer programming language for creating database management applications. This outstanding feature in dBASE III Plus is not shared by many other user-friendly database software programs designed for microcomputers.

dBASE III and dBASE III Plus also support processing in *interactive mode*. This mode of processing differs from batch processing in the way the commands are issued to the computer. In batch processing mode, the entire set of instructions is fed to the computer in one file. Interactive command processing requires that each command be entered from the keyboard. In interactive mode, the tasks of data processing and computation can be carried out and monitored step by step.

This immediate feedback from the computer is one advantage of interactive mode. The feedback helps nonprogrammers understand what is going on during the processing stage. The immediate interaction between the user and the computer also permits immediate correction of mistakes in the entry of commands. These advantages are among the chief reasons why many recent developers of database management programs have chosen interactive mode as the primary method for manipulating data. Interactive mode makes database management software more user-friendly for nonprogrammers. But because of the nature of interactive processing, a complex application cannot be carried out by means of easy-to-use menus, and an untrained user cannot operate complex programs effectively.

dBASE III Plus can be operated in both modes, however. By selecting the appropriate options from The Assistant menu or by entering dBASE III Plus commands at the dot prompt, you can easily set up and manipulate a database in interactive mode. Complex tasks can be performed effectively by a command program in batch processing mode. The two processing modes make dBASE III Plus a flexible, powerful, and easy-to-use database management system.

PLUS

# Organization of Data

As a relational database management system, dBASE III Plus stores all database information in a relational structure. The items are arranged in a data table consisting of rows and columns, where each row is a data record and each field is a column. Information in a data table is stored on disk as a data file.

Many different types of data files are available; each is reserved for storing a specific kind of data. A database can consist of several data files of different types. Because information in a database is usually stored on an external memory device, such as a floppy disk, a data file is often called a *disk file*.

PLUS

# Types of Disk Files

Because different types of information are used in a database application, different kinds of data structures are defined in disk files. The types of disk files that can be set up in dBASE III Plus are

> Database files
> Database memo files
> Index files
> Command or procedure files
> Format files
> Label files
> Memory files
> Report form files
> Text output files
> Catalog files
> Query files
> Screen files
> View files

## Database Files

A *database file* is equivalent to the relational data table in that the file is composed of records, and the records comprise fields containing the data elements. (A relational data table is described in Chapter 1.) The contents of a database file consist of information in one of four forms:

A string of alphanumeric characters, such as *James C. Smith* or *(206) 456-9873*

A date in the form of *mm/dd/yy*, such as *03/25/85*, where *mm*, *dd*, and *yy* are the numeric codes for month, day, and year

A numeric value, such as *135.78* or *−25.89*

A logical character: *T* for *true* or *F* for *false*, or *Y* for *yes* or *N* for *no*

New database files can be created by choosing the Create/Database file option from The Assistant menu or by entering the CREATE command at the dot prompt.

## Database Memo Files

A *database memo file*, which is similar to a database file, is used to store large blocks of text called *memos*. A database memo file provides supplementary storage space for a database file. The memo text can be defined as a data field in a database file, but the contents of the memo field are stored in a memo file that is separate from the database file itself.

## Index Files

Sorting data into the desired order is an important function in database management. dBASE III Plus indexes the contents of a database file according to the contents of a specified field; this operation achieves the effect of sorting. An *index file* provides the necessary working space for indexing. With an index file, a set of data can be viewed or processed in a logical order rather than the order in which the records were entered in the database.

## Command (or Procedure) Files

A *command file* stores a collection of commands that are to be processed in batch mode. Because the set of instructions is often called a program (or procedure), a command file is sometimes called a *command program file* or *procedure file*. A command file can be created either with the text-editing program that is a part of dBASE III Plus or with a word-processing program in nondocument mode.

## Format Files

A *format file* stores custom screen forms that are used along with the data items in a database for data entry and custom report generation. The contents of a format file are created by choosing the Create/Format menu options or by running a batch file of dBASE III Plus commands.

## Label Files

*Label files* contain information used for printing labels with the LABEL command. A label file, which is similar to a format file, stores the specifications for printed labels. The specifications can include the width and the height of a label, the spacing between labels, and so forth. The contents of a label file can be created by selecting the Create/Label menu options or by entering the MODIFY LABEL command at the dot prompt.

## Memory Files

A *memory file* stores the contents of active *memory variables*. Memory variables represent temporary memory locations that can hold the results of computations. The results stored in memory variables can be used again in subsequent processing. A memory variable can contain an alphanumeric string or a numeric value. These values are saved in a memory file with the SAVE command; the RESTORE command is used to "read" the values from disk and store them in memory variables. Memory variables play an important role in data manipulation. For example, they can be used to keep track of the last invoice number issued.

## Report Form Files

*Report form files* contain information used for generating reports with the REPORT command. Information in a report form file specifies the contents of reports and their format, such as the information which is to appear in the report heading and the data items that are to be used in the report. Report form files are created with the Create/Report menu options or with the MODIFY REPORT command.

## Text Output Files

A *text output file* stores text that can be "shared" with other computer programs. For instance, a table of data created with dBASE III Plus can be written to a text output file. After you have exited from dBASE III Plus, that file can then be read by other software, such as a word-processing program or another database-management program. A text output file provides the link for information exchange among different computer programs.

## Catalog Files

PLUS

A *catalog file* holds the names of a set of related database files and their related operational files (such as format, report form, and label files).

## Query Files

PLUS

*Query files* contain information about the filtering conditions for displaying data records in an existing database file. A query file is created with the Create/Query menu options. Once it has been created, a query file can be saved for future use.

## Screen Files

PLUS

*Screen files* contain information related to the screen layout of a custom data-entry form. Although the dBASE III commands used to create the form are stored in a format file, the screen file contents are needed to modify the data-entry form by means of the Modify/ Format menu options.

## View Files

PLUS

*View files* contain information used for relating different database files. View files hold the names of database files and their associated indexes, format files, and other information defining the relationships among all these files.

# Disk File Names

PLUS

Each dBASE III Plus disk file must be assigned a two-part file identification: a *file name* and an *extension*. A unique file name is assigned by the user. The extension indicates the file's type. The extension consists of a period (.) and any of the following letter combinations:

| | |
|---|---|
| .dbf or .DBF | Database file |
| .dbt or .DBT | Database memo file |
| .ndx or .NDX | Index file |
| .prg or .PRG | Command or procedure (program) file |
| .fmt or .FMT | Format file |
| .lbl or .LBL | Label file |
| .mem or .MEM | Memory file |

| | |
|---|---|
| .frm or .FRM | Report form file |
| .txt or .TXT | Text output file |
| .cat or .CAT | Catalog file |
| .qry or .QRY | Query file |
| .scr or .SCR | Screen file |
| .vue or .VUE | View file |

A *file name* consists of a string containing no more than eight characters. These characters can be letters, numbers, or the underscore character (_). No blank spaces are allowed in a file name. The following strings of characters are acceptable file names:

PHONES.DBF
Accounts.dbf
PAYCHECK.FMT
ID_NO.DBF
LETTERS.DBT
mailing.lbl
ATABLE.TXT
Billing.prg

A file name, together with its file extension (for example, .DBF or .PRG), constitutes a symbolic name for the disk file. The file name and extension provide a unique reference for the disk file.

## Types of Data Fields

A *data field* is a division of a data record. Five different types of data fields can be used in dBASE III Plus:

Character (or text) fields
Memo fields
Numeric fields
Logical fields
Date fields

Each type of data field is used to store one type of data. The type of the data field governs the form in which the data must be entered and the way in which the data can be used.

Character fields and memo fields store text, which can include letters, numerals, special symbols, and blank spaces. Most characters defined in the American Standard Code for Information Interchange (ASCII) can be text characters. (A list of the ASCII characters is given in Appendix A at the end of this book.) However, character fields and memo fields are different. A *character field* can store a short text, but only a *memo field* can store a large block of text. In addition, the text stored in these two fields is used differently. Details of these differences are the subjects of later chapters.

Any values or numbers in a database can be stored in a numeric field, whose contents are used for computational applications. *Numeric fields* are of two types: integer and decimal. The sign (positive or negative) associated with a number or value is considered a part of the field contents.

A *date field* is used to store dates, which can be represented in various forms. A common format for a date is *mm/dd/yy*, where *mm*, *dd*, and *yy* represent numeric codes for the month, day, and year, respectively. A date in dBASE III Plus is treated differently from text or a number. Date values must be used only as dates in data manipulation; they cannot be treated as normal alphanumeric strings. Without conversion, the numeric codes in dates cannot be used in formulas.

*Logical fields* hold a single character that represents a true (T) or false (F) condition. A logical field can therefore divide the contents of a database file into two groups: one for which the condition is true and another for which the condition is false. For example, a database consisting of a set of student records can include a logical field to identify the sex of a student. A *T* entered in the logical field MALE indicates that the student is male, whereas an *F* indicates that the student is female.

# System Requirements

dBASE III Plus is designed to run on the IBM Personal Computer, PC XT, PC AT, and Personal System/2™ machines, as well as the COMPAQ® and other IBM-compatible microcomputers. The minimum computer memory required is 256K. Because computer memory is used as a working space during data manipulation, more memory usually results in increased processing speed.

dBASE III Plus requires MS-DOS® or PC DOS Version 2.0 or later. The system should have either two 360K double-sided floppy disk drives or one 360K floppy drive and a hard disk drive. The computer program usually resides on one of the floppy disks, and the database files are stored on the other floppy disk or the hard disk. The maximum data storage on a floppy disk is about 360,000 characters. A system with two floppy disk drives may be sufficient for handling small-to-medium-size databases. However, for faster processing and larger databases, a hard disk is highly recommended. Other hardware requirements include a printer with a capacity of at least 80 columns.

# System Limitations

The type of processor used in the microcomputer and the amount of available memory limit the size of the database. The available storage space on the floppy disk determines the number of files that can be stored. Furthermore, both dBASE III Plus and the disk operating system limit the number of files that can be created and that can be open at one time. A maximum of 10 database (.DBF) files can be active at one time, and 7 index (.NDX) files can be created for a single database file. Only one format file can be specified for each database file. Still, a total of 20 different files of all types can be active at one time during processing. Note, however, that a database file containing a memo field is counted as two files.

A database (.DBF) file can contain as many as two billion characters of information or a maximum of one billion data records. Each data record can hold up to 4,000 characters and can be divided into as many as 128 data fields. However, each data record in a database memo (.DBT) file can store up to 512,000 characters of text.

A character field can store as many as 254 characters of information, whereas a memo field can hold only 4,096 characters. A numeric field can store up to 19 characters, which can include digits, decimal points, and the sign of a value (a + or −), but no commas. Smaller yet, a date field holds a string of eight characters (mm/dd/yy), and a logical field can contain only one character (T or F, Y or N).

# Chapter Summary

In late 1985, Ashton-Tate introduced dBASE III Plus. This relational database management program is friendlier and more powerful than dBASE III, released in 1984 for the IBM PC. Although dBASE III Plus evolved from dBASE II, the two programs have significant differences in their design philosophy and processing power.

Because of the type of processor used in the microcomputer and the amount of computer memory available, certain size limits are imposed. dBASE II was designed for 8-bit microprocessors, and its processing speed is much lower than that of dBASE III Plus; a dBASE II database is much smaller than a dBASE III Plus database.

The power of dBASE III Plus lies in its built-in programming language, which supports an effective batch processing mode. Because of such added features as help screens and ASSIST commands, dBASE III Plus can be used efficiently in both batch processing mode and in interactive mode.

dBASE III Plus organizes data elements in a relational database model. Data in a database is stored in disk files. Various types of data files can be used for holding different kinds of information in the database.

A database file, which is equivalent to the data table in a relational database, contains the database structure and all the data records. The data structure defines in detail the attributes of the data fields within a data record. A memo file is used to hold large blocks of text. Format files, label files, and report files are used to store the information needed for generating custom entry forms and reports. Batch-processing commands are stored in command files. Index files and memory files contain information that can be used in the operations of data manipulation. A text file can be used to save text that is to be "shared" with other computer programs. Other disk files include catalog, screen, view, and query files.

In dBASE III Plus, five different types of data fields are available for different kinds of data elements. Character/text fields and memo fields are reserved for holding alphanumeric data. Numeric values are stored in numeric fields. Dates are stored in date fields in the form *dd/mm/yy*. A logical field contains a character that represents a true or false (T or F, Y or N) condition.

# 3

# Getting Started

## An Overview

Because dBASE III Plus is specifically designed to run on an IBM
Personal Computer (PC) or compatible machine, a thorough
understanding of the computer system is vital for effective use of the
program. This chapter therefore is written for the reader who has
little prior knowledge of microcomputers. The chapter begins by
discussing the basic components of a personal computer system.
Next, the steps necessary to start the disk operating system (DOS)
are explained, followed by the procedures for formatting a data disk
and for activating the dBASE III Plus program itself.

Before you use it, however, the dBASE III Plus program must be
installed on your computer system. Furthermore, the disk you will
use to start the program must be prepared so that the system will
accommodate the maximum number of database files and data
buffers you will need. This operation is called *configuring the*

*system*. You need also to designate the *default disk drive*, in which the data disk is to be found when dBASE III Plus is running. These installation and configuration steps are explained in the latter part of this chapter, and you may want to verify them before you proceed to the rest of the book.

One of the new, user-friendly features offered by dBASE III Plus is the interactive mode of processing available with the Assistant menu. The menu's components and layout are discussed in this chapter, as is dBASE III's original interactive processing mode—entering commands at the dot prompt.

The special terms introduced in this chapter include:

    System unit
    Microprocessor
    Internal memory
    Auxiliary memory
    Read-only memory (ROM)
    Random-access memory (RAM)
    Data backup system
    Disk operating system (DOS)
    Booting a computer system
    System files
    Cold boot procedure
    Warm boot procedure
    Installing the dBASE III Plus program
    Configuring the DOS system disk
    Configuring the dBASE III Plus system disk
    The Assistant menu

The following disk operating system (DOS) commands are explained in this chapter:

    FORMAT
    dBASE
    COPY CON: CONFIG.SYS
    COPY CON: CONFIG.DB
    TYPE

# The Microcomputer System

Computers were originally developed to perform tedious, time-consuming, and often complex calculations. Now they are widely used to assist business managers in problem solving and database management functions. Over the years, various types of computers have been developed; but until recently, business computers were large and expensive and required specially trained operators. With the help of professional programmers, computers were used mostly for handling business managers' data-processing needs.

The procedures for using these types of computers were usually complicated and difficult for nonprogrammers to understand. Most business applications also required specially tailored computer programs. As a result, computers were not widely used as decision-making and problem-solving tools by management until the recent development of microcomputers.

The introduction of the IBM PC represented a milestone in computer development. Because of the machine's computational power and ease of use, IBM PCs have become an increasingly important tool for business applications, including word processing, accounting operations, financial analysis, and database management. The IBM Personal System/2 (PS/2) computers, introduced in April, 1987, promise even greater advances in personal computer technology.

# Basic Components of the IBM Personal Computer

The basic components of a microcomputer system usually include four parts: the input unit, the processing unit, auxiliary storage, and the output unit. The basic components of an IBM PC and their functional relationships are summarized in figure 3.1.

## The Input Unit: the Keyboard

Although there are different ways to enter information to a computer, the keyboard is the most important input device. Diagrams of the IBM PC keyboard and enhanced keyboard are shown in figures 3.2a and 3.2b.

Like an electric typewriter, the keyboard has a set of alphanumeric keys used to enter information. However, the PC also has a set of 10 special keys that are not found on a typewriter keyboard. These keys, called *function keys*, are located on the left side of the keyboard and are labeled F1 through F10. Computers in the PS/2 line have 12 function keys arranged across the top of the keyboard.

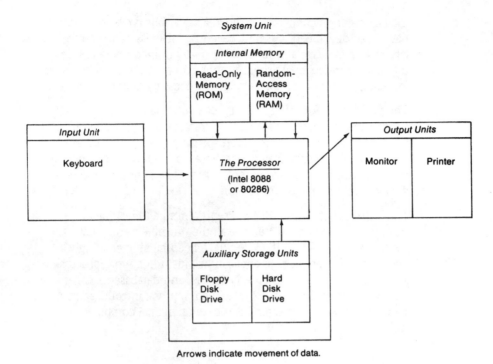

Arrows indicate movement of data.

Fig. 3.1. Basic components of a microcomputer system.

Fig. 3.2a. The IBM PC keyboard.

Fig. 3.2b. The IBM Enhanced Keyboard.

(The function keys are in a different location on some compatible machines. Consult your computer's manual if you are in doubt.) Each function key can be programmed to perform a predefined function. Several other keys, such as the Esc, Ctrl, and cursor (or arrow) keys are also unique to the computer keyboard. The functions of these keys in dBASE III Plus are summarized in Appendix C, and the uses of the keys are explained as the keys are introduced. (The current release of dBASE III Plus, version 1.1, "ignores" function keys F11 and F12.)

One important point to remember about using the PC keyboard is that when you enter information, the information appears on the monitor but goes no farther. The information is received, or "understood," by the computer only after the Enter key (which is marked with the ↵ symbol) has been pressed. You must therefore press the Enter key at the end of every command line.

## The System Unit and Microprocessors

The *system unit* of an IBM personal computer houses the "brain" of the computer. The main components of the system unit are the processing circuits, which use the Intel 8088 or 80286 microprocessor. Another part of the system unit is the control unit, which acts as a "traffic controller" regulating data flow within the computer system. Internal memory in the form of read-only memory (ROM) and random-access memory (RAM) is also part of the system unit. Auxiliary storage devices—floppy disk drives and a hard disk drive—are other components contained within the system unit.

All computations are carried out by the arithmetic unit of the *microprocessor*. Another part of the microprocessor, the logic unit, performs "decision-making" operations, such as comparing two values and determining whether one is greater than, less than, or equal to the other.

Most computer users do not need to understand the technical aspects of these microprocessors. The 8088 and 80286 microprocessors perform similar functions, except that the latter may perform faster computations and provide more accuracy in numeric manipulation.

### Read-Only Memory (ROM)

Two types of *internal memory* devices are contained in the system unit. The first, read-only memory (ROM), stores the programs and instructions necessary for controlling low-level operations of the computer. Because the information stored in ROM can only be read, or retrieved, you cannot modify the contents of ROM. They are normally set by the computer manufacturer and usually do not concern programmers or users.

### Random-Access Memory (RAM)

The second type of internal memory in the system unit is *random-access memory*, or RAM. The microprocessor can load, or "read," the contents of RAM and deposit, or "write," information to RAM. RAM therefore is used to store application programs and data. For instance, the code for interpreting dBASE III Plus processing commands and the contents of database files are stored in RAM during processing. Programs have full control of the contents of the random-access memory: they can create, modify, or delete any information in RAM.

The size of the memory is usually measured in bytes. A byte consists of 8 binary digits ("bits"), each of which can be represented by a digit, 0 or 1. Although the practice is not universal, most computers use 8 bits to represent a character; a byte therefore is the memory capacity needed for storing a single character.

The capacity of RAM in the personal computer is determined by the RAM chips available on the system circuit board. You can increase the amount of RAM by adding to the system a plug-in memory board with RAM chips. The maximum amount of RAM that can be used is also dictated by the disk operating system. To learn the maximum size of RAM for your computer, check the reference manual for your disk operating system.

## Auxiliary Storage Devices

To store large amounts of information, such as a large database, you need *auxiliary storage* devices to supplement the internal memory. Common external storage devices include floppy disk drives and hard disk drives. Floppy disks are one of the most commonly used storage media for the IBM PC. The disk drives in the IBM PC use 5 1/4-inch disks to record information, and the disk drives in PS/2 machines use 3 1/2-inch "microfloppy" disks. Floppy and microfloppy disks are an economic means for storing large amounts of information, such as programs and data files.

The amount of information that can be stored on a floppy disk is determined by the type of disk drive and by the *disk operating system*. IBM PCs use either single-sided or double-sided disk drives. The disk operating system for the IBM PC is PC DOS; different versions of DOS are identified by version numbers, such as V1.1 and V2.0. (With minor differences, MS-DOS is equivalent to PC DOS.) When used with a double-sided drive under PC DOS V2.0 or 2.1, a floppy disk holds 360K of information. A double-sided drive on the IBM Personal Computer AT under PC DOS V3.0 may store 1.2 million bytes (1.2 megabytes) of information on a high-density floppy disk. Microfloppy capacities are 720K and 1.44M.

The popularity of hard disks as auxiliary storage devices has recently increased dramatically because of their improved efficiency and reliability and their decreased cost. The storage capacity of a hard disk drive is much greater than that of a floppy disk. The amount of information that can be stored on a hard disk ranges from 5 megabytes to about 250 megabytes. A hard disk can transfer information from the disk to the processor much faster than a floppy drive. Because of these advantages, hard disks now are widely used on business computer systems.

## The Output Unit

The output unit in a computer system displays the results of computations or data processing. Output can be displayed temporarily on a monitor, or permanent "hard copy" can be produced on a printer.

### Display Monitors

The most common output device is a display monitor. Two types of display monitors can be used with the IBM PC: monochrome monitors and graphics monitors. With dBASE III Plus, either a monochrome monitor or a color monitor can be used.

### Printers

Printers are important output devices because they are used to generate a permanent copy of the output. In general, two types of printers are available. The types are differentiated by the way characters, or symbols, are generated. One type is the dot-matrix printer, which forms each character by a combination of dots (usually in a pattern of 7 columns by 9 rows, or 63 dots). Dot-matrix printers are fast and versatile and can print different type fonts. But because each character is formed by a pattern of discrete dots, the characters do not look as sharp as those produced by an electric typewriter.

With recent developments in printer technology, some printers use a high-density dot pattern. These printers produce what is called *correspondence-quality* print without sacrificing printing speed. In addition to text, many dot-matrix printers can produce graphics documents, with continuous lines and figures. Many of the more expensive printers can also produce charts, graphics, and text in color.

Another type of printer is the letter-quality printer. The printing mechanism of most letter-quality printers is a thimble-shaped printing element called a *daisywheel*. Letter-quality printers can generate output that looks as good as output from an electric typewriter. However, letter-quality printers are slow and have a limited number of type fonts.

# Data Backup System

Although hard disks are effective means of data storage for microcomputers, hard disks are vulnerable to hardware failures. Hard disk malfunctions often lock up the disk-retrieval mechanism. Consequently, none of the data on the disabled disk can be accessed, and repairs usually erase the contents of the disk. Regular systematic *data backup* therefore is essential to ensure that all data is maintained. Data backup means making an extra copy of the data and storing the backup copy in a safe place. Then, if the hard disk fails, the data on the backup disk can be used.

You can choose from a number of storage devices for backup. The most common is a streamer-tape unit that uses tape cartridges. Some units copy the contents of the entire hard disk to a tape cartridge; others provide the flexibility of copying the data file by file. The tape backup system is convenient and cost-effective for data backup.

# The Procedure for Starting a Microcomputer

The procedure used to start a microcomputer is usually referred to as *booting the computer*. Before a computer can perform any tasks, instructions must be sent to the processor. Some of these instructions are stored in ROM and are carried out by the processor as soon as the power is turned on. The computer must also have instructions for retrieving and processing the information stored on the disk drives. These instructions are in files called *system files,* which are part of the disk operating system (DOS).

# Starting DOS

The *disk operating system*, or DOS, is stored on a floppy disk that is usually supplied by the computer's manufacturer. The disk operating system, such as IBM's PC DOS V3.2, comes as a part of the contents of the disk labeled DOS System Disk. The system disk must be in a disk drive (usually in drive A) before the DOS program can be retrieved.

## The Cold Boot

DOS can be started two different ways. The first way to start the computer is called a *cold boot*. To perform a cold boot:

1. Put the disk operating system disk in drive A.

2. Turn on the computer's power switch.

As soon as the power is turned on, the processor is activated. Instructions stored in ROM cause the computer to perform various functions, such as checking the random-access memory (RAM) and activating the input and output devices (the keyboard, monitor, and printer). The computer then attempts to retrieve the DOS system files from the disk in the default disk drive, which is usually drive A. If found, the DOS system files are loaded into computer memory, and you are prompted to enter the current date and time. The following prompt then appears:

A>

This DOS prompt indicates that drive A is the active disk drive. At this point, the computer is ready to receive further instructions. If you are using a hard disk (on an IBM PC XT or Personal Computer AT, for example), you can copy the disk operating system to the hard disk, which may be designated as drive C or D; from then on, you can boot the computer from the hard disk.

## The Warm Boot

The second way of starting DOS, the *warm boot*, interrupts the current processing task and restarts the operating system. To perform a warm boot, you hold down the Ctrl key and the Alt key, then press the Del key. The current processing job is halted; DOS is reinitiated and the A> prompt appears. A warm boot takes less time because the processor does not check the RAM.

# Preparing a Data Disk

If you are using floppy disks, you need to prepare data disks to store the database files you will create with dBASE III Plus. A floppy disk cannot be used to store data until the disk has been formatted. When a disk is formatted, information is written on it that indicates to the disk drive where and how the information is to be saved on the disk.

## Formatting a Floppy Disk

If you are using a system with two floppy disk drives, you can follow these steps to format a disk:

1. Put the DOS disk (such as DOS V2.0, 2.1 or 3.0) in drive A.

2. Start the system with a cold boot or a warm boot.

3. Enter the date and time as requested by the computer.

4. When the A> appears, type the phrase

   *FORMAT B:*

   This command tells the computer to format a disk in drive B. Be sure to press the Enter key after each line you type.

5. Put a blank disk in drive B and follow the instructions displayed on the screen.

6. When formatting is finished, put the formatted disk away for later use.

## Formatting a Hard Disk

The storage space on a hard disk is usually divided into volumes.
You can think of each volume as being equivalent to a separate disk
drive in a floppy system; volumes are ordinarily designated as drives
C, D, E, and so on.

Formatting a hard disk volume is similar to formatting a floppy disk.
If you have a system with one floppy disk and one hard disk, a hard
disk volume (designated as drive C, for this example) is formatted
by following the first three steps given for the floppy disk, typing *C:*
instead of *B:* in step 4, and eliminating steps 5 and 6. You may also
format only a portion of a hard disk volume. Check your hard disk
reference manual for details.

# Installing dBASE III Plus

Before you start dBASE III Plus, you need to install it on your
computer system. Installation involves making a working copy of
the program that is set up for the configuration of your system. This
section gives instructions for installing version 1.1 of dBASE III Plus.
The procedures for installing version 1.0 are different because
version 1.0 is copy-protected, whereas version 1.1 is not copy-
protected.

dBASE III Plus version 1.1 is available in two disk formats: 3 1/2-
inch microfloppy disks and 5 1/4-inch floppy disks. Because of the
greater capacity of the 3 1/2-inch microfloppy disks, the files on the
5 1/4-inch disks labeled *System Disk #1* and *System Disk #2* are
shipped on a single 3 1/2-inch disk, which is labeled *System
#1/System #2*. If you are using the 3 1/2-inch disks, then you
should use use the disk labeled System #1/System #2 whenever the
instructions in this chapter or on your computer screen refer to
System Disk #1 or System Disk #2. Similarly, you should ignore
any on-screen instructions that tell you to replace System Disk #1
with System Disk #2 or vice versa.

The procedures for installing dBASE III Plus version 1.1 vary
substantially, depending on whether your computer has a hard disk.
If you are using a hard disk system, you should follow the
instructions in the section "Installing dBASE III Plus on a Hard Disk
System"; if you are installing the program on a floppy-disk system,
follow the instructions in the section "Installing dBASE III Plus on a
Floppy-Disk System." In either case, you should follow the

instructions in the next section, which tells how to run a program used for identifying ownership of your copy of dBASE III Plus.

# Running the ID Program

Before using dBASE III Plus, you must run a program that identifies you as the owner of your copy of dBASE III Plus. This program encodes your name, your company's name, and the serial number of your copy of dBASE III Plus and inserts that information in the dBASE III Plus program files.

First, jot down the serial number that appears on System Disk #1. Then follow these steps to run the ID program:

1. Start your computer.

2. Insert System Disk #1 in drive A of your computer.

3. Make drive A the default drive by typing *A:* and pressing Enter.

4. Start the ID program by typing *ID* and pressing Enter.

5. Follow the instructions that appear on the screen.

# Installing dBASE III Plus
# on a Hard Disk System

To install the contents of the two dBASE III Plus system disks on a hard disk, you must have about 540K of hard disk storage space. However, because you also need disk space for storing data tables and their related disk files, a minimum of about 1,000K (one megabyte) of disk space is highly recommended. To determine the amount of free disk space on your hard disk, you can use the DOS command CHKDSK:

*C>CHKDSK*

Before you type *CHKDSK* at the *C>* prompt, make sure that the DOS file CHKDSK.COM is located on the hard disk. If the file is not on the disk, an error message will appear:

`Bad command or file name`

Even if you intend to use only the hard disk for all your processing needs, you will need a floppy disk drive to install the program to the hard disk; all the dBASE III Plus system information is recorded on the system floppy disks. During the installation process, the floppy disk drive is designated as drive A and the hard disk drive as drive C.

To begin installing dBASE III Plus, have ready a DOS disk and the following disks from the dBASE III Plus package:

System disk #1
System disk #2

Then follow these steps:

1. Start the system with either a cold boot or a warm boot and wait for the DOS system prompt **C>** to appear. If you are starting the system from drive A, you can switch to drive C by typing *C:* at the **A>** prompt:

   **A>***C:*

   With this step you make hard disk drive C the current active disk. Unless specified otherwise, drive C remains the default disk drive. You are now in the main, or "root," directory of drive C.

2. If you will want to store the files related to dBASE III Plus in a subdirectory named *DBASE*, create the subdirectory by typing *MD* (for *make directory*) at the **C>** prompt:

   **C>***MD DBASE*

   When the **C>** reappears, you can verify the existence of the *DBASE* subdirectory by typing *DIR* at the prompt:

   **C>***DIR*

   The subdirectory will be displayed as:

   **DBASE        <DIR>        3-12-86 2:09p**

   (The date and time will of course be different.) You can change from the root directory to the DBASE subdirectory by typing *CD \DBASE* at the **C>** prompt (*CD* stands for *change directory*):

   **C>***CD \DBASE*

   Next, type *DIR* at the **C>** prompt to verify the subdirectory:

   **C>***DIR*

The DBASE subdirectory is then displayed:

```
Volume in drive C has no label
Directory of C:\DBASE
  .         <DIR>     3-12-86      2:09p
  ..        <DIR>     3-12-86      2:09p
```

3. Now insert System Disk #1 in drive A.

4. Make drive A the current drive by typing *A:* at the C>
   prompt:

   C>*A:*

5. When the A> appears, type *INSTALL C:*

   A>*INSTALL C:*

6. In response to that command, information appears on the
   screen as shown in figure 3.3. You are prompted to indicate
   whether you want to proceed; to do so, press *Y*. After you
   press *Y*, additional messages appear as files are copied to the
   hard disk. If you are installing dBASE III Plus from 5 1/4-inch
   disks, soon you are prompted to insert System Disk #2 in
   drive A and to press a key after you have changed disks.
   After changing disks, press the space bar to continue with
   installation.

```
              dBASE III PLUS VERSION 1.1
                 HARD DISK INSTALLATION

     You can copy dBASE III PLUS to your hard disk by following
     these installation instructions. You can also use these
     instructions to install dBASE ADMINISTRATOR.

     If you want to save a previously installed version of dBASE,
     uninstall it using that version's UNINSTAL program.

     If you choose not to save a previous version, install dBASE
     III PLUS Version 1.1 into the same directory. This will auto-
     matically erase the previous version of dBASE.

     dBASE III PLUS will be installed on drive c:

     Do you want to continue (Y/N)?
```

*Fig. 3.3. Initial screen of dBASE III Plus hard disk installation.*

7. Finally, the message

   **dBASE III PLUS has been successfully installed.**

   appears on the screen (see fig. 3.4). Now you can store your dBASE III Plus disks in a safe place.

```
Copying files to drive c:  . . .

        1 File(s) copied
        1 File(s) copied
        1 File(s) copied
        1 File(s) copied
        1 File(s) copied
        1 File(s) copied
        1 File(s) copied
        1 File(s) copied

dBASE III PLUS has been successfully installed.
A>
```

*Fig. 3.4. Completion of the installation process.*

# Uninstalling dBASE III Plus from the Hard Disk

If for some reason you want to remove the dBASE III Plus program files from your hard disk, follow the steps given in this section.

1. At the **C>** prompt, enter *CD \DBASE* (don't forget to press the Enter key at the end of each line):

   **C>***CD \DBASE*

2. Insert System Disk #1 in drive A and make it the default disk drive by entering *A:* at the **C>** prompt:

   **C>***A:*

3. When the **A:** prompt appears, enter *UNINSTAL C:*

   **A>***UNINSTAL C:*

   The uninstal procedure then appears, as shown in figure 3.5, and you are prompted to press *Y* to confirm that you want to uninstall dBASE III Plus.

4. After you press *Y*, further messages inform you that the dBASE III Plus files are being removed from the hard disk. Finally, you are informed of successful uninstallation, as shown in figure 3.6.

```
                    dBASE III PLUS VERSION 1.1
                   HARD DISK UNINSTALL PROCEDURE

        The UNINSTAL procedure allows you to remove a copy of dBASE III
        PLUS and dBASE ADMINISTRATOR from your hard disk.

        dBASE III PLUS will be uninstalled from drive c:

        Do you want to continue (Y/N)?
```

*Fig. 3.5. Initial screen of dBASE III Plus hard disk "uninstallation."*

```
        Do you want to continue (Y/N)?y

        Removing files from drive c: . . .

        dBASE III PLUS has been successfully uninstalled.

        A>
```

*Fig. 3.6. Completion of the "uninstall" process.*

# Installing dBASE III Plus on a Floppy-Disk System

If your system has two floppy disk drives, you can run dBASE III Plus from copies of the two system disks. (If your system has 3 1/2-inch microfloppy drives, remember that the contents of both system disks are contained on a single microfloppy labeled *System #1/System #2.*)

Preparing working copies involves two steps: making the copies, and copying certain DOS files to the working disks. Those procedures are explained in this section.

Before you begin, make sure you have your DOS disk, the dBASE III Plus system disks, and two blank floppy disks (or one blank microfloppy disk). Then follow these steps to prepare working copies of the dBASE III Plus system disks:

1.  Put the DOS disk in drive A, and boot up the system.

2.  When the **A>** prompt appears, type *DISKCOPY A: B:*

    **A>***DISKCOPY A: B:*

    to invoke DOS's DISKCOPY program.

3. The DISKCOPY program then displays the following prompts:

   `Insert source diskette in drive A:`

   `Insert target diskette in drive B:`

   `Strike any key when ready`

   (The messages may differ slightly, depending on the version of DOS you are using.)

4. Remove the DOS disk from drive A and insert System Disk #1 in drive A.

5. Put one of the blank disks in drive B, and press the space bar to begin copying System Disk #1.

6. When the disk has been copied, the message `Copy complete` appears. Then you see the message

   `Copy another (Y/N)?`

   If you are using 5 1/4-inch disks, press *Y* and then repeat steps 3, 4, and 5, this time inserting System Disk #2 in drive A. If you are using 3 1/2-inch microfloppy disks, press *N* to indicate that you have no more disks to copy.

7. Remove the disks from drives A and B, and label your working copies of the system disks. Put your original dBASE III Plus disks in a safe place.

Now you can copy the DOS files to your working copy of System Disk #1. Depending on the version of DOS you are using, your working disks may not have sufficient space for the DOS files. If you receive the error message `Insufficient disk space` as you perform any of the following steps, then you should delete the files

INITDB.BAT
INSTALL.BAT
UNINSTAL.BAT
YN.EXE
ID.EXE

from your working system disk (*not* the original system disk). Then you can repeat the procedure that caused the error message.

To copy the DOS files to your working system disk, follow these steps:

1. Put your DOS disk in drive A and the working copy of System Disk #1 in drive B.

2. At the A> prompt, enter the command *SYS B:* to copy DOS's system files to the working disk:

   A>*SYS B:*

   When the copying is complete, the message **System transferred** appears, and you can proceed.

3. At the A> prompt, enter the command *COPY COMMAND.COM B:* to copy the DOS command-interpreter file to the working disk:

   A>*COPY COMMAND.COM B:*

   After the message **1 File(s) copied** appears, you can remove the DOS disk from drive A.

# Configuring the dBASE III Plus System Disk

dBASE III Plus is designed to be used on a system with two floppy disk drives or with one floppy and one hard disk. During processing, the program "assumes" that one of the dBASE III Plus system disks is in drive A. The data files created by the program are stored either on the second floppy disk, which is designated as drive B, or on the hard disk, which is usually designated as drive C. During data manipulation, the program needs to know which is the data-disk drive.

You can specify the data disk drive in either of two ways: by providing the drive identification (drive B or drive C, for example) during processing or by recording the drive identification in a CONFIG.DB file on the dBASE III Plus system disk. The latter method is often preferred. When the dBASE III Plus system disk is configured with information about the data disk drive, data files will be saved automatically on the designated disk drive.

Normally, the CONFIG.DB file has been created and saved on the dBASE III Plus System Disk #1. That file contains processing commands that initiate certain operations when the program is first activated, but CONFIG.DB does not usually contain information about the data-disk drive. Therefore, you may want to specify the default data disk drive by modifying the CONFIG.DB file to include the command

   DEFAULT=<default disk drive>

You enter a letter in place of <default disk drive>.

If you plan to run dBASE III Plus from a hard disk, you may want to store both the dBASE III Plus program and the data files on the same disk drive (for example, drive C). In such a case, there is no need to identify the data-disk drive. By default, the program will always consider the drive on which you begin the program as the data disk drive. However, if you plan to use dBASE III Plus on a two floppy system, you will need to reserve drive B for storing your data files because there will not be enough room on the system disk for your data. In that case, you should specify drive B as the data disk drive in the CONFIG.DB file; this CONFIG.DB file must be present on the System Disk #1 before you start the dBASE III Plus program.

To specify the data disk drive in the CONFIG.DB file on System Disk #1, follow these steps:

1. Insert the installed System Disk #1 in drive A and boot up the system.

2. When the A> has appeared, enter *TYPE CONFIG.DB:*

   A>*TYPE CONFIG.DB*

3. The contents of the file then are displayed in response to the line typed in step 2:

   STATUS=ON
   COMMAND=ASSIST

   The message **File not found** will let you know if the CONFIG.DB file is not on System Disk #1. In either case, you may proceed; the CONFIG.DB file will be created in the following steps.

4. At the A> prompt, type *COPY CON: CONFIG.DB:*

   A>*COPY CON: CONFIG.DB*

5. Next, type the following three lines; press Enter at the end of each line:

   STATUS=ON
   COMMAND=ASSIST
   DEFAULT=B:

6. Press the F6 function key; ^Z appears when you do so. Then press Enter. The message **1 File(s) copied** will appear, and the configuration process is complete.

# System Configuration for dBASE III Plus

dBASE III Plus is a program that instructs the computer to perform the tasks required for managing a database. The computer program consists of a set of commands that are coded and stored on the dBASE III Plus system disk. Before dBASE III Plus is loaded into memory, the computer must be informed about the environment in which the program is to be operated. For example, the number of files to be used by the program and the amount of memory to be reserved for data storage must be specified before the program is loaded. The default disk drive for data storage must also be designated so that the disk operating system can locate the data files when they are needed. You provide this information in a procedure called *system configuration*.

System configuration involves specifying necessary parameters, such as the number of files and the size of reserved memory, and designating the default disk drive on the dBASE III Plus system disk.

Booting the computer begins the execution of instructions stored in ROM. The computer is instructed to initialize the input and output devices and to allocate memory space for normal processing. By default, DOS sets at 8 the number of files that can be open at one time; however, 5 files are used by DOS, leaving only 3 for the user's programs. Because dBASE III Plus can accommodate a total of 15 files, you must set the number of files to 20 during system configuration.

The processor sets aside a certain amount of computer memory as temporary working space for manipulation of disk data. This temporary working space is reserved in blocks of RAM that are called *buffers*. The more buffers you reserve, the faster processing is achieved. The total number of buffers is restricted by the amount of RAM available on the computer system. Because the dBASE III Plus program itself and the active data files used in the program compete with buffers for memory space, the number of buffers should not be set too high. Otherwise, you will not have enough memory for storing your database files during processing. With a minimum of 256K RAM in the computer, you should be safe to designate 15 memory buffers; that is the number recommended by the dBASE III Plus developers.

When settings other than the default settings are chosen, information about the number of files and the number of buffers is communicated to the computer through a file called CONFIG.SYS. dBASE III Plus supplies the CONFIG.SYS file on System Disk #1. If you are using the installed System Disk #1 to start the dBASE III Plus program, you therefore do not need to add another file to the disk.

However, if you install the dBASE III Plus program on a hard disk under the DBASE subdirectory, the CONFIG.SYS file must be saved in the main, or "root," directory. Therefore, you must copy the CONFIG.SYS file from System Disk #1 to the root directory of drive C. To do so, follow these steps:

1. Use either a warm boot or a cold boot to start up the computer. Move from the DBASE subdirectory to the root directory of drive C by typing *CD \* at the **C>** prompt:

   **C>***CD \*

2. When the **C>** prompt appears, insert System Disk #1 in drive A.

3. Type *COPY A:CONFIG.SYS:* at the **C>** prompt.

   **C>***COPY A: CONFIG.SYS*

4. The message **1 File(s) copied** indicates that the copying process is completed.

If you want to verify the configuration procedure and to examine the contents of the CONFIG.SYS file, enter the following command at the **C>** prompt:

**C>***TYPE CONFIG.SYS*

The contents of the CONFIG.SYS file will be displayed for verification:

**FILES=20**
**BUFFERS=15**

If you find errors in the file, you must either use a word-processing program to edit the contents of the file or re-create the file by following these steps:

1. At the **C>** prompt, type *COPY CON: CONFIG.SYS:*

   **C>***COPY CON: CONFIG.SYS*

2. Next, type the following two lines; press Enter at the end of each line:

   *FILES=20*
   *BUFFERS=15*

3. Press the F6 function key; ^Z appears when you do so. Then press the Enter key. When the message **1 File(s) copied** appears, the configuration process is completed.

# Starting the dBASE III Plus Program

After you have installed dBASE III Plus on your computer system and made certain that the system is configured properly with the CONFIG.DB and CONFIG.SYS files, you are ready to start using dBASE III Plus.

## Starting dBASE III Plus from System Disk #1

If you plan to run the dBASE III Plus program on a two floppy drive system, start the program with the following procedure:

1. Insert System Disk #1 in drive A and start the computer system with either a cold boot or a warm boot. Soon, the system will prompt you for the current date.

2. Enter the current date, and press the Enter key. Next, enter the current time when the system prompts you for new time.

3. When the A> prompt appears, type *DBASE:*

   A>*DBASE*

4. After a short time, the first dBASE III Plus message screen will appear (see fig. 3.7). Press Enter to continue.

5. When the message **Insert System Disk 2 and press ENTER....** appears at the bottom of the screen (see fig. 3.8), remove System Disk #1 from drive A, insert System Disk #2 in that drive, and press the Enter key.

```
                    dBASE III PLUS  Version 1.1
                    This Software is Licensed to:
                          Jane Q. Public
                          ABC Corporation
                          3650221-19

          Copyright (c) Ashton-Tate 1985, 1986. All Rights Reserved.
      dBASE, dBASE III PLUS and Ashton-Tate are trademarks of Ashton-Tate

      You may use the software and  printed materials in  the dBASE III
      PLUS package under the  terms of the  Software License Agreement;
      please  read it.   In summary,  Ashton-Tate grants you a paid-up,
      non-transferable,  personal license to use dBASE III  PLUS on one
      computer  work  station.   You  do  not become  the owner  of the
      package nor do  you have  the  right  to  copy  (except permitted
      backups of  the  software)  or  alter  the  software or printed
      materials.   You are legally accountable for any violation of the
      License Agreement and copyright, trademark, or trade secret law.
```

`Command Line   ‖<B:>‖                                        ‖Num`

```
      Press ↵ to assent to the License Agreement and begin dBASE III PLUS.
```

Fig. 3.7. Running dBASE III Plus from the floppy disk drive.

```
                    dBASE III PLUS  Version 1.1
                    This Software is Licensed to:
                       Product Development Dept.
                          Que Corporation
                          3650221-19

          Copyright (c) Ashton-Tate 1985, 1986. All Rights Reserved.
      dBASE, dBASE III PLUS and Ashton-Tate are trademarks of Ashton-Tate

      You may use the software and  printed materials in  the dBASE III
      PLUS package under the  terms of the  Software License Agreement;
      please  read it.   In summary,  Ashton-Tate grants you a paid-up,
      non-transferable,  personal license to use dBASE III  PLUS on one
      computer  work  station.   You  do  not become  the owner  of the
      package nor do  you have  the  right  to  copy  (except permitted
      backups of  the  software)  or  alter  the  software or printed
      materials.   You are legally accountable for any violation of the
      License Agreement and copyright, trademark, or trade secret law.
```

`Command Line   ‖<B:>‖                                        ‖Num`

```
      Insert System Disk 2 and press ENTER, or press Ctrl-C to abort.
```

Fig. 3.8. Prompt for inserting System Disk 2.

6. In response to the Enter keystroke, the Assistant menu's opening screen is displayed (see fig. 3.9). Now you are ready to use dBASE III Plus to perform data management operations.

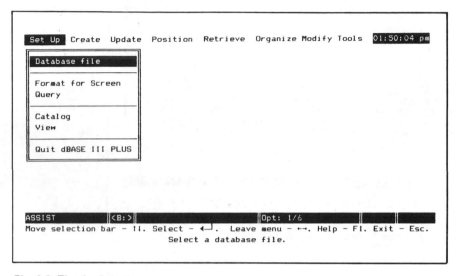

Fig. 3.9. The Assistant menu.

# Starting dBASE III Plus from the Hard Disk

If you plan to run dBASE III Plus from the hard disk on which the program has been installed (assumed to be drive C), you can start the program with the following procedure:

1. Start the computer system with either a cold boot or a warm boot, and move to the DBASE subdirectory by typing *CD \DBASE* at the C> prompt:

   C>*CD \DBASE*

2. When the C> prompt reappears, type *DBASE* at the prompt:

   C>*DBASE*

3. Soon, the first dBASE III Plus message screen will appear (see fig. 3.10). Press Enter to continue.

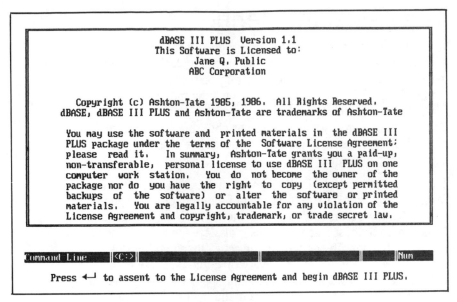

Fig. 3.10. Running dBASE III Plus from the hard disk.

4. In response to the Enter keystroke, the opening Assistant menu is displayed (see fig. 3.11). You are now ready to use dBASE III Plus.

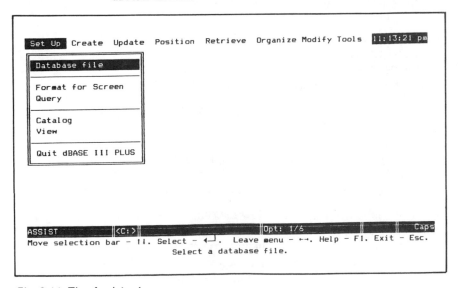

Fig. 3.11. The Assistant menu.

# The Assistant Menu

Whether you start the dBASE III Plus program from System Disk #1 or from the hard disk, the opening menu will look almost the same, except that the default data disk drive may be specified differently (compare figs. 3.9 and 3.11). After the opening menu is displayed, you enter one of the dBASE III Plus interactive processing modes. You can select a processing operation by choosing the appropriate option from the Assistant menu. The options are listed on the menu bar at the top of the menu.

The current active menu option (Set Up, in fig. 3.11) appears in reverse video, with dark text on a light background. (The figures in this book show reverse video as white text on a black background.) Notice that a list of submenu options is displayed in a box below the highlighted option. Depending on the active menu option, the number of submenu options may vary. In addition, some menu options lead to several levels of submenu options. Various levels of submenu options under the Retrieve menu option, as well as the other components of the Assistant menu, are illustrated in figure 3.12.

The basic components of the Assistant menu are

> The menu bar
> The submenu area
> The action line
> The status bar
> The navigation line
> The message line
> The current time window

The menu bar at the top of the screen displays the menu options available for performing various operations. The current active menu option is displayed in reverse video. The current menu option's submenu options are displayed immediately below the menu bar. This area is used also to display information about the current database file; that information can be helpful in data manipulations.

The action line, which appears below the submenu area, shows the dBASE III Plus command generated by the Assistant menu. The status bar, which is displayed in the lower portion of the menu screen, shows you which disk drive is active and which database file is in use. The status bar also displays the total number of records in the current file and the current record number. While you select

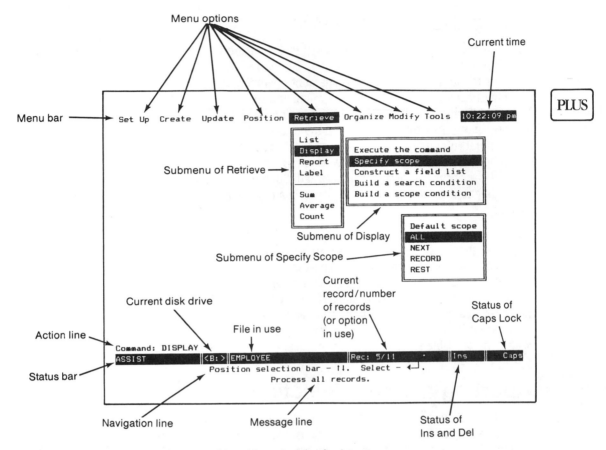

Fig. 3.12. Components and layout of the Assistant menu.

submenu options, the current option number is also shown in the status bar; it appears where the record number appears in figure 3.12. In addition, the status bar indicates whether the Ins (insert), Del (delete), or Caps Lock key has been pressed.

Located below the status bar, the navigation line shows you how to move between menu or submenu options. The message line at the bottom of the Assistant menu displays the current menu option. The current time is continuously updated and displayed in a window in the upper right corner of the menu screen.

## ⎡PLUS⎤ Using the Assistant Menu

One significant improvement of dBASE III Plus compared with dBASE III is the addition of the powerful, easy-to-use, pull-down Assistant menu. Most database management operations can be accomplished by selecting appropriate menu and submenu options. Detailed information displayed in the navigation line informs you at all times about how to move between menu and submenu options. As a general rule, you will use the ← and → keys to move between menu options. As you use the arrow keys to move along the menu bar, the current menu option is highlighted. Submenu options for the highlighted menu option are displayed in a box below the menu option.

To move within the list of submenu options, you use the ↑ and ↓ keys to highlight the option you want to select. Then you press the Enter key to select the option. You repeat this process to select several levels of submenu options. As soon as you have selected a submenu option, another list of submenu options (if there is one) is displayed in a double-bar box in the submenu area. These submenu boxes are laid out in relation to other existing submenu boxes within the available screen space.

## ⎡PLUS⎤ Aborting a Menu Selection

If you have made a mistake or have decided to abort the operation while selecting menu and submenu options, use the Esc (escape) key to undo the selection. Each time you press Esc, you are moved back one level to the previous submenu choice. However, if you are at the main menu (refer to figs. 3.9 and 3.11) when you press the Esc key, you leave the Assistant menu and enter "dot-prompt mode." As you will learn later, dot-prompt mode is another processing mode provided for database management with dBASE III Plus. When you have entered dot-prompt mode, the Assistant menu will disappear. The screen will be cleared of everything but the status bar, the message line, and the dot prompt, which appears directly above the status bar (see fig. 3.13).

If you have accidentally entered dot-prompt mode, however, you can return easily to the Assistant menu. Simply type *ASSIST* at the dot prompt (see fig. 3.14).

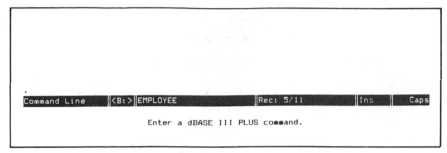

*Fig. 3.13. The dot-prompt screen.*

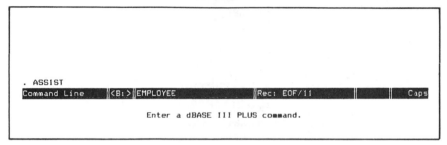

*Fig. 3.14. Returning to the Assistant menu from the dot prompt.*

# Menu Structure

PLUS

When you use the Assistant menu for data manipulation, you can perform the necessary operations by selecting a sequence of menu and submenu options. For instance, to display all the records in a database file named EMPLOYEE, you would choose (in a specific sequence) all the highlighted menu and submenu options shown in figure 3.12. The menu selection sequence for displaying all the records in the EMPLOYEE database file can be described with the following symbols:

Retrieve/Display/Specify scope/ALL

In this book, slashes are placed between menu and submenu options.

The first level of the submenu structure for the Assistant menu options is summarized in table 3.1. Appendix F contains a complete submenu structure for all the Assistant menu options.

## Table 3.1
## First-Level Submenu Options

| *Main-Menu Options* | *Submenu Options* |
|---|---|
| Set Up | Database file |
|  | Format for Screen |
|  | Query |
|  | Catalog |
|  | View |
|  | Quit dBASE III Plus |
| Create | Database file |
|  | Format |
|  | View |
|  | Query |
|  | Report |
|  | Label |
| Update | Append |
|  | Edit |
|  | Display |
|  | Browse |
|  | Replace |
|  | Delete |
|  | Recall |
|  | Pack |
| Position | Seek |
|  | Locate |
|  | Continue |
|  | Skip |
|  | Goto Record |
| Retrieve | List |
|  | Display |
|  | Report |
|  | Label |
|  | Sum |
|  | Average |
|  | Count |
| Organize | Index |
|  | Sort |
|  | Copy |

| Modify | Database file |
|--------|---------------|
|        | Format        |
|        | View          |
|        | Query         |
|        | Report        |
|        | Label         |
| Tools  | Set drive     |
|        | Copy file     |
|        | Directory     |
|        | Rename        |
|        | Erase         |
|        | List structure |
|        | Import        |
|        | Export        |

# The Dot Prompt

In interactive processing mode, you can manipulate data not only by using the Assistant menu but also by entering dBASE III Plus commands at the dot prompt. For example, you can display all the records in the current active database file out by entering the command *DISPLAY ALL* (see fig. 3.15).

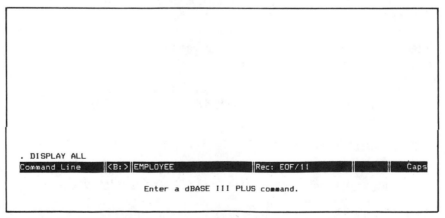

*Fig. 3.15. The DISPLAY ALL command, entered at the dot prompt.*

Entering dBASE III commands at the dot prompt is a quick, efficient way to manipulate data. For beginning users of dBASE III Plus, the Assistant menu seems an easy, natural way of manipulating the information in a database. After you have learned the basics of dBASE III Plus, however, you may find that entering the dBASE III commands at the dot prompt is the more efficient way. By selecting options from the Assistant menu and submenus you are in effect building a dBASE III command with various clauses. The dBASE III command that you are building is shown in the action line, directly above the menu screen's status bar. You achieve the same effect by entering the dBASE III command at the dot prompt. Whichever method you use, you can enjoy the tremendous processing power of the dBASE III Plus program.

# Getting Help

Help is available not only from the comprehensive dBASE III Plus user's manual but also from the program's built-in message system. If you have questions about the function of a specific command or menu option while you are processing data in dBASE III Plus, you can ask for help by pressing the HELP function key, F1. Whenever you press the F1 key, a message screen describing the current command or submenu option is displayed. For example, if you press F1 while the Display submenu option is highlighted under the Assistant menu's Retrieve option, the function of Display is described on the screen (see fig. 3.16).

After you have read the help message, you can return to the Assistant menu by pressing any key.

Whenever you make a mistake in entering a command in dot-prompt mode (such as misspelling *DISPLAY ALL* as *DISPLAY AL*), dBASE III Plus will ask:

   Do you want some help? (Y/N)

If you then type *Y*, a message screen explains the correct use of the command in question (DISPLAY) (see fig. 3.17). At this point, you can either return to the dot prompt by pressing the Esc key or you can ask for information about another command (such as LIST) by typing the command at the cursor (see fig. 3.18). After you type *LIST*, a screen message that describes the LIST command is displayed (see fig. 3.19).

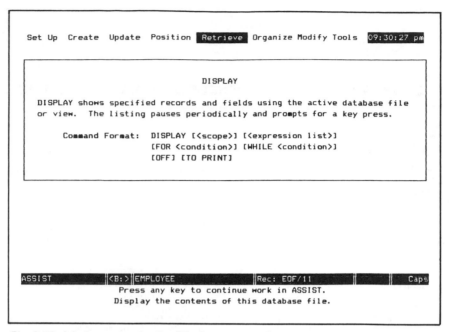

Fig. 3.16. A help screen for the Display menu option.

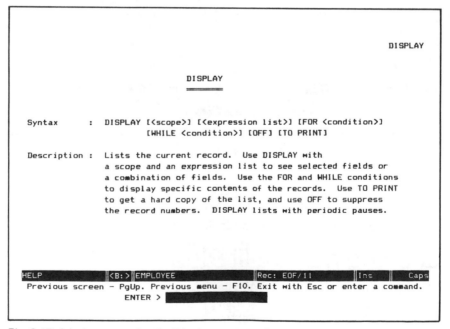

Fig. 3.17. A help screen for the Display command.

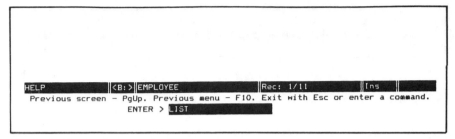

Fig. 3.18. Getting help on the LIST command.

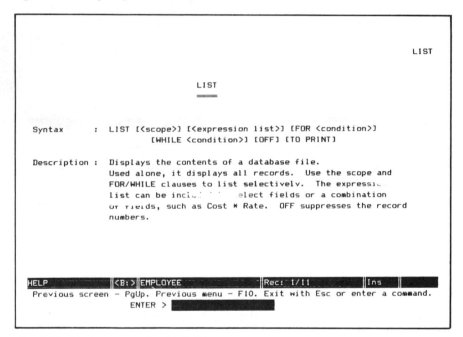

Fig. 3.19. A help screen for the LIST command.

You can return to the previous help screen by pressing the PgUp key. To go to the help-screen menu, press the F10 function key. The Help Main Menu screen is shown in figure 3.20.

PLUS
# Leaving dBASE III Plus

When you have finished using dBASE III Plus, you can exit the program by choosing the **Quit dBASE III Plus** option from the submenu of the Assistant menu's **Set Up** option (see fig. 3.21). If you are in dot-prompt mode and want to leave dBASE III Plus, type *QUIT* at the dot prompt and then press Enter (see fig. 3.22).

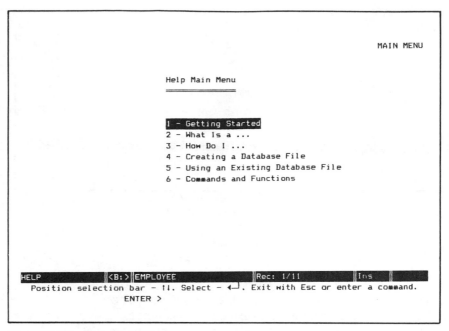

```
                                                                MAIN MENU


                         Help Main Menu
                         ═══════════════


                         1 - Getting Started
                         2 - What Is a ...
                         3 - How Do I ...
                         4 - Creating a Database File
                         5 - Using an Existing Database File
                         6 - Commands and Functions




 HELP            ║<B:>║EMPLOYEE            ║Rec: 1/11        ║║Ins  ║
      Position selection bar - ↑↓. Select - ←┘. Exit with Esc or enter a command.
                         ENTER >
```

Fig. 3.20. The Help Main Menu.

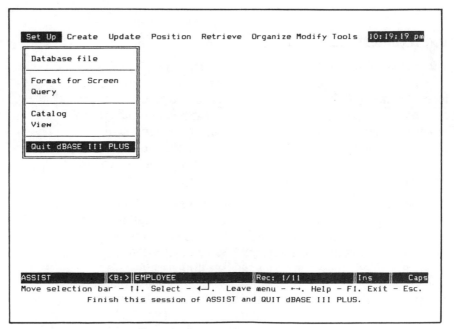

```
 Set Up  Create  Update  Position  Retrieve  Organize Modify Tools  10:19:19 pm
┌─────────────────────┐
│ Database file        │
├─────────────────────┤
│ Format for Screen    │
│ Query                │
├─────────────────────┤
│ Catalog              │
│ View                 │
├─────────────────────┤
│ Quit dBASE III PLUS  │
└─────────────────────┘








 ASSIST          ║<B:>║EMPLOYEE            ║Rec: 1/11        ║║Ins  ║   Caps
 Move selection bar - ↑↓. Select - ←┘.  Leave menu - ←→. Help - F1. Exit - Esc.
         Finish this session of ASSIST and QUIT dBASE III PLUS.
```

Fig. 3.21. Quitting dBASE III Plus in dot-prompt mode.

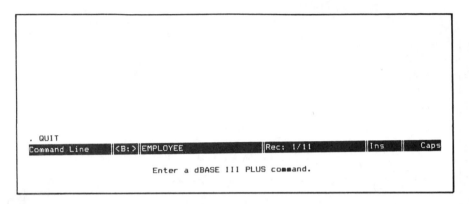

. QUIT
Command Line    <B:> EMPLOYEE                    Rec: 1/11          Ins        Caps

Enter a dBASE III PLUS command.

*Fig. 3.22. Quitting dBASE III Plus from the Assistant menu.*

It is of utmost importance to remember that you must use the Quit dBASE III Plus submenu option to exit the program from The Assistant, or the QUIT command to exit dot-prompt mode. Information in your database files may be lost if you attempt to exit the program by any other means.

# Chapter Summary

The four major IBM PC components are the input unit, which is the keyboard; the system unit, which contains the microprocessor and internal memory (ROM and RAM); the auxiliary storage unit, such as a floppy disk drive or a hard disk unit; and the output unit, which can be a monitor or a printer. An IBM keyboard has a set of alphanumeric keys by which information can be given to the computer and a set of keys unique to the computer that are used to perform various operations.

ROM and RAM hold information in a computer system. Some of the systems programs, such as those governing the operations of the input/output devices, are stored in ROM, or read-only memory. RAM, or random-access memory, holds some of the sytem programs, as well as user programs and data from files. Auxiliary storage units in the form of floppy disk drives or hard disk units are devices for storing user programs and data files as permanent records. A streamer-tape unit is a storage device that can back up a large amount of information, such as that stored on a hard disk.

The procedure for starting a computer system is called booting. You use a cold boot when you turn on power to the computer. You can restart the computer system by a warm boot, which interrupts the current processing task.

Before starting dBASE III Plus, you must prepare the computer for handling the computer program. Furthermore, data disks must be prepared and formatted before data can be saved on the disks. The computer must also be informed of the anticipated memory usage—that is, the number of files and the number of buffers to be used. You must also specify the default data disk. You accomplish these tasks by setting up the CONFIG.SYS file on the DOS system disk and the CONFIG.DBF file on the dBASE III Plus system disk. After these tasks have been completed, you can activate the dBASE III Plus program. When dBASE III Plus is successfully activated, the Assistant menu will be displayed. You now are in the world of dBASE III and can enter commands for performing database management functions.

The Assistant menu is a powerful, user-friendly interface between you and the program. In interactive mode, you can create your database files and manipulate them by selecting appropriate menu options. You can perform the same data-manipulation operations by using the Assistant menu or by entering dBASE III Plus commands at the dot prompt.

# Creating and
# Displaying Data

## An Overview

This chapter explains how to design and create a database file. You can use a database file to store data elements as simple as employee information or as complicated as an accounting system.

The chapter also highlights the simplicity of database management with the Assistant's easy-to-use menu and the dBASE III Plus commands. If you are a beginning user of dBASE III Plus, you may prefer the Assistant menu because most data-manipulation operations can be performed by selecting a sequence of menu and submenu options. However, processing data by entering dBASE III Plus commands at the dot prompt may prove a shortcut for many of these operations. In this chapter, you will see how one data-manipulation operation can be performed with either of these methods. You can choose whichever mode of processing best suits you.

The chapter explains how to

Create a new database file
Define the structure of a database file
Enter data in a newly created database file
Add or append new records to an existing database file
Display the database file directory
Display the structure and contents of a database file

The following dBASE III Plus commands are introduced in this chapter:

| Command | Function |
|---------|----------|
| CREATE | Creates a database file |
| USE | Activates a database file |
| APPEND | Adds records to a database file |
| DISPLAY, LIST | Displays data |
| DIR | Displays a file directory |

# Creating a Database File

A new database file can be created by choosing the **Create** option from the Assistant menu or by entering CREATE at the dot prompt. In either case, the creation of a new database file begins with the assignment of a new name to the file.

 ## Using the Assistant

If you want to use the Assistant menu, all you have to do is use the ← or → key to move the highlighting block until the **Create** option is selected (see fig. 4.1).

When you have selected the **Create** option, the first submenu option, **Database file,** is highlighted. The highlighting indicates that this is the current option. The current menu option also is indicated on the status bar as **Opt : 1/6.** Because you plan to create a new database file, you now select the highlighted submenu option by pressing the Enter key. In response to that keystroke, dBASE III Plus

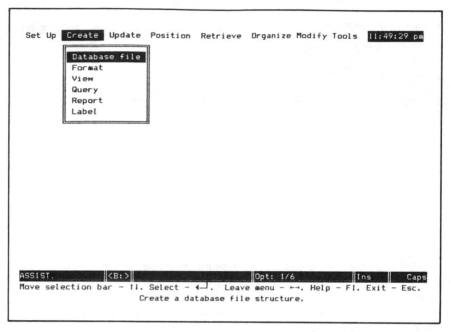

```
Set Up  Create  Update  Position  Retrieve  Organize Modify Tools  11:49:29 pm
        ┌──────────────┐
        │Database file │
        │Format        │
        │View          │
        │Query         │
        │Report        │
        │Label         │
        └──────────────┘
```
```
ASSIST.          <B:>                          Opt: 1/6              Ins      Caps
Move selection bar - ↑↓. Select - ◄┘.  Leave menu - ←→. Help - F1. Exit - Esc.
                        Create a database file structure.
```

*Fig. 4.1. Menu option for creating database file.*

prompts you to select the disk drive on which the database file is to be stored (see fig. 4.2).

Notice that **B**: is highlighted in the submenu and displayed on the status bar in figure 4.2. This happens because drive B was specified in the CONFIG.DB file as the default disk drive. (Refer to Chapter 3 for more information on the CONFIG.DB file.) If drive B had not been specified as the default drive, then the drive from which dBASE III Plus was initiated (drive A) would be indicated as the default drive. (Your screen may show different defaults if dBASE III Plus has been installed in a different configuration.)

After selecting the default disk drive, you are prompted to enter the name of the database file that is to be created. At the prompt, you enter the name; for this example, the name is EMPLOYEE (see fig. 4.3).

To correct any mistakes you make while entering the file name (but before pressing the Enter key), press the Backspace key to erase the characters entered. After you have pressed the Enter key, the only way to change the file name is to abort the file-creation process by

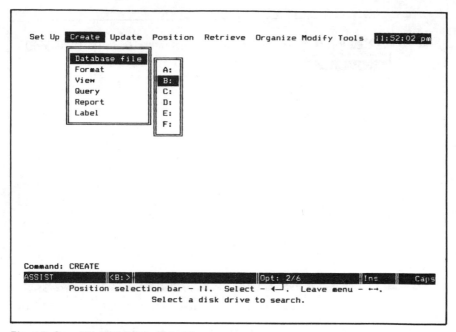

Fig. 4.2. Specifying default disk drive.

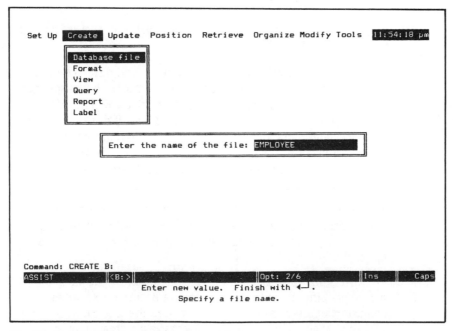

Fig. 4.3. Naming database file to be created.

pressing the Esc key. In response to that keystroke, a question will appear in the message window:

Are you sure you want to abandon operation? (Y/N)

If you press *y*, the file-creation process is aborted and you are returned to the Assistant menu. If you type *n*, you can continue creating the database file.

Notice that the action line in figure 4.3 (shown directly above the status line at the bottom of the screen) shows:

Command : CREATE B :

The action line shows the dBASE III Plus command the Assistant has "built." The menu and submenu options that have created this command are

Create/Database File/B:

# Entering Dot-Prompt Commands

If you want to create a new database file named EMPLOYEE by entering commands from the dot prompt, all you have to do is enter *CREATE B:EMPLOYEE* (see fig. 4.4).

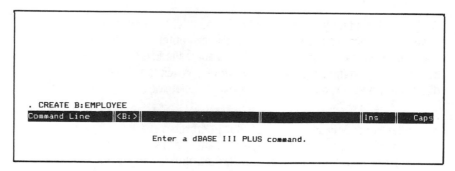

. CREATE B:EMPLOYEE

| Command Line | <B:> | | Ins | Caps |

Enter a dBASE III PLUS command.

*Fig. 4.4. Creating database file in dot-prompt mode.*

As you saw in Chapter 3, you can press the Esc key to enter dot-prompt mode from the first menu level of the Assistant menu. You can return to the Assistant menu by typing *ASSIST* at the dot prompt. The format of the CREATE command entered at the dot prompt is

. CREATE <database file name>

The less than (<) and greater than (>) symbols *signify* the name of the database file that is to be created. These symbols are not part of the command and should not be entered.

Whether you have selected the **Create** menu option from the Assistant or entered the CREATE dot-prompt command, the next step is to define the database file structure. However, before going any further you need to learn how to name a database file correctly.

# Naming a Database File

The name of a database file can include up to eight characters, the first of which must be a letter of the alphabet. The remaining characters can be letters, numeric digits, or the underscore (_). A few acceptable database file names are

EMPLOYEE
Directry
PHONES
INVENTRY
Accounts
ADDRESS
COURSES
ITEMSOLD

When naming a file, you can enter the name in either upper- or lowercase letters. To access a file, you also can enter the name in upper- or lowercase. For example, the database file EMPLOYEE can be recalled by typing *Employee* or *employee*. When the directory is displayed, however, all file names appear in uppercase.

A database file name cannot contain spaces or symbols other than the underscore. Because dBASE III Plus interprets a space as a separator between two data items, a file name with a space is not acceptable. The period (.), the slash (/), the colon (:), and the semicolon (;) are reserved for special functions in dBASE III Plus and should not be used in file names. Some examples of illegal file names are

PHONE NO
PART1;35
BUS/101
MODEL:A

If you enter an illegal file name, a **Syntax error** message will inform you that an item violates the syntax rules for a dBASE III Plus command. If you enter *CREATE PHONE NO*, for example, dBASE III Plus "reads" your input as two separate file names and displays an error message. Two database files cannot be created with one CREATE command.

No warning message is displayed if a database file name has more than eight characters, but only the first eight characters are saved. For example, when *PARTS_RCAVCRS* is entered as a file name, only the first eight characters (*PARTS_RC*) will be recognized and used.

# Defining the Structure
# of a Database File

PLUS

After you enter an acceptable file name, the field-definition form for the database structure appears on the screen (see fig. 4.5).

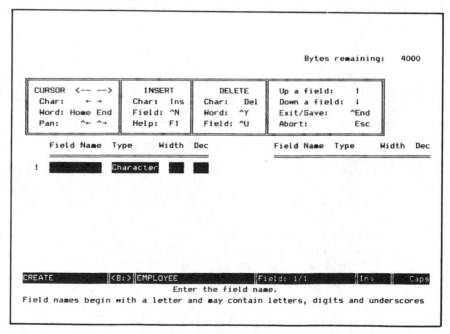

*Fig. 4.5. Defining database file structure.*

Displayed at the top of the screen is a summary of all the valid keystrokes that you can use during this operation. The upper right corner of the screen shows the amount of available memory in bytes. The name of the database file appears in the middle of the status bar, at the bottom of the screen. To indicate the type of file involved when the file is later saved on the data disk, dBASE III Plus will add a *.DBF* extension to the file name. The current field is shown in the status bar as **Field: 1/1**. Information in the status bar is updated as new fields are defined and added to the database structure. The main body of the form provides space for defining the specifications of each data field, such as its name, type, and width.

# Entering the Data Field Name

After you begin creating a database file, the cursor appears at the beginning of a data field on the field definition form. Now the name of the data field can be entered. A data field name can contain up to 10 characters, the first of which must be a letter. The remaining characters may be letters, numerals, or underscores. As in database file names, no blank spaces are allowed. Underscores often are used to separate words in a field name. Some examples of acceptable data field names are

FIRST_NAME
LAST_NAME
MIDDLE_INT
AREA_CODE
PHONE_NO
ACCOUNT_NO
GROSS_WAGE
BIRTH_DATE
ANNUAL_PAY

The definition form provides space for 10 characters in a field name. When that space is filled, the cursor automatically moves to the form's next data field, and a beep sounds. You can enter a field name with fewer than 10 characters. Pressing Enter after the last character of the field name causes the cursor to move to the next item on the form, and no beep is heard.

# Entering the Data Field Type

In dBASE III Plus, you can define five types of data fields in which to store different kinds of information. The five field types are

C Character/text fields
N Numeric fields
D Date fields
L Logical fields
M Memo fields

To define the field type, enter one of the five letters (*C, N, D, L,* or *M*) when the cursor is in the field type. The default field type is a character/text field; you can select it by pressing Enter. By pressing the space bar, you can choose a field type other than the one displayed. Each time you press the space bar, a different field type appears in the Type column. When the appropriate type appears, press Enter to select it.

# Entering the Data Field Width

The width of a data field is the maximum number of characters allowed in the field. In character/text or memo fields, the field width determines the length of the text that can be entered in the field. All letters, numeric digits, symbols, and spaces are considered part of the text. A memo field, like a character field, is used to hold alphanumeric data. Although you cannot sort the information in a memo field, you may want to use a memo field to store a large section of text that you do not plan to manipulate later. The contents of a memo field are saved in a separate file on the disk, thus conserving memory space.

A date field is always eight characters wide and stores the numeric codes for the month, the day, the year, and the slashes that separate the codes. The standard date format is *mm/dd/yy*.

Because a logical field accepts only one character indicating a true/false value, the width of the logical field is always one character.

The width of a numeric field is defined in two ways. First, you define the maximum number of digits allowed in the value, including the sign and the decimal point if those are to be used. Then you determine the number of digits to appear to the right of the decimal point. For example, to store values up to 9999.99, you set the width of the field to seven and define two decimal places. An integer value does not require decimal places defined in the field width. Commas or dollar signs (such as $9,999.99) cannot be entered as part of the value.

# A Sample Data Structure

To illustrate the process of defining the data structure, we have created a database file to store information about a firm's employees. Employee information is stored in each data record in the file. Each item shown in figure 4.6 can be defined as a data field.

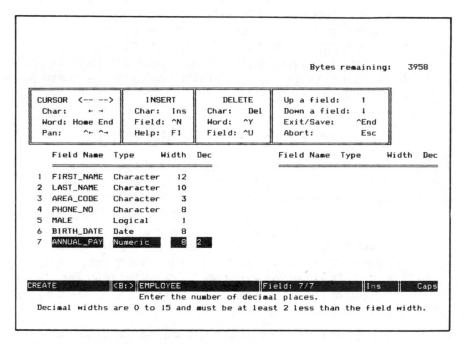

Fig. 4.6. Structure of EMPLOYEE.DBF file.

The data fields FIRST_NAME, LAST_NAME, AREA_CODE, and PHONE_NO are defined as character/text fields. These store the employee's name and phone number. The width of these fields is set to accommodate the maximum number of characters to be entered in the fields.

The logical field MALE identifies the sex of the employee, and accepts only a single character: *T* for true or *F* for false. Alternatively, you could define a character/text field named SEX to store a variable for male or female. However, a logical field can be searched more efficiently than a character/text field.

The date field BIRTH_DATE is defined to store an employee's birth date in the form *dd/mm/yy*. Remember that a date field is not a character/text field, although the date field may contain a string of alphanumeric characters. The contents of a date field can be manipulated only with date operators.

The numeric field ANNUAL_PAY is used to store the employee's annual salary. Because the maximum length of the numeric field is eight characters, you can enter values up to 99999.99.

When all the fields are defined, you terminate the process by pressing the Enter key or the Ctrl-End keystroke combination. (To use Ctrl-End, simply press and hold down the Ctrl key while you press also the End key.) After you press either of those keystrokes, you will see the following message:

**Press ENTER to confirm—any other key to resume**.

If you press Enter, the data structure is saved, and the following prompt appears at the bottom of the screen:

**Input data records now? (Y/N)**

# Entering Data in a Database File

If you press *y*, the program displays the data-entry form for the file you have just defined. For example, after you have defined the EMPLOYEE database file structure, dBASE III Plus displays the first data-entry form for that file. You then position the cursor in the desired field and enter data in the space provided on the entry form. When the field is full, the cursor moves to the next field. If your data item does not fill the field, you can move the cursor to the next field by pressing Enter after you enter the last character of the data item. After you have entered the information to the data field for the first record, the screen will look like figure 4.7.

As soon as the last data field is filled, a new data-entry form is displayed (see fig. 4.8).

During data entry, each data record you enter is assigned a record number. In figure 4.8, for example, the record indicator in the status bar shows **Rec : EOF/1**. The first part of the indicator shows the current record's position in the database file (in this instance, it is the last record or End of File, EOF). The number after the slash (/1) indicates the total number of records in the database file.

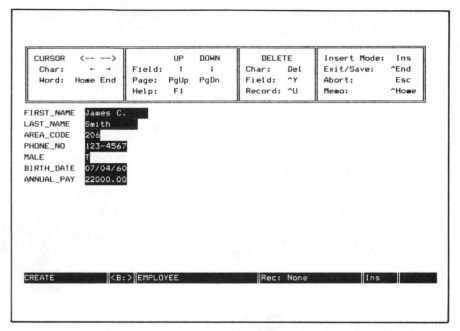

Fig. 4.7. Standard data-entry form for EMPLOYEE.DBF.

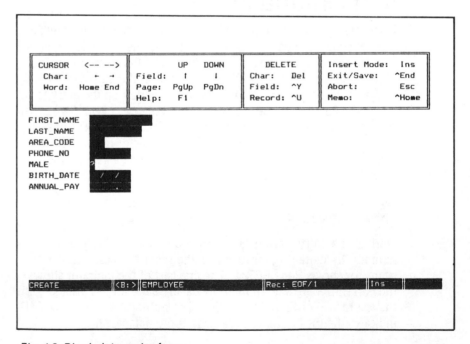

Fig. 4.8. Blank data-entry form.

Using the blank form, you can enter the next record to the database file. For this example, four data records have been entered:

| Field | Record 1 | Record 2 | Record 3 | Record 4 |
|---|---|---|---|---|
| FIRST_NAME | James C. | Albert K. | Doris A. | Harry M. |
| LAST_NAME | Smith | Zeller | Gregory | Nelson |
| AREA_CODE | 206 | 212 | 503 | 315 |
| PHONE_NO | 123-4567 | 457-9801 | 204-8567 | 576-0235 |
| MALE | T | T | F | T |
| BIRTH_DATE | 07/04/60 | 09/20/59 | 07/04/62 | 02/15/58 |
| ANNUAL_PAY | 22000.00 | 27900.00 | 16900.00 | 29000.00 |

During data entry, you can use the PgUp and PgDn keys to move between data records. Press the PgUp key to return to the previous record; to proceed to the next record, press the PgDn key.

# Terminating the Data-Entry Process

Data entered in a database file is saved record by record. As soon as the last field of a data record has been completed, that record is added to the database file. Then you can terminate the data-entry process.

To terminate data entry, you can press Enter when the cursor is on the first field of a new data-entry form. For example, when you have entered data in the last field of data record 4, the form for record 5 is displayed. At this point, the data from record 4 has already been added to the database file. Pressing Enter now will terminate the data-entry procedure. The last data record added to the database file would be record 4.

You can also use the Ctrl-End key combination to end the data-entry process. Ctrl-End saves the displayed data record and returns the program to the dot prompt or the Assistant menu. The Ctrl-End combination can be entered at any time, regardless of the cursor's position on the entry form. If Ctrl-End is pressed before all data fields are filled, the empty data fields are filled with blank spaces. If you press Ctrl-End when all the fields in the entry form are blanks, however, a new empty record will be added to the database. For now, do not worry if this should happen. You will learn later how to delete an unwanted record.

The Esc key can be used in dBASE III Plus to stop any function in progress and return to the Assistant menu or the dot prompt. However, that method should be used with care. Improper use of the Escape function can cause you to lose data.

When you press the Esc key, the computer "forgets" the most recent operation. What constitutes the most recent operation may vary from one type of procedure to another. For example, if you press the Esc key while entering data, any data entered to the current record is discarded. Data entered to the preceding record is not affected, however, because that data was saved before the current record was displayed.

#  Appending Data to the Database File

New data records can be added to the database file in one of two ways. One way is to *append* a new data record to the end of the file, and the other way is to *insert* a data record within the database file.

If you want to use the Assistant menu to add new records to the end of an existing database file, select **Append** from the Update options (first you select **Update,** and then you select **Append;** see fig. 4.9).

When you select **Append,** an entry form is displayed so that you can append the new record (see fig. 4.10).

Now, using the procedure described earlier, you can enter the remaining data records to the database file. For this example, the following records have been appended to the existing EMPLOYEE database file:

| Field | Record 5 | Record 6 | Record 7 | Record 8 | Record 9 |
|---|---|---|---|---|---|
| FIRST_NAME | Tina B. | Kirk D. | Mary W. | Charles N. | Winston E. |
| LAST_NAME | Baker | Chapman | Thompson | Duff | Lee |
| AREA_CODE | 415 | 618 | 213 | 206 | 503 |
| PHONE_NO | 787-3154 | 625-7845 | 432-6782 | 456-9873 | 365-8512 |
| MALE | F | T | F | T | T |
| BIRTH_DATE | 10/12/56 | 08/04/61 | 06/18/55 | 07/22/64 | 05/14/39 |
| ANNUAL_PAY | 25900.00 | 19750.00 | 24500.00 | 1350.00 | 34900.00 |

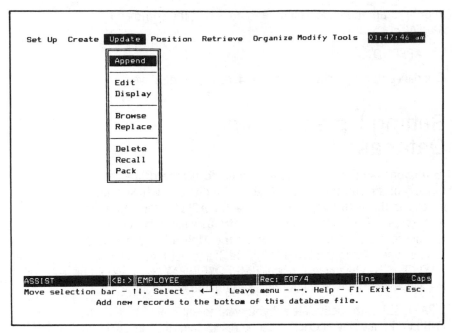

*Fig. 4.9. Appending new records to EMPLOYEE.DBF file.*

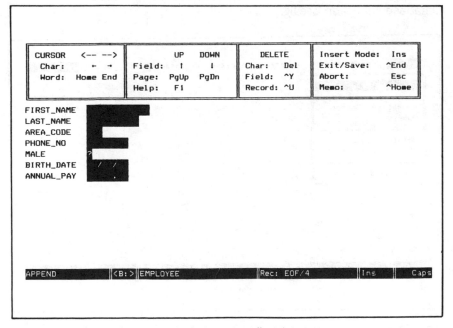

*Fig. 4.10. Standard data-entry form for appending data.*

In dot-prompt mode, all you have to do is type the command *APPEND*:

. APPEND

The data-entry form shown in figure 4.10 then is displayed.

# Setting Up an Existing Database File

As demonstrated in the previous example, data records are added to the end of the currently active database file (the one whose name appears in the status bar) when you use the APPEND operation. In the example, EMPLOYEE was the last database file activated, and that file remains active. If you now use the APPEND command, data will be appended to the EMPLOYEE file. If another file, such as PAYROLL, had been created after EMPLOYEE, PAYROLL would be the active file to which the APPEND command would add data.

If PAYROLL is the active file but you want to enter new data to the EMPLOYEE file, EMPLOYEE must be reactivated (or "set up") before you can enter APPEND. You can activate an existing database file (EMPLOYEE) from the Assistant menu by selecting the **Set Up/ Database file** option (see fig. 4.11).

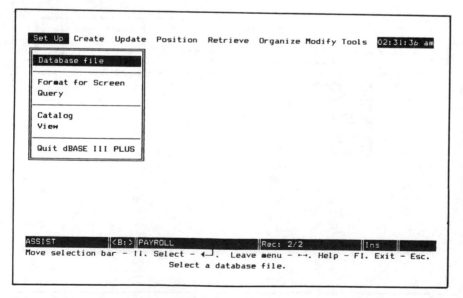

Fig. 4.11. Setting up database file for processing.

After you select the option, you are prompted to enter the name of the database file that is to be activated. The process of setting up the EMPLOYEE database file in default drive B can be summarized by the following sequence of menu and submenu options:

Set Up/Database file/B:/*EMPLOYEE.DBF*

Then you are prompted to answer the question:

**Is the file indexed? [Y/N]**

Because you have not previously indexed this database file, you answer *n*. (To *index* a database file is to rearrange its data records; that is discussed in a later chapter.) After the database file is set up, the name of the file appears in the status bar.

## Reactivating a File

If you are in dot-prompt mode, you can activate an existing database file by entering the USE command at the dot prompt:

. USE EMPLOYEE

Database files are usually saved in auxiliary storage, such as a floppy disk or a hard disk. To conserve memory, only active database files are stored in random-access memory (RAM), where the data can be quickly accessed. The USE command tells the computer to retrieve the contents of a file from the auxiliary storage and store the file contents in RAM. Although several database files may remain active, only one active file can be used at a time. The format of the USE command in dot-prompt mode is

. USE <database file name>

Because only database files can be accessed with USE, you do not need to enter the extension .DBF. After you enter USE, the contents of the database file are copied from the disk to RAM, and a dot prompt appears on the screen. Then you can enter other dBASE III Plus commands, such as APPEND.

## Performing File Operations with dBASE III Plus

Database files created in dBASE III or dBASE III Plus can be renamed, duplicated, copied to files with different names, or erased.

# Setting the Default Data Disk Drive

When dBASE III Plus is brought up, the default drive is indicated in the status bar as ⟨B:⟩. You can change the default drive by selecting the **Tools/Set drive** menu options. For example, if you want to change the current drive (B, for this example) to drive C, you select the following menu options:

>    Tools/Set drive/C:

The equivalent dot command for this operation is

>    . SET DEFAULT TO C

 # Renaming a File

By choosing **Tools/Rename**, you can give a file a different name without changing its contents. To rename EMPLOYEE.DBF to PERSONEL.DBF, for example, you make the following menu selections and keyboard entries:

>    Tools/Rename/*EMPLOYEE.DBF*/Enter the name of the file: *PERSONEL.DBF*

The equivalent dot command is

>    . RENAME ⟨current file name⟩ TO ⟨new file name⟩

Both the current and new file names must include the file name and the extension (such as .DBF). For example, the following command assigns the new name PERSONEL to the current database file named EMPLOYEE:

>    . RENAME EMPLOYEE.DBF TO PERSONEL.DBF

(The file name is "misspelled" because of the eight-character limitation for file names.) In most cases, the file identifier of the current file (.DBF) must be the same as that of the new file.

 # Copying Files

To copy the contents of a file to another file, choose the **Tools/Copy file** menu options. For example, if you want to copy the contents of the EMPLOYEE.DBF file to a new file named BACKUP.DBF, you make the following menu selections and keyboard entries:

Tools/Copy file/B:/*EMPLOYEE.DBF*/B:/Enter the name of the file: *BACKUP.DBF*

The equivalent dot prompt command is

. COPY FILE <source file name> TO <destination file name>

An example of the command is

. COPY FILE EMPLOYEE.DBF TO BACKUP.DBF

This command copies the contents of the source file to a destination file. If the destination file has not been created, a new file is made. If a file with the destination file name already exists, you see the warning

<destination file name> **already exists, overwrite it? (Y/N)**

If you answer *Y*, the contents of the existing file are replaced with the contents of the source file.

Active files cannot be used in a COPY FILE command. If you try to copy an active file, you will see the message

**File is already open**

A similar error message is displayed if you try to copy a file to an active file. As you can see, a file must be closed before it is used as a source file or a destination file in a COPY FILE command. To close a database file, use the following command:

. CLOSE DATABASES

You can also close other types of files. These are discussed in later chapters.

# Deleting a File

PLUS

A file in dBASE III Plus can be permanently deleted with the **Tools/ Erase** options from the Assistant menu. For example, to delete the BACKUP.DBF file, you make the following menu selections and keyboard entries:

Tools/Erase/B:/*BACKUP.DBF*

The equivalent dot command for the **Erase** option is

. ERASE <file name>

The file name should include the file extension, as in

. ERASE BACKUP.DBF

The ERASE command deletes the contents of a nonactive file, which includes the data structure and all the records in the file. Active files must be closed before being erased. Once the contents have been erased, the data cannot be recovered. For this reason, you should use extreme care in erasing files.

# [PLUS] Customizing a Data-Entry Form

During the data-entry process described earlier, dBASE III Plus provides a standard form for entry of values to the data fields. (Refer to fig. 4.8. for an example of such a standard form.) In the standard data-entry form, all data fields in the database structure are listed in sequence. The space provided for the field contents is shown in a reverse-video box. Such a standard form should be sufficient for most data-entry operations. However, dBASE III Plus also allows you to design a custom data-entry form. For example, figure 4.12 shows a custom data-entry form that you can use for entering information to data records in the EMPLOYEE database file.

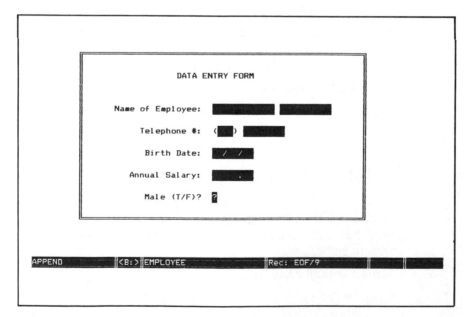

Fig. 4.12. Custom data-entry form for EMPLOYEE.DBF.

On the custom data-entry form, you can place the data fields anywhere on the screen and provide your own field labels. In addition to including instructional messages for the data-entry procedure (or other information), you can add graphic designs such as single or double-line boxes.

You can design and create a custom data-entry form by choosing the **Create** and **Format** options from the Assistant menu (see fig. 4.13).

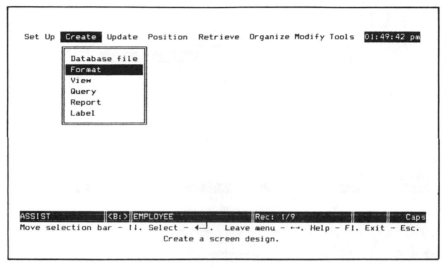

Fig. 4.13. Creating a custom data-entry form.

To create a custom data-entry form, you use the dBASE III Plus screen painter, which enables you easily to position fields on the screen. The screen painter creates a working file, which has the extension .SCR. The entry form that you design with the screen painter is saved in a format file. Although this file bears the same name as the screen file, the format file has the file extension .FMT. After selecting the **Create/Format** option from the menu, you are prompted to specify the name of the screen file and the name of the disk drive on which it is to be stored. The rules governing a screen file name are the same as those for a database file name. You may choose any legitimate name for the screen file. Because each screen file is unique and can be used only with the database file that is designated when you create the form, using the name of the database file for the screen file is advisable. Because database, screen, and format files are assigned different file extensions (.DBF, .SCR, and .FMT), they are saved individually on disk. You may therefore

specify EMPLOYEE as the name of the screen file for the custom
data-entry form you are creating (see fig. 4.14).

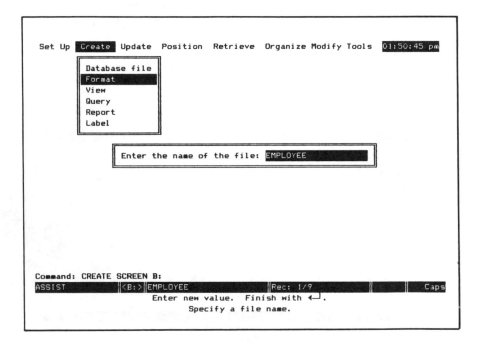

*Fig. 4.14. Naming the format and screen files.*

After entering the format file name, you are prompted to select a
database file from the **Set Up** menu (see fig. 4.15). Then you are
returned to the **Set Up** menu, and you can begin designing your
data-entry form.

The process of entry-form design can be summarized in a series of
steps:

1. Load the data fields that are to be included in the data-entry
   form.

2. Go to the screen-painter "blackboard" and position the fields
   on the form.

3. Modify field labels and add descriptive text and graphic
   elements such as boxes.

4. Save the data-entry form and end the operation.

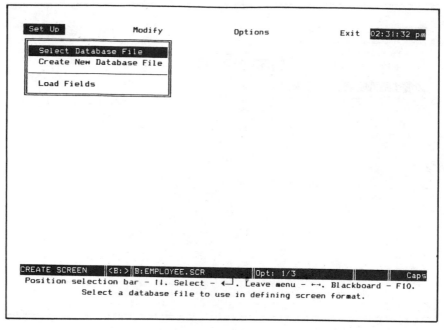

*Fig. 4.15. Setting up database file for custom data-entry form.*

# Loading Data Fields

PLUS

As you saw in figure 4.12, the major components of a data-entry form are

1.  Field labels, such as *Name of Employee*

2.  The fields themselves, which appear as reverse-video boxes

To select data fields for inclusion in the data-entry form, you choose the **Set Up/Load Fields** options from the menu. All the existing fields in the database file then are displayed as a list of submenu choices. You use the ↑ and ↓ keys to position the highlighting at a data field that you want to include on the form, and then press Enter. A small triangular marker then appears to the left of the selected data field (see fig. 4.16). To remove the selection marker so that you can select another field, highlight the previously selected field again and press the Enter key.

You can either select one data field at a time, returning to the menu for another after placing that field in the blackboard's data-entry form, or you can select all the data fields before moving to the

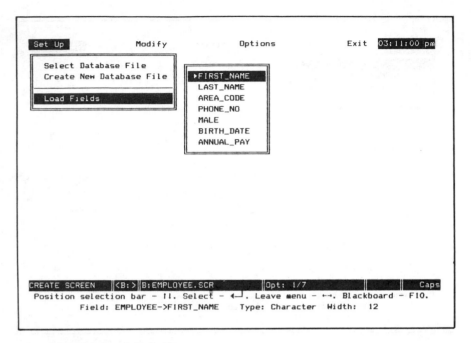

```
 Set Up            Modify           Options        Exit  03:11:00 pm

  ┌──────────────────────────┐
  │ Select Database File     │   ┌─────────────────┐
  │ Create New Database File │   │▶FIRST_NAME      │
  ├──────────────────────────┤   │ LAST_NAME       │
  │ Load Fields              │   │ AREA_CODE       │
  └──────────────────────────┘   │ PHONE_NO        │
                                  │ MALE            │
                                  │ BIRTH_DATE      │
                                  │ ANNUAL_PAY      │
                                  └─────────────────┘
```
```
 CREATE SCREEN   <B:> B:EMPLOYEE.SCR        Opt: 1/7                  Caps
   Position selection bar - ↑↓. Select - ←┘. Leave menu - ←→. Blackboard - F10.
          Field: EMPLOYEE->FIRST_NAME    Type: Character   Width:   12
```

Fig. 4.16. Selecting data fields.

blackboard. For the purpose of this example, you should now select all the fields from the submenu. After you have completed loading the data fields into the blackboard, you can move to the blackboard by pressing the F10 key. Your screen should then look like figure 4.17.

You can now rearrange the data fields in the blackboard by moving one field at a time from its default location to a new location. To move a data field in the form, you first position the cursor on the highlighted field and then use the arrow keys to "drag" the field to its new position. For example, if you want to move the ANNUAL_PAY field to the lower middle portion of the blackboard, you can move the cursor to the highlighted field (99999.99) by using the arrow keys. When the cursor is located anywhere in the highlighted field, a description of the field is displayed in the message line at the bottom of the screen. You then press the Enter key to select that field. Now you use the arrow keys to drag the field to the appropriate location. After positioning the field, you can anchor it by pressing Enter again. When you have positioned the ANNUAL-PAY field, your screen should look like the one shown in figure 4.18.

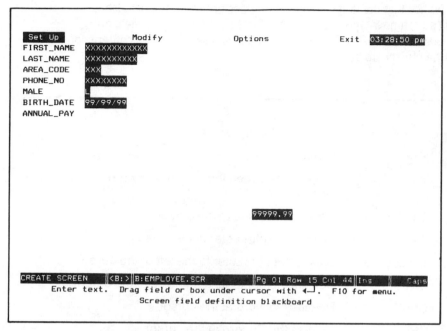

*Fig. 4.17. Blackboard, with loaded data fields.*

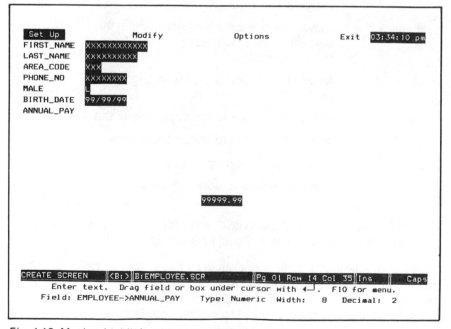

*Fig. 4.18. Moving highlighted field for ANNUAL_PAY.*

Notice that the dragging operation does not move the field label. You can now type in a new label for the ANNUAL_PAY field and erase the old label. The keys that you can use to edit the contents of the blackboard are shown in table 4.1.

**Table 4.1**
**Keys for Editing Screens**

| Key | Function |
|---|---|
| Ins | Switches between insert and overwrite modes |
| Ctrl-End | Inserts a new line at the cursor |
| Del | Deletes the character at the cursor |
| Backspace | Erases the character to the left of the cursor |
| Ctrl-Y | Deletes the contents of the field at the cursor |
| Ctrl-T | Deletes the word at the cursor |
| Ctrl-U | Deletes the Record at the cursor |
| Cursor key | Moves the cursor one character in the indicated direction |
| Home | Moves the cursor to the beginning of the current word, or to the beginning of the previous word |
| End | Moves the cursor to the beginning of the next word |
| Ctrl-Z | Moves the cursor to the beginning of the line |
| Ctrl-B | Moves the cursor to the end of the line |
| Ctrl-C | Scrolls the screen up 18 lines |
| Ctrl-R | Scrolls the screen down 18 lines |

When you have rearranged the data fields and added custom labels to the entry form, the blackboard should look like figure 4.19.

To make your form look better, you can draw a box (with single or double lines) around the data fields. To get to the menu press F10 and, when the menu appears, choose **Options/Double bar** (see fig. 4.20). Then return to the blackboard by pressing the Enter key. The blackboard reappears, and you can draw a double-bar box in the entry form by indicating the positions of the upper left and lower right corners. First you place the cursor where you want the upper left corner of the box to be, and press Enter. Then move the cursor to the position of the lower right corner and press Enter again. The result of these steps is a double-bar box like the one shown in figure 4.21.

You can move the box by positioning the cursor anywhere on the perimeter and pressing Enter. You can then drag the box and its contents to a new location in the same way you move a highlighted field. To erase an existing box, all you have to do is position the cursor anywhere on the box line and then press Ctrl-U (press the Ctrl key and hold it down as you press U).

# Saving the Data-Entry Form

PLUS

After you have completed designing the data-entry form, you can save it by first leaving the blackboard (press F10) and then choosing the **Exit/Save** menu options.

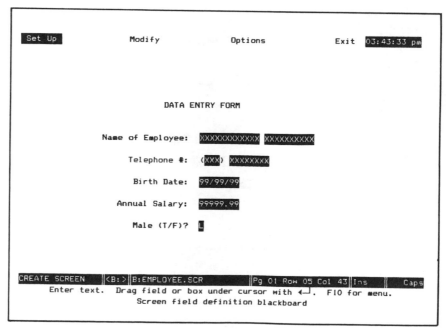

Fig. 4.19. Custom data-entry form.

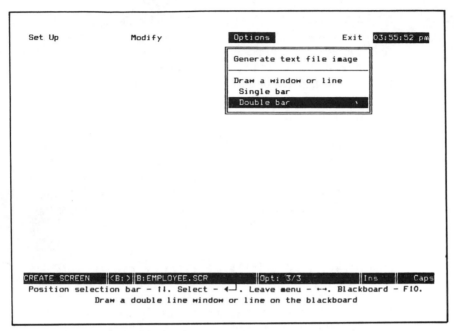

Fig. 4.20. Drawing a double-bar box.

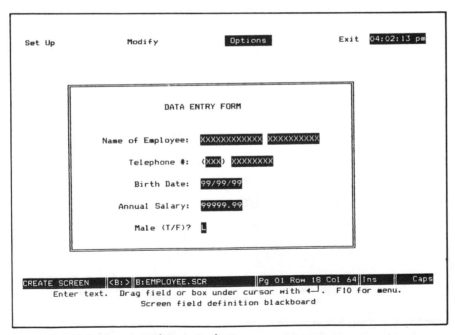

Fig. 4.21. Finished custom data-entry form.

# Modifying the Data-Entry Form

PLUS

To modify an existing data-entry form, choose the **Modify/Format** option sequence from the Assistant menu. To modify the data-entry form that you have designed for the EMPLOYEE database file, for example, you select the following menu and submenu options:

Modify/Format/B:/*EMPLOYEE.SCR*

When the setup screen shown in figure 4.22 appears, press the F10 key to go to the blackboard. The existing data-entry form then is displayed (see fig. 4.23).

You can modify any part of the form by following the previously described procedures for designing a data-entry form. After you have completed the modifications, you can save the modified form by choosing the **Exit/Save** options. If you find that you have made a mistake and you want to abort the modification process, you can do so by pressing the Esc key.

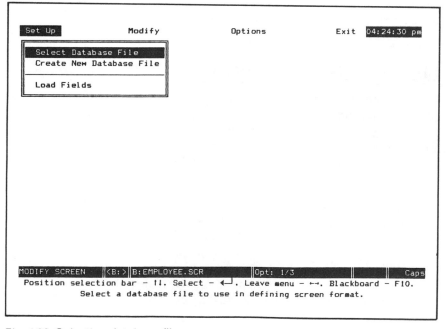

*Fig. 4.22. Selecting database file.*

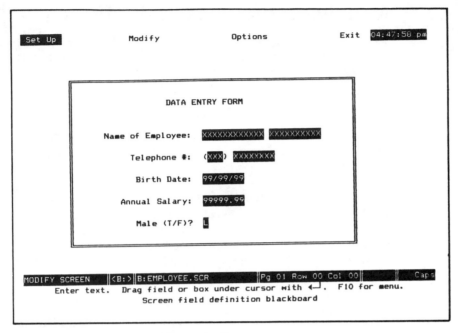

Fig. 4.23. Modifying custom data-entry form.

# PLUS  Using the Data-Entry Form

The data-entry form, which has been saved in a format file, can now
be used for appending or editing records in the database file. Before
using an existing data-entry form, however, you must set up the
form by retrieving the contents of the format file. To do so, choose
the **Set Up/Format for Screen** options from the Assistant menu
(see fig. 4.24).

For example, if you want to set up the data-entry form saved in the
EMPLOYEE.FMT file so that you can enter data to the EMPLOYEE
database file, select these menu and submenu options:

  Set Up/Format for Screen/B:/*EMPLOYEE.FMT*

Then, by choosing the **Update/Append** menu options, you can
append a new data record to the EMPLOYEE database.

First, be certain that the EMPLOYEE database file has been set up
and that it is shown as the current active file in the status bar. If not,
you can set up the database file by choosing:

  Set Up/Database file/B:/*EMPLOYEE*

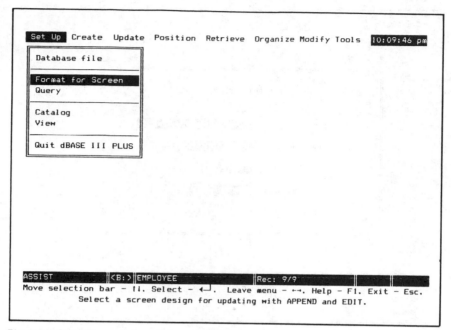

```
 Set Up  Create  Update  Position  Retrieve  Organize Modify Tools   10:09:46 pm
┌─────────────────────┐
│  Database file      │
│                     │
│  Format for Screen  │
│  Query              │
│                     │
│  Catalog            │
│  View               │
│                     │
│  Quit dBASE III PLUS│
└─────────────────────┘




ASSIST           <B:> EMPLOYEE              Rec: 9/9
Move selection bar - ↕. Select - ←┘.  Leave menu - ↔. Help - F1. Exit - Esc.
          Select a screen design for updating with APPEND and EDIT.
```

*Fig. 4.24. Selecting custom data-entry form.*

The blank custom entry form now is displayed (refer to fig. 4.12),
and you can enter information to the data fields just as you would in
a standard entry form. Now you can enter record 10 to the database
file by filling in the field values shown in figure 4.25. After entering
the data, you end the data-entry process by pressing Enter when the
blank entry form for record 11 appears.

# Displaying a Database File

After a database has been created, you can display the contents of
the file. A database file contains the data structure and the data
stored in records.

## Listing a File Directory

PLUS

To verify the existence of a disk file, you can display a directory of
the files saved on disk by choosing the **Tools/Directory** options
from the Assistant menu (see fig. 4.26). After selecting the
**Directory** submenu option, you are prompted to specify a disk
drive. Then you are prompted to select the type of disk file to be

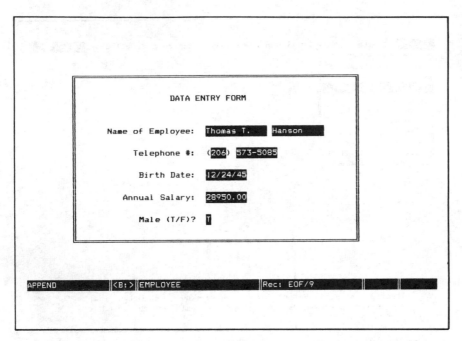

Fig. 4.25. Appending data.

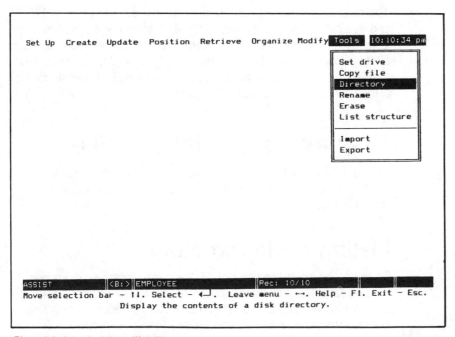

Fig. 4.26. Displaying a file directory.

listed (see fig. 4.27). If you want to list all the database files, select the **.dbf Database Files** submenu option. The directory of all the existing database files is then displayed (see fig. 4.28).

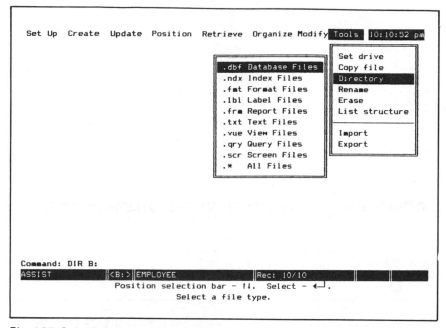

Fig. 4.27. Selecting type of file directory.

# Displaying the Database
# File Structure

PLUS

To examine or verify the active file's data structure, you select the **Tools/List Structure** option (see fig. 4.29). If you select the **Tools/List Structure** option while the EMPLOYEE.DBF file is in use, for example, the structure of that file is displayed on either the printer or the screen after you answer the prompt

**Direct the output to the printer? [Y/N]**

If you answer *n*, the structure of the EMPLOYEE database file is displayed on the screen. It will appear as in figure 4.30. After examining the database file structure, press Enter to exit the **List structure** operation.

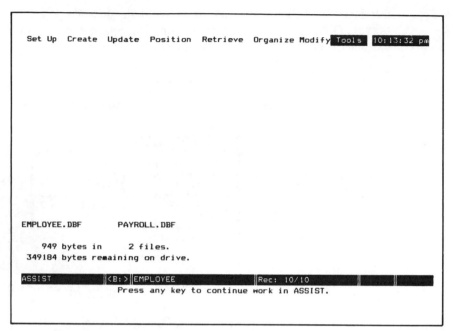

Fig. 4.28. Directory of all .DBF files in drive B.

Fig. 4.29. Listing database structure.

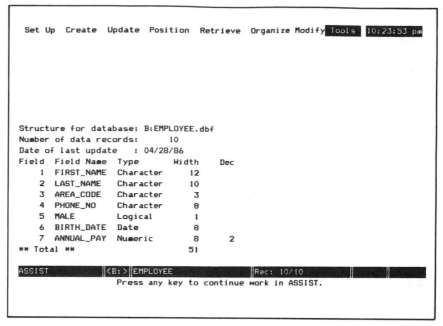

```
  Set Up  Create  Update  Position  Retrieve  Organize Modify Tools  10:23:53 pm




  Structure for database: B:EMPLOYEE.dbf
  Number of data records:      10
  Date of last update   : 04/28/86
  Field  Field Name  Type      Width    Dec
     1   FIRST_NAME  Character    12
     2   LAST_NAME   Character    10
     3   AREA_CODE   Character     3
     4   PHONE_NO    Character     8
     5   MALE        Logical       1
     6   BIRTH_DATE  Date          8
     7   ANNUAL_PAY  Numeric       8     2
  ** Total **                    51

 ASSIST            <B:> EMPLOYEE              Rec: 10/10
            Press any key to continue work in ASSIST.
```

*Fig. 4.30. Structure of EMPLOYEE.DBF file.*

# Displaying Data Records in a Database File

PLUS

Data records that have been stored in an existing database file can be displayed in several ways. You can display some or all of the data fields in the current record, in all existing records, or in selected records. To display one or more of the records in the active database file, you select the **Retrieve/Display** options from the Assistant menu (see fig. 4.31).

The **Retrieve/Display** options provide flexibility in choosing any subset of existing data records and data fields. When you select the **Display** option, you are shown a list of submenu options for specifying such a subset (see fig. 4.32).

## Executing the Command

PLUS

The **Execute the command** submenu option is used to perform the display operation after you have specified a subset of data records

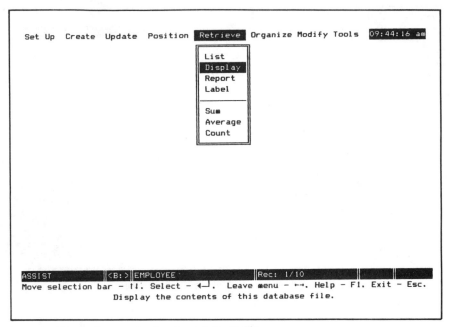

Fig. 4.31. Displaying contents of a database file.

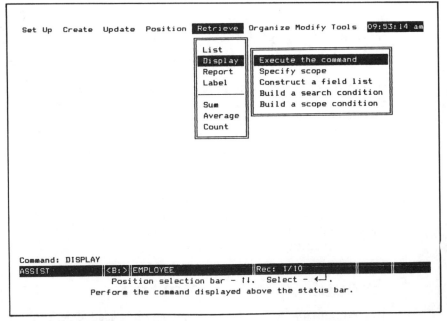

Fig. 4.32. Display option submenu.

and fields. You select this submenu option only after you have used other submenu options to specify the data subset.

# Selecting the Data Records To Be Displayed

Existing data records in the active database file can be selected for display according to one or more criteria:

By specifying the "scope," or the range of records within the database file

By selecting records that meet specified conditions

# Specifying Scope

PLUS

The **Display** operation's second submenu option, **Specify scope,** provides one way of defining the subset of data records that are to be displayed. Because each data record is assigned a sequential *record number* when it is entered to the database file, you can specify a set of data records by identifying a range of record numbers. When you select the **Specify scope** option from the submenu, another list of submenu options is displayed (see fig. 4.33).

The subsets of data records that are specified with these submenu options are summarized in table 4.2.

**Table 4.2**
**Options for Defining Scope**

| Submenu Option | Records Specified |
| --- | --- |
| Default scope | The current record |
| ALL | All existing records in the database file |
| NEXT | A specified number of records, beginning with the current record |
| RECORD | The record with the specified record number |
| REST | Every record, beginning with the current record |

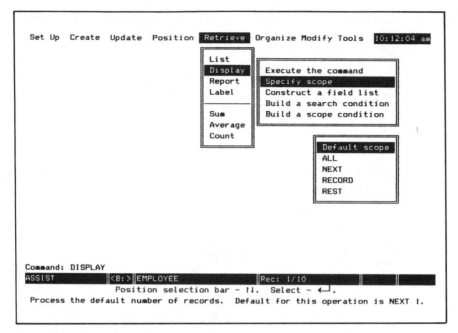

Fig. 4.33. Defining record scope.

To display all the existing records in the active database file, for example, you select the following options:

Retrieve/Display/Specify scope/ALL/Execute the command

The records displayed by selecting these options are shown in figure 4.34.

When more than 20 records are displayed, the program pauses after every 20 lines and prompts you to press any key to continue. If the record contains more than 80 characters of information, its contents wrap around to the next display line; a field may be broken up into two or more lines.

 # Constructing a Field List

The third submenu option of **Display, Construct a field list,** enables you to specify which data fields are to be displayed. All the existing data fields will be displayed unless a subset is specified with this option. However, the contents of memo fields are not displayed

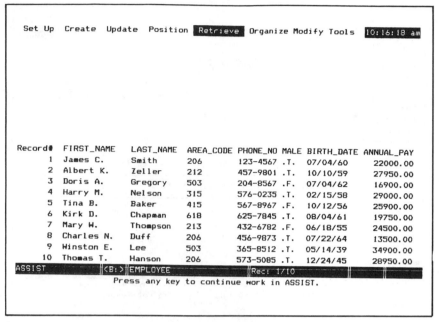

Fig. 4.34. Displaying all records in EMPLOYEE.DBF.

automatically unless you specify them in the field list. The contents of specified memo fields are displayed in a 50-column format.

When you have selected the **Construct a field list** submenu option, a list of the active database file's fields is displayed (see fig. 4.35).

From this field list you select the data fields that you want to display. You can select one or all of the existing fields in the database file. To select data fields one at a time, you first highlight the field and then press Enter. The sequence in which you select the data fields determines the order in which they are displayed. To produce a telephone directory from the EMPLOYEE database file, for example, you choose the following options:

> Retrieve/Display/Specify scope/ALL/Construct a field list /
> FIRST_NAME/LAST_NAME/AREA_CODE/PHONE_NO/
> Execute the command

The dBASE III Plus dot-prompt command for the display operation is

> DISPLAY ALL FIRST_NAME, LAST_NAME, AREA_CODE,
> PHONE_NO

The output generated by this operation is shown in figure 4.36.

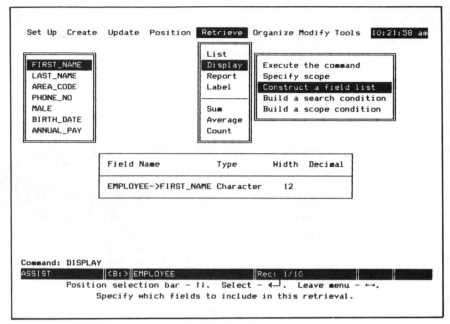

Fig. 4.35. Selecting data fields to be displayed.

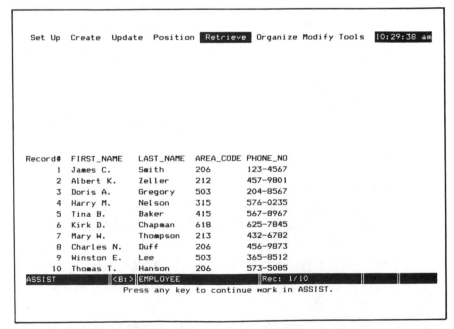

Fig. 4.36. Displaying contents of selected data fields.

# Specifying Selected Records

PLUS

In addition to selecting records by range, you can have dBASE III Plus search for records that meet specified conditions. To define these conditions, you select the **Build a search condition** option from the submenu of the **Display** option (see fig. 4.37).

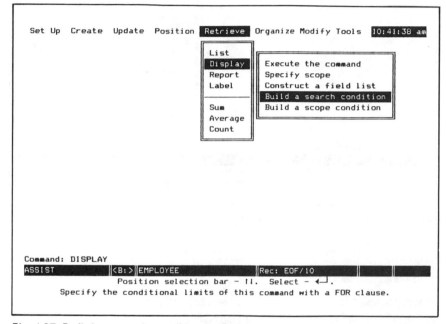

Fig. 4.37. Defining search condition for Display.

After selecting the submenu option, you are prompted to choose the data field for which you want to define a search condition. For example, if you want to display only those records with AREA_CODE fields that contain a certain value, such as 206, you select the AREA_CODE field from the submenu option list. A list of logical operators then is displayed (see fig. 4.38).

These logical operators are used to determine whether a particular data record will be chosen for display. If you select the = **Equal To** operator, the condition will be satisfied only when the contents of the search key and the search object are identical. If the object of the search is Smith, the condition will be met only if the LAST_NAME field (the search key) contains *Smith*. The condition will *not* be met if the field contains *smith* or *SMITH*. Because upper- and lowercase

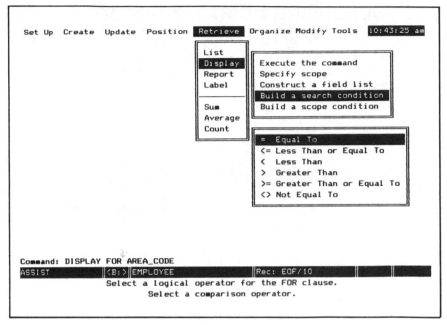

Fig. 4.38. Logical operators for defining search condition.

letters are treated as unique characters in a data record, the string
*Smith* is not equal to *smith*.

When you use the greater than (>) or less than (<) logical
operators, the strings are compared character by character to
determine which string has the greater or lesser value. The order of
alphanumeric characters as defined by the American Standard Code
for Information Interchange (ASCII) is listed in table 4.3. A character
with a high-order designation is greater than a character with a
low-order designation.

---

### Table 4.3
### The Order of Alphanumeric Characters

*Lower Order*

*(space) ! " # $ % & ' (apostrophe) ( ) * + , (comma) – .(period)
/ 0 . . . 9 : ; < = > ? @ A B C . . . X Y Z [ \ ] ^ a b c . . . x y z*

*Higher Order*

---

In keeping with the order defined in table 4.3, each of the following relations is true:

"smith" > "Smith"
"Samson" > "Sam"
"JOHN" < "john"
"ABC123" < "ABC12"
"(206)" < "206"
"Smith, James" <> "Smith,James"

Note that the string *smith* is greater than *Smith*. The first character of *smith*, *s*, has a higher order designation than does *S*.

When you use a logical operator to select data records in a date field, a later calendar date is evaluated as being greater than an earlier date. For example, 60/01/01 is greater than 59/12/31.

To use a logical field in a search, you need only select the data field (such as MALE). The search condition will be met when the value of the logical data field is *T*.

As you define the search condition, the dot-prompt command for the display operation is shown on the action line. If you want to display all data records whose AREA_CODE fields share the string *206*, for example, you would choose the following options:

Retrieve/Display/Build a search condition/AREA_CODE/= Equal to/*206*

As shown in figure 4.39, the equivalent dot-prompt command for the display operation is

DISPLAY FOR AREA_CODE = '206'

If you have no further search conditions to define, now you can execute the display command by choosing the following submenu options:

/No more conditions/Execute the command

The records that satisfy the search conditions are then displayed (see fig. 4.40).

Notice that all the records displayed in figure 4.40 have the value 206 in the AREA_CODE field.

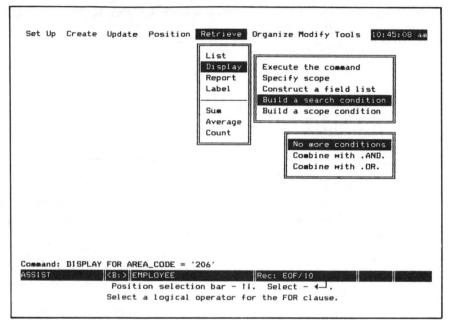

Fig. 4.39. Another level of logical operators.

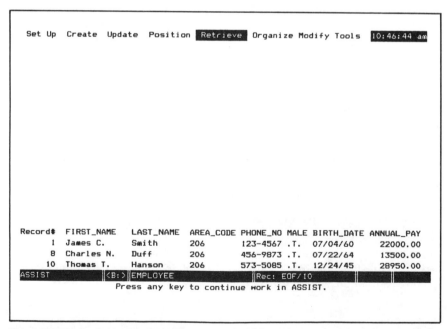

Fig. 4.40. Displaying records with area code 206.

## Multiple Search Conditions

When selecting data records for display, you can specify more than one condition for the search operation. Using the .AND. operator, you can form a search criterion that combines two logical operators. For example, you can have dBASE III Plus display those records in which

AREA_CODE = '206' .AND. ANNUAL_PAY > 20000

In this case, only those records whose field values meet both conditions are selected.

The menu and submenu options for this display operation are

Retrieve/Display/Build a search condition/AREA_CODE/= Equal to/*206*/Combine with .AND./ANNUAL_PAY/> Greater than/*20000*/No more conditions/Execute the command

As shown in figure 4.41, the dBASE III Plus command for this display operation is

DISPLAY FOR AREA_CODE = '206' .AND. ANNUAL_PAY > 20000

The records displayed with this command are shown in figure 4.42. Notice that the displayed records meet both conditions specified in the search criteria.

You can use the .OR. operator to select records in which either or both of the specified conditions are satisfied. To display the records of employees who were born before 1960 or whose annual incomes are greater than $20,000, for example, you would choose the following options:

Retrieve/Display/Build a search condition/BIRTH_DATE/< Less than/*60/01/01*/Combine with .OR./ANNUAL_PAY/> Greater than/*20000*/No more conditions/Execute the command

The corresponding dBASE III Plus command is

DISPLAY FOR BIRTH_DATE < CTOD('60/01/01') .OR. ANNUAL_PAY > 20000

CTOD is a built-in function that converts a string of characters ('60/01/01' in this example) to a date. (You will learn more about built-in functions in Chapter 7.) The records displayed by using these menu and submenu options are shown in figure 4.43.

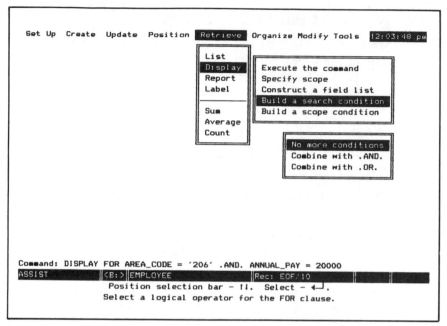

Fig. 4.41. Using .AND. in search condition.

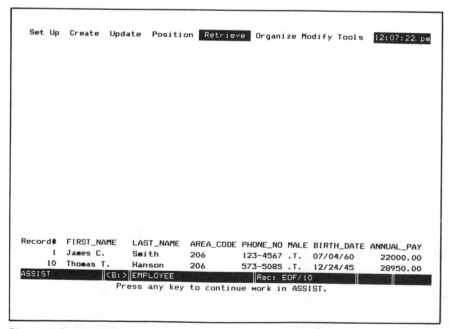

Fig. 4.42. Records displayed with .AND. in search condition.

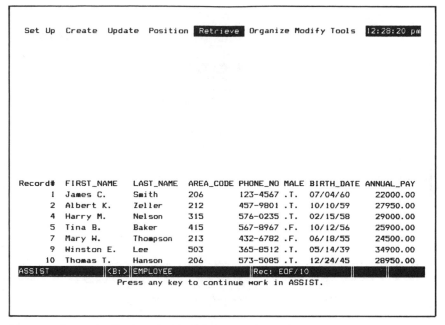

*Fig. 4.43. Records displayed with .OR. in search condition.*

## Defining the Scope in Search Conditions

PLUS

You define the scope of a search by selecting the **Specify scope** submenu option from the **Display** menu. Data records that meet the search condition are selected from those records that fall within the scope you specify. If you select **ALL**, the search applies to all existing records. Otherwise, the search operation applies only to those records falling within the specified range.

Not only can you define the record set from which the search conditions are to be applied, but you can also specify the record set by selecting **Build a scope condition** from the submenu of **Display** (see fig. 4.44).

This option provides an additional screening level for selecting the set of records to be displayed. When you use this submenu option to define the scope of the search, the search continues as long as the specified scope condition remains valid. If you set the search scope to MALE, for example, the search will continue as long as the value in the MALE fields remains true (.T.). However, as soon as a record

Fig. 4.44. Defining scope condition with WHILE clause.

fails to meet the scope condition, the display operation is terminated.

Here is an example of how to use **Build a search condition:**

Retrieve/Display/Specify scope/*ALL*/Build a search condition/ *AREA_CODE*/= Equal to/*206*/No more conditions/Build a scope condition/*MALE*/No more conditions/Execute the command

Figure 4.44 shows the dBASE III Plus command for this Display operation:

DISPLAY ALL FOR AREA_CODE = '206' WHILE MALE

The output produced by this **Display** operation is shown in figure 4.45. Instead of showing all the data records that satisfy both the search condition (AREA_CODE = '206') and the scope condition (MALE = .T.), the output displays only one data record. If you examine all the records in the EMPLOYEE database file (refer to fig. 4.34), you will notice that the value in the third record's MALE field is *.F.*. Therefore, when the scope condition (WHILE MALE) is applied in the search operation, the display operation is terminated at

the third record (the current record is indicated in the status bar as
**Rec : 3/10**). To display all the records for male employees, you
would group them together before applying this scope condition to
the search.

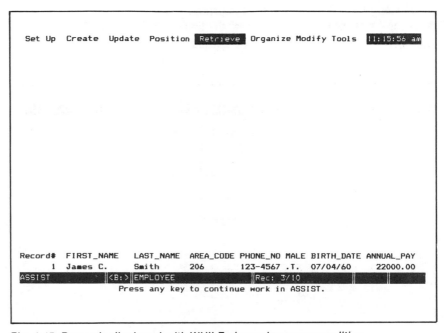

*Fig. 4.45. Records displayed with WHILE clause in scope condition.*

It is important to select **ALL** for the **Specify scope** option *before*
you define a scope condition if you want the program to start
searching from the first records in the database file. Otherwise, the
search process will begin from the current record. After many data-
manipulation or display operations, the current record could be
located at the end of the file (indicated by **Rec : EOF/10** in the status
bar). If you were to perform the display operation at that point, no
records would be found. One solution to this problem (if you don't
select **ALL** for the **Specify scope** option) is to position the current-
record pointer at the beginning of the file. (The procedure for
positioning the current-record pointer is discussed in Chapter 5.)

PLUS  # Listing Data Records

You can list the contents of records with the **Retrieve/List** options (see fig. 4.46), as well as the **Retrieve/Display** options. The functions of these options are similar, with two important differences. One difference is that the current record is the default range for the **Display** option, whereas the **List** option shows all existing records unless it is limited by a scope or search condition.

Fig. 4.46. Using List option.

Another major difference between the **Display** and **List** options is that the former displays data records 20 lines at a time, whereas the latter lists all the records continuously. If there are more than 20 records to be displayed, only the last 20 records will be shown on the screen after the **Display** operation is performed. However, you can halt a listing by pressing Ctrl-S. After examining the displayed records, you can resume the listing operation by pressing Enter.

# Displaying Data on a Printer

**Display** and **List** can be used to display the contents of a database file either on the screen or on hard copy. You choose the output medium by answering the prompt:

**Direct the output to the printer ? [Y/N]**

If you are in dot-prompt mode and want to print records, all you have to do is add the clause *TO PRINT* after the DISPLAY or LIST command. Examples are

. DISPLAY ALL TO PRINT
. DISPLAY ALL FOR AREA_CODE = '206' WHILE MALE TO PRINT
. LIST AREA_CODE,PHONE_NO FOR LAST_NAME="Baker" TO PRINT
. DISPLAY FOR .NOT. MALE .AND. ANNUAL_PAY>=20000 TO PRINT
. LIST ALL FIRST_NAME,LAST_NAME,BIRTH_DATE TO PRINT

Notice that single and double quotation marks can be used interchangeably to enclose a character string, and that you can use .NOT. (another logical operator) to set a search condition.

# Chapter Summary

Database files are created by choosing the **Create/Database** file options from the Assistant menu. In dot-prompt mode, the CREATE command is used. To create a database file, you must first specify the structure, which defines a data record's field attributes: field name, type, and width.

After the structure is specified, you can enter data records in several ways. Records can be added to the end of a file with the APPEND command.

The **Erase** option deletes the whole database file, including the structure and all the data records in the file. To erase the data records without disturbing the data structure, you can use the ZAP dot command. Both **Erase** and ZAP permanently delete the contents of a file.

All commands that involve editing, modifying, and displaying the contents of a database file affect only the active file. The **Set Up** option (or the USE dot command) must be used to activate the database file if the file is not active. You can switch from the current data disk drive to a different disk drive by choosing the **Tools/Set drive** menu options or the SET DEFAULT TO dot command. The contents of a database file can be copied to a file with another name by means of the **Copy file** option. You can rename a database file by selecting **Tools/Rename**. Before you can copy or rename a file, however, the file must be closed with the CLOSE DATABASES dot command.

Information related to an existing database file can be displayed and printed. The **Tools/Directory** options from the Assistant menu enable you to display a directory of various kinds of disk files on the default disk drive. You can display the structure of an existing database file by choosing the **Tools/List structure** options.

The contents of data records can be displayed by choosing the **Retrieve/Display** or **Retrieve/List** options from the Assistant menu; in dot-prompt mode, you use the DISPLAY or LIST commands. You can display all data records in a database file or, by using the **Specify scope, Construct a field list, Build a search condition,** and **Build a scope condition options,** select a set of data fields and records to be included in the display operation.

# 5

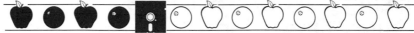

# Querying the Database and Editing Data

## An Overview

Chapter 4 explained how to use the **Display** and **List** options to display the contents and structure of a database file. This chapter introduces another way to display selected records: using the powerful query operation implemented in dBASE III Plus. The steps for creating and using a query file are discussed in this chapter.

This chapter also discusses how to position the record pointer to a specific record in the database file by using the Assistant's **Position** menu option. The **Position** submenu options are **Locate**, **Continue**, **Skip**, and **Goto Record**.

Editing the information related to a database file is also explained in this chapter. You can modify database structures and edit data records by using the Assistant menu or by issuing commands at the dot prompt. You will learn how to modify the database structure with the **Modify/Database file** menu options and how to edit selected records with the **Update** submenu options. These options are **Edit, Browse, Replace, Delete, Recall,** and **Pack.**

PLUS | # Using the dBASE III Plus Query Operation

One powerful feature offered by dBASE III Plus, which is not available in dBASE II or dBASE III, is the query operation. By querying the database, you can view the contents of data records that meet a set of conditions you define. These conditions can be specified and saved in a query file. After that, when you activate the query file by selecting **Setup**, only the records that satisfy the conditions will be accessible for data manipulations. For example, when you use one of the display options (such as **Retrieve/Display** or **Retrieve/List**) after setting up the query file, only the records that meet the query conditions will be shown. Records not meeting the conditions are in effect "filtered out" and are not accessible. All your data manipulations are performed upon the subset of records that meet the query conditions.

PLUS | # Creating a Query File

A query file stores the filter conditions that define a subset of records in the database file. To create a query file, you select the **Create/Query** options from the Assistant menu (see fig. 5.1). First, you are prompted to enter a name for the query file. Then a blank query form appears (see fig. 5.2); here, you define your query (or filter) conditions.

The menu bar in figure 5.2 shows that the default submenu option, **Set Filter,** is currently active. Now you can start defining query conditions. That process entails the following steps:

1. Select the data field for the query condition.

2. Select the logical operator to be used in the condition.

3. Specify the constant or expression for the condition.

4. Define the connecting logical operator if more than one condition is required.

5. Define nesting conditions, if necessary.

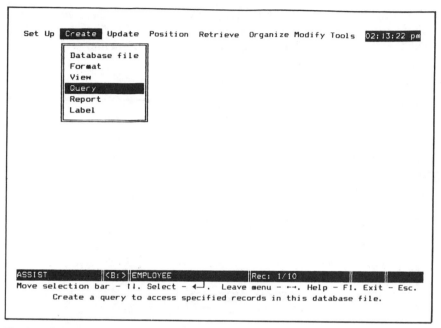

Fig. 5.1. Creating query file.

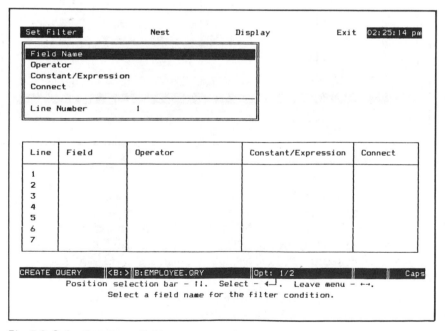

Fig. 5.2. Selecting query fields.

For example, you can select records from EMPLOYEE.DBF that hve the value 206 in AREA_CODE or a value greater than 20000 in ANNUAL_PAY by choosing the following menu and submenu options:

Set Filter/Field Name/AREA_CODE/Operator/= Matches/ Constant/Expression/*'206'*/Connect/Combine with .OR./ Field Name/ANNUAL_PAY/Operator/> More than/*20000*/ Connect/No combination

The resulting query table looks like the one shown in figure 5.3.

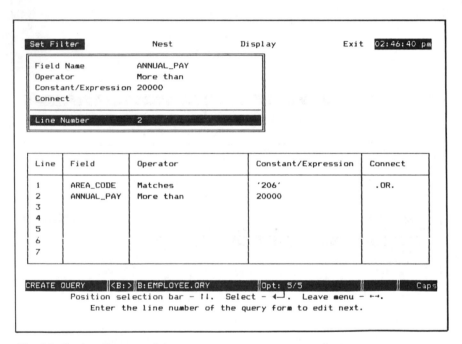

Fig. 5.3. Setting filter conditions.

Each query condition is defined on one row in the table; as many as seven conditions can be defined. A logical operator (such as .OR.) is used to link multiple conditions. When you define an expression for a character field (such as AREA_CODE), you must enclose the character string in single or double quotation marks (such as '206' or "206").

While you are creating the query table, you can experiment with these conditions and display different sets of records. To do this, press the → key until the **Display** menu option is highlighted, then press Enter (see fig. 5.4).

```
   Set Filter          Nest         ▐Display▌        Exit ▐02:56:50 pm▌




   ┌──────┬───────────┬───────────┬───────────────────┬──────────┐
   │ Line │ Field     │ Operator  │ Constant/Expression│ Connect  │
   ├──────┼───────────┼───────────┼───────────────────┼──────────┤
   │  1   │ AREA_CODE │ Matches   │ '206'             │ .OR.     │
   │  2   │ ANNUAL_PAY│ More than │ 20000             │          │
   │  3   │           │           │                   │          │
   │  4   │           │           │                   │          │
   │  5   │           │           │                   │          │
   │  6   │           │           │                   │          │
   │  7   │           │           │                   │          │
   │      │           │           │                   │          │
   └──────┴───────────┴───────────┴───────────────────┴──────────┘
▐CREATE QUERY    ▌ ▐<B:>▌▐B:EMPLOYEE.QRY                         ▐  Caps▌
              Select - ◄┘.   Leave prompt pad - ←→.
          Display records in the database that meet the query condition.
```

*Fig. 5.4. Choosing Display.*

The first record that meets the query condition is then displayed. In figure 5.5 the displayed records satisfy the condition

AREA_CODE = '206' .OR. ANNUAL_PAY>20000

You can display the next record that meets the query condition, if there is one, by pressing the PgDn key. Pressing PgDn at this point causes the record of Albert K. Zeller to be displayed (see fig. 5.6). Pressing the PgUp key causes the previous record to be displayed.

While you are displaying a record, you can blank out the query table by pressing F1. That way only the information about the record is shown (see fig. 5.7).

To display the query table again, press F1 once more. When you have examined the filtered records and are satisfied with the conditions defined in the query table, you can save the table by selecting the **Exit** menu option. You are then asked whether you want to save the query table or abandon the operation (see fig. 5.8).

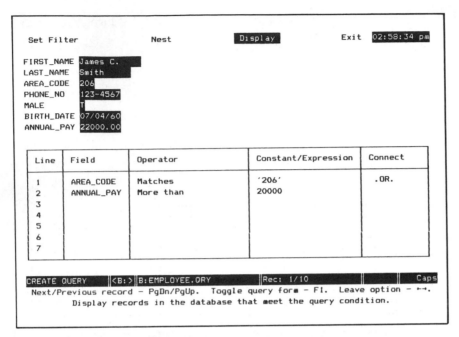

Fig. 5.5. Displaying first selected data record.

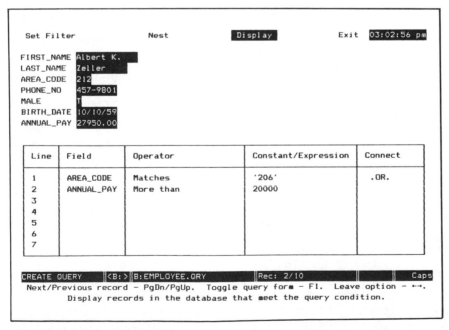

Fig. 5.6. Displaying next selected data record.

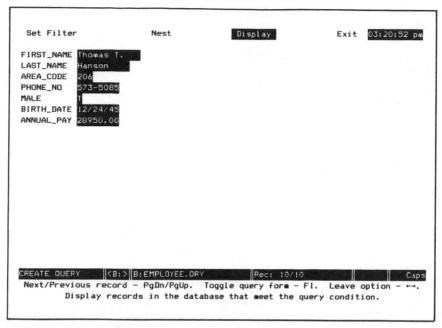

Fig. 5.7. Query table blanked out by pressing F1.

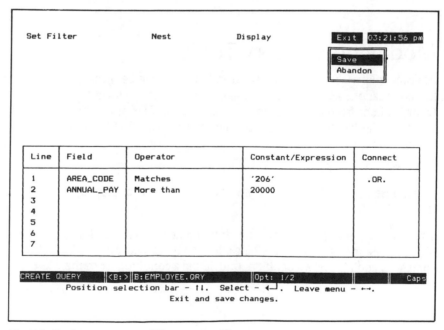

Fig. 5.8. Saving query conditions and exiting.

If you select **Save,** the query table is saved in the query file
EMPLOYEE.QRY.

In dot-prompt mode, you can create the EMPLOYEE.QRY query file
by entering CREATE QUERY (see fig. 5.9). The subsequent steps are
the same as when The Assistant is used.

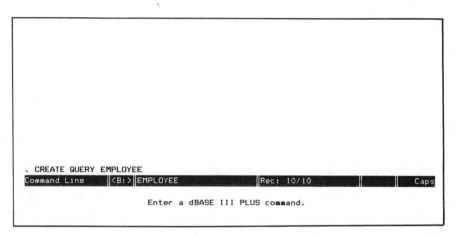

```
.  CREATE QUERY EMPLOYEE
Command Line      <B:> EMPLOYEE                      Rec: 10/10                          Caps

               Enter a dBASE III PLUS command.
```

*Fig. 5.9. Creating query file in dot-prompt mode.*

PLUS
# Modifying a Query Table

After the query table has been created and saved, it can be recalled
for modification. To recall a query table, simply select the **Modify/
Query** options from the Assistant menu (see fig. 5.10). For example,
you could display the query table created earlier (EMPLOYEE.QRY)
by choosing the following menu and submenu options:

   Modify/Query/B:/EMPLOYEE.QRY

In response to these menu selections, the query table is displayed
(see fig. 5.11).

You can now modify the query table, entering new conditions for
filtering. The modifications might include changing a query
condition, adding a new condition, or deleting a condition from the
table.

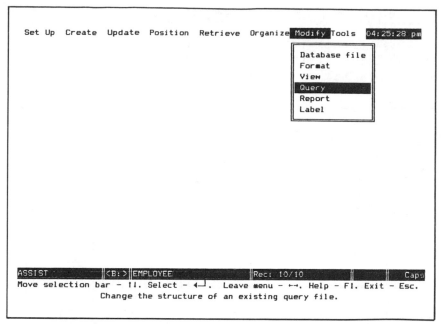

Fig. 5.10. Modifying query file.

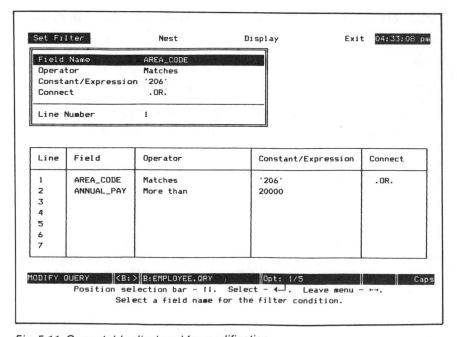

Fig. 5.11. Query table displayed for modification.

## PLUS Modifying Query Conditions

As shown in figure 5.11, each query condition is defined as a line in the table. To select the query condition to be modified, you enter its line number in the submenu of the **Set Filter** menu option.

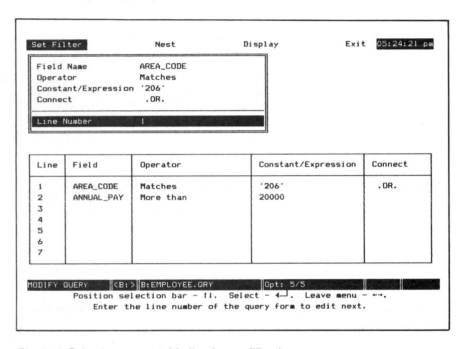

Fig. 5.12. Selecting query-table line for modification.

For example, if you want to modify the contents of the query condition for the ANNUAL_PAY field, first select the **Line Number** option (see fig. 5.12). The cursor is now positioned at the submenu option, and you can enter the line number of the query condition that is to be modified. After entering a line number (2, for this example), press the Enter key. The contents of the selected query line then are displayed as a list of submenu options (see fig. 5.13).

Now you can select the item to be changed by pressing the ↓ key until that item is highlighted. For example, to change the contents of ANNUAL_PAY from 20000 to 22000, select **Constant/Expression** and press Enter. When the cursor appears at the end of the item, use the backspace key to erase characters as necessary, then type the new expression value. After you press Enter, the modified query condition replaces the original one (see fig. 5.14).

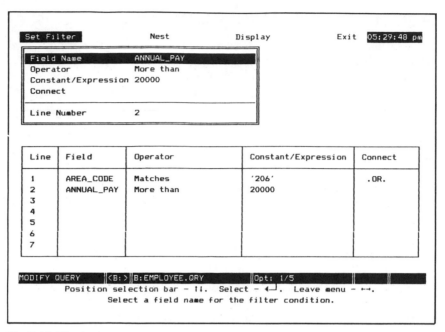

Fig. 5.13. Displaying current query field.

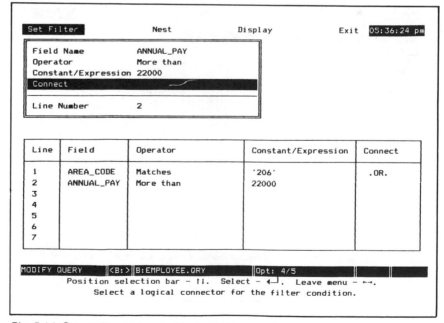

Fig. 5.14. Query-line contents displayed for modification.

# Adding a New Query Condition

To insert a new query condition, select the line number above which the new condition is to be inserted. For example, if you want to insert a new line above the first query line in the current table, go to line 1 by selecting the following menu and submenu options:

Set Filter/Line Number/*1*

When the query condition in line 1 is displayed, press Ctrl-N. A blank line is then inserted and all lines following that line are moved down (see fig. 5.15). The query condition for this new line can now be entered. For example, you could enter a new query condition to select records having the value .T. in the MALE field (see fig. 5.16).

You can add a new condition to the end of the query table by selecting the number of the line following the last existing query line. Suppose, for example, that you want to add a condition to select the records of employees born before January 1, 1960. You add such a new line to the query table by means of the following menu and submenu options and keyboard entries:

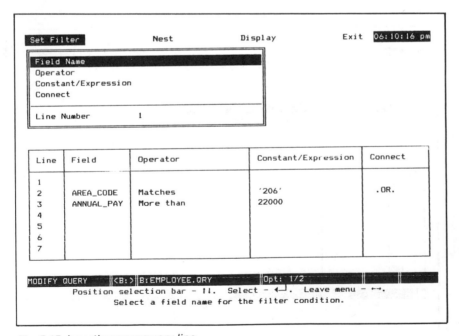

Fig. 5.15. Inserting new query line.

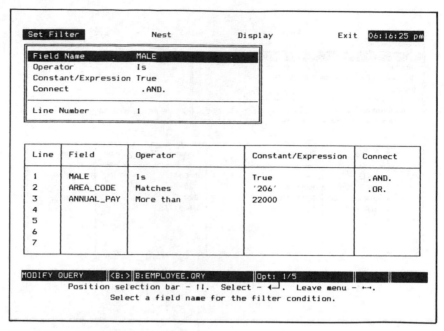

```
 Set Filter            Nest          Display          Exit  06:16:25 pm

  Field Name          . MALE                .
  Operator              Is
  Constant/Expression   True
  Connect               .AND.

  Line Number           1


 ┌───────┬───────────┬─────────────┬─────────────────────┬──────────┐
 │ Line  │ Field     │ Operator    │ Constant/Expression │ Connect  │
 ├───────┼───────────┼─────────────┼─────────────────────┼──────────┤
 │  1    │ MALE      │ Is          │ True                │ .AND.    │
 │  2    │ AREA_CODE │ Matches     │ '206'               │ .OR.     │
 │  3    │ ANNUAL_PAY│ More than   │ 22000               │          │
 │  4    │           │             │                     │          │
 │  5    │           │             │                     │          │
 │  6    │           │             │                     │          │
 │  7    │           │             │                     │          │
 └───────┴───────────┴─────────────┴─────────────────────┴──────────┘

 MODIFY QUERY     <B:> B:EMPLOYEE.QRY        Opt: 1/5
      Position selection bar - ↑↓.  Select - ↵.  Leave menu - ↔.
            Select a field name for the filter condition.
```

*Fig. 5.16. Defining new query line.*

Set Field/Line Number/*4*/Field Name/BIRTH_DATE/ Operator/< Less than/Constant/Expression/*01/01/60*/No combination

The revised query table should look like the one shown in figure 5.17. (Notice that the connecting operator in line 3 has also been changed to .AND.).

If you choose to display the records that meet the new query conditions, you will find that records 1, 2, 4, 5, 7, 8, 9, 10 are included. The conditions defined in the query table can be expressed as

MALE .AND. AREA_CODE = '206'.OR. ANNUAL_PAY > 20000 .AND. BIRTH_DAY < CTOD(01/01/60)

(CTOD, a built-in function that converts a character string to a date, is discussed in a later chapter.) Because you can compare a date field only with a date value, the character string must be converted to a date before the less-than operator (<) can be applied.

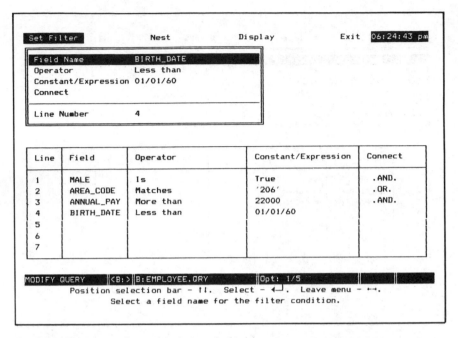

| Set Filter | Nest | Display | Exit | 06:24:43 pm |

| Field Name | BIRTH_DATE |
| Operator | Less than |
| Constant/Expression | 01/01/60 |
| Connect | |
| Line Number | 4 |

| Line | Field | Operator | Constant/Expression | Connect |
|------|-------|----------|---------------------|---------|
| 1 | MALE | Is | True | .AND. |
| 2 | AREA_CODE | Matches | '206' | .OR. |
| 3 | ANNUAL_PAY | More than | 22000 | .AND. |
| 4 | BIRTH_DATE | Less than | 01/01/60 | |
| 5 | | | | |
| 6 | | | | |
| 7 | | | | |

MODIFY QUERY    <B:> B:EMPLOYEE.QRY    Opt: 1/5

Position selection bar - ↑↓.  Select - ↵.  Leave menu - ←.
Select a field name for the filter condition.

*Fig. 5.17. New query line added at end of table.*

Unless you specify otherwise, query conditions are evaluated from
left to right and in the order of their appearance. The conditions in
the previous example are evaluated in the following order:

1. The records that satisfy the conditions MALE .AND.
   AREA_CODE = '206' are selected.

2. The records are selected that meet the conditions in step 1 or
   that have values in the ANNUAL_PAY field greater than
   20000.

3. The records are selected that satisfy the conditions in step 2
   and whose values in the BIRTH_DATE field are less (earlier)
   than the date 01/01/60.

Parentheses can be used to define a different evaluation sequence. In
mathematical equations, expressions enclosed in parentheses are
evaluated first. The use of parentheses in query conditions follows
the same conventions: expressions in inner parentheses are
evaluated before those in outer parentheses. The conditions
specified in the previous example are therefore interpreted as

(((MALE .AND. AREA_CODE = '206') .OR. ANNUAL_PAY > 20000) .AND. BIRTH_DAY < CTOD(01/01/60))

Because the parentheses indicate the order of precedence, a different set of records will be selected if you move the parentheses, as in

MALE .AND. (AREA_CODE = '206' .OR. (ANNUAL_PAY > 20000) .AND. BIRTH_DAY < CTOD(01/01/60)

In this case, the program will search first for the records in which ANNUAL_PAY is greater than 20000. Then the rest of the conditions will be evaluated.

To add parentheses to the conditions in the query table, select the **Nest** menu option. A list of submenu options is displayed; you can use these options to add or remove a left parenthesis (**Start**) or a right parenthesis (**End**), as shown in figure 5.18.

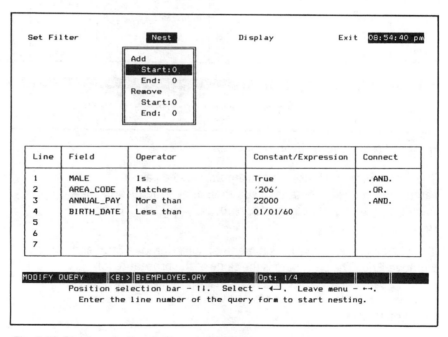

*Fig. 5.18. Placing starting (left) parenthesis.*

You can enclose in parentheses the first two lines of the query table by selecting these submenu options:

Nest/Add Start:/*2*/Add End:/*3*

Figure 5.19 shows that after you select the submenu options, an open parenthesis is placed at the beginning of line 2 (**Start:2**) and a closed parenthesis is inserted at the end of line 3 (**End:3**).

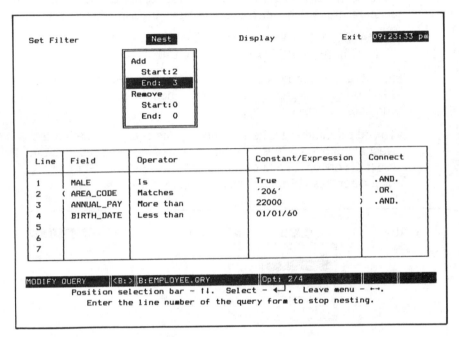

Fig. 5.19. Placing ending (right) parenthesis.

The same procedure is used to add another nested pair of parentheses to the query table. If you then display the records that meet the current query conditions, records 2, 4, 9, and 10 are shown.

To erase parentheses, use the submenu options **Remove Start** and **Remove End**. The procedure is the same as the procedure for inserting parentheses. Once you have finished modifying the query table, you can save the changed table by choosing the **Exit/Save** menu option.

# PLUS | Deleting a Query Condition

When you are modifying a query table, you can delete any of the conditions you have specified. To delete a query condition, simply move the cursor to the line containing the condition and press Ctrl-U. The condition then is removed from the table.

# Using the Query Table

PLUS

After the query table has been created and saved in a query file (such as EMPLOYEE.QRY), the conditions defined in the table can be used to select data records for further processing. To use the conditions in the query file, you must first activate the file by choosing **Set Up/ Query** from the Assistant menu (see fig. 5.20).

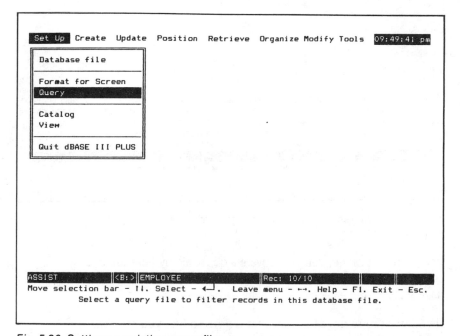

Fig. 5.20. Setting up existing query file.

After you have set up a query file, only the records that meet the query conditions are affected when you manipulate the data in the database file. For example, after setting up the EMPLOYEE.QRY file with

Set Up/B:/EMPLOYEE.QRY

you can choose to display all the records in the database file by selecting

Retrieve/List/Execute the command

Notice that only the records that satisfy the query conditions are listed (see fig. 5.21).

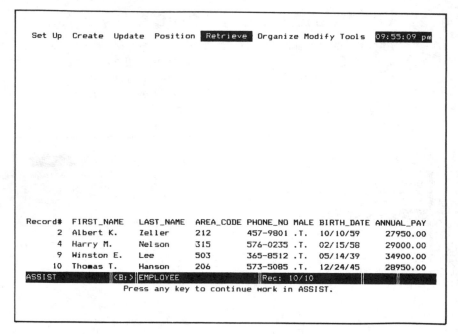

Fig. 5.21. Listing records that meet query conditions.

In dot-prompt mode, you can activate a query file by entering the command SET FILTER TO FILE <name of query file> after you have selected the database file (see fig. 5.22).

If you want to remove the query conditions so that you can again process all the data records in the database file, you have to set up the database file again. For example, to process all the records in the EMPLOYEE.DBF without any query conditions, you set up the database file as follows:

    Set Up/Database/File/B:/EMPLOYEE.DBF

If you then choose the **Retrieve/List** options from the Assistant menu, all 10 records in the database file are displayed with no filtering conditions in effect.

#  Using the Record Pointer

When manipulating data, you often need to know which record is the current record. When you use the **Display** option, for example,

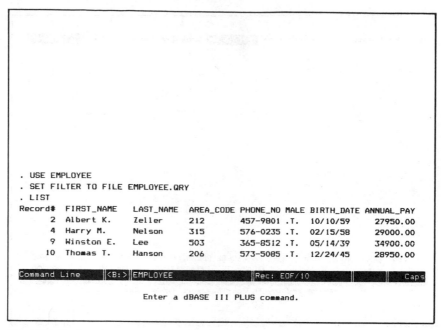

```
. USE EMPLOYEE
. SET FILTER TO FILE EMPLOYEE.QRY
. LIST
Record#  FIRST_NAME   LAST_NAME   AREA_CODE PHONE_NO MALE BIRTH_DATE ANNUAL_PAY
      2  Albert K.    Zeller      212       457-9801 .T.  10/10/59   27950.00
      4  Harry M.     Nelson      315       576-0235 .T.  02/15/58   29000.00
      9  Winston E.   Lee         503       365-8512 .T.  05/14/39   34900.00
     10  Thomas T.    Hanson      206       573-5085 .T.  12/24/45   28950.00
```

| Command Line | <B:> EMPLOYEE | Rec: EOF/10 | Caps |
|---|---|---|---|

```
            Enter a dBASE III PLUS command.
```

*Fig. 5.22. Performing query operation in dot-prompt mode.*

the current record is displayed by default unless you specify a search condition or a scope.

As you know, when a database file is created, the records are assigned numbers reflecting the order in which the records are entered. The first record in the database file, for example, is record 1, the next is record 2, and so on.

The record pointer stores number of the current record. The content of the record pointer is constantly updated to reflect the record being processed.

When you set up an existing database file (with **Set Up/Database/ File/B:/EMPLOYEE.DBF**, for example), the first record of the file is designated as the current record. Therefore, if you perform the Display operation (**Retrieve/Display/Execute the command**) the contents of the first record are displayed (see fig. 5.23).

If you want to display the contents of a different record (record 5, for example), you can move the record pointer to that record before displaying the record. To position the record pointer, you first select the **Position** option from the Assistant menu.

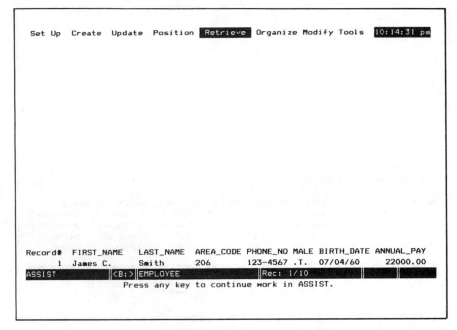

*Fig. 5.23. Displaying current record.*

By using the Position menu options, you can

Unconditionally position the record pointer at a specific record
by specifying the record number

Skip a number of records and position the record pointer at
the record following the skipped records

Position the record pointer at the record that satisfies a
specified search or scope condition

## PLUS Going to a Specific Record

To position the record pointer at a specific record, simply select the
**Position/Goto Record** options and enter the record number at the
prompt. For example, to position the record pointer at record 5,
select the following menu options (see fig. 5.24):

Position/Goto Record/Record/Enter a numeric value:*5*

The current record then is shown, and **Rec : 5/10** appears in the
status bar. If you select the Display operation now (**Retrieve/**

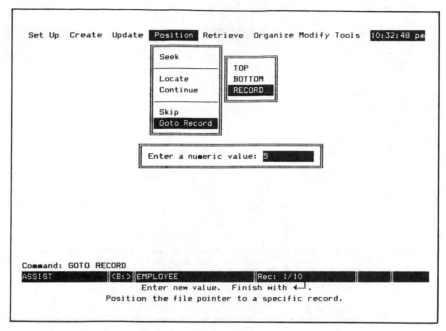

*Fig. 5.24. Going to fifth record in database file.*

Display/Execute the command), record 5 is displayed on the screen (see fig. 5.25).

Instead of using the Position submenu, you can move the pointer to a specific record by entering the GOTO command at the dot prompt, as in

. GOTO <data record number>

To position the pointer at record 5 in the EMPLOYEE.DBF file, for example, you enter the following commands:

. USE EMPLOYEE
. GOTO 5

While using the Position menu option, you can position the pointer at the beginning of the current database file by choosing the options

Position/Goto Record/TOP

Record 1 then becomes the current record. Similarly, you can move the pointer to the last record of the current database file by choosing the menu options

Position/Goto Record/BOTTOM

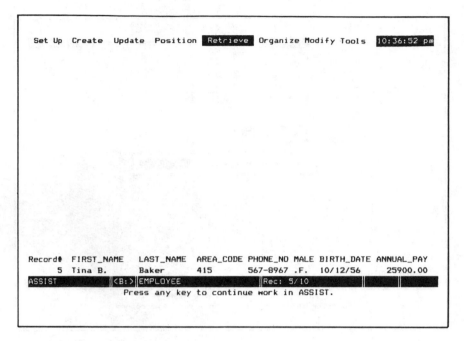

Fig. 5.25. Displaying current record.

If the current database has 10 records (as in this example), record 10 is made the current record, and **Rec ∶ 10/10** appears in the status bar.

In dot-prompt mode, the equivalent commands for these operations are

. GO TOP

and

. GO BOTTOM

 **Skipping Records**

Another **Position** submenu option is the **Skip**. You can use this option to skip forward or backward a number of records from the current record position and to place the record pointer at the next record. After choosing **Position/Skip**, you are prompted to specify the number of records to be skipped (see fig. 5.26).

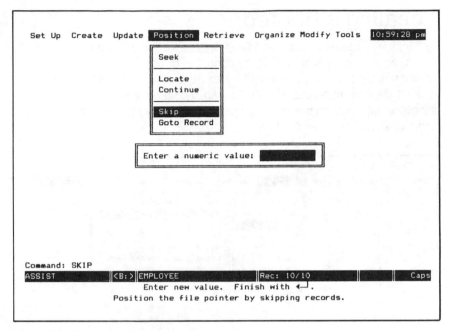

*Fig. 5.26. Skipping data records.*

Now you enter a number, which can be a positive or negative integer. Entering a positive integer (the plus sign is optional) causes the pointer to skip forward; entering a negative integer moves the pointer backward. For instance, if the current record number is 5, and you enter 3 (or +3), record 8 becomes the current record. On the other hand, if record 8 is the current record, and you enter –4, record 4 becomes the current record.

If you skip forward beyond the last record in the database file, the record pointer is placed at the end of file; the status bar indicates that the pointer is at EOF (**Rec**: **EOF/10**, for this example). However, if you attempt to skip backward past the first record, the record pointer is positioned at record 1.

In dot-prompt mode, the SKIP command has the following format:

. SKIP <number of records to skip>

To skip the next 3 records, for example, you enter

. SKIP 3

If you do not specify the number of records to be skipped, one record (+1) is skipped by default.

# PLUS Locating a Record

In addition to using the **Goto** and **Skip** options from the **Position** menu, you can use a search or scope condition to position the record pointer at a specific record. To locate a specific record and make it the current record, choose **Position/Locate**. A set of submenu options then is displayed, and you can specify the search and scope condition (see fig. 5.27).

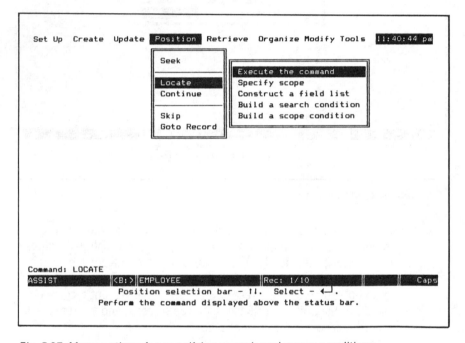

Fig. 5.27. Menu options for specifying search and scope conditions.

Specifying a search or scope condition is similar to using the **Retrieve** option, which is discussed in Chapter 4. To place the record pointer at the record that belongs to Mary Thompson, for example, you would choose the menu options

Position/Locate/Build a search condition/LAST_NAME/ = Equal to/*Thompson*/No more conditions/Execute the command

After you have selected the options, the following command is displayed on the command line:

Command: LOCATE FOR LAST_NAME = ' Thompson'

When this command is executed, the record that satisfies the search condition (record 7) is displayed above the status line at the bottom of the screen, and the current record is indicated as **Rec : 7/10** in the status bar. If you choose **Retrieve/Display/Execute**, record 7 is displayed (see fig. 5.28).

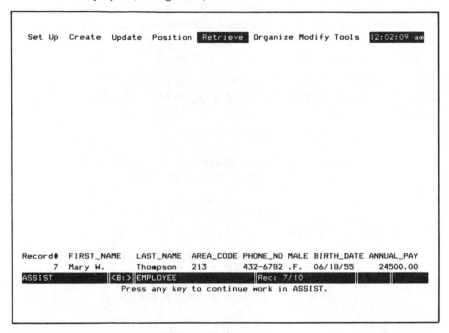

```
      Set Up   Create   Update   Position   Retrieve   Organize Modify Tools   12:02:09 am












      Record#  FIRST_NAME   LAST_NAME   AREA_CODE PHONE_NO MALE BIRTH_DATE ANNUAL_PAY
            7  Mary W.      Thompson     213       432-6782 .F.  06/18/55     24500.00
      ASSIST              <B:> EMPLOYEE                  Rec: 7/10
                      Press any key to continue work in ASSIST.
```

*Fig. 5.28. Displaying located data record.*

If no record is found that satisfies the search condition, the message **End of LOCATE scope** is displayed, and the record pointer is placed at the end of the file. If more than one record in the database file satisfies the search condition, the record pointer is placed at the first of those records. After processing the current record, you can go to the next record that meets the condition by selecting the **Continue** option from the **Position** submenu.

In dot-prompt mode, you can locate a specific record by using the LOCATE command with a qualifier, as in

    . LOCATE <qualifier>

The qualifier can be a scope or search condition. For instance, to find the employee record with *James C.* in the FIRST_NAME field, you enter

    . LOCATE FOR FIRST_NAME="James C."

When the command is executed, the records are searched, and the first record with the alphanumeric string *James C.* in the FIRST_NAME field is located. The record pointer is then set to the number of that record. The FIRST_NAME field may contain more than the alphanumeric string *James*, but if the first five characters match the search string, the record is selected; the characters after the first five characters are not examined. If more than one employee in the company has the first name *James* (even with a different middle initial), the first record containing *James* is selected.

The following LOCATE command finds the record of James C. Smith because EMPLOYEE.DBF has only one record with a first name beginning with *J*:

  . LOCATE FOR FIRST_NAME="J"

By using logical operators such as .AND. or .OR. in the LOCATE command qualifier, you can specify multiple relations. Some examples are

  . LOCATE FOR LAST_NAME="Smith" .AND.
  FIRST_NAME="James C."

  . LOCATE FOR MALE .AND. ANNUAL_PAY>=20000 .AND.
  AREA_CODE="315"

  . LOCATE WHILE AREA_CODE="206"FOR MALE .AND.
  ANNUAL_PAY>20000

When the pointer is positioned on the active record, you can use the CONTINUE command to move the pointer to the next record that satisfies the last search condition. The format for the CONTINUE command is simple:

  . CONTINUE

For example, suppose that record 6 was found by a LOCATE command. When you enter the CONTINUE command, the record pointer moves to record 7.

When you use the LOCATE command to search for records, the search begins with the current record and continues to the end of the file. Unless you are certain that the record you are looking for falls within that range, you may need to position the record pointer at the beginning of the file (by using the **Position/Goto Record/ TOP** menu options or the .GO TOP dot-prompt command). Then you can use the LOCATE command, and every record in the file will be searched.

# Editing a Database File

After a database file has been created, you can change its contents at any time. The contents of a database file are divided into two parts: the data structure, which defines the data fields in the file, and the actual contents of the data records.

# Modifying a Database Structure

Data fields can be redefined, changed, and deleted with the the **Modify** option of the Assistant menu. After the database file is set up (with **Set Up/Database file**), its structure can be recalled for modification. If the current database file is EMPLOYEE.DBF, for example, the structure of the database file can be displayed for examination or modification by choosing the following menu options (see fig. 5.29):

> Modify/Database file

The structure of the database file EMPLOYEE.DBF then is displayed (see fig. 5.30).

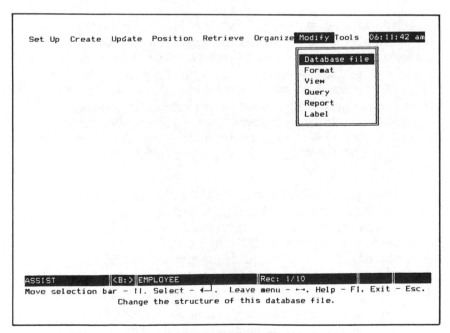

*Fig. 5.29. Menu options for modifying database file structure.*

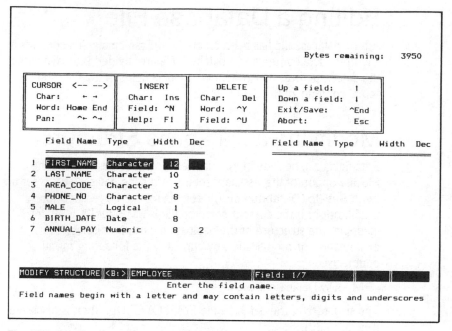

Fig. 5.30. Displaying existing database file structure.

To edit the database structure, use the cursor keys to position the cursor at the beginning of a field-definition area. You can then change such items as field name, field type, and field width. If the fields use more than one display screen, use the PgUp and PgDn keys to scroll through the field-definition areas. You can insert a new field by positioning the cursor at the desired location and pressing Ctrl-N. A blank field then is displayed, and the field definition can be entered. To delete a field, place the cursor at the beginning of the field and press Ctrl-U. When you have finished modifying the structure, press Ctrl-End.

When you begin to modify the structure of the database, dBASE III Plus automatically creates a backup file. The backup file has the same name, structure, and contents as the original database file, but instead of having the extension .DBF, the backup file has the extension .BAK. After you have edited the structure, dBASE III Plus adjusts the contents of the original file to conform to the new structure.

The contents of a character/text field remain in the same field regardless of whether you have modified the name. If the width of a numeric field is changed, the contents of the field are automatically adjusted to the new width. When a new field is added to the structure, blank spaces are written in the new field in all data records. When an existing data field is deleted from the structure, the contents of that field are erased automatically from the database file.

In dot-prompt mode, the structure of a database file can be recalled with the MODIFY STRUCTURE command. For example, if you want to change the structure of EMPLOYEE.DBF, enter the following commands at the dot prompt:

. USE EMPLOYEE
. MODIFY STRUCTURE

The structure of the active database file (EMPLOYEE.DBF) is then displayed for you to examine or modify.

 # Editing Records

You can edit, change, or replace the contents of a data record at any time by choosing the **Update/Edit** menu options.

When you select **Edit**, the contents of the current record are displayed. The number of the current record is always indicated in the status bar. If the displayed record is not the one you want to edit, use the **Position** option to move the pointer to the desired record before you select **Edit**. For example, if you want to edit the contents of the fifth record in EMPLOYEE.DBF, you can make record 5 the current record by choosing

Position/Goto Record/RECORD/Enter a numeric value: *5*

The record indicator in the status bar then shows **Rec : 5/10**, and you can edit the record by selecting the following menu options (see fig. 5.31):

Update/Edit

The current record, which is now record 5, is displayed in the work area for modification (see fig. 5.32).

Press the arrow keys to position the cursor on the data field you want to edit. As long as you move the cursor within the data fields shown, the current record remains on the screen. If you move the cursor beyond the current record, however, the previous record or the next record is displayed. For instance, if the cursor is positioned in the last field of record 5 and you press the ↓ key, the next data

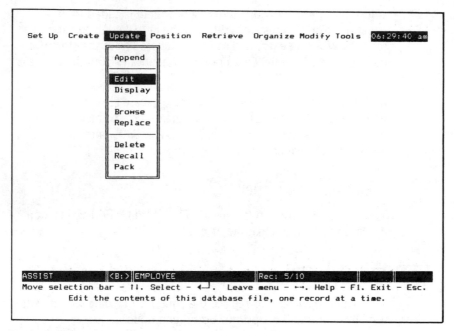

*Fig. 5.31. Menu options for editing records.*

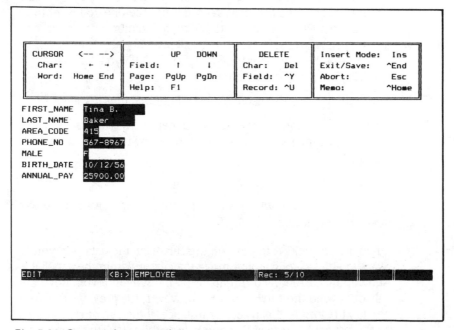

*Fig. 5.32. Current data record displayed for editing.*

record (record 6) is displayed. Similarly, when the cursor is on the first field of record 5, pressing ↑ moves the cursor to the previous record (record 4).

When you have finished modifying the record, you can either exit editing mode or move to the previous or next record. At any point during the editing process you can display the previous record by pressing PgUp or the next record by pressing PgDn.

You can leave editing mode in two ways. Pressing Ctrl-End causes the edited record to be saved and the program to return to the dot prompt or the Assistant menu. You can also press Esc to leave editing mode, but this alternative aborts the editing process and causes your modifications on the current record to be lost. (The record remains in its original form.)

In dot-prompt mode, you can edit the current record by simply entering the EDIT command:

. EDIT

To edit the contents of a specific record, specify its record number in the EDIT command line:

. EDIT RECORD <record number>

For example, you enter the following command to edit the contents of record 5:

. EDIT RECORD 5

The contents of record 5 are then displayed.

## Browsing Records

PLUS

In addition to displaying a single record at a time with **Update/Edit**, you can display multiple records for modification by selecting

Update/Browse

A set of records from the current database file then is displayed on-screen for reviewing or editing (see fig. 5.33). In figure 5.33, records 5 through 10 (end of file) have been displayed.

The **Browse** option displays up to 17 records in the working area. The current record is the first record displayed. Because of screen limitations, if a data record contains more than 80 characters, only the first 80 characters are displayed.

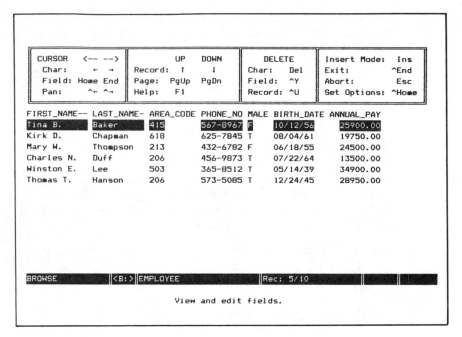

```
┌──────────────────────────────────────────────────────────────────────────┐
│  ┌─────────────────────┐┌─────────────────────┐┌────────────────┐┌──────────────────────┐
│  │ CURSOR    <-- -->   ││          UP   DOWN  ││  DELETE        ││ Insert Mode:   Ins   │
│  │ Char:      ←   →    ││ Record:   ↑     ↓   ││ Char:     Del  ││ Exit:         ^End   │
│  │ Field: Home End     ││ Page:   PgUp  PgDn  ││ Field:    ^Y   ││ Abort:         Esc   │
│  │ Pan:     ^← ^→      ││ Help:    F1         ││ Record:   ^U   ││ Set Options:  ^Home  │
│  └─────────────────────┘└─────────────────────┘└────────────────┘└──────────────────────┘
│
│  FIRST_NAME-- LAST_NAME- AREA_CODE PHONE_NO MALE BIRTH_DATE ANNUAL_PAY
│  Tina B.      Baker      415       567-8967 F    10/12/56   25900.00
│  Kirk D.      Chapman    618       625-7845 T    08/04/61   19750.00
│  Mary W.      Thompson   213       432-6782 F    06/18/55   24500.00
│  Charles N.   Duff       206       456-9873 T    07/22/64   13500.00
│  Winston E.   Lee        503       365-8512 T    05/14/39   34900.00
│  Thomas T.    Hanson     206       573-5085 T    12/24/45   28950.00
│
│
│  BROWSE        <B:>  EMPLOYEE              Rec: 5/10
│
│                    View and edit fields.
└──────────────────────────────────────────────────────────────────────────┘
```

*Fig. 5.33. Browsing data records.*

When records are displayed, the keystrokes you can use to edit the text are displayed at the top of the screen. The current record is highlighted in reverse video. If you want to change the current record, use the ↑ and ↓ keys to move through the records one at a time. The ↓ key can also be used to scroll beyond the first 17 records; simply press that key until the last record is displayed.

The ← and → keys can be used to "pan" across the fields of the current record. After positioning the cursor at the desired field, you can enter new data to replace the existing contents of the field. To move to the next field, press Enter. You can press PgDn to skip to the last record in the database and PgUp to move to the first record.

Records can be added to the database with the **Browse** option. When you press the ↓ key to move the cursor beyond the last record, the message **Add new record? (Y/N)** appears at the top of the screen. If you press *Y*, blank spaces representing data fields are displayed at the bottom of the screen, and new data can be entered in the corresponding fields. You can use this method to append as many data records as necessary. Although a record can be added to the end of the file, a new record cannot be inserted in the middle of the file during the Browse procedure.

The **Browse** operation can also be used to delete records. Two steps are required for deleting a record from the current database file. The first step is to mark the data record that is to be deleted. The second step is to remove the record from the database file. The second step is performed with the **Pack** operation, which is discussed in the following section.

To mark a data record for deletion, position the cursor at the data record and press Ctrl-U. The short message **∗DEL∗** appears at the top of the screen, indicating that the current data record is marked for deletion. To erase the deletion mark, press Ctrl-U once more. The **∗DEL∗** message disappears, and the data record is recovered.

The dot command for the Browse operation is

. BROWSE

As mentioned earlier, only the first 80 characters are displayed if a record contains more than 80 characters. However, you can display only selected field contents in order to keep the display within the screen size limit. To display selected data fields, specify the field names on the BROWSE FIELDS command, as in

. BROWSE FIELDS <field name 1>, <field name 2>, . . .

For example, if you want to display only the names and telephone numbers in the EMPLOYEE.DBF database file, you enter the BROWSE FIELDS command in the format

. GO TOP
. BROWSE FIELDS FIRST_NAME,LAST_NAME,AREA_CODE,PHONE_NO

The result of the BROWSE FIELDS command is shown in figure 5.34.

## Replacing Values in Records

PLUS

Contents of one or more records can be modified by replacing their field values with new values. For example, you can replace the last name of a specific employee with a new last name. You can also replace all the 206 area codes in the EMPLOYEE.DBF file with a new area code of 216. The data replacement operation can be carried out by selecting

Update/Replace

from the Assistant menu (see fig. 5.35).

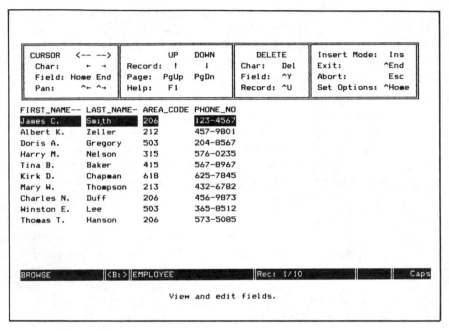

Fig. 5.34. Browsing selected data fields.

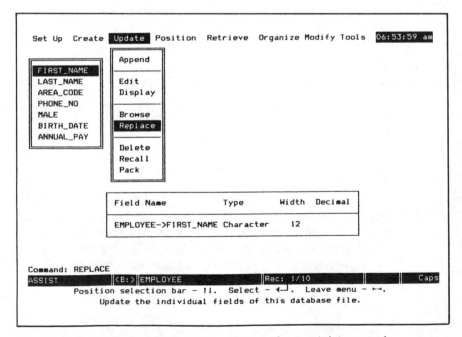

Fig. 5.35. Menu options for replacing contents of current data record.

A listing of the fields in the current database (EMPLOYEE.DBF) is then displayed to the left of the submenu box, and a description of the highlighted data field appears below the submenu box. Now you specify the field whose value is to be replaced. For example, to replace the value in the AREA_CODE field with the new value 216, first select that field by pressing the ↓ key until AREA_CODE is highlighted; then press Enter (see fig. 5.36).

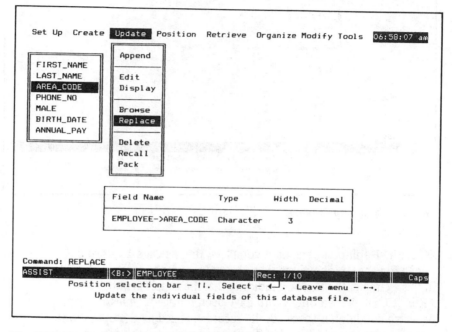

*Fig. 5.36. Replacing contents of AREA_CODE field.*

You can now enter the new value at the prompt

**Enter a character string (without quotes):**

The data type of the new information must be the same as that of the existing information. For example, only an alphanumeric string can replace the contents of a character/text field.

As the field list reappears on the screen, you can select another field to replace if you need to change more than one field. After you have defined the fields to be replaced, you can execute the replacement operation by pressing →. The field list disappears, a command submenu box appears to the right of the Update submenu box, and you can select **Execute the command** to replace the old field contents with the new ones (see fig. 5.37).

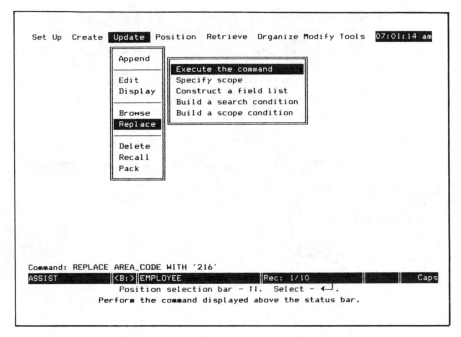

Fig. 5.37. Executing Replace.

When the **Replace** operation is complete, the message **1 record replaced** appears above the status bar at the bottom of the screen. In this example, the message indicates that the contents of the AREA_CODE field in one record have been replaced. Unless a scope or search condition is specified, the record changed by the operation is the current record (**Rec : 1/10**). If you now display the records in EMPLOYEE.DBF, you will see that the contents of AREA_CODE in record 1 have been replaced with the new value 216 (see fig. 5.38).

In addition to replacing a field value of the current record, you can replace all values in the same field of the current database file with one **Replace** operation. To do so, select the set of records by specifying the necessary search or scope condition. For example, to replace all 206 area codes with a new value of 216, you make the following menu selections and keyboard entries:

Update/Replace/AREA_CODE/Enter a character string (without quotes): *216*/Build a search condition/ AREA_CODE= Equal to/Enter a character string (without quotes): *206*/No more conditions/Execute the command

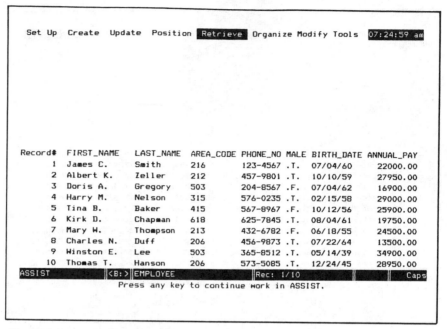

```
   Set Up  Create  Update  Position  Retrieve  Organize Modify Tools   07:24:59 am




   Record#  FIRST_NAME   LAST_NAME   AREA_CODE  PHONE_NO  MALE  BIRTH_DATE  ANNUAL_PAY
        1   James C.     Smith       216        123-4567  .T.   07/04/60    22000.00
        2   Albert K.    Zeller      212        457-9801  .T.   10/10/59    27950.00
        3   Doris A.     Gregory     503        204-8567  .F.   07/04/62    16900.00
        4   Harry M.     Nelson      315        576-0235  .T.   02/15/58    29000.00
        5   Tina B.      Baker       415        567-8967  .F.   10/12/56    25900.00
        6   Kirk D.      Chapman     618        625-7845  .T.   08/04/61    19750.00
        7   Mary W.      Thompson    213        432-6782  .F.   06/18/55    24500.00
        8   Charles N.   Duff        206        456-9873  .T.   07/22/64    13500.00
        9   Winston E.   Lee         503        365-8512  .T.   05/14/39    34900.00
       10   Thomas T.    Hanson      206        573-5085  .T.   12/24/45    28950.00
   ASSIST          <B:> EMPLOYEE                      Rec: 1/10                  Caps
                    Press any key to continue work in ASSIST.
```

*Fig. 5.38. Records after one value has been replaced.*

Figure 5.39 shows the records in EMPLOYEE.DBF after the **Replace** operation has been performed. As you can see, all 206 area codes have been replaced with the new value 216.

In dot-prompt mode, data replacement operations can be performed with the REPLACE command also. The format for the REPLACE command is

. REPLACE <name of field> WITH <new field value>

For example, the replacement operation previously mentioned would be written in dot prompt mode as

. REPLACE AREA_CODE WITH "216"

The REPLACE command can also be used with a qualifier, as in

. REPLACE <name of field> WITH <new field value> FOR <qualifier>

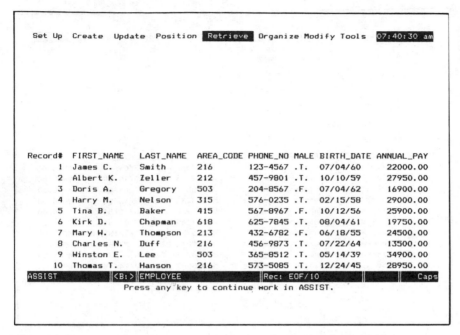

```
Set Up  Create  Update  Position  Retrieve  Organize Modify Tools  07:40:30 am




Record#  FIRST_NAME   LAST_NAME   AREA_CODE  PHONE_NO  MALE  BIRTH_DATE  ANNUAL_PAY
      1  James C.     Smith       216        123-4567  .T.   07/04/60    22000.00
      2  Albert K.    Zeller      212        457-9801  .T.   10/10/59    27950.00
      3  Doris A.     Gregory     503        204-8567  .F.   07/04/62    16900.00
      4  Harry M.     Nelson      315        576-0235  .T.   02/15/58    29000.00
      5  Tina B.      Baker       415        567-8967  .F.   10/12/56    25900.00
      6  Kirk D.      Chapman     618        625-7845  .T.   08/04/61    19750.00
      7  Mary W.      Thompson    213        432-6782  .F.   06/18/55    24500.00
      8  Charles N.   Duff        216        456-9873  .T.   07/22/64    13500.00
      9  Winston E.   Lee         503        365-8512  .T.   05/14/39    34900.00
     10  Thomas T.    Hanson      216        573-5085  .T.   12/24/45    28950.00
ASSIST            <B:>|EMPLOYEE              |Rec: EOF/10                    Caps
              Press any key to continue work in ASSIST.
```

Fig. 5.39. Records after all 206 area codes have been changed to 216.

Some examples of the REPLACE command used with qualifiers are

. REPLACE AREA_CODE WITH "216" FOR AREA_CODE="206"

. REPLACE ANNUAL_PAY WITH ANNUAL_PAY*1.10 FOR MALE

. REPLACE ANNUAL_PAY WITH ANNUAL_PAY*1.15 FOR
.NOT. MALE .AND. AREA_CODE="503"

The qualifier in the REPLACE command can also be a scope and search condition. The qualifier defines which search and scope conditions will be used to select those data records that are the objects of the replacement operations.

## Inserting Records

In addition to appending records at the end of a file, you can insert new records between existing records. The Assistant menu does not offer the capability of inserting records, however, so the insertion must be carried out in dot-prompt mode. The syntax for the command is

. INSERT

The INSERT command adds a new data record after the current record and places the program in the EDIT mode. To add a data record before the current record, enter the following command:

. INSERT BEFORE

To add a new record between the third and fourth record of the active file, use one of the following sets of commands:

. GOTO 3
. INSERT

or

. GOTO 4
. INSERT BEFORE

Both of these command sequences display the entry form for data record 4 and place dBASE III Plus in editing mode. New data can then be entered on the data-entry form. After entering the data, be sure to press Ctrl-End to save the inserted record.

## Deleting Records

Deleting data records involves two steps, which may or may not be carried out consecutively. First you mark the data record for deletion, and then you cause the marked records to be removed from the database file. One way to mark records is to use the **Browse** operation (discussed earlier in this chapter); another way is discussed in this section. The procedure for removing marked records is discussed in the next section.

Deletions can also be performed by choosing the **Update/Delete**. Then you are prompted to specify a scope or search condition, which will be used to select the set of records for deletion (see fig. 5.40).

In dot-prompt mode, you can remove records by using the DELETE command. The syntax of this command is

. DELETE RECORD <record number>
. DELETE ALL
. DELETE <qualifier>

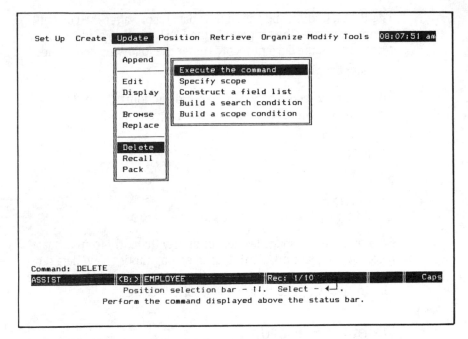

*Fig. 5.40. Marking records for deletion.*

Some examples of using DELETE are

. DELETE RECORD 5
. DELETE ALL
. DELETE FOR AREA_CODE="503"
. DELETE FOR MALE
. DELETE FOR LAST_NAME="Smith".AND. ANNUAL_PAY>20000

The **Delete** operation does not actually remove the records permanently from the database file. It simply places a deletion mark (✻) in front of the specified records. The records marked for deletion can later be recalled or unmarked. The marked records are removed from the database file only when you perform the **Pack** operation, which is discussed in the next section.

## PLUS Removing Records Permanently

After data records have been marked for deletion, you can use the **Pack** operation to remove them from the database file. To perform this operation, select **Update/Pack** from the Assistant menu (see fig. 5.41).

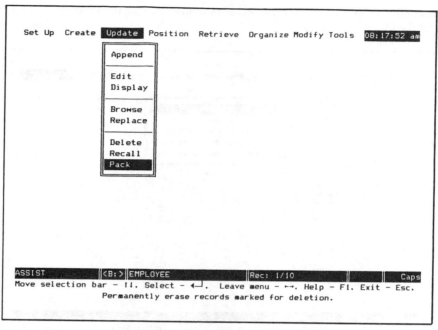

*Fig. 5.41. Removing marked records with Pack.*

All records that have been marked by means of **Delete** now are permanently removed from the database file. The remaining records are then "repacked": the disk space formerly occupied by marked records is allocated for the remaining records, which are in effect packed more tightly within the file. Using **Pack** can therefore reduce the disk space required for your database files.

*A word of caution:* Always be sure to back up your database files before using the Pack operation. After **Pack** is executed, the marked records are removed permanently.

The equivalent dot command is

. PACK

## Undeleting Records

PLUS

As you know now, records marked for deletion are removed only when you select **Update/Pack** from the Assistant menu or enter PACK at the dot prompt. You can remove the deletion marks by using the **Recall** option of the **Update** submenu. After selecting **Update/Recall**, you are prompted to specify the scope and search

conditions that will be used to select a set of marked records to be
recalled (see fig. 5.42).

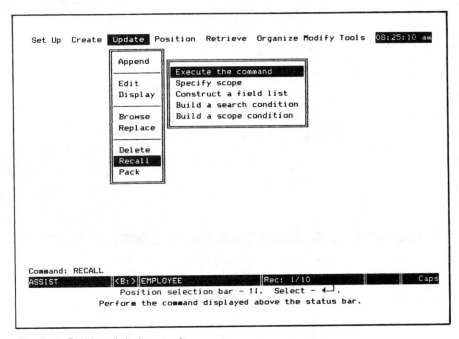

*Fig. 5.42. Erasing deletion marks.*

In dot-prompt mode, you erase deletion marks by using the
RECALL command. The syntax for the RECALL command is

    . RECALL RECORD <record number>
    . RECALL ALL
    . RECALL <qualifier>

Some examples are

    . RECALL RECORD 5
    . RECALL ALL
    . RECALL FOR AREA_CODE="503"
    . RECALL FOR MALE
    . RECALL FOR LAST_NAME="Smith".AND. ANNUAL_PAY>20000

## Emptying a Database File

All records can be removed from a database file with the dot-prompt ZAP command. The format for the command is simply

. ZAP

When you use this command, the records are deleted but the data structure is left intact. The ZAP command achieves the same effect as a combination of the following two commands:

. DELETE ALL
. PACK

When you enter the ZAP command, dBASE III Plus requests confirmation. The following message is displayed

**ZAP B:EMPLOYEE. DBF? (Y/N)**

If you answer *N*, the ZAP command is aborted. Remember that once the data records are zapped, the records are erased from the file and cannot be recovered.

# Chapter Summary

Once data is saved in a database file, the contents of the file can be recalled for viewing or modifying. The data can be displayed selectively by fields or by records. With the powerful query operations offered by dBASE III Plus, you can view the contents of existing data records that meet a set of predefined conditions. These conditions can be saved in a query file so that they can be used repeatedly for data manipulation operations.

The contents of a data record can be modified with the **Edit** option. With the **Browse** option, several data records can be viewed and modified on the same screen. The contents of an active record field can be modified with the **Replace** option.

Because many data manipulation operations are directed by default to the current data record, it is important to know which record is the current record. dBASE III Plus uses a record pointer to keep track of the active data record. You can use dot commands such as GOTO, GO TOP, GO BOTTOM, SKIP, LOCATE, and CONTINUE to position the record pointer at the desired data record. These commands can also be accessed from the Assistant menu under the **Position** option.

Part or all of the contents in a database file can be marked for removal with the **Delete** option. The **Pack** option actually removes the marked data records from the database file. Marked data records can be recovered with the **Recall** option. To erase the data records without disturbing the data structure, you can use the ZAP dot command. Both ZAP and **Erase** permanently delete the contents of a file.

# 6

# Sorting, Indexing, and Summarizing Data

## An Overview

This chapter, which explains how to arrange data so that you can perform data management functions, introduces two important operations: sorting and indexing. Also introduced are commands for generating summary statistics, such as totals and averages. The major topics discussed in this chapter are

Sorting data records in a database file
Indexing a database file on its data fields
Organizing data records with an indexed database file
File sorting versus file indexing
Organization of a sorted file
Structure of an indexed file
Applications of sorted files

Applications of indexed files
Counting data records
Summing numeric fields

Using The Assistant's **Organize/Index** and **Organize/Sort** options, you can perform sorting and indexing operations. The equivalent dot commands for these operations are

| *Commands* | *Functions* |
|---|---|
| SORT TO . . . ON . . . | Sort data records |
| SORT TO . . . ON . . . FOR . . . | |
| INDEX ON . . . TO . . . | Index a database file |
| USE INDEX | |
| SET INDEX TO . . . | |
| REINDEX | |
| FIND | Locate a data record |
| SEEK | |
| COUNT | Count data records |
| COUNT FOR . . . | |
| COUNT FOR . . . TO . . . | |
| SUM | Accumulate values |
| SUM . . . FOR . . . | |
| AVERAGE | Compute averages |
| AVERAGE FOR . . . | |
| CLOSE INDEX | Perform file operations |
| DIR *.NDX | |

# Organizing Data in a Database File

The contents of a database file are organized by data fields and data records. Definitions of the data fields are specified when the file is created. Data records are stored in a file in the order in which they are entered. For example, the 10 data records stored in the EMPLOYEE database file are arranged in the order in which they were entered (see fig. 6.1). Each record is assigned a number, which you can use for later reference.

```
          Set Up   Create   Update   Position   Retrieve  Organize Modify Tools   06:40:37 am




          Record#  FIRST_NAME    LAST_NAME   AREA_CODE PHONE_NO MALE BIRTH_DATE ANNUAL_PAY
                1  James C.      Smith       216       123-4567 .T.  07/04/60   22000.00
                2  Albert K.     Zeller      212       457-9801 .T.  10/10/59   27950.00
                3  Doris A.      Gregory     503       204-8567 .F.  07/04/62   16900.00
                4  Harry M.      Nelson      315       576-0235 .T.  02/15/58   29000.00
                5  Tina B.       Baker       415       567-8967 .F.  10/12/56   25900.00
                6  Kirk D.       Chapman     618       625-7845 .T.  08/04/61   19750.00
                7  Mary W.       Thompson    213       432-6782 .F.  06/18/55   24500.00
                8  Charles N.    Duff        216       456-9873 .T.  07/22/64   13500.00
                9  Winston E.    Lee         503       365-8512 .T.  05/14/39   34900.00
               10  Thomas T.     Hanson      216       573-5085 .T.  12/24/45   28950.00
          ASSIST           <B:> EMPLOYEE                    Rec: 1/10                    Caps
                         Press any key to continue work in ASSIST.
```

Fig. 6.1. Records of EMPLOYEE.DBF in order of their entry.

Data records organized in this way may not be suitable for your needs. Because the files are not arranged alphabetically, a listing of the records in the EMPLOYEE.DBF database file would not produce a satisfactory employee roster. As you can see, data records must often be rearranged.

# Sorting Data Records on a Single Key Field

You can use a sorting operation to arrange data records in ascending or descending order according to the contents of a specified field or fields, which are called *key fields*. Before the sorting process begins, a working file is created; this is known as the *target file*. The records to be sorted are copied to the target file so that the original files remain intact while the sort is performed on the target file records. After you complete the sorting operation, the data records in the target file are arranged as specified in the key field(s).

PLUS | # Sorting Records in Ascending Order

To sort records in the current database file, you can select the **Organize/Sort** menu options from the Assistant menu. After selecting these options, you are prompted to specify the key field(s) on which the data records are to be arranged (see fig. 6.2).

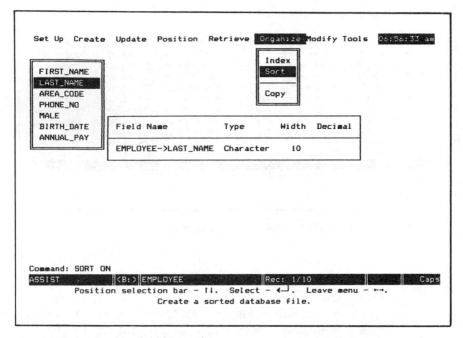

*Fig. 6.2. Selecting key field for sorting.*

If you want to produce a roster by arranging the EMPLOYEE.DBF records according to the employees' last names, for example, you make the following menu selections:

    Organize/Sort/LAST_NAME

After you have specified the key field (LAST_NAME), you can specify the name of the target file by pressing the → key, designating the disk drive (B:), and entering the file name *ROSTER.DBF* (see fig. 6.3).

Next, the sorting begins. dBASE III Plus monitors the progress of the sort and displays the percentage of data records sorted. At the end of the sorting process, the message

    **100% Sorted . . . 10 Records sorted**

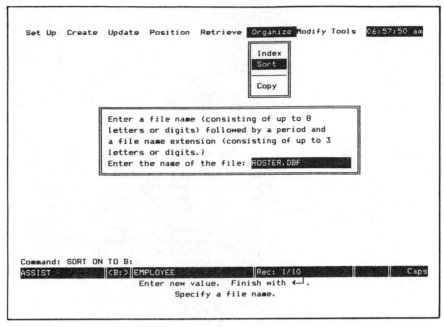

*Fig. 6.3. Specifying target file for sorted records.*

is displayed above the status bar at the bottom of the screen. When you see the message, you know that the sorted records have been saved in the ROSTER.DBF target file.

To display the sorted roster, you set up the ROSTER.DBF file (**SetUp/B:/ROSTER.DBF**) and then select **Retrieve/List**. The sorted ROSTER.DBF records are shown in figure 6.4.

If you want to arrange the EMPLOYEE.DBF records in order by the employees' ages, you can use the BIRTH_DATE field as the sorting key. Because you have displayed the ROSTER.DBF file, you need again to set up EMPLOYEE.DBF as the current database file. Then use the following options to order the records chronologically:

Organize/Sort/BIRTH_DATE/B:/Enter the name of the file: *BDATES.DBF*

Figure 6.5 shows the resulting list of employees, sorted by birth date.

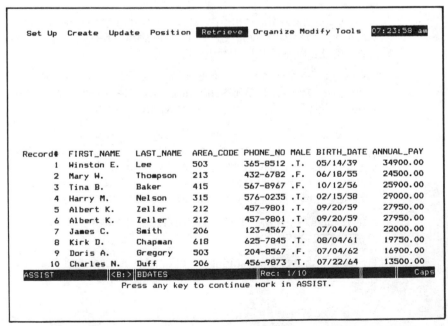

Fig. 6.4. Records in sorted file ROSTER.DBF.

Fig. 6.5. Records sorted by contents of BIRTH_DATE.

Similarly, you can rearrange the EMPLOYEE.DBF records by using the ANNUAL_PAY field as a sorting key:

Organize/Sort/ANNUAL_PAY/B:/Enter the name of the file: *PAYRANK.DBF*

The records of PAYRANK.DBF are shown in figure 6.6.

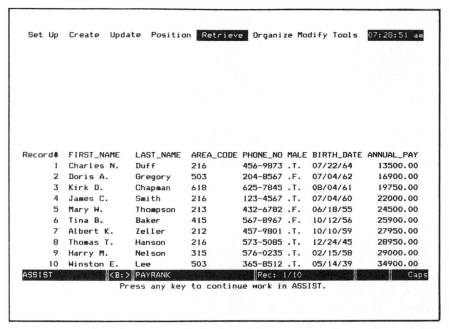

| Record# | FIRST_NAME | LAST_NAME | AREA_CODE | PHONE_NO | MALE | BIRTH_DATE | ANNUAL_PAY |
|---|---|---|---|---|---|---|---|
| 1 | Charles N. | Duff | 216 | 456-9873 | .T. | 07/22/64 | 13500.00 |
| 2 | Doris A. | Gregory | 503 | 204-8567 | .F. | 07/04/62 | 16900.00 |
| 3 | Kirk D. | Chapman | 618 | 625-7845 | .T. | 08/04/61 | 19750.00 |
| 4 | James C. | Smith | 216 | 123-4567 | .T. | 07/04/60 | 22000.00 |
| 5 | Mary W. | Thompson | 213 | 432-6782 | .F. | 06/18/55 | 24500.00 |
| 6 | Tina B. | Baker | 415 | 567-8967 | .F. | 10/12/56 | 25900.00 |
| 7 | Albert K. | Zeller | 212 | 457-9801 | .T. | 10/10/59 | 27950.00 |
| 8 | Thomas T. | Hanson | 216 | 573-5085 | .T. | 12/24/45 | 28950.00 |
| 9 | Harry M. | Nelson | 315 | 576-0235 | .T. | 02/15/58 | 29000.00 |
| 10 | Winston E. | Lee | 503 | 365-8512 | .T. | 05/14/39 | 34900.00 |

*Fig. 6.6. Records sorted by contents of ANNUAL_PAY.*

The ascending sorting order (the default order) is the same as ASCII order shown in Chapter 4, table 4.3. Sorting rearranges the active file's data records in ascending order based on the contents of the key field. As you have seen, you can use sorting to arrange data records alphabetically, chronologically, or numerically by the key field you specify.

When you sort an alphanumeric string in ascending order, the sorted strings are arranged in order from A to Z. If you use a date as the key field with the **Sort** option, records with earlier dates will be placed before records with later dates. When numeric values are sorted in ascending order, records with smaller values are placed before those with larger values.

In dot-prompt mode, you can sort the records in a database file by using the SORT command:

. SORT ON <name of key field> TO <name of sorted file>

or

. SORT TO <name of sorted file> ON <name of key field>

To sort records in dot-prompt mode rather than from the Assistant menu, you can use the following commands:

. USE EMPLOYEE
. SORT ON LAST_NAME TO ROSTER.DBF
. SORT TO BDATES.DBF ON BIRTH_DATE
. SORT ON ANNUAL_PAY TO PAYRANK.DBF

## Sorting Records in Descending Order

You can sort records in descending order by adding /D after the key field name:

. SORT TO <name of sorted file> ON <name of key field>/D

or

. SORT ON <name of key field>/D TO <name of sorted file>

For example, by including the /D operator in the SORT command you can arrange the records in descending order by the values stored in the ANNUAL_PAY key field (see fig. 6.7).

The target file for this sorting operation is named PAYRANK. To conserve disk memory space, a single target file can be used repeatedly to store the contents of a sorted file. When an existing name (such as PAYRANK.DBF) is used for a sorted file, a warning message is displayed:

PAYRANK.DBF already exists, overwrite it? (Y/N)

If you answer *Y*, the contents of the existing PAYRANK.DBF file will be erased and the file is used as the target file for the current SORT command.

 ## Sorting Selected Records

During the sorting operation, all the records are sorted according to the contents of the key field. However, you can sort only a selected

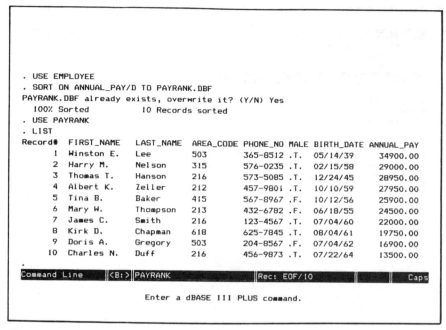

```
. USE EMPLOYEE
. SORT ON ANNUAL_PAY/D TO PAYRANK.DBF
PAYRANK.DBF already exists, overwrite it? (Y/N) Yes
   100% Sorted          10 Records sorted
. USE PAYRANK
. LIST
Record#   FIRST_NAME   LAST_NAME   AREA_CODE  PHONE_NO  MALE  BIRTH_DATE  ANNUAL_PAY
       1   Winston E.   Lee          503       365-8512  .T.   05/14/39     34900.00
       2   Harry M.     Nelson       315       576-0235  .T.   02/15/58     29000.00
       3   Thomas T.    Hanson       216       573-5085  .T.   12/24/45     28950.00
       4   Albert K.    Zeller       212       457-9801  .T.   10/10/59     27950.00
       5   Tina B.      Baker        415       567-8967  .F.   10/12/56     25900.00
       6   Mary W.      Thompson     213       432-6782  .F.   06/18/55     24500.00
       7   James C.     Smith        216       123-4567  .T.   07/04/60     22000.00
       8   Kirk D.      Chapman      618       625-7845  .T.   08/04/61     19750.00
       9   Doris A.     Gregory      503       204-8567  .F.   07/04/62     16900.00
      10   Charles N.   Duff         216       456-9873  .T.   07/22/64     13500.00
.
Command Line      <B:> PAYRANK                    Rec: EOF/10              Caps

             Enter a dBASE III PLUS command.
```

*Fig. 6.7. Using SORT in dot-prompt mode.*

set of records if you first create a query file that specifies the conditions for selecting records. For example, if you want to sort only those EMPLOYEE.DBF records that belong to male employees, you can set up a query file named ALLMALES.QRY. To do so, make EMPLOYEE.DBF the current data file; then make the following menu selections and keyboard entries:

Create/Query/B:/*ALLMALES*

The query table used for this sorting operation is shown in figure 6.8.

After you have created the ALLMALES.QRY file, you can set it up in order to filter the records in the EMPLOYEES.DBF files (see fig. 6.9). Only the records that meet the query condition (MALE is True) will be active when you carry out the sorting operation.

If you sort the EMPLOYEE.DBF records after you have set up the ALLMALES.QRY file, only those records filtered by the query conditions will be sorted. To sort the male employees' records in the EMPLOYEE.DBF file, you can therefore choose the following menu options:

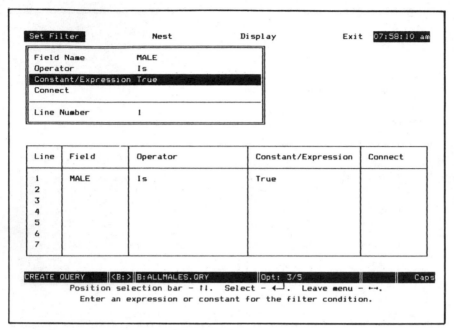

Fig. 6.8. Defining query conditions.

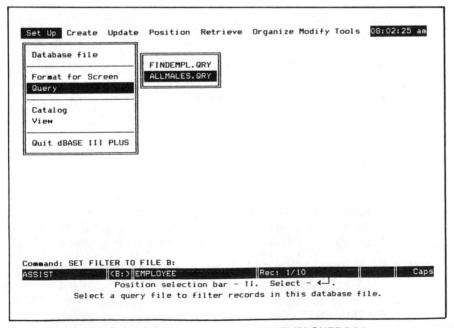

Fig. 6.9. Using ALLMALES.QRY to filter records in EMPLOYEE.DBF.

Organize/Sort/LAST_NAME/B:/Enter the name of the file: *MALES.DBF*

After the sorting operation is carried out, you will notice that the status message shows only seven sorted records. The reason is that only seven records contain .T. in the MALE data field. A listing of records in the sorted file MALES.DBF is shown in figure 6.10.

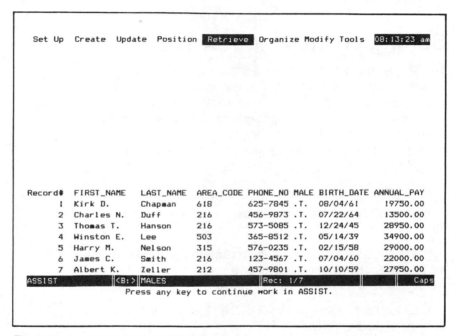

```
      Set Up  Create  Update  Position  Retrieve  Organize Modify Tools   08:13:23 am




      Record#  FIRST_NAME   LAST_NAME   AREA_CODE PHONE_NO MALE BIRTH_DATE ANNUAL_PAY
            1  Kirk D.      Chapman     618       625-7845 .T.  08/04/61   19750.00
            2  Charles N.   Duff        216       456-9873 .T.  07/22/64   13500.00
            3  Thomas T.    Hanson      216       573-5085 .T.  12/24/45   28950.00
            4  Winston E.   Lee         503       365-8512 .T.  05/14/39   34900.00
            5  Harry M.     Nelson      315       576-0235 .T.  02/15/58   29000.00
            6  James C.     Smith       216       123-4567 .T.  07/04/60   22000.00
            7  Albert K.    Zeller      212       457-9801 .T.  10/10/59   27950.00
      ASSIST              <B:> MALES                   Rec: 1/7                  Caps
                 Press any key to continue work in ASSIST.
```

Fig. 6.10. Records in sorted file MALES.DBF.

In dot-prompt mode, you can use a conditional SORT command to sort portions of data in a database file. A subset of the database file can be defined with a qualifier (FOR . . . ). When you execute the command, only those records that meet the condition(s) in the qualifier are sorted. The syntax of a conditional SORT command is

. SORT TO <sorted file> ON <key field> FOR <a qualifier>

A few examples of conditional SORT commands are

. SORT TO MALEPAY ON ANNUAL_PAY/D FOR MALE

. SORT TO FEMALES ON LAST_NAME FOR .NOT. MALE

. SORT TO FONELIST ON PHONE_NO/D FOR
AREA_CODE="503" .OR. AREA_CODE="206"

. SORT TO SORTED ON FIRST_NAME FOR
AREA_CODE>="212"

## PLUS | Sorting on Multiple Key Fields

You have seen examples in which a single key field is used for
sorting records in a database file. Records in the current database file
can be sorted also on the basis of several key fields. By specifying
multiple key-field names, you can perform multiple sortings. Using
the **Organize/Sort** options, you can specify the names of these key
fields in the desired order. **Organize/Sort** sorts the file on the first
key field and temporarily stores the results in the target file. The
contents of the sorted file then are sorted again on the next key
field. The sorting operation is repeated for each key field and, after
all the key fields have been sorted, the results are saved in the target
file.

For example, if you want to sort the records in the EMPLOYEE.DBF
file by area code and then by telephone number, you can specify
AREA_CODE and PHONE_NO (in that order) as the key fields:

Organize/Sort/AREA_CODE/PHONE_NO/B:/Enter the
name of the file: *FONELIST.DBF*

The sorted file FONELIST.DBF is shown in figure 6.11.

The equivalent dot command for this sorting operation is

. SORT ON <key field 1>, <key field 2>, <key field 3>,
. . . TO <sorted file>

or

. SORT TO <sorted file> ON <key field 1>, <key field 2>,
<key field 3>, . . .

To sort records by area code and then by phone number, you would
use this dot command:

. SORT ON AREA_CODE, PHONE_NO TO FONELIST.DBF

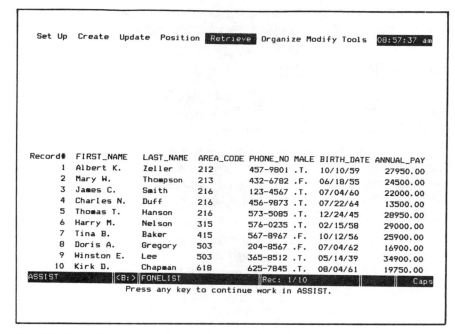

*Fig. 6.11. Records in sorted file FONELIST.DBF.*

You can also add a qualifier (FOR . . . ) to a conditional SORT command so that only a subset of the records is affected.

Some examples of conditional SORT commands with multiple key fields are

. SORT TO ROSTER ON ANNUAL_PAY/D, LAST_NAME FOR MALE

. SORT TO BDATES ON BIRTH_DATE, LAST_NAME FOR .NOT. MALE

. SORT TO LISTS ON ANNUAL_PAY, LAST_NAME FOR LAST_NAME<="Smith"

. SORT TO PAYLIST ON LAST_NAME,ANNUAL_PAY FOR MALE .AND. ANNUAL_PAY>=20000

# Indexing a Database File

The SORT command creates a sorted file that contains the data fields of the ordered data records. If there are many data fields in each record, sorting can be a long process. File indexing is another way to organize records, and indexing takes less time than sorting.

## PLUS | Single-Field Indexing

The file-indexing operation uses one or more data fields as key field(s) on which to generate an index file. You use the index file to reorganize the contents of the database file.

The indexing operation creates a target file that contains the key-field entries and their corresponding record numbers. The contents are in ascending alphabetical, chronological, or numerical order, according to the contents of the specified key field. The target file has the file extension .NDX.

The names of the key indexing field and the target index file are specified during the indexing operation. To begin indexing the current database file, you select the **Organize/Index** menu options. You are then prompted to enter an index key expression (see fig. 6.12).

*Fig. 6.12. Specifying key field for indexing.*

The index key expression can be a single key field, a set of key fields, or an expression. An expression contains data fields (or other data elements such as memory variables) and symbols such as the plus sign (+) that define operations performed upon the data. If you use a single key field, the key field can be a character/text field, a date field, or a numeric field. Logical and memo fields *cannot* be used as key fields in the indexing operation. To arrange the records in the EMPLOYEE.DBF file by the values in the LAST_NAME field, for example, you can select the following menu options:

Organize/Index/Enter an index key expression: *LAST_NAME*

You then are prompted to specify the name of the index file:

/B:/Enter the name of the file: *LASTNAME.NDX*

The database file will be indexed accordingly. When the indexing operation is completed, you will see the message:

**100% indexed        10 Records indexed**

If you display the contents of the current database records at this point, you will notice that the records have been arranged alphabetically by the values in the LAST_NAME key field (see fig. 6.13).

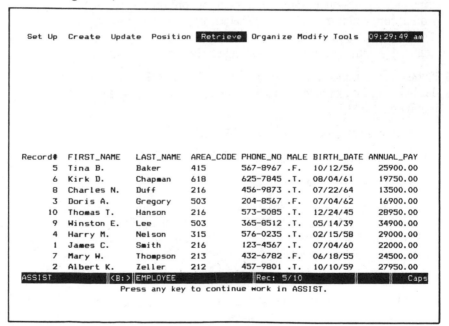

Fig. 6.13. Records in indexed file EMPLOYEE.DBF.

The LASTNAME.NDX index file created by the indexing operation contains the LAST_NAME field entries and their corresponding record numbers. You cannot use the **Display** and **List** options to display the contents of an index file because these options show only the records of a database file (.DBF).

The dot command for indexing is

. INDEX ON <name of key field> TO <name of index file>

You can use the command in this way, for example:

. INDEX ON LAST_NAME TO LASTNAME.NDX

## PLUS Setting Up an Existing Index File

The indexing operation creates a working copy of the database file and arranges the records in this working file. Remember that the indexing operation affects *only* the records in the original database file that is saved on disk.

After you have indexed an active database file, the records (arranged in the order specified in the index file) remain active in RAM for further processing. However, if you activate another database by using either the **Set Up/Database** menu options or the USE dot-prompt command, the indexed file is lost. Because the contents of the file on disk are not affected by INDEX, you can reorganize the original file with an index file by setting up the indexed database file.

If you want to reindex the records in the original EMPLOYEE.DBF database file, for example, you set up the file by choosing the usual menu options:

Set Up/Database file/B:/*EMPLOYEE.DBF*

The following prompt then appears:

**Is the file indexed? [Y/N]**

In this case, you answer *Y*. When you are asked to identify the index file with which you want to index the current database file, specify /LASTNAME.NDX. Press the → key to leave the menu, and the database file will be reindexed.

The equivalent dot command for the indexing operation is

. USE <database file> INDEX <name of existing index file>

You can reindex the database file by using the command:

. USE EMPLOYEE.DBF INDEX LASTNAME.NDX

You can also reactivate an index file with a SET INDEX TO command at the dot prompt. The format of this command is

. SET INDEX TO <name of existing index file>

The SET INDEX TO command tells the computer to rearrange the data records by using an existing index file. Assuming that the EMPLOYEE.DBF is in use, for example, the command to reactivate the LASTNAME.NDX file is

. SET INDEX TO LASTNAME

## Multiple-Field Indexing

Multiple keys are used frequently to sort the records in a database file. But instead of sorting the file, you can achieve the same result by using several fields as a combined key field in the indexing operation. To use multiple index key fields, you specify all the key fields in response to the following prompt:

**Enter an index for expression**:

If you want use two key fields (AREA_CODE AND PHONE_NO, for example) to index the EMPLOYEE.DBF file, for example, you make the following menu selections and keyboard entries:

Organize/Index/Enter an index key expression:
*AREA_CODE+PHONE_NO*/B:/Enter the name of the file:
*FONELIST.NDX*

The equivalent dot command for such an indexing operation is

. INDEX ON <field 1>+ <field 2> + . . . TO <index file>

An example of the use of this command form is

. INDEX ON AREA_CODE+PHONE_NO TO FONELIST.NDX

Note that whether you use menu options or an INDEX ON command, you must use plus signs to join the names of fields that you use as an indexing key.

# Searching for Data in an Indexed Database File

With an indexed database, you can search quickly for records whose contents are the same as those of the index key field. For example, if the EMPLOYEE.DBF file is indexed on the AREA_CODE field, all the records with the same area code are arranged consecutively in one block. The record you are searching for will be found and made the current record if its index field has a unique value. If the values in the index fields of several records match the search value, the record pointer will be placed at the first of these records.

To find a specific record by the value of its index key field, use the **Position/Seek** option. Before you can begin the Seek operation, you must index the database file with the appropriate key field. For example, if you want to find James C. Smith's record you must index the EMPLOYEE.DBF file by the LAST_NAME field:

> Organize/Index/Enter an index key expression:
> *LAST_NAME*/B:/*LASTNAME.NDX*

If the LASTNAME.NDX file already exists, you can reindex the EMPLOYEE.DBF file simply by setting up the index file:

> Set up/B:/*EMPLOYEE.DBF*/Is the file indexed? [Y/N]
> *Y*/LASTNAME.NDX

After the database file has been indexed by the LAST_NAME key field, you can find a record according to the value of the key field. For example, to find the record for an employee whose last name is Smith, you can choose the following menu options:

> Position/Seek/Enter an expression: *"Smith"*

When you search the records in an indexed file, the values of the index field's records are compared with the value specified in the search expression. In other words, the indexed records are searched until a record is found that has in the index key field (LAST_NAME) a value matching the value of the search expression. The record found becomes the current record and its record number is displayed in the status bar. At this point, you can select the **Retrieve/Display** menu options to display the contents of the record.

You can specify an alphanumeric string, a numeric value, or a date as the search expression. When you use an alphanumeric string (such as "Smith") as the search expression, the string must be enclosed in quotation marks. A record will be selected if the first part of the alphanumeric string in the record's index field matches the first part of the alphanumeric string in the search expression. The match need not be exact. If you specify *"Sm"* as the search expression, for example, records whose values in the LAST_NAME field begin with *"Sm"* (Smith, Smyth, Smithers, etc.) will be considered as a match.

If you use a date for the search expression, you must enter the date as an alphanumeric string (enclosed in quotation marks) that you convert to a date by using the CTOD (character to date) function. For example, if you have indexed the database file by the values in the BIRTH_DATE field and you want to find the record whose value in the key field is 07/04/62, you enter *CTOD("07/04/62")* as the search expression:

Position/Seek/Enter an expression: *CTOD("07/04/62")*

When you use a numeric value or a date as a search expression, there must be an exact match between the expression and the field value for a record to be selected.

The dot command for the Seek operation is

. SEEK <searching expression>

You might use, for example,

. SEEK "Smith"
. SEEK 25900
. SEEK CTOD("07/04/62")

Additionally, in dot-prompt mode you can use the FIND command with an alphanumeric search expression to search the data records in an indexed file. The syntax of the FIND command is

. FIND <alphanumeric string>

The FIND command searches the indexed database file for the first record with a character string that matches the contents of the key field. When a record with the specified string is found, the record pointer is set to that record. The FIND command and the SEEK command work the same way; the former, however, can be used only with alphanumeric fields, whereas the latter can be used for alphanumeric, numeric, and date fields.

## Reindexing a Database File

Index files must be updated to reflect any changes made to the contents of their data records. You can rebuild an index file by performing another indexing operation or, alternatively, by using the REINDEX dot command. The format of this command is

. REINDEX

Before you use the REINDEX command, however, the database file must be activated and referenced with the index file. To rebuild the LASTNAME.NDX index file after the records in the EMPLOYEE.DBF file have been modified, for example, you enter the following dot commands:

. USE EMPLOYEE
. SET INDEX TO LASTNAME.NDX
. REINDEX

 # Counting and Summarizing Data Records

Summarizing data is one of dBASE III Plus's most important functions. For example, you may need to count the number of employees listed in EMPLOYEE.DBF whose annual salaries fall within a certain range. Or perhaps you need to find the average annual salary for all male employees. The dBASE III Plus **Count, Sum, Average,** and **Total** summary operations can help you accomplish those tasks.

 # Counting Records

You can tally the records in a database file with a **Count** operation. The menu options are

Retrieve/Count

You are then prompted to select menu options to specify the desired scope and search condition. If no scope or search condition is defined, all the records in the current database file are counted, and the number of records is displayed at the bottom of the screen. For example, to count all the records in the EMPLOYEE.DBF file, you would select the menu options shown in figure 6.14:

Retrieve/Count/Execute the command

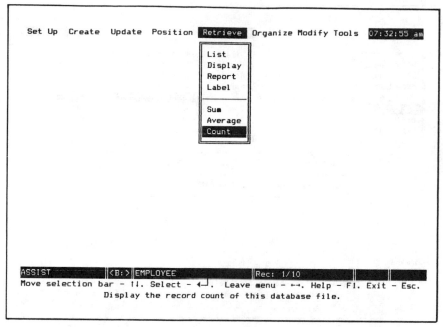

Fig. 6.14. Selecting Retrieve/Count.

The number of records (10) then is displayed on the screen above the status bar.

If you specify scope or search conditions when using the **Count** option, only those records that meet the conditions will be counted. For example, you can count all the male employees in the EMPLOYEE.DBF file by choosing the menu options shown in figure 6.15:

Retrieve/Count/Build a search condition/MALE

After you have defined the search condition (MALE is true), you can execute the operation by choosing **/No more conditions/Execute the command** from the Assistant menu. The number of records counted (7) is then displayed.

In dot-prompt mode, you can carry out the counting operation by entering the COUNT command, either with or without a qualifier:

. COUNT

or

. COUNT <a qualifier>

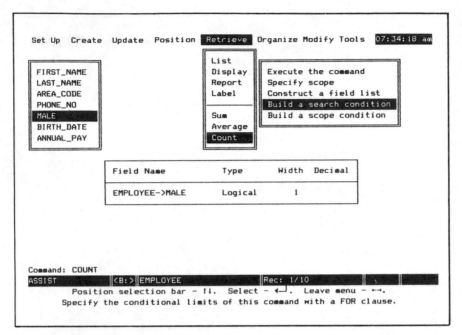

```
Set Up  Create  Update  Position  Retrieve  Organize Modify Tools  07:34:18 am
                                  List
                                  Display  Execute the command
   FIRST_NAME                     Report   Specify scope
   LAST_NAME                      Label    Construct a field list
   AREA_CODE                               Build a search condition
   PHONE_NO                       Sum      Build a scope condition
   MALE                           Average
   BIRTH_DATE                     Count
   ANNUAL_PAY

           Field Name          Type      Width  Decimal

           EMPLOYEE->MALE       Logical     1




Command: COUNT
ASSIST          <B:>EMPLOYEE              Rec: 1/10
          Position selection bar - ↑↓.  Select - ↵.  Leave menu - ↔.
          Specify the conditional limits of this command with a FOR clause.
```

Fig. 6.15. Specifying search condition for Count.

Figure 6.16 shows several examples of using the COUNT command.

# PLUS Summing Numeric Values

You can add all the values in numeric fields of the current database file by choosing the menu options shown in figure 6.17:

Retrieve/Sum/Execute the command

Unless otherwise specified, all the values for each numeric field are added and their sums are displayed on the screen when the **Sum** operation is carried out. To get the sum of selected field values, you specify the numeric fields whose values are to be summed. You can also define scope and search conditions for selecting a set of records that will be the subject of the Sum operation. For example, if you want to sum all the male employees' annual salaries you could select these menu options:

Retrieve/Sum/Construct a field list/ANNUAL_PAY/Build a search condition/MALE/No more conditions/Execute the command

```
. USE EMPLOYEE
. COUNT FOR AREA_CODE = "216"
      3 records
. COUNT FOR AREA_CODE = "216" .OR. AREA_CODE = "503"
      5 records
. COUNT FOR ANNUAL_PAY >=20000 .AND. ANNUAL_PAY <= 30000
      6 records
. COUNT FOR BIRTH_DATE >= CTOD("01/01/60")
      4 records
.
```

| Command Line | \<B:\> EMPLOYEE | Rec: EOF/10 | Caps |

Enter a dBASE III PLUS command.

*Fig. 6.16. Examples of using COUNT.*

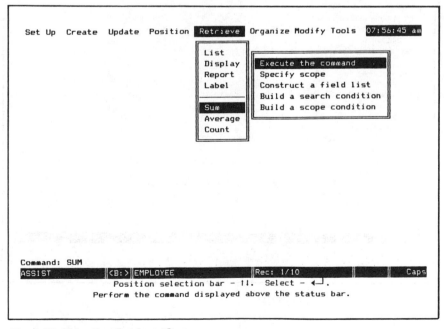

*Fig. 6.17. Selecting Retrieve/Sum.*

In response to these menu selections, the following results will be displayed:

```
2 records summed
ANNUAL PAY
1706050.00
```

You can perform the summing operation in dot-prompt mode by entering a SUM command in one of the following formats:

. SUM

or

. SUM <numeric field 1>, <numeric field 2>, . . .

or

. SUM <numeric field 1>, <numeric field 2> , . . . FOR <qualifier>

Figure 6.18 shows different examples of using the SUM command.

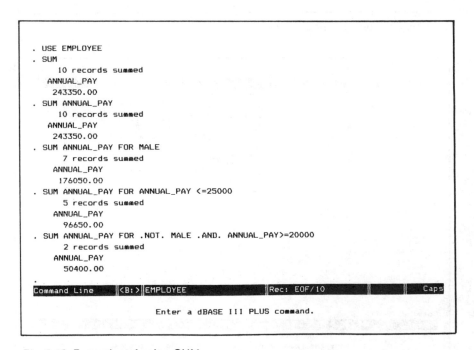

Fig. 6.18. Examples of using SUM.

# Computing Averages

An average value (arithmetic mean) of the contents of a numeric field can be computed and displayed with the **Average** option. As shown in figure 6.19, the menu options for averaging are

Retrieve/Average/Execute the command

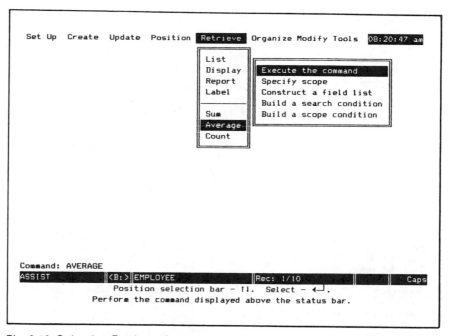

Fig. 6.19. Selecting Retrieve/Average.

If no scope or search condition is specified, averages are calculated and displayed for all the values in each numeric field. However, you can define scope and search conditions for selecting a set of records whose values are to be averaged. For example, to compute the average annual salary for male employees you select these menu options:

Retrieve/Average/Construct a field list/ANNUAL_PAY/Build a search condition/MALE/No more conditions/Execute the command

In response to these menu selections, the following results are displayed:

```
7 records averaged
ANNUAL PAY
   25150.00
```

You can perform the averaging operation in dot-prompt mode by
entering the AVERAGE command in one of the following formats:

. AVERAGE

or

. AVERAGE <field 1>, <field 2>, . . .

or

. AVERAGE <field 1>, <field 2>, . . . FOR <qualifier>

Figure 6.20 shows examples of using the AVERAGE command.

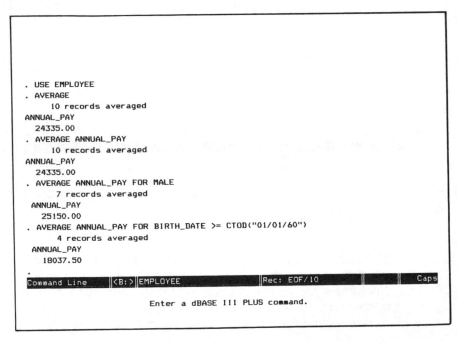

Fig. 6.20. Examples of using AVERAGE.

# Saving Totals to a File

Records whose key fields contain the same data can be processed in groups. Values stored in the numeric fields in those groups can be totaled and saved as summary statistics in another database file. Because this operation is not available from the Assistant menu, you use a dot-prompt command to total field values and save the totals to a file.

Before you can enter the TOTAL command, you must use a sorting or indexing command to arrange the records of the database file in ascending or descending order. The records must be sorted or indexed on the key field you will use with the TOTAL command.

The format of the TOTAL command is

. TOTAL ON <key field> TO <name of summary file>

The TOTAL command sums the active database file's numeric fields and saves the results to the summary file. All the numeric fields in the database file are totaled unless you specify otherwise. The summary file's numeric fields contain totals for all the records whose key fields contain the same data. The structure of the summary file is copied from that of the database file.

If a field in the summary file is not large enough for the total, an error message is displayed and an asterisk (*) is placed in the data field.

A new database file, QTYSOLD.DBF, has been created to illustrate totaling of field values. The QTYSOLD.DBF file contains a small television store's weekly sales figures for December, 1984. The file's structure is shown in figure 6.21, and its data records are shown in figure 6.22.

You can see that each data record shown in figure 6.22 contains a date (DATE), a model number (MODEL), and the quantity sold (UNITS_SOLD) during the week ending with that date. To generate weekly totals of television sets sold, you enter the TOTAL command as in figure 6.23.

For each group of records containing the same value in the DATE field, the contents of the UNITS_SOLD field have been totaled and saved as one data record in the summary file QTYWEEK.DBF. For example, four records in QTYSOLD.DBF have 12/07/84 in the DATE field; the records contain values of 2, 5, 4, and 3 in

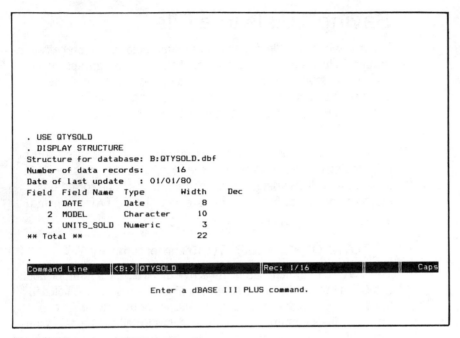

```
. USE QTYSOLD
. DISPLAY STRUCTURE
Structure for database: B:QTYSOLD.dbf
Number of data records:      16
Date of last update   : 01/01/80
Field  Field Name  Type      Width   Dec
    1  DATE        Date         8
    2  MODEL       Character   10
    3  UNITS_SOLD  Numeric      3
** Total **                   22

.
Command Line    |<B:>|QTYSOLD              |Rec: 1/16      |       | Caps

          Enter a dBASE III PLUS command.
```

Fig. 6.21. Structure of QTYSOLD.DBF.

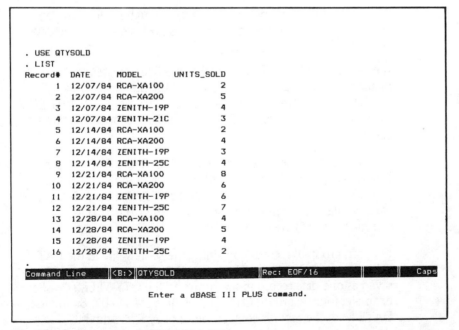

```
. USE QTYSOLD
. LIST
Record#  DATE     MODEL      UNITS_SOLD
      1  12/07/84 RCA-XA100        2
      2  12/07/84 RCA-XA200        5
      3  12/07/84 ZENITH-19P       4
      4  12/07/84 ZENITH-21C       3
      5  12/14/84 RCA-XA100        2
      6  12/14/84 RCA-XA200        4
      7  12/14/84 ZENITH-19P       3
      8  12/14/84 ZENITH-25C       4
      9  12/21/84 RCA-XA100        8
     10  12/21/84 RCA-XA200        6
     11  12/21/84 ZENITH-19P       6
     12  12/21/84 ZENITH-25C       7
     13  12/28/84 RCA-XA100        4
     14  12/28/84 RCA-XA200        5
     15  12/28/84 ZENITH-19P       4
     16  12/28/84 ZENITH-25C       2
.
Command Line    |<B:>|QTYSOLD              |Rec: EOF/16    |       | Caps

          Enter a dBASE III PLUS command.
```

Fig. 6.22. Data records in QTYSOLD.DBF.

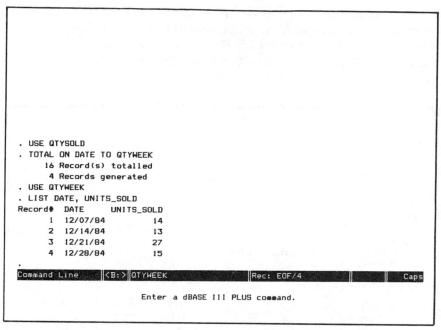

```
. USE QTYSOLD
. TOTAL ON DATE TO QTYWEEK
      16 Record(s) totalled
       4 Records generated
. USE QTYWEEK
. LIST DATE, UNITS_SOLD
Record#   DATE       UNITS_SOLD
       1  12/07/84          14
       2  12/14/84          13
       3  12/21/84          27
       4  12/28/84          15
.
```

Command Line     <B:> QTYWEEK              Rec: EOF/4              Caps

Enter a dBASE III PLUS command.

*Fig. 6.23. Totaling units sold by date.*

UNITS_SOLD. The total of those values is in the UNITS_SOLD field
of QTYWEEK.DBF:

| *In QTYSOLD.DBF* | | | | *In QTYWEEK.DBF* | | |
|---|---|---|---|---|---|---|
| Record # | DATE | UNITS_SOLD | | Record # | DATE | UNITS_SOLD |
| 1 | 12/07/84 | 2 | | 1 | 12/07/84 | 14 |
| 2 | 12/07/84 | 5 | | . . . | | |
| 3 | 12/07/84 | 4 | | | | |
| 4 | 12/07/84 | 3 | | | | |
| . . . | | | | | | |

To total the field values in a subset of the data records, you can add
a qualifier so that the TOTAL command applies only to those data
records that meet a certain condition. The format of the conditional
TOTAL command is

.  TOTAL ON <key field> TO <name of summary file> FOR
<qualifier>

The example in figure 6.24 uses the qualifier *MODEL<ZENITH*. In
comparisons of alphanumeric values, any value beginning with *RCA*
is evaluated as less than the value *ZENITH*. Consequently, only
those records containing RCA-XA100 or RCA-XA200 will be totaled.

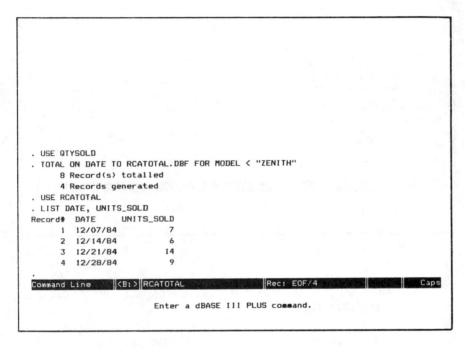

```
. USE QTYSOLD
. TOTAL ON DATE TO RCATOTAL.DBF FOR MODEL < "ZENITH"
      8 Record(s) totalled
      4 Records generated
. USE RCATOTAL
. LIST DATE, UNITS_SOLD
Record#  DATE      UNITS_SOLD
      1  12/07/84         7
      2  12/14/84         6
      3  12/21/84        14
      4  12/28/84         9
.
Command Line    <B:> RCATOTAL                Rec: EOF/4              Caps
              Enter a dBASE III PLUS command.
```

*Fig. 6.24. Generating weekly totals.*

The same logic can be used to generate a monthly summary of the
television models sold. Before the database file QTYSOLD.DBF is
totaled, however, you must use the SORT or INDEX command to
arrange the data records in ascending or descending order according
to the contents of the MODEL field. Figure 6.25 shows how a
monthly summary can be produced with INDEX and TOTAL.

The results show that each record in the summary file
QTYMONTH.DBF contains the total number sold during
December, 1984, for one model of television set. You can then use
the SUM command to find the monthly total for all television sets
sold:

    . SUM UNITS_SOLD

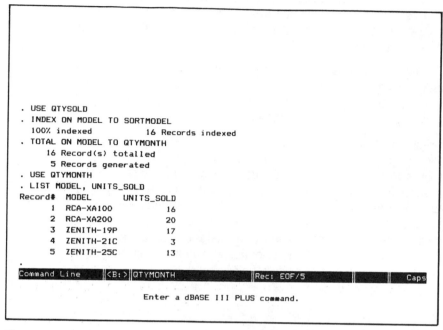

```
. USE QTYSOLD
. INDEX ON MODEL TO SORTMODEL
  100% indexed            16 Records indexed
. TOTAL ON MODEL TO QTYMONTH
      16 Record(s) totalled
       5 Records generated
. USE QTYMONTH
. LIST MODEL, UNITS_SOLD
Record#  MODEL        UNITS_SOLD
      1  RCA-XA100            16
      2  RCA-XA200            20
      3  ZENITH-19P           17
      4  ZENITH-21C            3
      5  ZENITH-25C           13
.
Command Line    <B:> QTYMONTH                  Rec: EOF/5                     Caps

            Enter a dBASE III PLUS command.
```

Fig. 6.25. Producing monthly summary with INDEX and TOTAL.

The same results will be achieved whether the SUM command is applied to the original QTYSOLD.DBF database file or to either of the summary files (QTYWEEK.DBF or QTYMONTH.DBF).

# Chapter Summary

This chapter has introduced Index and Sort, the two most useful options on the Assistant menu, and their corresponding dot commands. You can use the Sort option in an active database file to arrange data records according to the contents of one or more key fields. The result of the sorting operation is a target file that contains the ordered data records.

The Index option is similar to Sort, but indexing is much faster than sorting. Indexing creates an index file that contains only key-field values and their corresponding record numbers. The index file is used to rearrange data records in the active database file.

Sorting and indexing give you the option of accessing all or part of a database file's records. To select a subset of the data records for sorting or indexing, you can define scope and search conditions. In dot-prompt mode, you can affect a selected set of records in the database file by adding a qualifier clause (FOR . . . ) to the SORT or INDEX command.

Sorting and indexing do not change the order of data records in the disk file; target files are created to store the arranged data fields or records. If the contents of the database file have been changed, you must re-sort or reindex the database file.

Using the Assistant menu and dot-prompt commands, you can sum, average, and count records. These summarizing operations can be applied to a selected subset of records or to all the records in the database file. In dot-prompt mode, you use the TOTAL command to sum the active database file's numeric fields and save the results in a summary file. The numeric fields of the summary file contain the totals for all the data records whose key fields contain the same value. Before using the TOTAL command, you must rearrange the data records in ascending or descending order.

# 7

Memory Variables,
Expressions, and
Functions

## An Overview

Often, in addition to storing data in a database, you need to retain
the intermediate results of data manipulation procedures so that the
values can be used for further processing. Instead of storing the
values as records in a file, you can save them as variables. A *memory
variable* is a memory location that is set aside to store a data
element. Memory variables are important in data manipulation
because they take up little memory space and their contents can be
recalled almost instantly. This chapter explains how memory
variables are defined and used in database management.

This chapter also discusses the use of expressions and functions in data manipulation. An *expression* is a combination of data field values and memory variables that is used to define the operations performed on specified data elements. *Functions* are predefined operations whose results (such as numbers and alphanumeric strings) can be used in expressions. For example, you can use a function to find the square root of a number and then use the square root for further processing.

The following commands for processing memory variables are introduced in this chapter:

| Commands | Functions |
|---|---|
| STORE = | Enters data into memory variables |
| ? DISPLAY MEMORY | Displays memory variables |
| SAVE TO | Saves memory variables to disk file |
| RELEASE ERASE | Discards memory variables |
| RESTORE | Retrieves memory variables from disk file |

The following are some of the commonly used built-in functions of dBASE III Plus:

| Functions | For |
|---|---|
| CDOW, CMONTH, DATE, DAY DOW, MONTH, TIME, YEAR | Time and date processing |
| CTOD, DTOC, VAL, STR | Field/Variable conversion |
| AT, LEFT, LEN, LTRIM RIGHT, RTRIM SPACE, STUFF SUBSTR, TRIM | Character string manipulation |
| ABS, EXP, INT, LOG, MAX MIN, MOD, ROUND, SQRT | Mathematical operation |
| RECNO | Current record pointer |
| COL, PCOL, ROW, PROW | Displaying a location |

# Memory Variables

The term *variable* is used in algebra to mean a quantity that may assume different values. In dBASE III Plus, a *variable* is a name assigned to a memory location that can be used to hold a data element. The value stored in a memory variable can be the value in a data field or some other data item. Alphanumeric strings, numeric values, and dates can be stored in memory variables.

Memory variables are stored temporarily in RAM during processing. Contents of memory variables are stored outside the structure of a database file and are not considered part of the database contents.

Memory variables are the major components of formulas. Intermediate results from computations or data manipulations are often stored in memory variables to be recalled and used in further calculations or report generation.

## Determining the Type of Memory Variable

dBASE III Plus offers four types of memory variables: alphanumeric (character), numeric, date, and logical. The type is determined when data is stored in the variable: if a numeric value is assigned to a variable, for example, then the type of that variable is numeric. The contents of memory variables can be used only in expressions appropriate to the type of the variable. Alphanumeric variable contents can be processed only by alphanumeric operators and functions, for example, and mathematical computations can be performed only on numeric values.

You can change the variable type by assigning a different kind of data. For instance, when an alphanumeric string is placed in a variable, that variable becomes an alphanumeric variable. If you later assign a numeric value to the same variable, it becomes a numeric variable.

## Naming the Variable

A memory variable name can consists of up to 10 characters. As with field names, these 10 characters may be a combination of letters, digits, and the underscore character (_). However, the first character of a memory variable name must be a letter. The following are acceptable memory variable names:

| SALES | Grosspay | DISCOUNT |
|---|---|---|
| SaleDate | WEEKLYHRS | PAY_RATE |
| ACCOUNTNO | UNITSSOLD | TAXRATE |

The same name should not be used for a variable and a data field in the same application. When the same name is assigned to a variable and to a field, the name is recognized only for the field when the file containing the field is activated.

Because memory variables are often needed to retain the field contents for further computation, you may want to assign a variable name that is related to the corresponding field name. For example, if the field name contains an underscore, such as ACCOUNT_NO, then the name without the underscore, ACCOUNTNO, can be used for the variable. If the field name does not contain an underscore, you may want to create a memory variable name consisting of the field name preceded by the letter M. For instance, you can use the name MSALES for the memory variable to hold the contents of the data field SALES.

# Entering Data in a Memory Variable

You can enter data in a memory variable by entering data from the keyboard, by assigning to it the contents of a data field from the active record, or by copying the contents from another memory variable.

## The = Command

The equal sign (=) is a command entered from the keyboard. This command assigns an alphanumeric string, a value, or a logical state (.T. or .F.) to a memory variable. Use the following form:

. <name of memory variable>=<data element>

The equal sign (=) is interpreted differently in dBASE III Plus than in normal mathematical use. Instead of stating that two quantities are equal, the equal sign signifies an action: the memory variable on the left side of the equal sign is assigned the value of the data element on the right.

The data element assigned to the memory variable must be defined in a specific form, depending on the kind of data element. To avoid ambiguity, you must enclose alphanumeric strings in quotation marks. Contents of a logical variable must be specified in the form .T. or .F. (or .Y. or .N.). Be sure to include the two periods. Numbers entered in numerical variables can be integers or decimal values (see fig. 7.1). A date cannot be entered in a date variable with the = command.

```
. TESTSTRING="This is a test string"
This is a test string
. MEMBERSHIP=.T.
.T.
. HOURS=32
32
. PAYRATE=7.50
7.50
.
```

*Fig. 7.1. Assigning data to memory variables.*

*Note:* In figure 7.1 and other figures in this chapter, you may notice that the status bar is not shown on the screen display. The status bar can be removed by entering the SET STATUS OFF dot command. To display the status bar again, enter SET STATUS ON.

If the memory variable name and the data element have been defined correctly, the data element is assigned to the variable. Unless ECHO has been turned off, the program confirms the command by echoing the contents of the variable immediately after the = command is executed. If an error is made in the = command, the error message **\*\*\* Unrecognized command verb \*\*\*** is displayed.

Contents of a data field in the active data record (including character, numeric, logical, and date fields) can also be assigned to a memory variable with the = command. Use the following format:

. <name of memory variable>=<name of data field>

Figure 7.2 illustrates use of the = command to assign the contents of data fields in the EMPLOYEE database file to memory variables.

```
. USE EMPLOYEE
. GO TOP
. FIRSTNAME=FIRST_NAME
James C.
. MMALE=MALE
.T.
. BIRTHDATE=BIRTH_DATE
07/04/60
. ANNUALPAY=ANNUAL_PAY
22000.00
.
```

*Fig. 7.2. Assigning contents of data field to memory variable.*

## The STORE Command

The STORE command also assigns to a memory variable a data element or the contents of a data field of the active record. In fact, you can use the = and STORE commands interchangeably. The STORE command has the following formats:

. STORE <data element> TO <name of memory variable>
. STORE <name of data field> TO <name of memory variable>

The first format is used for entering data from the keyboard. This STORE command assigns alphanumeric, numeric, and logical memory variables but not dates (see fig. 7.3).

```
. STORE "This is a test string" TO TESTSTRING
This is a test string
. STORE .T. TO MEMBERSHIP
.T.
. STORE 32 TO HOURS
32
. STORE 7.5 TO PAYRATE
7.5
.
```

*Fig. 7.3. Using STORE.*

The second format of the STORE command assigns to a memory variable the content of a data field of the active record, regardless of the field type. The variable type becomes that of the data field when the STORE command is executed. The example in figure 7.4 illustrates assignment of contents of data fields in the EMPLOYEE database file to corresponding variables.

```
. USE EMPLOYEE
. LOCATE FOR FIRST_NAME="Doris"
Record =        3
. DISPLAY
Record#  FIRST_NAME    LAST_NAME    AREA_CODE PHONE_NO MALE BIRTH_DATE ANNUAL_PAY
      3  Doris A.      Gregory      503       204-8567 .F.  07/04/62     16900.00
. STORE FIRST_NAME TO FIRSTNAME
Doris A.
. STORE MALE TO MMALE
.F.
. STORE BIRTH_DATE TO BIRTHDATE
07/04/62
. STORE ANNUAL_PAY TO ANNUALPAY
16900.00
.
```

Fig. 7.4. Using another form of STORE.

# Displaying Memory Variables

When you enter data into memory variables, the variables are stored temporarily in RAM. You can display the contents of all the variables at any time during data manipulation.

## The DISPLAY MEMORY Command

The DISPLAY MEMORY command can be used to display detailed information about all active memory variables. Enter the command as

. DISPLAY MEMORY

When you enter this command, all active memory variables are displayed in the order they were last updated. DISPLAY also shows the type of data stored in each variable and the variable contents (see fig. 7.5).

The abbreviation *pub* after a variable name indicates that the variable is a public variable. All variables are either *public* or *private*. A private variable can be accessed only by the program module in which it is defined. The contents of a public variable can be accessed by every part of the program. This distinction, however, is useful only for batch command processing (discussed in Chapter 11). All variables defined in interactive mode are public variables.

The DISPLAY MEMORY command also displays summary statistics regarding the number of variables defined, the amount of memory

```
. DISPLAY MEMORY
TESTSTRING    pub    C    "This is a test string"
MEMBERSHIP    pub    L    .T.
HOURS         pub    N          32  (           32.00000000)
PAYRATE       pub    N          7.5 (            7.50000000)
FIRSTNAME     pub    C    "Doris A.      "
MMALE         pub    L    .F.
BIRTHDATE     pub    D    07/04/62
ANNUALPAY     pub    N       16900.00 (       16900.00000000)
      8 variables defined,        77 bytes used
    248 variables available,    5923 bytes available
```

Fig. 7.5. Results of DISPLAY MEMORY command.

used, and the numbers of variables and bytes of memory still
available.

## The ? Command

Instead of displaying all existing variables as a group, you can display
a single variable by entering the ? command in the form

. ? <name of memory variable to be displayed>

Figure 7.6 shows how the ? command can be used to display the
contents of several different types of memory variables.

```
. ? TESTSTRING
This is a test string
. ? MEMBERSHIP
.T.
. ? HOURS
        32
. ? PAYRATE
       7.5
. ? FIRSTNAME
Doris A.
. ? BIRTHDATE
07/04/62
. ? ANNUALPAY
    16900.00

.
```

Fig. 7.6. Example using ? command.

# Saving Memory Variables on Disk

Memory variables are stored temporarily in RAM and can be accessed at any stage of the data manipulation process. When you leave dBASE III Plus, however, the variables are erased (or released) from memory. If you want to use these variables in different dBASE III Plus applications, you must therefore store the variables permanantly. The SAVE command is used to store in a disk file the contents of the active memory variables.

The SAVE command stores all or part of the current set of memory variables to a disk file. To save all the active memory variables, use the SAVE command in the following form:

. SAVE TO <name of memory file>

To save the active variables to a file called VARLIST, for example, you enter

. SAVE TO VARLIST

This command tells the computer to copy all the memory variables to a file named VARLIST. Unless you specify otherwise, the file extension for the memory file created by this command is .MEM; the file name therefore is VARLIST.MEM.

You can also elect to save only some of the variables. To select the variables you want to save, use a selection clause such as ALL LIKE or ALL EXCEPT:

. SAVE ALL LIKE <variable description> TO <name of memory file>

. SAVE ALL EXCEPT <variable description> TO <name of memory file>

The symbol <*variable description*> refers to the "skeleton" of a variable name. dBASE III has two symbols (called *wild cards*) that can be substituted for the characters in a variable name. The question mark (?) substitutes for a single character, and the asterisk (*) stands for a string of characters of any length. A skeleton contains the alphanumeric characters and wild-card symbols necessary for specifying a set of variables. For instance, to save in the file NETVARS.MEM all the active memory variables with names beginning with the letters *NET* (NETREVENUE, NETCOST, NETPROFIT, etc.), you can use a skeleton containing the asterisk:

. SAVE ALL LIKE NET* TO NETVARS

The asterisk (∗) in the variable description stands for any series of characters; the program therefore saves every variable whose name begins with *NET*.

The ? wild-card symbol simplifies definition of memory variable sets. Suppose, for example, that you want to save all memory variables with six-character names including *RATE* as the second through fifth characters (WRATE1, MRATE2, YRATE3, etc.). You can use the question-mark wild-card symbol as follows:

. SAVE ALL LIKE ?RATE? TO RATES

The variable-name skeleton *?RATE?* instructs dBASE III Plus to store all variables with six-character names and *RATE* in the second through fifth positions, regardless of what characters occupy positions 1 and 6.

Skeletons can be used to exclude specific variables from a memory disk file. For example, if you want to exclude memory variables whose names begin with the letters *NET*, you can use the ALL EXCEPT clause in the SAVE command:

. SAVE ALL EXCEPT NET????? TO MEMVARS
. SAVE ALL EXCEPT NET∗ TO MEMVARS

The first command saves all memory variables that have names beginning with *NET* followed by any five alphanumeric characters. The second command saves all memory variables to the file except those that have names beginning with *NET* followed by any alphanumeric characters.

# Deleting Memory Variables

Memory variables can be deleted from the active list of memory variables. The RELEASE command permanently removes from memory some or all of the active memory variables. As with the SAVE command, the clauses ALL, ALL LIKE, and ALL EXCEPT can be used to select the memory variables to be released:

. RELEASE ALL
. RELEASE ALL LIKE <variable-name description>
. RELEASE ALL EXCEPT <variable-name description>

The wild-card symbols * and ? can be used for deletion in the same way they were used with the SAVE command. Following are some examples:

. RELEASE ALL LIKE *NET
. RELEASE ALL LIKE ?RATE?
. RELEASE ALL EXCEPT *NET
. RELEASE ALL EXCEPT NET?????

The RELEASE command removes the specified active memory variables from RAM, not from a memory file. To delete a memory file that has been saved on disk, use the ERASE command:

. ERASE <name of memory file to be erased>

For instance, the following command removes the memory file MEMVAR.MEM:

. ERASE MEMVAR.MEM

# Loading Memory Variables from Memory Files

Memory variables that have been saved in a memory file can be copied back to RAM. The RESTORE command retrieves all the memory variables in a memory file and places them in the computer's memory. The format for this command is

. RESTORE FROM <name of memory file>

The following command places in RAM the memory variables from the RATES.MEM memory file:

. RESTORE FROM RATES.MEM

When you use the RESTORE command, all memory variables currently in RAM are erased before the memory variables from RATES.MEM are restored. To retain the current memory variables, you must combine the ADDITIVE clause with the RESTORE command:

. RESTORE FROM <name of the memory file> ADDITIVE

For example, to retrieve all variables in VARLIST.MEM and add them to the current active memory list, you use the following command:

. RESTORE FROM VARLIST.MEM ADDITIVE

# Expressions

Besides serving as temporary storage, memory variables can be used in processing operations. A memory variable can be specified in an expression in order to define a procedure, to describe a qualifier phrase in a command, or to serve as an output element.

Depending on the application, different types of expressions can be used in dBASE III Plus. An expression can include a data field, a memory variable, a constant, or a combination of these elements. All elements in an expression must be the same type, however. If an expression contains data elements of different types, the error message **Data type mismatch** is displayed.

## Using Arithmetic Expressions

The most common expression is the arithmetic expression, which can contain a value, a memory variable, a numeric data field, or combinations of these joined by one or more arithmetic operators (+, −, *, /, etc.)

The following are arithmetic expressions:

```
32
HOURS
ANNUAL_PAY
HOURS*PAYRATE
ANNUAL_PAY + 0.05*ANNUAL_PAY
```

HOURS and PAYRATE are names of memory variables, and * is the symbol for multiplication. The expression HOURS*PAYRATE indicates that the contents of the variable HOURS are to be multiplied by the contents of PAYRATE.

Expressions are useful for arithmetic calculations. An expression can be used to assign a value to a memory variable, for example, or to place a new value in a numeric data field. In figure 7.7, the arithmetic expressions entered at the dot prompt assign values to the memory variables whose names are entered to the left of the equal signs.

The multiplication symbol (*) in the arithmetic expression is called an *arithmetic operator*. Other arithmetic operators are +, −, /, and ^ for the operations of addition, subtraction, division, and raising the power, respectively. When more than one arithmetic operator is

```
.  HOURS=32
32
.  PAYRATE=7.5
7.5
.  GROSSPAY=HOURS*PAYRATE
                  240.0

.
```

*Fig. 7.7. Arithmetic expressions assigning values to variables.*

included in an expression, the expression is evaluated from left to right according to the following series:

Highest priority        ^
Second priority        *, /
Lowest priority        +, −

This order of evaluation sometimes is called the *order of precedence*.

You can use parentheses in an arithmetic expression to define the evaluation sequence and alter the normal order of precedence. Material within parentheses is always evaluated first. When pairs of parentheses are nested in an arithmetic expression, the expression within the inner parentheses is evaluated first. Then the expressions within the outer parentheses are evaluated. Arithmetic operators within parentheses are evaluated from left to right following the normal order of precedence. For example, the arithmetic expression

(QTYA+QTYB)*PRICE*((1-DISCOUNT)/100)

is evaluated as follows.

1. Evaluate (1-DISCOUNT).

2. Evaluate (QTYA+QTYB).

3. Evaluate ((1-DISCOUNT)/100). (The result of step 1 is used in place of 1-DISCOUNT.)

4. Evaluate (QTYA+QTYB)*PRICE. (The result of step 2 is used in this step.)

5. Evaluate the entire equation: (QTYA+QTYB)*PRICE*((1-DISCOUNT)/100). (This is the result of step 4 multiplied by the result of step 3.)

You can also use the contents of numeric data fields in an arithmetic expression. The values are taken from fields in the active record. Figure 7.8 shows that the numeric field UNITS_SOLD in QTYSOLD.DBF can be used in an arithmetic expression to compute the total price for units sold.

```
. USE QTYSOLD
. LOCATE FOR MODEL="RCA-XA200"
Record =        2
. DISPLAY
Record#  DATE      MODEL        UNITS_SOLD
      2  12/07/84 RCA-XA200             5
. UNITPRICE=495.90
495.90
. TOTALPRICE=UNITPRICE*UNITS_SOLD
        2479.50
.
```

Fig. 7.8. Numeric data field used in arithmetic expression.

Similarly, as shown in figure 7.9, an arithmetic expression can be used with a DISPLAY command to compute record totals (UNITPRICE*UNITS_SOLD) for all records of QTYSOLD.DBF containing *RCA-XA200* in the MODEL field.

```
. USE QTYSOLD
. UNITPRICE=495.90
495.90
. DISPLAY DATE,UNITS_SOLD,UNITPRICE*UNITS_SOLD FOR MODEL="RCA-XA200"
Record#  DATE     UNITS_SOLD  UNITPRICE*UNITS_SOLD
      2  12/07/84          5               2479.50
      6  12/14/84          4               1983.60
     10  12/21/84          6               2975.40
     14  12/28/84          5               2479.50
.
```

Fig. 7.9. Arithmetic expression used with DISPLAY.

By using an arithmetic expression with the REPLACE command, you can adjust the contents of the numeric fields in the active record (see fig. 7.10). To raise by 5 percent all the employees' annual salaries (in the numeric field ANNUAL_PAY), you use the REPLACE command and the expression ANNUAL_PAY*1.05. The command causes the value in ANNUAL_PAY to be replaced by a value 5 percent higher.

```
. USE EMPLOYEE
. REPLACE ALL ANNUAL_PAY WITH ANNUAL_PAY*1.05
      10 records replaced
. LIST LAST_NAME,ANNUAL_PAY
Record#   LAST_NAME   ANNUAL_PAY
       1   Smith         23100.00
       2   Zeller        29347.50
       3   Gregory       17745.00
       4   Nelson        30450.00
       5   Baker         27195.00
       6   Chapman       20737.50
       7   Thompson      25725.00
       8   Duff          14175.00
       9   Lee           36645.00
      10   Hanson        30397.50
.
```

Fig. 7.10. Arithmetic expression with REPLACE.

# Using Alphanumeric Expressions

Alphanumeric expressions (sometimes called character expressions) are also used frequently in dBASE III and dBASE III Plus. An alphanumeric expression may contain an alphanumeric string enclosed in quotation marks, an alphanumeric memory variable, an alphanumeric data field, or a combination of these joined by the + sign.

For example, each of the following phrases is an alphanumeric expression:

"Employee's Name"
FIRST_NAME
LAST_NAME
"Employee's Name"+"is"+FIRST_NAME+LAST_NAME

Alphanumeric expressions often are used to assign an alphanumeric data element to a memory variable. For instance, either of the following commands assigns the contents of the alphanumeric expression to an alphanumeric variable:

. LONGSTRING=STRING A+STRING B+STRING C
. STORE STRINGA+STRINGB+STRINGC TO LONGSTRING

You can use an alphanumeric expression to combine data fields in the records of the active database file and show the result with a DISPLAY or LIST command. For example, in figure 7.11 an alphanumeric expression combines contents of two fields

```
. USE EMPLOYEE
. DISPLAY FIRST_NAME+LAST_NAME FOR MALE
Record#   FIRST_NAME+LAST_NAME
      1   James C.    Smith
      2   Albert K.   Zeller
      4   Harry M.    Nelson
      6   Kirk D.     Chapman
      8   Charles N.  Duff
      9   Winston E.  Lee
     10   Thomas T.   Hanson
. LIST LAST_NAME+", "+FIRST_NAME FOR .NOT. MALE
Record#   LAST_NAME+", "+FIRST_NAME
      3   Gregory    ,Doris A.
      5   Baker      ,Tina B.
      7   Thompson   ,Mary W.
  .
```

Fig. 7.11. Alphanumeric expression with DISPLAY and LIST.

(FIRST_NAME and LAST_NAME). The result of the expression is a string consisting of the employee's first and last names.

In addition, the REPLACE command can be used to substitute the result of an alphanumeric expression for the contents of a field in active records of the database. In figure 7.12, the contents of the variable NEWCODE have replaced the contents of the AREA_CODE field in EMPLOYEE.DBF.

```
. USE EMPLOYEE
. NEWCODE="513"
513
. REPLACE AREA_CODE WITH NEWCODE FOR AREA_CODE="503"
      2 records replaced
. LIST ALL LAST_NAME, AREA_CODE
Record#   LAST_NAME   AREA_CODE
      1   Smith       216
      2   Zeller      212
      3   Gregory     513
      4   Nelson      315
      5   Baker       415
      6   Chapman     618
      7   Thompson    213
      8   Duff        216
      9   Lee         513
     10   Hanson      216
  .
```

Fig. 7.12. Alphanumeric expression with REPLACE.

# Displaying Expressions

Results of alphanumeric and numeric expressions can be displayed in a number of ways. For example, a DISPLAY or a LIST command can be used with an alphanumeric expression to display the contents of the variable IDLABEL along with the name of an employee (see fig. 7.13).

```
. USE EMPLOYEE
. LOCATE FOR LAST_NAME="Gregory"
Record =        3
. DISPLAY
Record#  FIRST_NAME    LAST_NAME   AREA_CODE PHONE_NO MALE BIRTH_DATE ANNUAL_PAY
      3  Doris A.      Gregory       513        204-8567 .F.  07/04/62     17745.00
. IDLABEL="Employee's Name ..... "
Employee's Name .....
. DISPLAY IDLABEL+FIRST_NAME+LAST_NAME
Record#   IDLABEL+FIRST_NAME+LAST_NAME
      3  Employee's Name ..... Doris A.      Gregory
. LIST IDLABEL+LAST_NAME+", "+FIRST_NAME
Record#   IDLABEL+LAST_NAME+", "+FIRST_NAME
      1  Employee's Name ..... Smith      , James C.
      2  Employee's Name ..... Zeller     , Albert K.
      3  Employee's Name ..... Gregory    , Doris A.
      4  Employee's Name ..... Nelson     , Harry M.
      5  Employee's Name ..... Baker      , Tina B.
      6  Employee's Name ..... Chapman    , Kirk D.
      7  Employee's Name ..... Thompson   , Mary W.
      8  Employee's Name ..... Duff       , Charles N.
      9  Employee's Name ..... Lee        , Winston E.
     10  Employee's Name ..... Hanson     , Thomas T.
.
```

*Fig. 7.13. Displaying alphanumeric and numeric expressions.*

You can also use the ? command to display the results of an alphanumeric expression (see fig. 7.14). Notice that with the ? command, a comma is used to separate the alphanumeric string "Total Sale . . . " from the numeric expression UNITS_SOLD*UNITPRICE. Each is considered a separate expression.

```
. USE QTYSOLD
. LOCATE FOR MODEL="ZENITH-19P"
Record =        3
. DISPLAY
Record#  DATE     MODEL       UNITS_SOLD
      3  12/07/84 ZENITH-19P          4
. UNITPRICE=259.5
259.5
. ? "Total Sale .......   ", UNITS_SOLD*UNITPRICE
Total Sale .......        1038.0
.
```

*Fig. 7.14. Using ? command to display result of alphanumeric expression.*

An expression must contain only data elements of the same type. An alphanumeric expression and a numeric expression cannot be joined with a plus sign, for example. The following expression will result in the error message **Data type mismatch** because UNITS_SOLD*UNITPRICE is a numeric expression.

? "Total Sale . . . " +UNITS_SOLD*UNITPRICE

However, you can use the STR function, which is discussed later in this chapter, to convert the result of UNITS_SOLD*UNITPRICE to an alphanumeric value. That value can then be concatenated with the alphanumeric string "Total Sale . . . "

# Functions

Functions in dBASE III and dBASE III Plus provide a "built-in" way of performing mathematical and string manipulations. A function takes values (called *arguments*) that are "passed" to it and performs an operation on those values. The function then "returns" the value resulting from the operation it has performed. The arguments of functions can be either the contents of data fields or the results of expressions.

Functions are divided into groups according to the types of data they return and the kinds of operations they perform. Mathematical functions can round a decimal number to the integer, compute the square root of a value, and perform many other actions. String functions can select parts of an alphanumeric string for use in searching, sorting, and indexing operations. Other string functions can insert blank spaces in an alphanumeric string or trim off unwanted blank spaces. Functions for data-type conversion change data elements from one type to another. These functions can convert a date to an alphanumeric string, a numeric field value to an alphanumeric string, or the contents of an alphanumeric variable to a numeric value. The time and date functions display date and time in a number of formats that are used in business data processing applications.

# Format of a Function

A function, which is designed to perform a special operation, must have a function name. The argument of the function is enclosed in parentheses. The format of a function therefore is

. <name of function>(<argument>)

In the example

. INT(3.7415)

the INT function returns the integer portion of the decimal value 3.7415, which is the argument of the function. The result of the function INT(3.7415) is the numeric value 3. As shown in figure 6.15, this function may be used as an expression in a ? command or as part of an arithmetic expression.

```
. ? INT(3.7415)
    3
. ANSWER=1200/INT(3.7415)
    400.00
.
```

*Fig. 7.15. Example using INT function.*

Many functions are available for manipulating data elements of different types. These functions are summarized by their operations in the following sections.

# Mathematical Functions

As stated earlier, a mathematical function performs a mathematical operation on numeric data elements that are passed to the functions. The arguments can be numeric values or the contents of numeric data fields. The results of mathematical functions are always returned as numeric data. In addition to INT (explained in the preceding section), the types of mathematical functions supported by dBASE III Plus are ROUND, SQRT, LOG, and EXP.

## The ROUND Function

The ROUND function rounds a decimal value to the number of decimal places specified by the argument <n>. The decimal value argument can be the contents of a memory variable or numeric data field, or the result of a numeric expression. The format of the ROUND function is

. ROUND(<numeric expression>,<n>)

Note that the result and the argument of the function always have the same number of decimal places (see fig. 7.16). The argument <n> controls not the number of decimal places displayed, but the number of places to which the decimal argument is rounded. Consequently, the command

. ?ROUND(3.7415,0)

returns the value 4.0000, which is 3.7415 rounded to zero places after the decimal point. The command

. ?ROUND(3.7415,1)

returns 3.7000; the result is the original value rounded to one place after the decimal point.

```
. ? ROUND(3.7415,0)
 4.0000
. ? ROUND(3.7415,1)
 3.7000
. ? ROUND(3.7415,3)
 3.7420
. HOURS=39.5
39.5
. PAYRATE=9.75
9.75
. ? HOURS*PAYRATE
               385.125
. ? ROUND(HOURS*PAYRATE,2)
                385.130

.
```

Fig. 7.16. Example using ROUND function.

## The SQRT Function

The SQRT function returns the square root of the value in the argument. The format is

. SQRT(<numeric expression>)

The square root returned by the function has a minimum of two decimal places. The maximum number of decimal places in the square root is the same as the number of decimal places in the argument. If more decimal places are desired, extra zeros must therefore be added to the end of the value (see fig. 7.17).

```
. ? SQRT(100)
      10.00
. ? SQRT(2)
       1.41
. ? SQRT(2.00)
       1.41
. ? SQRT(2.00000000)
1.41421356
. A=3.125
3.125
. B=1567.89
1567.89
. ? SQRT(A*B)
   69.99754

.
```

*Fig. 7.17. Example using SQRT function.*

## The LOG Function

Two types of logarithms are used in mathematics and statistics. One is the base-10 (or *common*) logarithm, which is denoted as *log10x*. The other type of logarithm is the base-e (or *natural* logarithm, where e = 2.71828183. . . This logarithm is denoted by the symbol *ln x*.

In dBASE III and dBASE III Plus, only the natural logarithm (LOG) is available, but you can easily calculate the common logarithm of a value by using the LOG function. To calculate the natural logarithm of a value, just provide the value as a numeric expression in the argument:

. LOG(<numeric expression>)

Figure 7.18 shows a few examples of using the LOG function.

```
. ?LOG(2.71828183)
1.00000000
. ?LOG(10)
      2.30
. ?LOG(10.000000)
   2.302585

.
```

*Fig. 7.18. Example using LOG function.*

With the following conversion formula, the natural LOG function can be used to calculate the common logarithm of a value:

$$\log_{10}x = \frac{\ln x}{\ln 10}$$

To compute the common logarithm of the value of 1,000, use the LOG function as follows:

LOG(1000)/LOG(10)

## The EXP Function

EXP is the exponential function. When passed the argument $x$, the function returns the value $e^x$ ("e to the x power"). The format of the EXP function is

. EXP(<numeric expression>)

Figure 7.19 shows some examples. The command ?EXP(1.00) causes the value of $e^1$, 2.72, to be displayed. Because the argument of the function is displayed with two decimal places (1.00), the result returned by the function also has two decimal places. If you use more decimal places in the argument, as in the command ?EXP(1.00000000), you'll get a more accurate answer. You can also use a numeric expression as the argument for the EXP function, as shown in the third command, ?EXP(A*B).

```
.  ?EXP(1.00)
       2.72
.  ?EXP(1.00000000)
2.71828183
.  A=2
2
.  B=4
4
.  ?EXP(A*B)
     2980.0'
.
```

Fig. 7.19. Example using EXP function.

## PLUS  The ABS Function

ABS is the absolute value function. When you specify a numeric expression as an argument, the function returns the absolute value of the expression. The format is

.ABS(<numeric expression>)

Figure 7.20 shows examples of using the ABS function. Notice that even when the value of the expression is negative, the ABS function returns a positive value.

```
.  A=2
2
.  B=4
4
.  ?ABS(-3.4567)
 3.4567
.  ?(A-B)
          -2
.  ?ABS(A-B)
           2
.
```

*Fig. 7.20. Example using ABS function.*

## The MAX Function

PLUS

The MAX function returns the larger value of two numeric expressions that are supplied as arguments. The form of the MAX function is

.MAX(<numeric expression 1>,<numeric expression 2>)

In figure 7.21, the MAX function evaluates the two numeric expressions A+B and A*B and returns the larger of the two values.

```
.  A=10
10
.  B=20
20
.  ?MAX(A+B, A*B)
                  200
.
```

*Fig. 7.21. Example using MAX function.*

PLUS ## The MIN Function

The MIN function, the opposite of MAX, evaluates the two numeric expressions supplied as arguments and returns the smaller value. The format is

.MIN(<numeric expression 1>,<numeric expression 2>)

In figure 7.22, the MIN function evaluates the two numeric expressions A+B and A∗B and returns the smaller of the two values (A+B, or 30).

```
.  A=10
10
.  B=20
20
.  ?MIN(A+B, A*B)
         30
.
```

*Fig. 7.22. Example using MIN function.*

# String Manipulation Functions

Several functions are available for manipulating alphanumeric strings in various ways. For instance, characters in a string can be converted from uppercase to lowercase letters. Blank spaces in a character field can be removed or added. Any character in an alphanumeric string can be isolated for displaying or for sorting and indexing operations.

## The LOWER Function

The LOWER function converts to lowercase characters all the capital letters in an alphanumeric string. Numeric digits and other symbols are not changed, however. The argument of the LOWER function is an alphanumeric expression, which can be a combination of alphanumeric strings in quotation marks and the contents of character data fields. The format is

. LOWER(<alphanumeric expression>)

Figure 7.23 shows several examples of using the LOWER function.

```
. ?LOWER("THIS IS A SAMPLE PHRASE IN CAPITAL LETTERS")
this is a sample phrase in capital letters
. USE EMPLOYEE
. ?LOWER(FIRST_NAME)
james c.
. ?LOWER(LAST_NAME+", "+FIRST_NAME)
smith      ,james c.
.
```

*Fig. 7.23. Example using LOWER function.*

The LOWER function is effective for searching. To locate the record containing a particular value in a character field, for example, use LOWER to convert all contents of that character field into lowercase letters. Then you can find the string by specifying the search key in all lowercase letters, regardless of whether the string was entered in the field in lowercase or uppercase letters. In figure 7.24, the LOCATE command is used with the LOWER function to find the

```
. USE EMPLOYEE
. LOCATE FOR LOWER(LAST_NAME)="smith"
Record =        1
. DISPLAY LAST_NAME, FIRST_NAME
Record#  LAST_NAME  FIRST_NAME
     1   Smith      James C.
.
```

*Fig. 7.24. Example using LOWER function with LOCATE command.*

records that contain a last name in the forms of *SMITH*, *Smith*, *smith*, or any other combination of upper- and lowercase letters.

Without the LOWER function, the following LOCATE command finds only records with *smith* in the LAST_NAME field.

. LOCATE FOR LAST_NAME="smith"

## The UPPER Function

PLUS

The UPPER function performs a string conversion opposite to that of the LOWER function. UPPER converts to uppercase letters the lowercase letters in the alphanumeric string (see fig. 7.25). The format of the UPPER function is

. UPPER(<alphanumeric expression>)

```
. ?UPPER("This is an alphanumeric string!")
THIS IS AN ALPHANUMERIC STRING!
. USE EMPLOYEE
. LOCATE FOR UPPER(LAST_NAME)="SMITH"
Record =          1
. DISPLAY LAST_NAME+", "+FIRST_NAME
Record#  LAST_NAME+", "+FIRST_NAME
       1  Smith        , James C.
. ?UPPER(LAST_NAME+", "+FIRST_NAME)
SMITH        , JAMES C.
.
```

*Fig. 7.25. Example using UPPER function.*

Figure 7.25 shows that by using UPPER(LAST_NAME) in the LOCATE command, you can convert to uppercase letters the string stored in the LAST_NAME field. Consequently, you can use *SMITH* as the search key for locating the data record.

## The TRIM Function

The TRIM function removes any trailing spaces from a character string. The argument of the function is an alphanumeric expression, which may contain a combination of alphanumeric strings and character/text data-field contents. The format of the TRIM function is

. TRIM(<alphanumeric expression>)

Because the width of a character/text field is preset when the structure is defined, trailing spaces are automatically added to the end of any character string shorter than the field width. When the strings are displayed together, the blank spaces may make the display too wide. For instance, when the contents of the FIRST_NAME and LAST_NAME fields are displayed on the same line, several spaces separate the characters in the two fields (see fig. 7.26). When you use the TRIM function to remove the trailing spaces from the first field, FIRST_NAME, the display looks more attractive.

In figure 7.26, the TRIM function is used to remove all blank spaces in FIRST_NAME before it is concatenated with a single space and the contents of LAST_NAME.

```
. USE EMPLOYEE
. LOCATE FOR FIRST_NAME="Doris"
Record =       3
. ?FIRST_NAME+LAST_NAME
Doris A.    Gregory
. ?TRIM(FIRST_NAME)+LAST_NAME
Doris A.Gregory
. ?TRIM(FIRST_NAME)+" "+LAST_NAME
Doris A. Gregory
.
```

*Fig. 7.26. Example using TRIM function.*

## The RTRIM Function

PLUS

The RTRIM function performs an operation identical to that of the TRIM function. RTRIM removes the trailing blanks from the right of the alphanumeric expression in the argument. The format of the function is

.RTRIM(<alphanumeric expression>)

The TRIM and RTRIM functions can be used interchangeably to produce the same result.

## The LTRIM Function

PLUS

The LTRIM function removes all the leading blanks from the left of the alphanumeric expression in the argument. The format of the function is

.LTRIM(<alphanumeric expression>)

Figure 7.27 shows use of the LTRIM function to remove the spaces to the left of the characters in the memory variable named B.

```
. A="John J. "
John J.
. B="        Smith"
         Smith
. ?A+B
John J.           Smith
. ?A+LTRIM(B)
John J. Smith
.
```

*Fig. 7.27. Example using LTRIM function.*

## The SPACE Function

The SPACE function creates an alphanumeric string containing the number of blank spaces specified in the argument. The format of the function is

. SPACE(<number of blank spaces>)

The SPACE function can be used to create a memory variable that contains a specified number of spaces. You can also use this function to insert a number of spaces between data elements that are to be displayed (see fig. 7.28).

```
. STORE "ABC" TO STRINGA
ABC
. STORE "XYZ" TO STRINGB
XYZ
. STORE SPACE(10) TO TENBLANKS

. ?STRINGA + TENBLANKS + STRINGB
ABC          XYZ

.
```

Fig. 7.28. Example using SPACE function.

## The SUBSTR Function

The SUBSTR (substring) function extracts a part of an alphanumeric string. The arguments of the function include the alphanumeric string, the starting position of the substring, and the number of characters to be extracted:

. SUBSTR(<alphanumeric expression>,<starting position>,<number of characters>)

In figure 7.29, the first SUBSTR function returns the substring *CD* from the string *ABCDEFG*. The second argument gives the starting position (character 3 of the string), and the third argument specifies that two characters are to be extracted.

As shown in figure 7.30, the SUBSTR function can extract a part of an alphanumeric string from a data field and assign the substring to a memory variable. The substring (the first three characters of PHONE_NO) is stored to the memory variable PREFIX, and that variable is used in an alphanumeric expression with the ? command.

```
. ?SUBSTR("ABCDEFG",3,2)
CD
. ?SUBSTR("ABCDEFG",2,4)
BCDE
.
```

Fig. 7.29. Example using SUBSTR function.

```
. USE EMPLOYEE
. GOTO 5
. DISPLAY PHONE_NO
Record#  PHONE_NO
      5  567-7777
. STORE SUBSTR(PHONE_NO,1,3) TO PREFIX
567
. ?"The telephone prefix is "+PREFIX
The telephone prefix is 567
.
```

Fig. 7.30. Result of SUBSTR function assigned to memory variable.

With SUBSTR functions, you can even rearrange the characters in an alphanumeric string. Figure 7.31 shows how to use SUBSTR TO move the last three characters of the variable XSTRING to the beginning of the string. Two substrings, SUBSTR(XSTRING,4,3) and SUBSTR(XSTRING,1,3), are combined by means of an alphanumeric expression, and the result is assigned to the variable XSTRING.

```
. XSTRING="ABCDEFG"
ABCDEFG
. XSTRING=SUBSTR(XSTRING,4,3)+SUBSTR(XSTRING,1,3)
DEFABC
. ?XSTRING
DEFABC
.
```

Fig. 7.31. Using SUBSTR to rearrange characters.

The SUBSTR function enables you to use a part of the contents of an alphanumeric data field for locating, sorting, or indexing operations. For example, the following commands illustrate the use of SUBSTR functions with the LOCATE, DISPLAY, LIST, SORT, and INDEX operations (EMPLOYEE.DBF is the active database file):

. LOCATE FOR SUBSTR(PHONE_NO,5,4)="5085"

. DISPLAY LAST_NAME FOR
SUBSTR(LAST_NAME,1,1)="G"

. LIST AREA_CODE, PHONE_NO FOR
SUBSTR(PHONE_NO,1,3)="123"

. SORT ON SUBSTR(PHONE_NO,1,3) TO SORTPRFX

. INDEX ON SUBSTR(PHONE_NO,1,3) TO INDXPRFX

In the first three commands, a substring—for example, (PHONE_NUMBER,5,4) or (LAST_NAME,1,1)—is used for specifying the condition in the qualifier clause (FOR . . . ) of a LOCATE, DISPLAY, or LIST command. The last two commands use a substring, (PHONE_NO,1,3), as the key data field for sorting and indexing.

## PLUS The LEFT Function

The LEFT function allows you to extract a substring of a specified number of characters from the alphanumeric expression in the argument. The format of the function is

.LEFT(<alphanumeric expression>, <numeric expression>)

The value of the numeric expression determines the number of characters to be extracted from the left of the character string. The extracted substring can be displayed or assigned to another string. Figure 7.32 shows some examples of using the LEFT function.

As shown in figure 7.32, LEFT(FIRSTNAME,5) extracts five characters from the left of the character string *Doris Y.* The result is the substring *Doris.*

## PLUS The RIGHT Function

Similar to the LEFT function, the RIGHT function extracts a specified number of characters from the right of the character string represented by the alphanumeric expression in the argument:

.RIGHT(<alphanumeric expression>,<numeric expression>)

```
. FIRSTNAME="Doris Y."
Doris Y.
. LASTNAME="Taylor"
Taylor
. ?LEFT(FIRSTNAME,5)
Doris
. FULLNAME=LASTNAME+", "+LEFT(FIRSTNAME,5)
Taylor, Doris
. ?FULLNAME
Taylor, Doris
.
```

*Fig. 7.32. Example using LEFT function.*

The value of the numeric expression determines how many
characters are to be extracted from the right of the character string.
The extracted substring can be displayed or assigned to another
string. An example of using the RIGHT function (used with the
LEFT and SUBSTR functions) is shown in figure 7.33.

```
. FULLNAME="Doris Y. Smith"
Doris Y. Smith
. LASTNAME=RIGHT(FULLNAME,5)
Smith
. FIRSTNAME=LEFT(FULLNAME,5)
Doris
. INITIAL=SUBSTR(FULLNAME,7,2)
Y.
. ?FIRSTNAME, INITIAL, LASTNAME
Doris Y. Smith
.
```

*Fig. 7.33. Example using RIGHT function.*

## The STUFF Function

PLUS

The STUFF function can be used to replace a portion of a character
string with another character string. The portion to be replaced is
identified by the beginning character position and the number of
characters to be replaced. The format of the STUFF function is

.STUFF(<1st character string>,<beginning
position>,<number of characters to be replaced>,<2nd
character string>

Figure 7.34 shows an example of using the STUFF function.
Beginning with the sixth character, four characters in the string
*Mary Jane Smith* (represented by OLDNAME) are replaced by the
string *Kay* (NEWINITIAL).

```
. OLDNAME="Mary Jane Smith"
Mary Jane Smith
. NEWINITIAL="Kay"
Kay
. ?STUFF(OLDNAME,6,4,NEWINITIAL)
Mary Kay Smith

.
```

*Fig. 7.34. Example using STUFF function.*

## The AT Function

The AT function is used to search an alphanumeric string for a
specified substring. If the substring is found, the function returns a
number that indicates the starting position of the substring within
the string. If the alphanumeric string does not contain the substring,
the function returns a value of zero. The format of the AT
function is

. AT(<key substring>,<alphanumeric string>)

In figure 7.35, the number returned by the first AT function (7)
indicates that the substring *M.* begins at the seventh position in the
alphanumeric string *Harry M. Nelson*. Using the same logic, you
can locate the names of all employees with the middle initial *M.*
(see fig. 7.36).

```
. ? AT("M.", "Harry M. Nelson")
       7
. ? AT("son", "Harry M. Nelson")
        13

.
```

*Fig. 7.35. Example using AT function.*

```
. USE EMPLOYEE
. LOCATE FOR AT("M.",FIRST_NAME)<>0
Record =        4
. ?"The name found is "+TRIM(FIRST_NAME)+" "+LAST_NAME
The name found is Harry M. Nelson
.
```

*Fig. 7.36. Using AT function with LOCATE.*

# Data Type Conversion Functions

Data type conversion functions change data elements from one type to another. For instance, these functions can convert a numeric value or the contents of a numeric field to a character string. Similarly, contents of a date field can be converted to a character string, which may then be used in searching or indexing operations.

## The VAL Function

The VAL function converts an alphanumeric string of digits to a numeric value. You specify the alphanumeric string of digits in the argument, and the function returns a numeric value. If the alphanumeric string contains nonnumeric characters, however, the VAL function returns a zero. The format of the function is

. VAL(<alphanumeric string>)

The VAL function can be used to enter the contents of an alphanumeric string of digits in a numeric variable or expression (see fig. 7.37). If a string containing a decimal number, such as 123.789, is converted to a value by the VAL function, the rounded integer value of the string, such as 124, is returned (see fig. 7.38).

```
. XSTRING="1234"
1234
. VALUEX=VAL(XSTRING)
      1234
. VALUEY=VALUEX+VAL("2345")
      3579
.
```

*Fig. 7.37. Example using VAL function.*

```
. ?VAL("123.456")
        123
. ?VAL("123.789")
        124
. ?VAL("1995.95")
       1996
.
```

Fig. 7.38. Results of VAL function with decimal arguments.

## The STR Function

The STR function is used to convert numeric data to an alphanumeric string. The STR function returns an alphanumeric string representing the numeric value that is passed as the argument (see fig. 7.39). The alphanumeric string can be used in an alphanumeric expression. The format of the function is

. STR(<numeric expression>)

```
. ?STR(1234)
       1234
. ASTRING=STR(5678)
       5678
. ?"The converted string is "+ASTRING
The converted string is      5678
.
```

Fig. 7.39. Example using STR function.

In figure 7.39 the STR function converts the numeric value 5678 to the alphanumeric string. An alphanumeric expression then combines that string with the label *The converted string is*, and the result is displayed with the ? command.

The contents of numeric data fields can also be used as arguments for the STR function. This function enables you to convert the results of numeric fields and then use alphanumeric expressions to combine the results with the contents of alphanumeric fields. The results can then be displayed with a ? command (see fig. 7.40).

```
. USE EMPLOYEE
. LOCATE FOR LAST_NAME="Thompson"
Record =        7
. ?TRIM(FIRST_NAME)+" "+TRIM(LAST_NAME)+"'s salary is "+STR(ANNUAL_PAY)
Mary W. Thompson's salary is         25725
.
```

*Fig. 7.40. Displaying results of STR function with ? command.*

The STR function is important in data manipulation because you cannot mix numeric and alphanumeric values in commands. For example, the following command will produce an error message because ANNUAL_PAY is a numeric field.

. ?TRIM(FIRST_NAME)+" "+TRIM(LAST_NAME)+"'s salary is "+ANNUAL_PAY

The error can be avoided by converting the contents of ANNUAL_PAY to an alphanumeric string before issuing the ? command.

## The DTOC Function

In dBASE III and dBASE III Plus, dates are stored in date fields. Many restrictions apply to the use of dates in data manipulation. For example, the contents of a date field cannot be used as a key in the LOCATE FOR, DISPLAY FOR, and LIST FOR commands. You cannot mix dates or date variables with alphanumeric strings for displaying. However, you can use a DTOC (date-to-character) function to convert a date into a character string. Then the string can be used to perform operations that can be carried out only with alphanumeric strings. The format of the DTOC function is

. DTOC(<date>)

The date specified in the argument of the function must be the contents of a date variable or a date field. For instance, if you enter

. ?DTOC("03/08/85")

the error message **Invalid function argument** is displayed because the argument is an alphanumeric string.

Figure 7.41 shows how to display a date along with an alphanumeric string (such as a label). The contents of the date field BIRTH_DATE are first assigned to a date variable (BIRTHDATE). The contents of either the field or the variable can then be converted to an alphanumeric string and included in an alphanumeric expression.

```
. USE EMPLOYEE
. GO BOTTOM
. STORE BIRTH_DATE TO BIRTHDATE
12/24/45
. ?"Contents of the date field is "+DTOC(BIRTH_DATE)
Contents of the date field is 12/24/45
. ?"Contents of the date variable is "+DTOC(BIRTHDATE)
Contents of the date variable is 12/24/45

.
```

*Fig. 7.41. Example using DTOC function.*

After converting a date field into a character string, you can use all or a part of the character string to carry out different searching operations. For example, to search for all employees who were born in or before 1960, use the SUBSTR function to select a substring of the character string DTOC(BIRTH_DATE); then use the resulting substring as the qualifier for the LIST command (see fig. 7.42).

```
. USE EMPLOYEE
. LIST LAST_NAME,BIRTH_DATE FOR SUBSTR(DTOC(BIRTH_DATE),7,2)<="60"
Record#   LAST_NAME   BIRTH_DATE
      1   Smith       07/04/60
      2   Zeller      09/20/59
      4   Nelson      02/15/58
      5   Baker       10/12/56
      7   Thompson    06/18/55
      9   Lee         05/14/39
     10   Hanson      12/24/45

.
```

*Fig. 7.42. Using DTOC with LIST.*

In figure 7.42, the DTOC function converts the contents of the date field BIRTH_DATE to an alphanumeric string. The string contains the date in the form *mm/dd/yy*. The substring containing the seventh and eighth characters (yy) is extracted by the SUBSTR function and used as a qualifier for the selective LIST operation.

## The CTOD Function

Dates can be entered in a date field only with the APPEND, BROWSE, or EDIT commands. A date cannot be entered in a date variable with the STORE or = commands. The following commands will therefore result in an error:

. STORE 01/25/85 TO ADATE
. STORE "01/25/85" TO ADATE
. ADATE=01/25/85
. ADATE="01/25/85"

The commands "confuse" the program because the type of data element you intend to assign to a date variable has not been clearly identified. When you put quotation marks around the date, it is treated as a character string. On the other hand, without the quotation marks, the date may be misinterpreted as an arithmetic expression (dividing the value of 01 by 25, for instance). Fortunately, the CTOD (character-to-date) function solves some of these problems. The CTOD function converts an alphanumeric string to a date. The format of a CTOD function is

. CTOD(<alphanumeric string>)

For example, the following STORE command uses a CTOD function to enter a date (01/25/85) in the date variable ADATE:

. STORE CTOD("01/25/85") TO ADATE

Similarly, as shown in figure 7.43, you can use the REPLACE command to replace the contents of a date field (BIRTH_DATE) with a date that is converted from an alphanumeric string (such as 10/10/60).

```
. USE EMPLOYEE
. LOCATE FOR LAST_NAME="Zeller"
Record =        2
. DISPLAY BIRTH_DATE
Record#  BIRTH_DATE
     2   09/20/59
. REPLACE BIRTH_DATE WITH CTOD("10/10/59")
     1   record replaced
. DISPLAY BIRTH_DATE
Record#  BIRTH_DATE
     2   10/10/59
.
```

*Fig. 7.43. Example using CTOD with REPLACE.*

## The CHR Function

The CHR function returns an ASCII character (see Appendix A) when that character's numeric code is specified in the argument of the function. The format of the function is

. CHR(<numeric code of an ASCII character>)

You can display the ASCII characters by simply specifying their numeric codes as arguments for the CHR function (see fig. 7.44).

```
.  ?CHR(83)
S
.  ?CHR(109)
m
.  ?CHR(105)
i
.  ?CHR(116)
t
.  ?CHR(104)
h
.  ?CHR(83),CHR(109),CHR(105),CHR(116),CHR(104)
S m i t h
.
```

*Fig. 7.44. Results of CHR function.*

ASCII characters include control characters, letters, numbers, and symbols. You use a control character, such as CHR(12), to send a "form feed" code to the printer so that it will eject a page. Most control characters are invisible when you enter them at the keyboard. Some require multiple keystrokes. In such cases, the ASCII numeric code for the control character can be printed with a ? command to perform the control operation. For instance, if the printer is activated, the command

. ?CHR(12)

will cause the printer to advance the paper to the top of the next page.

## The ASC Function

The CHR function returns the ASCII character whose numeric code is provided in the argument; ASC does the reverse. When you specify an ASCII character in the argument, the ASC function returns the corresponding numeric code for the character (see fig. 7.45). The format of the function is

. ASC(<ASCII character>)

```
. ?ASC("S")
  83
. ?ASC("S"),ASC("m"),ASC("i"),ASC("t"),ASC("h")
  83   109   105   116   104
.
```

*Fig. 7.45. Results of ASC function.*

# Time/Date Functions

dBASE III Plus has a set of functions for processing dates and time. Some of these functions require an argument, and others do not. Although the input data type is a date, the data elements returned by these functions can be numeric values or alphanumeric strings. The date/time functions include TIME, DATE, CDOW, CMONTH, DOW, DAY, MONTH, and YEAR.

The TIME and DATE functions always use as input the current time and date stored in the internal system clock and therefore do not need arguments. Their formats are

TIME()
DATE()

The other functions require arguments, which can be the contents of date fields or of date memory variables:

<name of function>(<date field/variable>)

Descriptions of these functions are given in table 7.1. The contents of the BIRTH_DATE field in James C. Smith's record is used as the sample date.

**Table 7.1**
**Descriptions of Time/Date Functions**

| Function | Example | Returned Data Element | Returned Data Type |
|---|---|---|---|
| TIME | . ?TIME( ) | Current system time | Alphanumeric |
| DATE | . ?DATE( ) | Current system date | Alphanumeric |
| CDOW | . ?CDOW(BIRTH_DATE) | Character date of the week | Alphanumeric |
| CMONTH | . ?CMONTH(BIRTH_DATE) | Character month of the year | Alphanumeric |
| DOW | . ?DOW(BIRTH_DATE) | Numeric code for day of the week | Alphanumeric |
| DAY | . ?DAY(BIRTH_DATE) | Numeric code for day of the month | Numeric |
| MONTH | . ?MONTH(BIRTH_DATE) | Numeric code for month of the year | Numeric |
| YEAR | . ?YEAR(BIRTH_DATE) | Numeric code for year | Numeric |

# The ROW, COL, PROW, and PCOL Functions

dBASE III Plus has four functions that find the current cursor position on the screen and the printing position on the printer paper: ROW, COL, PROW, and PCOL. The ROW and COL functions return the row and column positions of the cursor. Similarly, the current printing position on the printer can be found by using the PROW and PCOL functions. These functions are often used in batch-processing mode to controlling the output position on the screen or the printer paper; these functions therefore are discussed in later chapters.

# A Summary Example

Functions play an important role in data manipulation. As a summary of the frequently used functions, figure 7.46 provides an example that calculates the ending balance on a beginning principal of $10,000.

```
. DATE1=CTOD("01/25/85")
01/25/85
. DATE2=CTOD("01/25/86")
01/25/86
. DAYS=DATE2-DATE1
        365
. YEARRATE=0.12000000
0.12000000
. DAILYRATE=YEARRATE/365
          0.00032877
. PRINCIPAL=10000
10000
. ENDBALANCE=PRINCIPAL*(1+DAILYRATE)^DAYS


                      11274.74615638
. ?"Ending Balance = ",ROUND(ENDBALANCE,2)
Ending Balance =        11274.75000000
.
```

*Fig. 7.46. Using functions to calculate loan balance.*

The example computes the ending balance on 01/25/86 (DATE2) of a savings account that begins with a deposit of $10,000 (PRINCIPAL) on 01/25/85 (DATE1). The annual interest rate (YEARRATE) is assumed to be 12 percent (0.12 in decimal form). Interest earned by the account is compounded daily at the rate of 0.032877 percent (DAILYRATE, determined by dividing the annual rate of 12 percent by 365 days). The number of days elapsed between 01/25/85 and 01/25/86 (DAYS) is computed by taking the difference between the two dates:

DAYS = DATE2 – DATE1

The ending balance (ENDBALANCE) is then computed with the following formula:

ENDBALANCE = PRINCIPAL × $(1 + DAILYRATE)^{DAYS}$

# Chapter Summary

This chapter introduces the concept of memory variables. A memory variable is a name assigned to a memory location that is used to store a data element temporarily. Four types of memory variables can be used: alphanumeric, numeric, date, and logical. The type of a memory variable is determined by the data element stored in the variable. The name of a memory variable can be up to 10 characters long; the first character must be a letter. The other characters can be letters, digits, or the underscore (_).

Data elements can be entered in alphanumeric, numeric, and logical memory variables with the STORE or = command. However, you cannot assign a string like "03/08/85" to a date variable with the STORE or = command. The date must be converted from an alphanumeric string to a date with the CTOD function before the date can be assigned to a date variable or a date field.

All or part of the active memory variables can be permanently saved in a memory file by using the SAVE command. Contents of a memory file can be recalled in part or in whole with the RESTORE command. Active memory variables can be deleted from memory by using the RELEASE command.

Expressions in dBASE III Plus define the operations to be carried out on specified data elements. dBASE III Plus has two types of expressions. Arithmetic expressions contain one or more numeric variables or data fields joined by one or more arithmetic operators (+, −, *, /, ^). Arithmetic expressions are often used to assign a value to a memory variable or to replace the contents of a numeric data record. Alphanumeric expressions consist of one or more alphanumeric strings, alphanumeric variables, or data fields joined by plus signs. An alphanumeric expression is used to enter an alphanumeric string in an alphanumeric variable or to replace the contents of a character data field.

This chapter also introduces all the dBASE III Plus functions that you use to convert data elements from one type to another, to manipulate character strings, and to perform mathematical operations. The basic form of a function consists of the name of the function followed by the arguments, if any, enclosed in parentheses. Some functions, such as DATE, TIME, RECNO, ROW, COL, PROW, and PCOL, do not require an argument. Other functions usually require that an argument be specified within the parentheses.

In this chapter only those commonly used functions were discussed. For a complete list of dBASE III Plus built-in functions, see Appendix E.

# Generating Reports

## An Overview

In the preceding chapters, you have seen how dot commands can be used to print or display on-screen the contents of data records and memory variables. This chapter introduces more flexible and powerful ways of displaying your data, using custom labels and reports.

One method is to display the label or report by issuing one of the following dBASE III Plus dot commands:

```
?
@ . . . SAY
SET PRINT ON/OFF
SET DEVICE TO PRINT/SCREEN
```

Using these commands to produce custom labels and reports can be tedious. The second method is easier, however. By using the label and report generators provided by dBASE III Plus, you can easily produce sophisticated, detailed report forms. The label and report generators can be accessed either through the Assistant menu or by the following dot commmands:

CREATE LABEL
MODIFY LABEL
LABEL FORM
CREATE REPORT
MODIFY REPORT
REPORT FORM

# Displaying Data on the Screen

You can use the ? dot command as one way to display items on the screen and send them to the printer. This command can be used to display one or more data items of different types. Because each item can be a memory variable, a data record, or an expression, you can display an alphanumeric string, a character data field, a date field, and a numeric memory variable all with one command (see fig. 8.1).

```
. SET PRINT OFF
. USE EMPLOYEE
. STORE ANNUAL_PAY TO YEARLYPAY
23100.00
. ?"Employee's last name is ",LAST_NAME,BIRTH_DATE,YEARLYPAY
Employee's last name is  Smith        07/04/60        23100.00
.
```

Fig. 8.1. Displaying label with ? command.

Commas must separate data items when they are of different types. As shown in figure 8.2, the plus sign (+) or space cannot be used as a separator. The first error message, **Data type mismatch**, results from combining an alphanumeric string ("Annual Salary is ") with a numeric variable (YEARLYPAY). The second error message, **Unrecognized phrase/keyword in command** is caused by the presence of a space instead of a comma between the label "Employee's Birth Date is " and the date field BIRTH_DATE.

```
. USE EMPLOYEE
. STORE ANNUAL_PAY TO YEARLYPAY
23100.00
. ?"Annual salary is "+YEARLYPAY
Data type mismatch
                                    ?
?"Annual salary is "+YEARLYPAY
Do you want some help? (Y/N) No
. ?"Employee's birth date is " BIRTH_DATE
Unrecognized phrase/keyword in command
                                    ?
?"Employee's birth date is " BIRTH_DATE
Do you want some help? (Y/N) No
.
```

*Fig. 8.2. Incorrect label entry without commas to separate items.*

Because the ? command always displays output immediately below the command line, this command lacks flexibility: you cannot position the display at a specific screen location. Another type of display command is needed to select a particular screen location for display of data or results. The dBASE III Plus command for this function is the @ . . . SAY command. The @ . . . SAY command displays a data item of a given type at a given location on the screen or printed copy.

The format for the @ . . . SAY command is

.@<row>, <column> SAY <data item to be displayed>

The screen location is specified by a row number and a column number. The computer screen is divided into 25 rows and 80 columns. Row 1 is at the top of the screen, and column 1 is the leftmost column. Row 1, column 1, is the upper left corner of the screen; row 25, column 80 is the lower right corner of the screen.

An example of using the @ . . . SAY command is

.@5,10 SAY LAST_NAME

Unlike the ? command, which can be used to display multiple data items, the @ . . . SAY command displays only one data item. The data item in an @ . . . SAY command must be in one of the following forms:

1. An alphanumeric expression, which may consist either of one alphanumeric variable or character field or of several

alphanumeric variables and/or character fields joined by plus signs.

> @5,10 SAY LAST_NAME+FIRST_NAME+AREA_CODE
> @10,5 SAY LAST_NAME+FIRSTNAME

(FIRSTNAME is a character variable in this example.)

2. A numeric variable, a numeric data field, or an expression involving more than one numeric variable and/or data field.

> @5,5 SAY ANNUAL_PAY
> @10,10 SAY YEARLYPAY*1.10
> @7,5 SAY QTY_SOLD*UNITPRICE

(YEARLYPAY and UNITPRICE are numeric variables; ANNUAL_PAY and QTY_SOLD are numeric data fields.)

3. A date field or a date variable (BILLDATE).

> @5,10 SAY BIRTH_DATE
> @10,5 SAY BILLDATE

4. A logical data field or a logical variable (MEMBERSHIP).

> @10,10 SAY MALE
> @5,5 SAY MEMBERSHIP

Row and column numbers in the @ . . . SAY command can also be results of arithmetic expressions. Using a memory variable as a row number, for example, causes the output to be displayed at different locations when the value of the variable changes:

> . STORE 5 TO ROW
> . STORE 10 TO COLUMN
> . @ROW,COLUMN SAY . . .

The ROW() and COL() functions return the current row and column positions of the cursor. Although that information does not play a significant role in interactive processing, these functions provide great flexibility in placement of output during batch processing.

An @ command followed by a row and column number without the SAY clause can be used to erase part of a screen display. For instance, the following command erases the fifth line, beginning at column 10:

> . @5,10

Another important feature of the @ . . . SAY command is its capability to employ a user-defined template for displaying output. The template defines which types of characters or symbols are to be displayed and how they should appear. You define the template by adding a PICTURE clause after the output element specified in the @ . . . SAY command:

. @5,10 SAY ANNUAL_PAY PICTURE "$##,###.##"

The string *"$##,###.##"* following the word *PICTURE* is a template: it "draws a picture" of the way the value in ANNUAL_PAY is to appear when the number is displayed. The $ and # symbols determine the type of character. The $, for example, tells the program to display a dollar sign instead of leading zeros. The # symbols indicate that only digits, spaces, and signs of a value can appear at the positions marked with these symbols. The comma and decimal point indicate that these symbols are to be placed at the corresponding positions when the value is displayed. Assume that the value in the data field ANNUAL_PAY is 28950.95; the number is printed differently when different pictures are given in the @ . . . SAY commands. The following list provides some examples.

| *If the PICTURE is defined as* | *The printed number is* |
| --- | --- |
| "$##,###.##" | $28,950.95 |
| "$##,###.#" | $28,950.9 |
| "$##,###" | $28,950 |
| "$###,###.##" | $$28,950.95 |

Note that *"$##,###"* produces an integer ($28,950) by suppressing the digits after the decimal point. The value is not rounded to the closest integer. To round the value of ANNUAL_PAY to the closest integer ($28,951), you must use one of the following commands:

@5,10 SAY ANNUAL_PAY+0.5 PICTURE "$##,###"
@5,10 SAY ROUND(ANNUAL_PAY,0) PICTURE "$##,###"

Be sure to enter enough symbols (#) for the total number of digits in a value. If the picture does not provide sufficient space, ********** is displayed.

Other symbols can also be used in a template. Most of the symbols are used in specifying a picture for an input command, but the following symbols are used for displaying output with the @ . . . SAY command:

| Symbol | Effect |
|---|---|
| ! | Displays lowercase letters as uppercase letters |
| 9 | Displays signs and digits in a value |
| * | Displays an asterisk in front of a value when the asterisk is followed by 9s; displays asterisks in place of leading zeros when the asterisk is followed by # symbols |

To see how these symbols are used in a template to produce custom-formatted output, assume that the following memory variables have these values:

ASTRING="ABCxyz"
BALANCE=−1345.87

In the following examples, the output produced by the sample @ . . . SAY commands is shown next to the corresponding command.

| Command | Output |
|---|---|
| @ . . . SAY ASTRING PICTURE "!!!!!!" | ABCXYZ |
| @ . . . SAY BALANCE PICTURE "99999" | −1345 |
| @ . . . SAY BALANCE PICTURE "999,999.9" | −1,345.8 |
| @ . . . SAY BALANCE PICTURE "*99,999.99" | *  −1,345.87 |
| @ . . . SAY BALANCE PICTURE "*##,###.##" | *−1,345.87 |

Because the @ . . . SAY command can display an alphanumeric expression, the command can show a label along with a data element. The label is enclosed in quotation marks in the command (see fig. 8.3). Note, however, that an alphanumeric string cannot form a label for a numeric or a date variable or date field with the @ . . . SAY command. Numeric data must be converted to an alphanumeric string with the STR function and then displayed as an alphanumeric expression:

@5,10 SAY "Annual Salary is "+STR(ANNUAL_PAY)

Similarly, the DTOC function can be used to convert a date field or date variable to an alphanumeric string and to display the string with a label:

@5,10 SAY "The birth date is "+DTOC(BIRTH_DATE)

The contents of a logical variable or logical data field cannot be converted to an alphanumeric string because dBASE III Plus lacks a

```
. USE EMPLOYEE
. LOCATE FOR LAST_NAME="Nelson"
Record =          4
. @8,5 SAY "Employee's last name is "+LAST_NAME


      Employee's last name is Nelson

.
```

*Fig. 8.3. Using @ . . . SAY to display label.*

built-in function for this conversion. An @ . . . SAY command
therefore cannot display the contents of logical fields with a label.

# Printing Data on a Printer

When you display output (which could be data or reports) from the
Assistant menu, you are prompted to indicate whether the output is
to be displayed on the printer. If you want to display the output on a
printer, all you have to do is answer *Y* to the prompt:

> `Direct the output to the printer? [Y/N]`

In dot-prompt mode, output of the ? and @ . . . SAY commands is
displayed on the screen; the output can be sent to a printer, as well.
The SET PRINT ON and SET DEVICE TO PRINTER dot commands
are used to activate the printer. The two commands are used
differently and produce different results.

# The SET PRINT
# ON/OFF Commands

Let's assume that you will be using dot-prompt commands to display
data on the printer. In dot-prompt mode, the printer must first be
turned on and connected to the computer. Failure to do so will lock
up the computer. In most cases, connecting and turning on the
printer unlocks the computer; otherwise, you must reboot the
computer and restart the dBASE III Plus program.

The SET PRINT ON command activates the printer and directs to
the printer all output except that of the @ . . . SAY command. The

printer remains activated until it is turned off with the SET PRINT OFF command (see fig. 8.4). The output printed includes the results of the ? command and all commands (except @ . . . SAY) entered after the printer is activated.

```
. USE EMPLOYEE
. GO BOTTOM
. SET PRINT ON
. ?"Employee's name is "+TRIM(FIRST_NAME)+" "+LAST_NAME
Employee's name is Thomas T. Hanson
. SET PRINT OFF
.
```

Fig. 8.4. Using SET PRINT ON/OFF commands.

When the printer is activated with SET PRINT ON, anything you enter from the keyboard is reproduced on the printer. Consequently, errors and corrections (such as using the backspace key to delete and reenter characters) appear on the printed copy.

To begin a new page on the printer paper, enter the EJECT command before the ? command:

```
. SET PRINT ON
. EJECT
. ?"Employee's name is "+TRIM(FIRST_NAME)+" "+LAST_NAME
```

The SET PRINT ON command is used mainly for directing to the printer the output generated by a ? command. A different command must be used to display output produced by an @ . . . SAY command.

# The SET DEVICE TO PRINT/ SCREEN Commands

The main purpose of the SET DEVICE TO PRINT command is to route to the printer all output generated by @ . . . SAY commands. The SET DEVICE TO PRINT command sends to the printer any output specified in an @ . . . SAY command.

The printed page is treated as if it were a screen: the first print line corresponds to the first row on the screen, and the horizontal

printing position is the same as a column. When SET DEVICE TO
PRINT is first invoked, the printer automatically ejects enough paper
to move to the top of a page. In the example in figure 8.5, the
output generated by the @ . . . SAY command is printed on the fifth
line from the top of the page, beginning at the tenth position on that
line. The commands themselves are not printed. The printer is
deactivated by the command SET DEVICE TO SCREEN.

```
. USE EMPLOYEE
. LOCATE FOR PHONE_NO="432-6782"
Record =         7
. SET DEVICE TO PRINT
. @5,10 SAY "Phone no."+PHONE_NO+" belongs to "+TRIM(FIRST_NAME)+" "+LAST_NAME
. SET DEVICE TO SCREEN
.
```

*Fig. 8.5. Using SET DEVICE TO commands.*

# Creating Custom Labels

PLUS

Designing a label to display the contents of data records with the ?
and @ . . . SAY commands can be tedious. Fortunately, dBASE III
Plus provides a tool for creating a custom label. The design of the
label can be saved on disk in a label file (.LBL). The label file contains
all the data fields whose contents will be used for making up the
labels. It also contains specifications such as the label's width and
length. After a label file has been created and saved, it can be
recalled whenever you want to create a label displaying the contents
of a data record.

You can create a custom label file in one of two ways. If you want to
use The Assistant, select the **Create/Label** option from the
Assistant menu. You then are prompted to enter a file name with
the extension .LBL, such as EMPLOYEE.LBL (see fig. 8.6).

In the example, the active database file, EMPLOYEE.DBF, and the
label file, EMPLOYEE.LBL, have the same name. Because the file
names have different extensions, however, the files are treated as
unique disk files, and the similar names should not cause any
problem. In fact, unless you have more than one label file for a
database file, using the same file name may provide a clearer
reference than using an entirely different name.

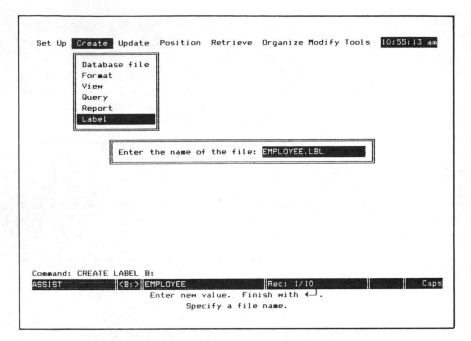

*Fig. 8.6. Naming label file.*

After entering the label-file name, you are prompted to specify the format for the custom label. The information is entered in a two-screen form. As shown in figure 8.7, on the first screen you select the size of the label; the default label size is 3 1/2 inches by 15/16 of an inch. You specify also the label's width in characters and the its height in lines. Additionally, you can specify the desired margin and spaces (in number of characters) between labels.

To enter these specifications, use the arrow keys to position the cursor at the desired location before you press Enter. Notice that a summary of the editing keys is displayed at the bottom of the screen. A completed label-specification form is shown in figure 8.8.

To specify the data fields whose values will be displayed on the label, you select the **Contents** option. Four lines (the number specified on the first screen) are presented. On those lines you will enter the field contents (see fig. 8.9).

On each of these lines you enter an expression, which can consist of data field names, labels for the fields' values, and functions or operators for manipulating those values. You can enter as many characters as you want for each line. Even though the width of the

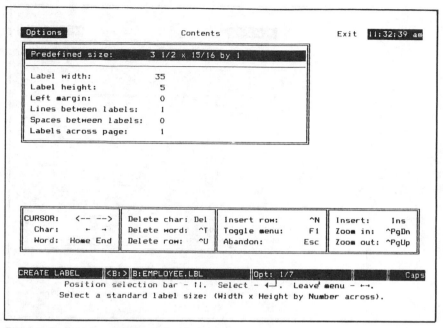

Fig. 8.7. Screen for defining label format.

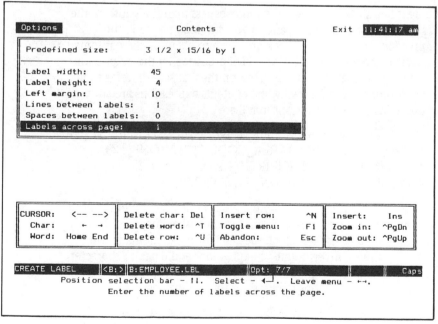

Fig. 8.8. Custom label format.

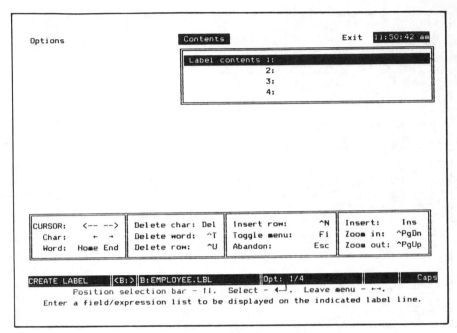

*Fig. 8.9. Second screen for defining custom label.*

content line shown on the screen may be less than the width of the
expression, the line will expand as you continue typing in the
expression. (You can scroll back and forth to examine the contents.)
However, the width of the actual label produced by the expression
is limited to the label width specified on the first screen (refer to fig.
8.8). Portions of the following line-contents expressions are shown
in figure 8.10; the expressions in full are

```
"      Employee: "+TRIM(FIRST_NAME)+" "+TRIM(LAST_NAME)
" Telephone No: "+"("+AREA_CODE+") "+PHONE_NO
"    Birth Date: "+DTOC(BIRTH_DATE)
"Annual Salary: $"+STR(ANNUAL_PAY,8,2)
```

As shown in the preceding example, you specify the contents of the
label lines on the label design form. On each label line, an
alphanumeric expression can be specified for the contents of the
label. You must convert numeric expressions and dates to character
strings before including them in an alphanumeric expression. The
STR and DTOC functions are used for those purposes.

After you have entered the label contents, you can save the
information and leave the label creation operation by selecting **Exit/**

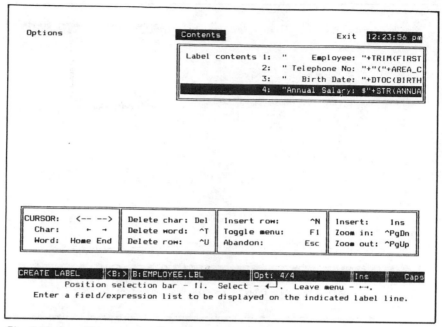

*Fig. 8.10. Specifying contents of label.*

**Save** from the menu. The EMPLOYEE.LBL label file will then be saved on disk. This file can later be used to display the records in the EMPLOYEE.DBF database file.

To create a label file in dot-prompt mode, you use the CREATE LABEL command, whose format is

. CREATE LABEL <name of the label file>

An example is

. CREATE LABEL EMPLOYEE.LBL

Then you create the label file by filling out the two screens discussed previously in this section.

# Modifying an Existing Label File

PLUS

At any time, you can recall and modify a label file that has been saved on disk. To recall an existing label file, you select the **Modify/Label** options from the Assistant menu (see fig. 8.11). Then you identify the label file that is to be modified.

*Fig. 8.11. Modifying existing label.*

To modify the contents of the EMPLOYEE.LBL file, for example, you select the following menu options:

Modify/Label/B:/*EMPLOYEE.LBL*

The first screen of the label specification form then is displayed (see fig. 8.12). You can now specify the label format again and continue to the next screen to modify the contents of the label lines. If you do not want to change any portion of the label file, you can leave the label modification operation by selecting the **Exit/Abandon** options.

To edit the contents of an existing label file in dot-prompt mode, you use the following dot command:

. MODIFY LABEL <name of the label file>

For example, when the command

. MODIFY LABEL EMPLOYEE.LBL

is invoked, the label design form in EMPLOYEE.LBL is displayed. At this point, you can modify the design form by using the same procedures you used to create it.

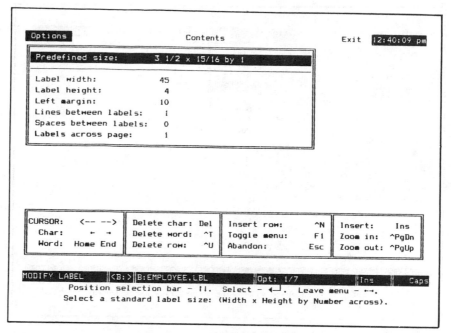

```
  Options                    Contents              Exit  12:40:09 pm
 ┌─────────────────────────────────────────────────────────────────┐
 │ Predefined size:        3 1/2 x 15/16 by 1                        │
 │                                                                   │
 │ Label width:            45                                        │
 │ Label height:            4                                        │
 │ Left margin:            10                                        │
 │ Lines between labels:    1                                        │
 │ Spaces between labels:   0                                        │
 │ Labels across page:      1                                        │
 └─────────────────────────────────────────────────────────────────┘



 ┌──────────────────┬──────────────────┬──────────────────┬──────────────┐
 │ CURSOR:  <-- -->  │ Delete char: Del │ Insert row:   ^N │ Insert:   Ins│
 │  Char:    ← →     │ Delete word:  ^T │ Toggle menu:  F1 │ Zoom in: ^PgDn│
 │  Word:  Home End  │ Delete row:   ^U │ Abandon:     Esc │ Zoom out: ^PgUp│
 └──────────────────┴──────────────────┴──────────────────┴──────────────┘
 ┌─────────────────────────────────────────────────────────────────┐
 │MODIFY LABEL    <B:> B:EMPLOYEE.LBL       Opt: 1/7      Ins    Caps│
 └─────────────────────────────────────────────────────────────────┘
      Position selection bar - ↕↓. Select - ←┘. Leave menu - ←→.
      Select a standard label size: (Width x Height by Number across).
```

Fig. 8.12. Displaying existing label-format screen.

# Using the Custom Label

A label file that has been saved as a disk file (EMPLOYEE.LBL, for example) can be used to display or print the contents of the data records. To display the data records with the custom label specified in a label file, you select the **Retrieve/Label** options from the Assistant menu (see fig. 8.13).

After selecting these options, you are prompted to identify the label file you want to use. For example, if you want to display the records in the EMPLOYEE.DBF with the custom labels defined in the EMPLOYEE.LBL file, you make the following menu selections and keyboard entries:

Retrieve/Label/B:/*EMPLOYEE.LBL*

Then you are prompted to specify scope and search conditions for selecting data records. If you want to display or print all the records in the database file, select **Execute the command.** You can select only the records with the value 216 in the AREA_CODE field by choosing the following menu options:

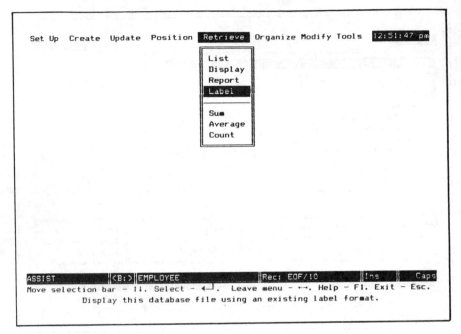

*Fig. 8.13. Menu options for using custom label.*

/Build a search condition/*AREA_CODE*/= Equal to/Enter a character string (without quotes): *216*/No more conditions / Execute the command

At this point, you are prompted to indicate whether you want the output directed to the printer:

**Direct the output to the printer? [Y/N]**

If you answer *Y*, the records are printed in the format defined in the label file (see fig. 8.14).

```
        Employee: James C. Smith
    Telephone No: (216) 123-4567
      Birth Date: 07/04/60
   Annual Salary: $22000.00

        Employee: Charles N. Duff
    Telephone No: (216) 456-9873
      Birth Date: 07/22/64
   Annual Salary: $13500.00

        Employee: Thomas T. Hanson
    Telephone No: (216) 573-5085
      Birth Date: 12/24/45
   Annual Salary: $28950.00
```

*Fig. 8.14. Printed output using custom label form.*

In dot-prompt mode, you can accomplish this task by entering the LABEL FORM dot command, whose format is

. LABEL FORM <name of label file>

or

. LABEL FORM <name of the label file> FOR <qualifier>

Here are some examples of using the LABEL command:

. USE EMPLOYEE
. LABEL FORM EMPLOYEE.LBL

and

. USE EMPLOYEE
. LABEL FORM EMPLOYEE.LBL FOR AREA_CODE="216"

To direct the output to the printer, add the clause TO PRINT to the LABEL FORM dot command. For instance, the output is directed to the printer by the following command:

. LABEL FORM EMPLOYEE FOR AREA_CODE="216" TO PRINT

# Creating the Custom Report Form

PLUS

A complete report form can be created and saved in a report form file (.FRM). The report form specifies the details of the headings and their locations in the report. You can create a custom report by selecting the appropriate options from the Assistant menu or, in dot-prompt mode, by entering the appropriate dot commands.

The database file QTYSOLD.DBF is used to illustrate the creation of a custom report form. A listing of the data records in this database file is shown in figure 8.15. Notice that the file has been sorted on the DATE field, whose contents will be used to define groups in the report. Whenever you create a report using group expressions, you must ensure that the file has been sorted on the grouping field. The custom report (the finished product) is shown in figure 8.25.

This sales summary is produced by showing the weekly subtotal for the units sold; the subtotal is identified by the end-of-week date (12/07/84, 12/14/84, etc.).

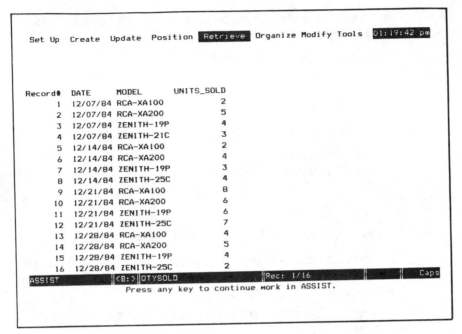

Fig. 8.15. Records in QTYSOLD.DBF.

If you intend to use the Assistant menu to create a custom report, you can select the **Create/Report** options from the menu. You are then prompted to enter the name of the report file. For example, if you want to create the weekly sales summary by using the data records in the QTYSOLD.DBF database file, you would make the following menu selections and keyboard entries (see fig. 8.16):

Create/Report/B:/*WEEKLY.FRM*

The first screen of the report design form is then displayed (see fig. 8.17). On this screen, you specify information related to the report format. The items specified on the format screen include the report's title, its width (in characters), and its page length (in lines), as well as margin and spacing information. Additionally, you can control the printer by specifying when and if you want to advance the paper to a new page.

To enter information on this screen, use the ↑ and ↓ keys to move the highlighting to the desired item, then select the item by pressing Enter. A summary of the editing keys is displayed on the screen for a handy reference.

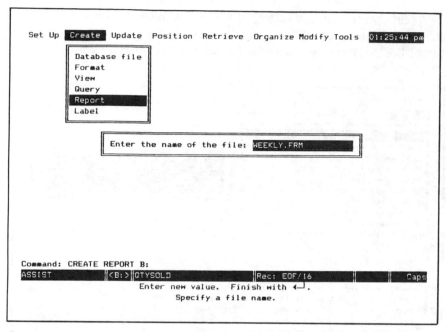

Fig. 8.16. Menu options for creating custom report file.

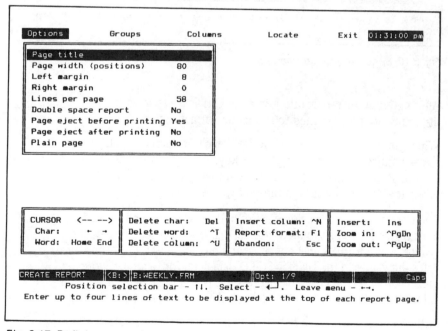

Fig. 8.17. Defining report format.

To specify the report title, you select the **Page title** option and then enter the title in the box that appears. The box will expand automatically as you type in the title. A sample report title is shown in figure 8.18.

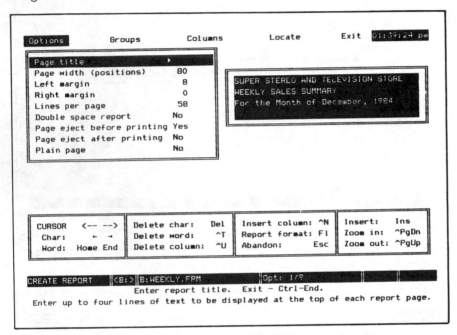

*Fig. 8.18. Specifying report heading.*

After entering the report title, press the Ctrl-End key to save the title. You are then returned to the report format options.

When you have completed the design form's first screen, you can go to the next screen by pressing the → key. You are now at the Groups screen. On this screen, you can specify how you want to group the data field values in the report (see fig. 8.19).

The Groups screen gives you a set of options with which to specify how values are to be grouped, the desired labels or headings for the groups, and information about subgrouping. If you want to group by dates the values in the UNITS_SOLD data field, for example, you specify DATE as the grouping expression. (The DATE field in QTYSOLD.DBF holds the end-of-week date for weekly sales.)

With the **Group heading** option, you label the grouped data as *Week of:*. Because you want your report to list all the models and

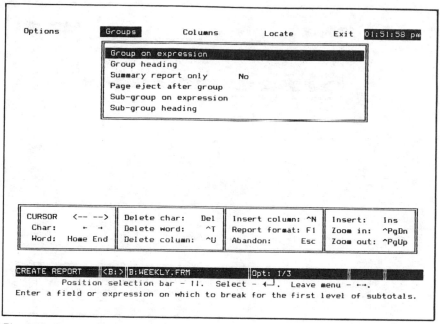

```
      Options              Groups          Columns          Locate        Exit  01:51:58 pm

                   ┌──────────────────────────────────────────────┐
                   │ Group on expression                          │
                   │ Group heading                                │
                   │ Summary report only          No              │
                   │ Page eject after group                       │
                   │ Sub-group on expression                      │
                   │ Sub-group heading                            │
                   └──────────────────────────────────────────────┘




   ┌─────────────────────┬──────────────────────┬────────────────────────┬──────────────────────┐
   │ CURSOR   <-- -->    │ Delete char:    Del  │ Insert column: ^N      │ Insert:     Ins      │
   │ Char:      ←  →     │ Delete word:    ^T   │ Report format: F1      │ Zoom in:    ^PgDn    │
   │ Word:   Home End    │ Delete column:  ^U   │ Abandon:        Esc    │ Zoom out:   ^PgUp    │
   └─────────────────────┴──────────────────────┴────────────────────────┴──────────────────────┘

   CREATE REPORT     <B:> B:WEEKLY.FRM                   Opt: 1/3
                 Position selection bar - ↕↓.  Select - ↵.  Leave menu - ←→.
     Enter a field or expression on which to break for the first level of subtotals.
```

*Fig. 8.19. Groups definition screen.*

units sold for each week, specify *No* for the **Summary report** only option. Otherwise, only the subtotal figures (the total units sold for each date, with no breakdown of models and units sold) will be displayed.

Selecting *No* for the **Page eject after group** option causes all the subtotals to be printed on the same page. In this example, the heading for the group is *Week of*; you enter this heading in the space provided. Because you do not have a second level of subtotals within a week, you can ignore the options for subgrouping (see fig. 8.20).

The next step in designing the form is to specify the data fields whose contents are to be displayed within each group. The sales summary shows the models and units sold each week (refer to fig. 8.25). You therefore need to specify, in the next part of the design form, the field names containing data on the models and units sold. A field definition form is required for each data field selected. The first field definition form (see fig. 8.21) is displayed as soon as you press the → key to select the **Columns** menu option.

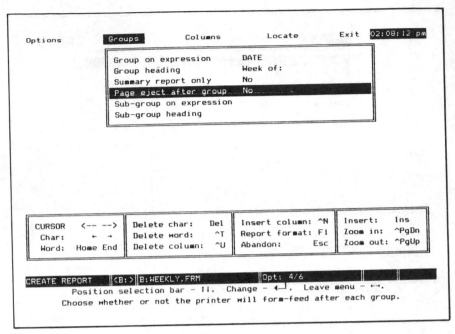

Fig. 8.20. Grouping records by DATE.

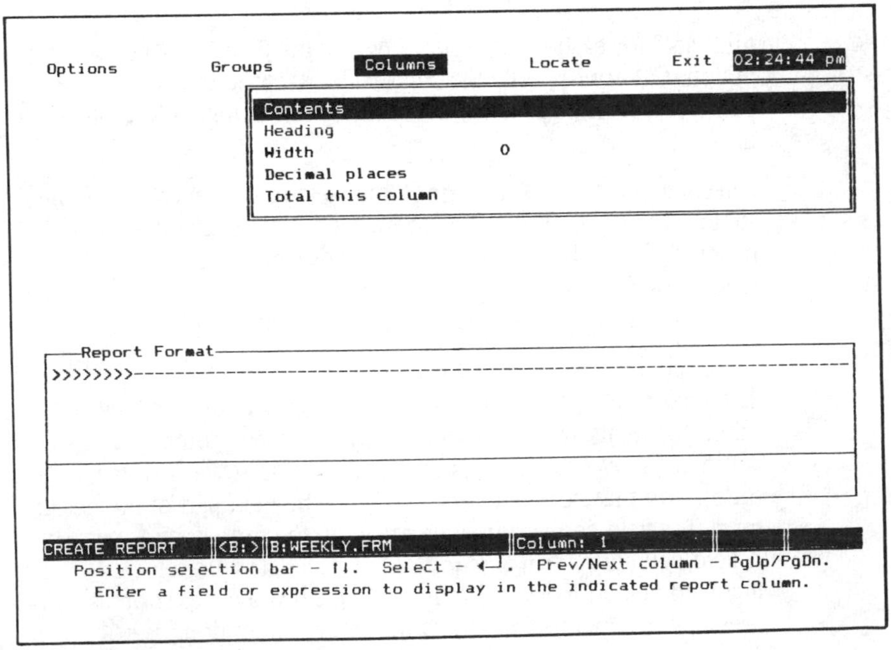

Fig. 8.21. Defining report columns.

In the **Contents** line, you enter the name of one or more data fields. If only one data field is to be used, you enter the name of that data field. Multiple data fields can be used if their names are combined by means of an alphanumeric or numeric expression. If the field contains a numeric data element, specify the number of decimal places to be displayed. If the contents are to be totaled, select *Y* at the **Total this column** prompt.

The two fields selected for the sales summary report are MODEL and UNITS_SOLD. The fields can be defined in sequence; the definition of the MODEL field is shown in figure 8.22. Because MODEL is a character field, no decimal places are needed and you cannot total the values in the field. The lines for those options are therefore left blank in the definition form.

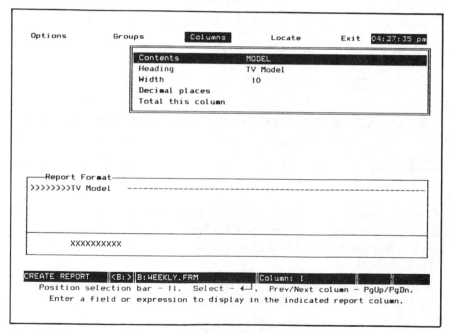

Fig. 8.22. Specifying MODEL as first report column.

When you define a report field, each column you define is displayed in the Report Format window at the bottom of the screen as soon as you enter the column's contents and heading. The string of Xs (XXXXXXXXXX) shown below the column heading (TV Model) in figure 8.22 represents the contents of the column in the report.

After defining the first report column, press the PgDn key to define the next. A blank form is provided in which you can specify the next report column. Figure 8.23 shows the completed form for the report's second column.

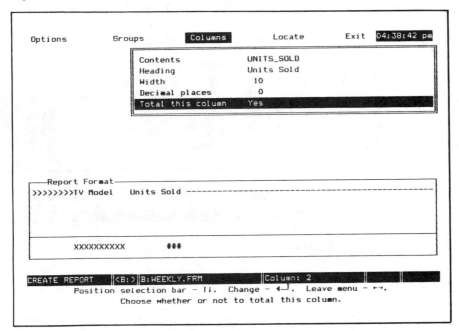

Fig. 8.23. Specifying UNITS_SOLD as second report column.

When you have finished defining all the report columns, you can save the report form by selecting the **Exit/Save** options from the Assistant menu. The custom report will be saved in a report file (.FRM) for later use.

You can create a custom report in dot-prompt mode by using the CREATE REPORT command, whose format is

. CREATE REPORT <name of report form file>

For example, you can create the weekly summary report by using the following commands:

. USE QTYSOLD
. CREATE REPORT WEEKLY.FRM

When you enter the CREATE REPORT command, the screen of the report-design form is displayed (refer to fig. 8.17). You can follow the previously described steps to create the custom report form.

# Producing a Custom Report PLUS

After a custom report form has been created and saved in a.FRM file, you can use the form to display the custom report on the screen or on a printout. To produce such a custom report, you select the **Retrieve/Report** options from the Assistant's menu (see fig. 8.24).

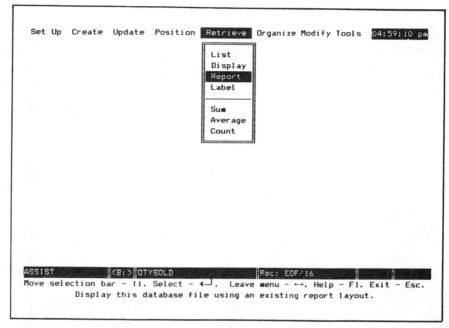

Fig. 8.24. Menu selections for producing custom report.

After selecting these options, you will be asked to specify the name of the report form file with which you will produce the report. For example, to produce the weekly sales summary report whose form was created in the preceding section, you select the following menu options (assuming that the current database file is QTYSOLD.DBF):

Retrieve/Report/B:/*WEEKLY.FRM*

Now you are prompted to specify the desired scope and search condition for selecting the data records that are to be included in the summary report. If you want to use all the data records in the database file, you select **Execute the command**. You are then prompted to specify whether the report is to be displayed on the printer:

**Direct the output to the printer? [Y/N]**

If you answer *Y* to the prompt, a custom report with the specifications defined in the WEEKLY.FRM file will be printed. A copy of the custom report is shown in figure 8.25.

```
Page No.
06/27/86
                    SUPER STEREO AND TELEVISION STORE
                          WEEKLY SALES SUMMARY
                    For the Month of December, 1984


  TV Model    Units Sold


** Week of: 12/07/84
  RCA-XA100           2
  RCA-XA200           5
  ZENITH-19P          4
  ZENITH-21C          3
** Subtotal **
                     14

** Week of: 12/14/84
  RCA-XA100           2
  RCA-XA200           4
  ZENITH-19P          3
  ZENITH-25C          4
** Subtotal **
                     13

** Week of: 12/21/84
  RCA-XA100           8
  RCA-XA200           6
  ZENITH-19P          6
  ZENITH-25C          7
** Subtotal **
                     27

** Week of: 12/28/84
  RCA-XA100           4
  RCA-XA200           5
  ZENITH-19P          4
  ZENITH-25C          2
** Subtotal **
                     15
*** Total ***
                     69
```

*Fig. 8.25. Custom report produced with WEEKLY.FRM.*

In dot-prompt mode, you can produce this custom report by using the REPORT FORM dot command:

. REPORT FORM <name of the report form file>

or

. REPORT FORM <name of the report form file> <qualifier>

If you want to display the custom report on the screen, enter the following dot commands:

```
. USE QTYSOLD
. REPORT FORM WEEKLY.FRM
```

If you want to direct the output to the printer, add the clause *TO PRINT* at the end of the command line:

```
. REPORT FORM WEEKLY.FRM TO PRINT
```

To include only a selected set of data records in the report, you can add a qualifer to the REPORT FORM command:

```
. REPORT FORM WEEKLY.FRM FOR MODEL="RCA-
XA100".OR. MODEL="RCA-XA200"
```

```
. REPORT FORM WEEKLY FOR
DTOC(DATE)<="12/21/84" TO PRINT
```

With the added FOR qualifier, the first command produces a summary report for two television models, RCA-XA100 and RCA-XA200. The second command selects and prints all QTYSOLD.DBF records containing dates before 12/21/84 in the DATE field.

Because the last two digits of all the date fields in the database file are 84, only the first five characters (mm/dd) determine the chronological order of the data records. This could cause a problem if QTYSOLD.DBF contained any records with dates later than 12/31/84, because dBASE III Plus compares alphanumeric strings from left to right and the date 01/01/85 consequently is considered less than 12/01/84. You can solve this problem by changing the dates to the form *yy/mm/dd*; 85/01/01 is not considered less than 84/12/01.

# Modifying an Existing Custom Report Form

PLUS

After you have designed a report form and saved it to a disk file (WEEKLY.FRM, for example), you can recall it for any necessary modifications. From the Assistant menu, you can recall an existing report form by selecting the **Modify/Report** menu options. To change the report specification in the WEEKLY.FRM file, for example, you select the following menu options:

Modify/Report/B:/*WEEKLY.FRM*

The first screen of the report form then is displayed (see fig. 8.26).

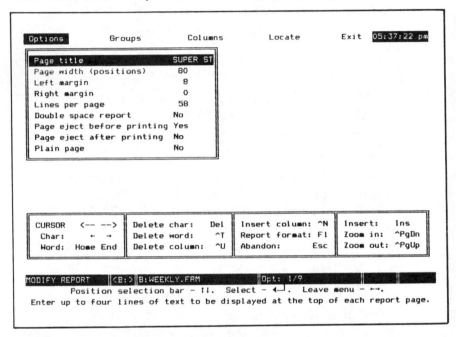

Fig. 8.26. Modifying existing custom report.

Now you can modify the report form by following the previously described procedures for defining the report format and columns.

The existing WEEKLY.FRM file contains definitions for two columns (MODEL and UNITS_SOLD), which were defined in the report. You can look at the column definition forms by first selecting the **Column** option from the menu. When the definition form for the first column is displayed, you can use the PgUp and PgDn keys to move between the different column definition forms. This method is sufficient for locating a column easily if the report contains only a few columns. If many columns have been defined in the report, however, you can move directly to a specific column by using the **Locate** option. When you select **Locate,** the list of defined columns will be displayed (see fig. 8.27).

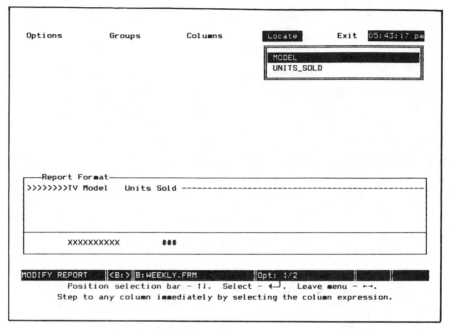

*Fig. 8.27. Locating existing report column.*

From this list, you can select the column that you want to examine or modify by using the ↑ or ↓ keys to highlight the column and then pressing Enter. As a result of these keystrokes, the definition form for the selected column is displayed.

While redefining the columns, you can delete the currently displayed column by pressing Ctrl-U. The current column then is removed from the report form, the next column is displayed as the current column, and the report format is adjusted accordingly. Similarly, you can add a new column to the report by pressing Ctrl-N. A form for the new column then is displayed and space for the new column opens in the report.

After making any necessary modifications to the report, you can exit and save the modified report form by choosing the **Exit/Save** menu options. If you select **Exit/Abandon**, any changes you have made are *not* saved, and the report form file remains as it was before you began modifying it.

In dot-prompt mode, you modify an existing report form file by issuing the MODIFY REPORT command:

. MODIFY REPORT <name of report form file>

An example of this command is

. USE QTYSOLD.DBF
. MODIFY REPORT WEEKLY.FRM

The preceding example, WEEKLY.FRM, generated a report in which single data fields (DATE and UNITS_SOLD) supplied the data for report columns. However, the contents of several data fields can also be combined to produce the contents of one report column. With this method, the report generator can be used to create an employee roster from EMPLOYEE.DBF (see fig. 8.28).

```
Page No.       1
06/27/86
                         SUPER STEREO AND TELEVISION STORE
                                 Employee Roster

Employee's Name                 Telephone Number Birth Date Annual Salary


Smith, James C.                 (216) 123-4567    07/04/60        23100.00
Zeller, Albert K.               (212) 457-9801    10/10/59        29347.50
Gregory, Doris A.               (503) 204-8567    07/04/62        17745.00
Nelson, Harry M.                (315) 576-0235    02/15/58        30450.00
Baker, Tina B.                  (415) 567-8967    10/12/56        27195.00
Chapman, Kirk D.                (618) 625-7845    08/04/61        20737.50
Thompson, Mary W.               (213) 432-6782    06/18/55        25725.00
Duff, Charles N.                (216) 456-9873    07/22/64        14175.00
Lee, Winston E.                 (503) 365-8512    05/14/39        36645.00
Hanson, Thomas T.               (216) 573-5085    12/24/45        30397.50
*** Total ***
                                                                255517.50
```

*Fig. 8.28. Another example of custom report.*

The name of the report form file is ROSTER.FRM. The design forms used to generate the employee roster are displayed in figures 8.29 through 8.35.

In figure 8.32, an alphanumeric expression combines the contents of the data fields LAST_NAME and FIRST_NAME. The result of the expression forms the contents of the report field labeled *Employee's Name*. The expression is

. TRIM(LAST_NAME)+", "+TRIM(FIRST_NAME)

Similarly, AREA_CODE and PHONE_NO are combined to form the contents of the report field labeled *Telephone Number* (see fig. 8.33).

Numeric expressions, as well as alphanumeric expressions, can be used to produce the contents of a report field. For instance, you can use a numeric expression and the contents of ANNUAL_PAY to

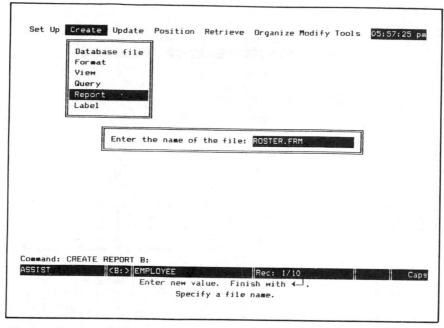

Fig. 8.29. Defining ROSTER.FRM custom report.

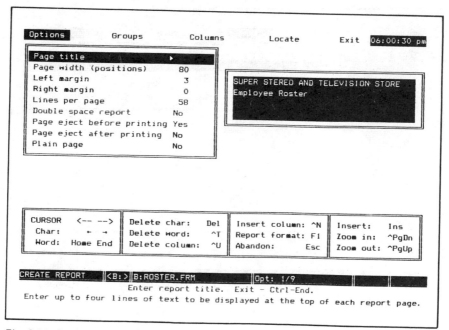

Fig. 8.30. Specifying report heading.

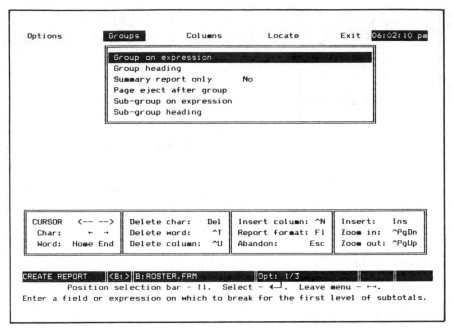

Fig. 8.31. Specifying groups expression.

```
Options         Groups         Columns         Locate         Exit    06:04:10 pm

                     Contents          TRIM(LAST_NAME)+", "+TRIM(FIRST_NAME
                     Heading           Employee's Name
                     Width             24
                     Decimal places
                     Total this column



     ┌─Report Format─────────────────────────────────────────────────────
     >>>Employee's Name         ──────────────────────────────────────────



          XXXXXXXXXXXXXXXXXXXXXXXX


 CREATE REPORT    <B:> B:ROSTER.FRM              Column: 1
   Position selection bar - ↕↓.  Select - ◄┘.  Prev/Next column - PgUp/PgDn.
     Enter up to four lines of text to display above the indicated column.
```

Fig. 8.32. Specifying first report column.

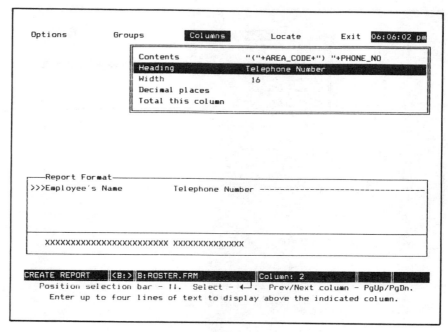

Fig. 8.33. Specifying second report column.

```
Options           Groups        Columns         Locate        Exit   06:07:49 pm
                         ┌──────────────────────────────────────────────┐
                         │ Contents          BIRTH_DATE                  │
                         │ Heading           Birth Date                  │
                         │ Width             10                          │
                         │ Decimal places                               │
                         │ Total this column                            │
                         └──────────────────────────────────────────────┘




      ┌─Report Format─────────────────────────────────────────────────────────┐
      │>>>Employee's Name        Telephone Number Birth Date ----------------- │
      │                                                                         │
      │                                                                         │
      ├─────────────────────────────────────────────────────────────────────── │
      │  XXXXXXXXXXXXXXXXXXXXXXXXX XXXXXXXXXXXXXX    mm/dd/yy                    │
      └─────────────────────────────────────────────────────────────────────── ┘
 CREATE REPORT    <B:> B:ROSTER.FRM            Column: 3
      Position selection bar - ↕↓.  Select - ◄┘.  Prev/Next column - PgUp/PgDn.
      Enter up to four lines of text to display above the indicated column.
```

Fig. 8.34. Specifying third report column.

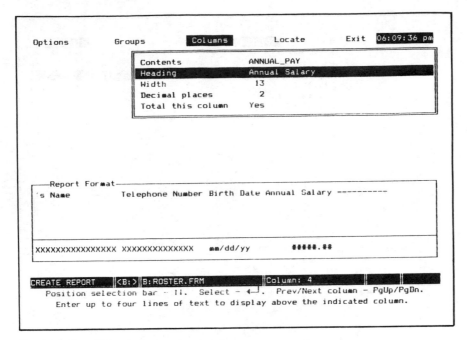

Fig. 8.35. Specifying last report column.

generate a salary projection. Using an assumed inflation rate of 5 percent for computing the employees' pay raises, you can define the projected 1986 salaries by multiplying 1985 salaries (ANNUAL_PAY) by 1.05:

ANNUAL_PAY*1.05

The salary projection report shown in figure 8.36 is generated with the report form file PROJECTN.FRM. The definition forms shown in figures 8.37 through 8.43 are used to define the fields of the report fields.

```
Page No.        1
06/27/86
                           SUPER STEREO AND TELEVISION STORE
                                     Salary Projections
                                For the Years of 1986-1987
                                (Annual Inflation Rate = 5%)

Name of Employee                    1985            1986            1987


James C. Smith                  23100.00        24255.00        25467.75
Albert K. Zeller                29347.50        30814.88        32355.62
Doris A. Gregory                17745.00        18632.25        19563.86
Harry M. Nelson                 30450.00        31972.50        33571.12
Tina B. Baker                   27195.00        28554.75        29982.49
Kirk D. Chapman                 20737.50        21774.38        22863.09
Mary W. Thompson                25725.00        27011.25        28361.81
Charles N. Duff                 14175.00        14883.75        15627.94
Winston E. Lee                  36645.00        38477.25        40401.11
Thomas T. Hanson                30397.50        31917.38        33513.24
*** Total ***
                               255517.50       268293.38       281708.04
```

Fig. 8.36. Another custom report.

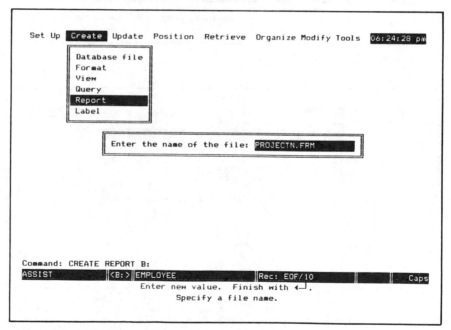

Fig. 8.37. Defining PROJECTN.FRM custom report.

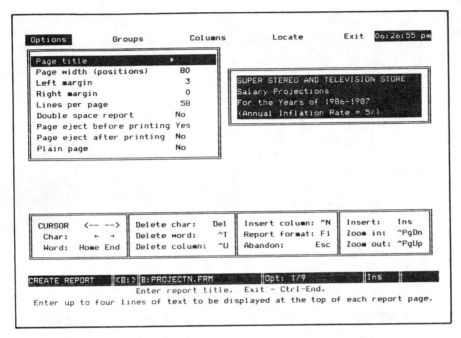

Fig. 8.38. Specifying report heading.

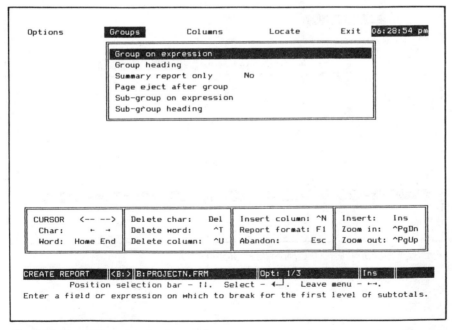

Fig. 8.39. Specifying groups expression.

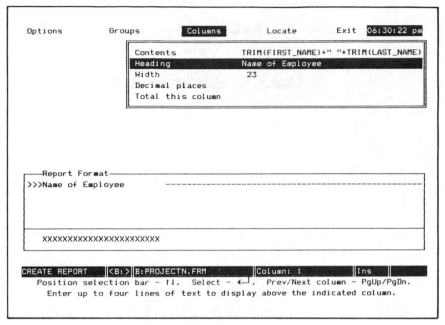

Fig. 8.40. Specifying first report column.

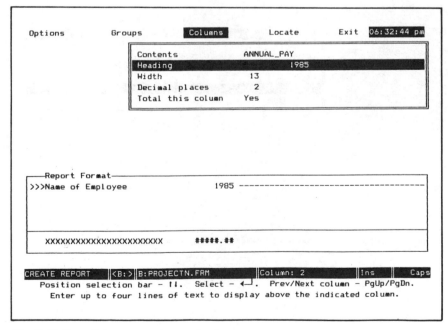

Fig. 8.41. Specifying second report column.

```
   Options          Groups          Columns            Locate          Exit   06:34:28 pm

                         Contents               ANNUAL_PAY*1.05
                         Heading                          1986
                         Width                  15
                         Decimal places          2
                         Total this column      Yes



        ┌─Report Format─────────────────────────────────────────────────────────┐
        │>>>Name of Employee              1985            1986 ─────────────────── │
        │                                                                         │
        │                                                                         │
        │   XXXXXXXXXXXXXXXXXXXXXXXXX      #####.##        #########.##            │
        └─────────────────────────────────────────────────────────────────────────┘
   CREATE REPORT   │<B:>│B:PROJECTN.FRM         │Column: 3        │Ins  │  Caps
      Position selection bar – ↑↓.  Select – ◄┘.  Prev/Next column – PgUp/PgDn.
            Enter the number of decimal places to display for this column.
```

Fig. 8.42. Specifying third report column.

```
   Options          Groups          Columns            Locate          Exit   06:36:40 pm

                         Contents               (ANNUAL_PAY*1.05)*1.05
                         Heading                          1987
                         Width                  14
                         Decimal places          2
                         Total this column      Yes



        ┌─Report Format─────────────────────────────────────────────────────────┐
        │mployee                 1985            1986            1987 ──────────── │
        │                                                                         │
        │                                                                         │
        │XXXXXXXXXXXXXX      #####.##        #########.## ###########.##           │
        └─────────────────────────────────────────────────────────────────────────┘
   CREATE REPORT   │<B:>│B:PROJECTN.FRM         │Column: 4        │Ins  │  Caps
      Position selection bar – ↑↓.  Select – ◄┘.  Prev/Next column – PgUp/PgDn.
            Enter the number of decimal places to display for this column.
```

Fig. 8.43. Specifying last report column.

# Chapter Summary

You have learned how to use the ? command to display the contents of a data record or a memory variable. This command is powerful but, because it always begins the display from the leftmost position, lacks flexibility. One solution to the problem is to use the @ . . . SAY command to position an output item at a specified location. By specifying the row and column position, you can place an output element anywhere you choose on the screen or the printer paper. As a result, you can use the ? and @ . . . SAY commands to design and produce custom labels and reports.

Producing labels and reports with the ? and @ . . . SAY commands, however, can be tedious. Instead, you can use the dBASE III Plus label and report generators to easily generate custom labels and reports.

With the label generator, you can design a label form for displaying the contents of data fields. With the report generator, you can design a complete report form, including text labels and data field contents. Label and report designs created with these generators can be saved on disk as label and report files. The files can be recalled for displaying data records in an active database file during processing.

# 9

Fundamentals of Command-File Programming

## An Overview

You have been using dBASE III Plus commands in interactive mode. Although it is easy to use, this mode of processing is not efficient for repetitive tasks. This chapter presents command-file programming, the batch-processing mode of data manipulation. This processing mode is more efficient for repetitive operations and for complex database management tasks.

Because the scope of command-file processing is broad, this chapter begins by introducing the fundamentals of creating and processing a command file. Then the text explains how a program can be created and edited in the dBASE III Plus text editor and saved to a disk file.

The dBASE III Plus commands discussed in this chapter include:

MODIFY COMMAND
DO
SET PRINT ON/OFF
TYPE
TYPE TO PRINT
COPY FILE
ERASE
SET TALK ON/OFF
SET ECHO ON/OFF

# Defining a Program

A dBASE III Plus program is a set of dBASE III Plus commands designed to perform a particular task.

As the preceding chapters have demonstrated, dBASE III Plus is effective for database management applications. Data in a database file can be manipulated or processed by means of dBASE III Plus commands in interactive mode. The commands for performing a data management task are entered from the keyboard or selected from the Assistant menus and are executed one by one in sequence. You can monitor your results as each command is executed. This mode of processing, however, can be tedious, time-consuming, and inefficient for a repetitive task.

You can solve some of these problems by switching to batch-processing mode. Batch processing involves the creation of a file containing all the dBASE III Plus commands needed to accomplish a particular task. The collection of commands constitutes a program, which is saved on the disk as a command file (or program file). The whole program can then be executed at any time.

## A Sample Program

In interactive mode, you can enter the commands needed to search the EMPLOYEE database file for the record of an employee whose telephone area code is 216 (see fig. 9.1). The result of each command is shown when the command has been executed.

```
.  USE EMPLOYEE
.  LOCATE FOR AREA_CODE="216"
Record =          1
.  ? "Employee's Name ........ ", FIRST_NAME, LAST_NAME
Employee's Name ........  James C.      Smith
.  ? "Area Code, Phone Number. ", AREA_CODE, PHONE_NO
Area Code, Phone Number.  216 123-4567
.
```

Fig. 9.1. Commands entered in interactive mode.

The same set of commands can be entered in a command (or program) file, whose contents are shown in figure 9.2. When this set of commands is executed as a batch (in other words, as a program file), the output shown in figure 9.3 is produced.

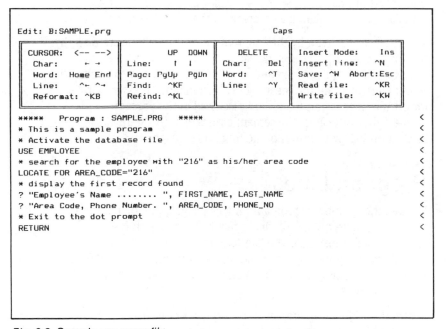

Fig. 9.2. Sample program file.

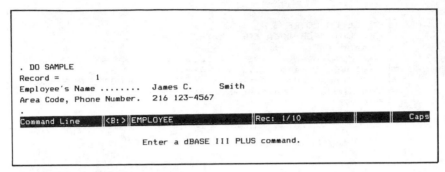

```
. DO SAMPLE
Record =        1
Employee's Name ........   James C.     Smith
Area Code, Phone Number.  216 123-4567
.
┌──────────────┬─────┬──────────┬─────────────┬──────────┬──────┐
│Command Line  │<B:> │EMPLOYEE  │         Rec: 1/10       │     Caps│
└──────────────┴─────┴──────────┴─────────────┴──────────┴──────┘
              Enter a dBASE III PLUS command.
```

*Fig. 9.3. Output from program file.*

# Program Format

A program consists of lines containing dBASE III Plus commands, each of which instructs the computer to perform a specific operation. The operation may be as simple as displaying a data field or as complicated as calculating a complex mathematical formula.

The instructions given by the programmer must be "understood" by the computer. To avoid errors, each command must follow the syntax rules that govern legitimate program format and the semantic rules that determine the meaning of a command. The syntax rules for dBASE III Plus commands are discussed in the preceding chapters. In most cases, the semantic rules of a dBASE III Plus instruction follow the rules of the English language.

# Program Lines

Unlike other computer programming languages, the format for a command line in dBASE III Plus is relatively free, with few restrictions. For instance, you can use any number of spaces to separate words within a command line. However, dBASE III Plus has one important requirement: You must end every command line by pressing Enter.

A dBASE III Plus program contains two types of instruction lines: *comment lines* and *command lines*. Comment lines are remarks describing the nature of the program and the operations it performs. Using comments to document the program and make it more readable is always a good practice.

A comment line can consist of any information, but the comment line must always begin with an asterisk (✳). The following line is a comment line:

✳✳✳✳✳    Program:  SAMPLE.PRG    ✳✳✳✳✳

Because comment lines do not play any part in manipulating the database, the computer ignores them when the program is executed.

Command lines, the other type of line contained in a program, instruct the computer to carry out specific operations. The syntax rules of dBASE III Plus require that each command line begin with a verb, which can be a word, such as USE or LOCATE, or a symbol, such as the question mark (?). The following lines are examples of command lines:

USE EMPLOYEE
LOCATE FOR AREA_CODE = "216"
?"Employee's Name . . . ", FIRST_NAME, LAST_NAME

The command verb can begin at the first position on the line, or the verb can be indented for easier reading. You can use both upper- and lowercase letters in an instruction line. The maximum length of an instruction line is 256 characters, and spaces are counted as characters.

# Creating a Program
# with MODIFY COMMAND

The text editor provided by dBASE III Plus can be used to create a program. With the text editor, you type the command lines one at a time; they appear on the screen as you type them. The program lines can then be edited or modified before they are saved to disk as a program file.

To create a new program file with the text editor, use MODIFY COMMAND and the name of the file. Enter the command and the file name at the dot prompt, in the same way that you have been entering other commands:

. MODIFY COMMAND <name of program file>

The file created by MODIFY COMMAND is a command file with the extension .PRG. For example, to create a new file named

SAMPLE.PRG, which consists of the instruction lines shown previously, you first invoke the text editor by typing

. *MODIFY COMMAND SAMPLE*

The file extension .PRG is automatically assigned when you use MODIFY COMMAND, but you can also create or modify other types of files with this command. In such cases, you must include the file identifier in the file name.

After you enter MODIFY COMMAND, the text editor is invoked and the following message appears at the top of the screen:

Edit: SAMPLE. PRG

You can immediately start entering the first line of your program. The line begins at the cursor position. When you press the Enter key at the end of the program line, the cursor moves to the beginning of the next screen line so that you can enter the next program line. Each time you press Enter, a 〈 symbol, indicating the end of a program line, is displayed at the right edge of the screen. You must end each program line with the Enter keystroke (also called a carriage return or a line feed).

If you have a program line longer than 80 characters, keep typing; press Enter only at the end of the program line. Lines longer than 80 characters "wrap around" to the next line. Even though the wrapped line may not look neat, the content of the line is not affected. The maximum number of characters for one program line is 256; but to make a program more readable, you should write short program lines unless long lines are absolutely necessary. When you must write long program lines, you can either let the lines wrap around or enter a semicolon (;) at the end of the screen line to indicate that the program line continues on the next screen line.

While creating a program file, you can use the arrow keys to move the cursor anywhere on the screen so that you can edit the lines. Pressing the Ins (insert) key toggles between insert and overwrite modes. When you are in insert mode, the characters you type are inserted at the cursor position; existing characters are moved aside. When insert mode is off, typed characters overwrite the characters at the cursor position. In addition, you can use the Del key to delete characters. You can scroll the screen up or down one section at a time with the PgDn and PgUp keys, respectively. A summary of the functions of the keys that can be used for cursor movements and screen editing is given in table 9.1.

**Table 9.1**
**Keystrokes Used for Editing with MODIFY COMMAND**

| *Keystroke* | *Function* |
|---|---|
| Left arrow (←) | Moves cursor left one character |
| Right arrow (→) | Moves cursor right one character |
| Up arrow (↑) | Moves cursor up one line |
| Down arrow (↓) | Moves cursor down one line |
| Home | Moves cursor to previous word |
| End | Moves cursor to next word |
| Ins | Toggles between insert and overwrite modes |
| Ctrl-N (^N) | Inserts line at cursor |
| Backspace (←) | Deletes character to left of cursor |
| Del | Deletes character at cursor |
| Ctrl-Y (^Y) | Deletes line at cursor |
| Ctrl-T (^T) | Deletes from cursor to next word |
| PgUp | Scrolls screen down 18 lines |
| PgDn | Scrolls screen up 18 lines |
| Esc | Exits from text editor without saving file |
| Ctrl-W (^W) | Writes (saves) contents to disk and exits to dot prompt |
| Ctrl-KR (^KR) | Reads another text file into file at cursor position |
| Ctrl-KW (^KW) | Writes (saves) file to another file |

The upper portion of the screen displays a summary table of keystrokes you can use to edit the program. The summary table can be removed or redisplayed by pressing the F1 key.

Users who are familiar with WordStar may be glad to learn that they can use that word processor to create and edit a dBASE III Plus program. Many of the editing commands used by WordStar can be used also in the dBASE III Plus text editor.

# Saving a Program

When all the program lines are in the form you want, press Ctrl-W to save the program to disk. The program file is saved under a name specified with MODIFY COMMAND. The file created with the MODIFY COMMAND SAMPLE command, for example, is named SAMPLE.PRG.

# Executing a Program with the DO Command

After the program has been saved to disk, you can recall the program for modification or for processing. To execute a program that is saved as a program file, use the DO command.

The DO command instructs the computer to "do" a certain task by performing the operations specified in a program file. The object of a DO command must be a program file. The format of the command is

. DO <name of program file>

To execute the program named SAMPLE.PRG, which was created earlier, enter

. *DO SAMPLE*

Because the DO command is reserved for program files, you do not need to include the .PRG file extension.

The DO command retrieves the specified program file and places its contents in RAM. The computer then interprets and executes each instruction line in the file. The output displayed on-screen by the SAMPLE program is shown in figure 9.3.

# Displaying and Printing a Program Directory

To verify the existence of the program files currently saved on the disk, use either the DIR or the TYPE command. The DIR command displays a directory of the files on the default disk drive. For example, the command

. DIR *.PRG

produces a directory of all the program (.PRG) files on the default disk drive (see fig. 9.4). The asterisk (*), which is called a *wild-card character*, stands for any set of permissible characters. dBASE III Plus displays a directory of the program files, along with information about the total disk space used and the total number of files.

# Printing a Directory

You have several alternatives for obtaining a printed copy of the displayed directory. One way to produce a hard copy of the screen display is to use the "print screen" (PrtSc) key. Make sure that the printer is turned on; then press and hold down the Shift key while you press the PrtSc key. This keystroke combination reproduces the screen display (except for some special symbols or lines) through the printer. This process is sometimes called *doing a screen dump*.

# Using the SET PRINT ON/OFF Commands

Another way to obtain a hard copy of the program file directory is to use the SET PRINT ON command to activate the printer before you enter the DIR command.

When dBASE III Plus is first brought up, the printer is usually not activated, and the displays are directed only to the screen. However, you can choose to have the results of dBASE III Plus commands sent to both the printer and the screen. You can activate the printer with the SET PRINT ON command at any time, and the printer remains on until it is turned off with the SET PRINT OFF command.

```
. DIR *.PRG
SAMPLE.PRG

    512 bytes in      1 files.
  49152 bytes remaining on drive.
.
```

*Fig. 9.4. Directory display.*

To produce a hard copy of the program file directory shown in the last section, use the following commands:

. SET PRINT ON
. DIR *.PRG

When you enter these two commands, the file directory generated by DIR *.PRG is displayed on the screen and printed at the same time. After printing the directory, enter the SET PRINT OFF command to turn off the printer.

# Displaying the Contents of a Program File

After you have written a program and saved it in a program file, you may want to examine the file's contents. The DIR command displays only the file directory, not the files themselves. You have several ways to display the actual contents of the files, however. A program file can be displayed for examination or modification with MODIFY COMMAND. You can also display the contents of a program file with a TYPE command, but you cannot edit the file's contents. The TYPE command is entered at the dot prompt in the following format:

. TYPE <name of program file>

As shown in figure 9.5, the TYPE command produces on the screen the complete contents of SAMPLE.PRG.

```
***** Program: SAMPLE.PRG *****
* This is a sample program
* Activate the database file
USE EMPLOYEE
* Search for the employee with "206" as his/her area code
LOCATE FOR AREA_CODE="206"
* Display the first record found
? "Employee's Name ........ ", FIRST_NAME, LAST_NAME
? "Area code, Phone Number: ", AREA_CODE, PHONE_NO
* Exit to the dot prompt
RETURN
```

Fig. 9.5. Listing of SAMPLE.PRG after the TYPE command.

# Printing the Contents of a Program File

A printed copy of the program listing can be obtained in several ways. With Shift-PrtSc, you can print the program lines that are currently on-screen during the MODIFY COMMAND process. You can also activate the printer with the SET PRINT ON command before you invoke MODIFY COMMAND. After the printer is activated, the program can be simultaneously displayed on the screen and printed.

The text editor can display only one screen full of program lines at a time. You must therefore scroll the screen to list a program that takes more than one screen to display. Consequently, using Shift-PrtSc or SET PRINT ON to obtain a printed copy of the program may not produce a complete listing of the program.

To produce the entire listing of a program, use the TYPE TO PRINT command. The command's format is

. TYPE <name of program> TO PRINT

For example, the command

. TYPE SAMPLE.PRG TO PRINT

prints a complete listing of the program SAMPLE.PRG. Other effects of the TYPE TO PRINT and the SET PRINT ON commands are significantly different. The latter command activates the printer and keeps it ON until the printer is turned off by the SET PRINT OFF command. The TYPE TO PRINT command, however, activates the printer and then automatically deactivates it after the program is printed.

# Modifying a Program

Program files can be easily modified. To recall a program from the disk, use MODIFY COMMAND. The program file is retrieved and displayed in the text editor. To modify an existing program file, just type the name of the program file in the command. The format of the command is

. MODIFY COMMAND <name of the existing program file>

For example, when the command

. MODIFY COMMAND SAMPLE

is entered, the program named SAMPLE (the .PRG file extension
again is assumed) is displayed in the text editor. If you do not want
to change the program after examining the program listing, you can
exit from the text editor by pressing the Esc key. If modifications are
necessary, however, you can now edit the program. Use the
keystrokes summarized in table 9.1. After making all the necessary
changes, press Ctrl-W. The version of the file currently displayed in
the text editor replaces the version that was saved on the disk.

# Copying a Program

You have seen that a program can be modified and saved with
MODIFY COMMAND. However, the original program is lost when
the new version is saved on the disk file under the same file name. If
you need to retain a copy of the original version of the program, you
need a different approach. One approach is to create a duplicate copy
of the program under a new file name. Then, without disturbing the
contents of the original program, you can make the modifications on
the duplicate copy.

To copy a program file to another file with a new name, you can use
the COPY FILE command (introduced in Chapter 5):

. COPY FILE <existing program name> TO <new program
name>

An example of the command is

. COPY FILE SAMPLE.PRG TO SAMPLE1.PRG

With the COPY FILE command, you must include in the command
the file name extensions (.PRG) for the program names. Making the
new program the same type as the original program helps to avoid
confusion (although this step is not mandatory). dBASE III Plus treats
the new program, SAMPLE1.PRG, as though it had been created in
the text editor. The new program can be examined or modified
with MODIFY COMMAND.

# Deleting a Program

You can delete a program file from the disk with the ERASE command (see Chapter 5):

   . ERASE <name of program>

When the command

   . ERASE SAMPLE1.PRG

is executed, for example, the following message is displayed to indicate that the program has been permanently deleted from the disk:

   **File has been deleted**

Remember that the ERASE command is irreversible. Once erased, a program cannot be recovered.

# Controlling Program Output

As you have seen from the screen displays, two types of results are displayed in response to the command DO SAMPLE. The first type consists of interactive messages between dBASE III Plus and the programmer. These messages provide detailed information about a program step. For instance, the message

   **Record =        1**

is an interactive message that describes the current contents of the record pointer.

The second type of result is generated by the instructions specified in the program. These messages include lines such as:

   Employee's Name . . . James C. Smith
   Area Code, Phone Number. 216 123-4567

See figure 9.6 for other examples of interactive messages that result from executing a program. The values 38 and 9.5, for instance, are interactive messages that describe the values assigned to the two memory variables (HOURS and PAYRATE). This kind of message, although useful for tracing program execution, can be distracting. In batch processing, then, those messages should usually be suppressed to make the program results more readable. The command to suppress these interactive messages is the SET TALK OFF command.

```
. TYPE SAMPLE1.PRG
*****    Program: SAMPLE1.PRG   *****
* Program to illustrate interactive messages
HOURS=38
PAYRATE=9.5
?"GROSS PAY =",HOURS*PAYRATE
RETURN

. DO SAMPLE1
38
9.5
GROSS PAY =                   361.0
.
```

Fig. 9.6. File with interactive messages displayed.

Note that in this and following figures, the purpose of the screen
print is to show the listing of the program but not the steps needed
to create the program.

# Using the SET TALK
# OFF/ON Commands

The SET TALK OFF command eliminates all the interactive
messages during the processing stage. Only the results produced by
the display commands (such as DISPLAY, LIST, and ?) are shown
on-screen. You can either enter SET TALK OFF at the dot prompt or
include it as an instruction line within a program. To illustrate the
effect of the SET TALK OFF command, you can use SAMPLE1.PRG
revised as SAMPLE2.PRG (see fig. 9.7).

```
. TYPE SAMPLE2.PRG
*****    Program: SAMPLE2.PRG   *****
* Show effects of SET TALK OFF
SET TALK OFF
HOURS=38
PAYRATE=9.5
?"GROSS PAY =",HOURS*PAYRATE
RETURN

. DO SAMPLE2
GROSS PAY =                   361.0
.
```

Fig. 9.7. Effect of SET TALK OFF.

The only output displayed by SAMPLE2.PRG is that produced by the ? command. All the interactive messages have been suppressed by the inclusion of a SET TALK OFF command which, when invoked, remains in effect until SET TALK ON is executed. SET TALK ON instructs the computer to display all the interactive messages during the processing stage. SET TALK ON is usually the default setting for dBASE III Plus.

# Tracing Program Errors during Execution

Some interactive messages are undesirable and should be removed by use of the SET TALK OFF command, but other interactive messages are helpful for locating errors during program execution. You can display these messages by using the SET ECHO ON command.

SET ECHO ON causes each command line to be displayed as it is executed. These interactive messages leave a "trail," enabling you to locate a program error in a specific command line. To illustrate the usefulness of this command, two errors are intentionally incorporated in the program shown in figure 9.8.

```
. TYPE SAMPLE3.PRG
*****    Program: SAMPLE3.PRG    *****
* A sample program with two errors
SET TALK OFF
HOURS-38
PAYRATE=9.5
? "GROSS_PAY = "; HOURS*PAYRATE
RETURN

.
```

Fig. 9.8. Program with errors.

The two errors introduced to instruction lines in the program are

1. A minus sign (–) is used for assigning a value (38) to the memory variable HOURS in the instruction, as in:

   HOURS–38

   An equal sign (=) should be used instead of the minus sign.

2. A semicolon (;) separates the string *GROSS PAY* = from the results of the formula HOURS∗PAYRATE:

    ? "GROSS PAY = "; HOURS∗PAYRATE

A comma (,) should be used instead of the semicolon.

When you execute the program with the DO SAMPLE3 command, you see the results shown in figure 9.9.

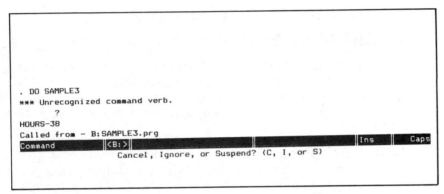

```
. DO SAMPLE3
*** Unrecognized command verb.
        ?
HOURS-38
Called from - B:SAMPLE3.prg
Command          <B:>                                    Ins      Caps
            Cancel, Ignore, or Suspend? (C, I, or S)
```

Fig. 9.9. First error message.

The first error message, **∗∗∗ Unrecognized command verb**, is displayed when the first error is encountered. The line

    Called from - B:SAMPLE3.PRG

indicates that the error came from the program SAMPLE3.PRG on the default disk drive, B. When an error in the program is encountered, you can cause program execution to skip over the erroneous command line by typing *I* in response to the question

    Cancel, Ignore, or Suspend ? (C, I, or S)

When you type *I*, the next program line will be executed, whereas *C* will cancel and *S* will suspend program execution. The first error message does not show the program line where the error was detected (see fig. 9.10). For more information about the error, you can use the SET ECHO ON command to display each command line as it is executed. If an error is found, the command line is displayed with the error message. To illustrate this application, a SET ECHO ON command is added to the beginning of the program SAMPLE4.PRG (see fig. 9.11).

```
. DO SAMPLE3
*** Unrecognized command verb
Called from - B:SAMPLE3.prg
Terminate command file? (Y/N)
```

*Fig. 9.10. File with SET ECHO ON.*

```
. TYPE SAMPLE4.PRG
*****    Program: SAMPLE4.PRG    *****
* Show effects of SET ECHO ON
SET TALK OFF
SET ECHO ON
HOURS-38
PAYRATE=9.5
? "GROSS_PAY = "; HOURS*PAYRATE
RETURN


.
```

*Fig. 9.11. Results of SET ECHO ON.*

When you execute the program, you see the results shown in figure 9.12. Each command line is displayed as it is executed, and program execution of the can be monitored step by step. Because the first error message is shown immediately after the command line **HOURS-38**, for instance, you can tell where the error is.

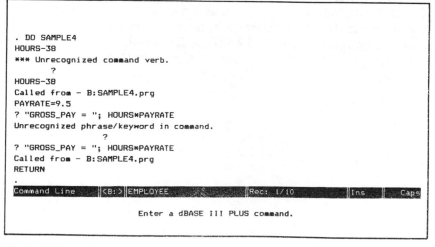

```
. DO SAMPLE4
HOURS-38
*** Unrecognized command verb.
        ?
HOURS-38
Called from - B:SAMPLE4.prg
PAYRATE=9.5
? "GROSS_PAY = "; HOURS*PAYRATE
Unrecognized phrase/keyword in command.
              ?
? "GROSS_PAY = "; HOURS*PAYRATE
Called from - B:SAMPLE4.prg
RETURN
.
Command Line    <B:> EMPLOYEE              Rec: 1/10        Ins      Caps
                   Enter a dBASE III PLUS command.
```

*Fig. 9.12. Results of SAMPLE4.PRG.*

The information contained in the second error message is far more precise in pointing to the exact location of the error found in a command line. The second error message, `Unrecognized phrase/keyword in command`, is displayed with a question mark (?) above the line where the error is found. The question mark points to the character following the semicolon (the error in this example).

# Chapter Summary

This chapter introduces another approach to data manipulation with dBASE III Plus. Instead of using the interactive mode of processing, you can perform data processing tasks by collecting all the necessary commands to form a command (or program) file. The commands in the program file are then executed as a batch by means of the DO command.

To create a new program file, you begin by invoking the dBASE III Plus text editor with MODIFY COMMAND. The same command can be used for editing existing program files. After a program has been edited, you can save the program on the disk file. The program can later be recalled for further modification or for execution.

This chapter introduces a number of ways in which a program file can be displayed or printed. You can print hard copy of the program file by using the TYPE TO PRINT command. The SET PRINT ON command activates the printer, and SET PRINT OFF turns off the printer. A hard copy of the screen display can also be made by doing a screen dump. To provide intermediate monitoring of the execution process, you can use the SET TALK ON command. To trace a program error during execution, use the SET ECHO ON command.

# 10

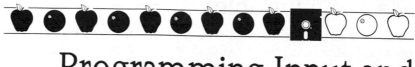

# Programming Input and Output Operations

## An Overview

This chapter explains how to use input commands to enter and modify data. The new commands are

CLEAR
ACCEPT TO
INPUT TO
WAIT TO
APPEND BLANK
@ . . . SAY . . . GET
READ

The two basic commands for displaying output (? and @ . . . SAY) were introduced in Chapter 8. This chapter explains how to print custom reports by using these commands with the SET PRINT ON and SET DEVICE TO PRINT commands.

# Entering Data in Memory Variables

Memory variables are important in data manipulations. Variables are often used to store the results of a calculation so that the results can be used again. Memory variables can also store data that will replace the contents of another data record. In some cases, a set of memory variables can even be used as a small database file.

Values are assigned to memory variables in many different ways. The STORE and = commands assign a numeric value or an alphanumeric string to a numeric, character/text, or logical variable:

```
. STORE 123.45 TO VALUEX
VALUEX=123.45

. STORE "Mary J. Smith" TO BUYERNAME
BUYERNAME="Mary J. Smith"

. STORE .T. TO MEMBERSHIP
MEMBERSHIP=.T.
```

When a value is assigned to a variable by means of the STORE or = command, the command line must contain the value. For example, the program in figure 10.1 assigns an alphanumeric string ("216") to the memory variable AREACODE. The variable AREACODE is used later as a search key in the LOCATE command line. The output from this program is shown in figure 10.2.

Whenever AREACODE.PRG is executed, the alphanumeric string "216" is assigned to the memory variable AREACODE. To search for a data record with the area code 415, you change the command line that assigns the alphanumeric string to the memory variable AREACODE:

```
AREACODE="415"
```

To enter the change, you must use the text editor to modify the program. Changing the alphanumeric string whenever you want to search for a new area code is inefficient. With the ACCEPT command, however, the same program can be made to search for different area codes.

```
.TYPE AREACODE.PRG
***** Program: AREACODE.PRG *****
* Find the first record with area code of "206"
SET TALK OFF
SET ECHO OFF
* Specify the area code to be located
AREACODE="206"
* Select the database file
USE EMPLOYEE
* Search for such an area code
LOCATE FOR AREA_CODE=AREACODE
* Show the data record found
DISPLAY
RETURN
.
```

*Fig. 10.1. Program using memory variables.*

```
. DO AREACODE
Record# FIRST_NAME LAST_NAME AREA_CODE PHONE_NO MALE BIRTH_DATE ANNUAL_PAY
     1  James C.    Smith       206     123-4567 .T.  07/04/60    22000.00
.
```

*Fig. 10.2. Output generated by memory variable program.*

# ACCEPT TO

The ACCEPT TO command assigns an alphanumeric string to a memory variable outside the program. ACCEPT TO enters the string in an alphanumeric memory variable and can be used with or without a prompting message. The prompt must be enclosed in quotation marks:

. ACCEPT "<prompt>" TO <name of alphanumeric memory variable>

Examples of using ACCEPT TO are

. ACCEPT TO AREACODE

. ACCEPT "Enter the area code to be searched for:" TO AREACODE

Figure 10.3 shows use of the ACCEPT TO command in a program. This program produces the output shown in figure 10.4. When the program is executed, the prompt and a blinking cursor appear. Now you can enter an answer to the prompt. As soon as you press Enter,

the data element you have entered is assigned to the memory
variable AREACODE. Then the memory variable is used as a search
key for the LOCATE command. You do not need to modify the
program PROMPT.PRG in order to search for a different area code.

```
. TYPE PROMPT.PRG
*****   Program: PROMPT.PRG   *****
* Find the first record with an area code keyed in
SET TALK OFF
SET ECHO OFF
* Prompt for the area code to be located
ACCEPT "Enter the area code to be searched .... " TO AREACODE
USE EMPLOYEE
LOCATE FOR AREA_CODE=AREACODE
DISPLAY
RETURN

.
```

*Fig. 10.3. Program using ACCEPT command.*

```
. DO PROMPT
Enter the area code to be located .... 415
Record#  FIRST_NAME    LAST_NAME   AREA_CODE PHONE_NO MALE BIRTH_DATE ANNUAL_PAY
      5  Tina B.       Baker       415       567-7777 .F.  10/12/56     27195.00
. DO PROMPT
Enter the area code to be located .... 212
Record#  FIRST_NAME    LAST_NAME   AREA_CODE PHONE_NO MALE BIRTH_DATE ANNUAL_PAY
      2  Albert K.     Zeller      212       457-9801 .T.  10/10/59     29347.50
. DO PROMPT
Enter the area code to be located .... 513
Record#  FIRST_NAME    LAST_NAME   AREA_CODE PHONE_NO MALE BIRTH_DATE ANNUAL_PAY
      3  Doris A.      Gregory     513       204-8567 .F.  07/04/62     17745.00

.
```

*Fig. 10.4. Output from program using ACCEPT.*

The ACCEPT command cannot be used to assign values to numeric
or logical variables. Only an alphanumeric string can be assigned to a
character variable. However, a numeric value can be entered in a
numeric variable if the value is entered as an alphanumeric string.
That alphanumeric variable can then be converted to a numeric
variable with the VAL function (see Chapter 8).

The program shown in figure 10.5 is an example. The values 123
and 234 are assigned as alphanumeric strings to the variables X and

```
. TYPE XPLUSY.PRG
*****  Program: XPLUSY.PRG  *****
* A program to add X and Y
* Prompt for values of variables X and Y
ACCEPT "Enter value for X =" TO X
ACCEPT "      value for Y =" TO Y
* Convert strings X and Y to numeric values
X=VAL(X)
Y=VAL(Y)
? "Sum of X and Y =",X+Y
RETURN

. DO XPLUSY
Enter value for X =123
      value for Y =234
Sum of X and Y =          357
.
```

*Fig. 10.5. Converting string to numeric variable.*

Y, respectively. Then the alphanumeric variables are converted to numeric variables with the VAL function:

    X=VAL(X)
    Y=VAL(Y)

The VAL function converts the alphanumeric strings to numeric values and assigns those values to the variables X and Y.

The VAL function retains the decimal digits in the variable, however, even though the decimal point and the digits to the right of the decimal point are not shown (see fig. 10.6). The first ? command displays the contents of the alphanumeric string X. The second and third ? commands show that the value returned by the VAL function is 124 (123.85 rounded to the nearest integer). The fourth ? command, which displays the result of multiplying VAL(X) by 100, shows that the decimal digits have been retained.

With the help of the VAL function, the ACCEPT command can be used to assign a decimal value to a numeric variable. For instance, the following instruction lines can be used to assign the value of 123.85 to the numeric variable X:

    ACCEPT "Enter a value for X . . . " TO X
    X=VAL(X)*100/100

```
. TYPE VALUEOFX.PRG
*****    Program: VALUEOFX.PRG    *****
* Illustrate effects of VAL function
X="123.85"
* X is an alphanumeric string
? VAL(X)
? VAL(X)+200
? VAL(X)*100
RETURN

. DO VALUEOFX
       124
        324
          12385

.
```

Fig. 10.6. Results of VAL function.

The value of VAL(X)*100 is 12385. The value is then divided by 100, and the result (123.85) is entered in the variable X.

As you can see, entering a value in a numeric variable is a lengthy procedure with ACCEPT. Fortunately, another command can be used to enter numeric data or an alphanumeric string in a memory variable. This command is the INPUT command.

# INPUT TO

The INPUT command, designed for programs that request entry of data from the keyboard, assigns a numeric value to a memory variable. The command has the following form:

. INPUT "<prompt>" TO <name of memory variable>

An example of the INPUT command is

. INPUT "Enter Employee's Last Name : " TO LASTNAME

The prompt tells you what data is to be entered. Possible data elements include

An alphanumeric string enclosed in quotation marks
A numeric value
A date
A logical state (T or F)

The type of the variable is determined when you enter the data element. If the data element is an alphanumeric string, you must enclose it in quotation marks. To enter a date to a memory variable, you must use the CTOD function to convert the input from a character string to a date. A logical field requires an answer in the form of *.T.* or *.F.* (including the periods).

The program in figure 10.7 demonstrates entry of various data elements in different memory variables. When you run the program, the prompts appear and you enter the values for the INPUT statements (see fig. 10.8).

An alphanumeric string must be enclosed in quotation marks before it is assigned to a variable. A date entered as "03/15/85" is an alphanumeric string.

```
*****    Program: INPUTING.PRG    *****
* A program show how to use an INPUT command
SET TALK OFF
SET ECHO OFF
?
?
?
INPUT "  Enter:      Today's Date .... " TO DATE
?
INPUT "            Customer's Name .... " TO CUSTOMER
?
INPUT "          Amount of Purchase ... " TO AMOUNT
?
INPUT "   Cash Purchase (.T. or .F.)? " TO CASH
?
?
?
? "      Contents of variables:"
? "         DATE ="+DTOC(DATE)
? "    CUSTOMER ="+CUSTOMER
? "      AMOUNT = "+STR(AMOUNT,5,2)
? "        CASH = ",CASH
RETURN

.
```

*Fig. 10.7. Using INPUT TO to enter data elements to memory variables.*

```
.  DO INPUTING


   Enter:       Today's Date .... CTOD("03/15/85")

              Customer's Name .... "Adam S. Smith"

            Amount of Purchase ... 95.55

       Cash Purchase (.T. or .F.)? .T.



       Contents of variables:
          DATE =03/15/85
      CUSTOMER =Adam S. Smith
        AMOUNT = 95.55
          CASH =  .T.
  .
```

*Fig. 10.8. Contents of memory variables.*

# WAIT TO

The WAIT command is used to enter a single character to an alphanumeric variable. The format of WAIT is

. WAIT "<prompt>" TO <name of memory variable>

as in

. WAIT "Do You Want to Continue (Y/N)?" TO CHOICE

The WAIT command is similar to the ACCEPT command except for minor differences. With the WAIT command, you can enter only one character to a variable, whereas the ACCEPT command assigns alphanumeric strings of any size. The ACCEPT command requires that you end the data element by pressing Enter, but the Enter keystroke is not necessary with the WAIT command.

WAIT is often used in programs that prompt for the answer to a decision variable. The answer is applied to conditional transfer commands, such as IF . . . ENDIF and DO CASE. The next chapter demonstrates more uses of the WAIT command.

# Editing Data Records

The ACCEPT command can also be used in a program to locate a specific data record. By using a number of ACCEPT commands, you can enter values in several memory variables. Those values then are used as search keys in a LOCATE command. The data record that meets the search conditions is displayed for editing.

For example, suppose that you need to modify a specific data record in the EMPLOYEE.DBF database file. To find the data record for the employee, use FIRSTNAME and LASTNAME as the memory variables for the search keys (see fig. 10.9). When the program is executed, a prompt appears for the variables FIRSTNAME and LASTNAME (see fig. 10.10). After you enter the data elements, the program finds the record that meets the conditional qualifier FOR LAST_NAME=LASTNAME .AND. FIRST_NAME=FIRSTNAME.

```
. TYPE EDITIT.PRG
*****    Program: EDITIT.PRG    *****
* Program to edit an employee's record
SET TALK OFF
SET ECHO OFF
*  Clear the screen
CLEAR
USE EMPLOYEE
*  Get the employee's name
ACCEPT "Enter Employee's First Name .... " TO FIRSTNAME
ACCEPT "                Last Name ..... " TO LASTNAME
*  Search for the employee's record
LOCATE FOR LAST_NAME=LASTNAME .AND. FIRST_NAME=FIRSTNAME
*  Edit current record
EDIT RECNO()
RETURN

.
```

Fig. 10.9. Using memory variables as search keys.

```
Enter Employee's First Name .... Doris
                Last Name ..... Gregory
```

Fig. 10.10. Results of the editing program.

You can display and edit the contents of the record with the following commands:

. EDIT RECNO()
. EDIT

The RECNO() function returns the number of the current data record. If record 4 has been found, for example, the command EDIT RECNO() is the same as EDIT 4. With EDIT RECNO(), you can display the current record for editing (see fig. 10.11). (Procedures for editing records are explained in Chapter 5.) After you have finished editing, you can press Ctrl-End to save the edited record and exit the program.

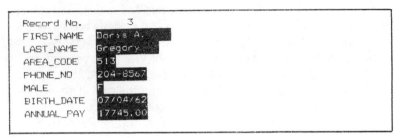

*Fig. 10.11. Record to be edited.*

As you can see in figure 10.11, the data fields are labeled with the field names specified in the data structure. Because a data field name is limited to 10 characters, the name may not provide a clear description of the data field. To solve that problem, you can use a set of custom labels defined with the @ . . . SAY command (see Chapter 8). The @ . . . SAY command specifies the row-and-column number of the label to be displayed. The label is enclosed in quotation marks, following the word SAY. Then a GET command links the label with a specific data field in the record to be edited, as in

@5,10 SAY "Employee's First Name : " GET FIRST_NAME

When the command is executed, the label

**Employee's First Name** :

is displayed at row 5, column 10. Following the label, blank spaces are displayed in which you can enter a value for the FIRST_NAME field. The number of blank spaces depends on the length of the data field. The program in figure 10.12 shows how to design a custom form.

After you enter the data for the variables (FIRSTNAME, LASTNAME), the editing screen is displayed (see fig. 10.13). As a result of the READ command, the cursor is positioned at the first data field.

```
. TYPE EDITIT1.PRG
*****    Program: EDITIT1.PRG    *****
* Another program to edit an employee's record
* using custom labels for data fields
SET TALK OFF
SET ECHO OFF
CLEAR
USE EMPLOYEE
ACCEPT "Enter Employee's First Name .... " TO FIRSTNAME
ACCEPT "                 Last Name ..... " TO LASTNAME
LOCATE FOR LAST_NAME=LASTNAME .AND. FIRST_NAME=FIRSTNAME
* Create custom labels for data fields
@5,10  SAY "Employee's First Name : " GET FIRST_NAME
@7,10  SAY "            Last Name : " GET LAST_NAME
@9,10  SAY "            Area Code : " GET AREA_CODE
@11,10 SAY "            Phone No. : " GET PHONE_NO
@13,10 SAY "           Male?(T/F) : " GET MALE
@15,10 SAY "           Birth Date : " GET BIRTH_DATE
@17,10 SAY "        Annual Salary : $" GET ANNUAL_PAY
READ
RETURN

.
```

Fig. 10.12. Creating custom labels.

```
Enter Employee's First Name .... Harry
                 Last Name ..... Nelson


        Employee's First Name :  Harry M.

                    Last Name :  Nelson

                    Area Code :  315

                    Phone No. :  576-0235

                   Male?(T/F) :  T

                   Birth Date :  02/15/58

                Annual Salary : $ 30450.00
```

Fig. 10.13. Editing screen.

When a READ command is encountered in a program, the cursor is positioned at the first character of the field specified in the @ . . . GET instruction line. The program then waits for you to enter a new data element in the data field. The arrow keys can be used to move the cursor to another data field for editing. Be careful, however, not to move the cursor off the screen before all data items have been entered. When the cursor is moved beyond the limits of the screen, the program saves the entered data and returns to the dot prompt.

The set of @ . . . SAY commands in the program EDITIT1.PRG can be saved as a template in a format file (.FMT) and used again in other programs. A format file can be created with the text editor, using the command

. MODIFY COMMAND <name of format file>

as in

. MODIFY COMMAND EDITFORM.FMT

To avoid confusion, the file extension of a format file (.FMT) should be attached to the file name. When the text editor is invoked, the @ . . . SAY commands can be entered (see fig. 10.14).

```
dBASE Word Processor
*****    A Format File : EDITFORM.FMT    *****
*  Create a format file for editing an employee's record
@5,10  SAY "Employee's First Name : " GET FIRST_NAME
@7,10  SAY "          Last Name : " GET LAST_NAME
@9,10  SAY "          Area Code : " GET AREA_CODE
@11,10 SAY "          Phone No. : " GET PHONE_NO
@13,10 SAY "        Male?(T/F) : " GET MALE
@15,10 SAY "         Birth Date : " GET BIRTH_DATE
@17,10 SAY "      Annual Salary : $" GET ANNUAL_PAY
```

*Fig. 10.14. Format file with @ . . . SAY commands.*

# Adding New Data Records

New data records can be added to a database file by means of a program that performs the necessary steps. For example, the following program uses the APPEND command to add a new data record to EMPLOYEE.DBF (see fig. 10.15).

```
. TYPE APENDIT.PRG
*****   Program: APENDIT.PRG   *****
*  Program to append an employee's record
SET TALK OFF
SET ECHO OFF
*  Clear the screen
CLEAR
*  Select the database file
USE EMPLOYEE
*  Append new record to active database file
APPEND
RETURN

.
```

*Fig. 10.15. Program to append records.*

When you execute the program, the data-entry form is displayed (see fig. 10.16). At this point, you can enter a new set of data items. As soon as the data record is added, you can press the Ctrl-End key combination to save the new record and exit from the program.

*Fig. 10.16. Data-entry form.*

# APPEND BLANK

An APPEND BLANK command displays a data-entry form without data field labels and appends a blank record to the file. You can attach custom labels to data fields to provide detailed descriptions. Labels can be defined by @ . . . SAY commands and can be used either as a part of the program or to format a file that has been saved on disk. Figure 10.17 shows how to design a custom screen to append a new record to EMPLOYEE.DBF with @ . . . SAY commands.

```
. TYPE APENDIT1.PRG
*****    Program: APENDIT1.PRG    *****
*   Another program to append an employee's record
SET TALK OFF
SET ECHO OFF
USE EMPLOYEE
CLEAR
*   Append new record with custom labels
APPEND BLANK
*   Show current record number
? "Enter Data for Record No.", RECNO()
@5,10  SAY "Employee's First Name : " GET FIRST_NAME
@7,10  SAY "           Last Name : " GET LAST_NAME
@9,10  SAY "           Area Code : " GET AREA_CODE
@11,10 SAY "           Phone No. : " GET PHONE_NO
@13,10 SAY "          Male?(T/F) : " GET MALE
@15,10 SAY "          Birth Date : " GET BIRTH_DATE
@17,10 SAY "       Annual Salary : $" GET ANNUAL_PAY
READ
RETURN

.
```

Fig. 10.17. Using @ . . . SAY to create custom screen.

When the program is executed, the custom labels for the new record appear (see fig. 10.18). You can also use the format file EDITFORM.FMT to create custom labels (see fig. 10.19). The results of APENDIT1.PRG (fig. 10.19) are identical to the results of APENDIT1.PRG (fig. 10.17).

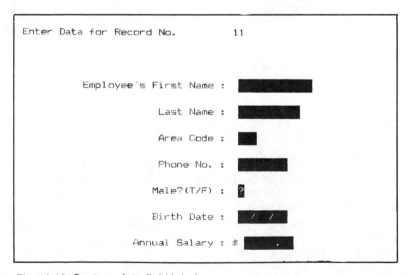

```
Enter Data for Record No.          11



            Employee's First Name :  ▮▮▮▮▮▮▮

                       Last Name :  ▮▮▮▮▮▮▮

                       Area Code :  ▮▮

                       Phone No. :  ▮▮▮▮▮

                      Male?(T/F) :  ?

                      Birth Date :    /  /

                  Annual Salary : $  ▮▮▮▮.
```

Fig. 10.18. Custom data field labels.

```
. TYPE APENDIT2.PRG
*****   Program: APENDIT2.PRG   *****
*   Aappend employee's record with a format file
SET TALK OFF
SET ECHO OFF
USE EMPLOYEE
*   Append new record with custom labels in EDITFORM.FMT
SET FORMAT TO EDITFORM.FMT
APPEND BLANK
READ
RETURN

.
```

*Fig. 10.19. Program using EDITFORM.FMT.*

In the preceding examples, the entry form for editing a data field is displayed in reverse video. The data field on the entry form is shown by a shaded block. For example, a data-entry form on an IBM monochrome monitor will show black characters on a bright green background, while other text is displayed as green characters on a black background. dBASE III Plus displays the data field in reverse video by default. However, you can change the display mode with the SET DELIMITER command.

# SET DELIMITER ON/OFF

With the SET DELIMITER ON/OFF command, you can use a pair of symbols to indicate the width of a data field on the data-entry form. To set the delimiter, use the following two commands:

. SET DELIMITER ON
. SET DELIMITER TO <delimiter symbol(s)>

An example of the command is

. SET DELIMITER TO "[]"

When dBASE III Plus is started, reverse video is used to mark a data field because the delimiter is *off*. To choose a different delimiter, you must activate the delimiter with the SET DELIMITER ON command. When the delimiter is set *on*, you can specify the symbol to mark a data field. Symbols such as [ ], { }, or quotation marks can be used to mark the beginning and end of a data field. You can also specify only one symbol (such as #) as the delimiter. In this case, the same symbol will be used to mark the beginning and the end of the data field. For example, the following program uses the symbols [ and ] to mark the data fields for the editing operation (see fig. 10.20).

```
. TYPE APENDIT3.PRG
*****  Program: APENDIT3.PRG  *****
*  Another program to append an employee's record
SET DELIMITER ON
*  Set brackets [] as delimiter
SET DELIMITER TO "[]"
USE EMPLOYEE
CLEAR
*  Append new record with custom labels
APPEND BLANK
*  Show current record number
? "Enter Data for Record No.", RECNO()
@5,10  SAY "Employee's First Name : " GET FIRST_NAME
@7,10  SAY "          Last Name : " GET LAST_NAME
@9,10  SAY "          Area Code : " GET AREA_CODE
@11,10 SAY "          Phone No. : " GET PHONE_NO
@13,10 SAY "          Male?(T/F) : " GET MALE
@15,10 SAY "          Birth Date : " GET BIRTH_DATE
@17,10 SAY "        Annual Salary : $" GET ANNUAL_PAY
READ
RETURN

.
```

Fig. 10.20. Program setting the delimiter to [ ].

When you execute the program, the entry form in figure 10.21 is displayed.

```
Enter Data for Record No.            11


        Employee's First Name :  [              ]

              Last Name :  [          ]

              Area Code :  [    ]

              Phone No. :  [          ]

              Male?(T/F) :  [?]

              Birth Date :  [  /  /  ]

           Annual Salary : $ [       .   ]
```

Fig. 10.21. Results of APENDIT3.PRG.

If you are using a monitor with a graphics interface card, you should see the display shown in the figure. With an IBM monochrome monitor, you may need to enter SET INTENSITY OFF before entering SET DELIMITER ON in order to eliminate the reverse video.

# Deleting Data Records

As you have seen, programs can be used to edit and append data records. A program to delete data records can also be written. The program in figure 10.22 deletes a data record from the EMPLOYEE.DBF file after you enter the employee's first and last names. Then the database file is rewritten by the PACK command (see fig. 10.23).

```
. TYPE DELETEIT.PRG
*****    Program: DELETEIT.PRG    *****
*   Program to delete an employee's record
SET TALK OFF
SET ECHO OFF
*   Clear the screen
CLEAR
*   Select the database file
USE EMPLOYEE
*   Get the employee's name
ACCEPT "Enter Employee's First Name .... " TO FIRSTNAME
ACCEPT "              Last Name ..... " TO LASTNAME
*   Search for the employee's record
LOCATE FOR LAST_NAME=LASTNAME .AND. FIRST_NAME=FIRSTNAME
*   Delete the current record
DELETE
PACK
RETURN

.
```

*Fig. 10.22. Program to delete data records.*

# Displaying Output

The dBASE III Plus display commands ? and @ . . . SAY were introduced in the preceding chapters. The @ . . . SAY command

```
Enter Employee's First Name .... Doris
              Last Name ..... Gregory
. LIST
Record#   FIRST_NAME    LAST_NAME   AREA_CODE  PHONE_NO  MALE  BIRTH_DATE  ANNUAL_PAY
     1    James C.      Smith       206        123-4567  .T.   07/04/60     22000.00
     2    Albert K.     Zeller      212        457-9801  .T.   10/10/59     27950.00
     3    Harry M.      Nelson      315        576-0235  .T.   02/15/58     29000.00
     4    Tina B.       Baker       415        567-8967  .F.   10/12/56     25900.00
     5    Kirk D.       Chapman     618        625-7845  .T.   08/04/61     19750.00
     6    Mary W.       Thompson    213        432-6782  .F.   06/18/55     24500.00
     7    Charles N.    Duff        206        456-9873  .T.   07/22/64     13500.00
     8    Winston E.    Lee         503        365-8512  .T.   05/14/39     34900.00
     9    Thomas T.     Hanson      206        573-5085  .T.   12/24/45     28950.00
.
```

Fig. 10.23. File repacked after using DELETE.

(see Chapter 8) displays output at the specified location on the
display medium. The screen is divided into 25 rows and 40
columns, where a row equals one print line, and a column equals
one character. The print line on most printers ranges from 40 to 80
characters, although some printers can print up to 132 characters on
a line. dBASE III Plus is often used with an 80-column matrix or
letter-quality printer.

A PICTURE clause can be added to the @ . . . SAY command to
generate a special output format. A collection of @ . . . SAY
commands can be used in a program to display an employee's
personnel file (see fig. 10.24).

After you enter the first and last names, you see the output shown
in figure 10.25.

To obtain a printed copy of the report, add the commands SET
DEVICE TO PRINT and EJECT at the beginning of the program (see
fig. 10.26).

The SET DEVICE TO PRINT command sends the output to the
printer. The EJECT command sends a form-feed instruction to the
printer to advance the paper by one page. As a result of that
command, the report generated by the @ . . . SAY commands is
printed at the top of a new page. The SET DEVICE TO SCREEN
command redirects the output to the screen.

```
. TYPE CARDFILE.PRG
*****    Program: CARDFILE.PRG    *****
* Produce an employee's personnel file
SET TALK OFF
SET ECHO OFF
* Get employee's name
CLEAR
@5,1 SAY " Enter Name of the Employee:"
@7,1 SAY " "
ACCEPT "                    Last Name ...... " TO LASTNAME
ACCEPT "                    First Name ..... " TO FIRSTNAME
* Find the employee's record
USE EMPLOYEE
LOCATE FOR FIRST_NAME=FIRSTNAME .AND. LAST_NAME=LASTNAME
* Display output on screen
CLEAR
@5,7 SAY "EMPLOYEE'S PERSONAL DATA SHEET"
@7,5  SAY "Name (Last, First)  :  "+TRIM(LAST_NAME)+", "+TRIM(FIRST_NAME)
@9,5  SAY "Home Telephone No.  :  ("+AREA_CODE+") "+PHONE_NO
@11,5 SAY "           Birth Date :  "+DTOC(BIRTH_DATE)
@13,5 SAY "        Annual Salary :  "
@13,26 SAY ANNUAL_PAY PICTURE "$##,###.##"
RETURN

.
```

Fig. 10.24. Using @ . . . SAY to display output.

```
            EMPLOYEE'S PERSONAL DATA SHEET

     Name (Last, First) : Nelson, Harry M.

     Home Telephone No. : (315) 576-0235

              Birth Date : 02/15/58

           Annual Salary : $30,450.00

    .
```

Fig. 10.25. Output from @ . . . SAY commands.

# The ? Command

The display command ? is used to display one or more output elements in a command. If the elements are separated by commas, output elements of mixed types can be included in the same command, as in

. ?"Name of Employee ",FIRST_NAME+
LAST_NAME,BIRTH_DATE,ANNUAL_PAY

```
*****   Program: PRNTCARD.PRG   *****
* Print an employee's personnel file on printer
 SET TALK OFF
 SET ECHO OFF
CLEAR
@5,1 SAY " Enter Name of the Employee:"
@7,1 Say " "
ACCEPT "                    Last Name ...... " TO LASTNAME
ACCEPT "                    First Name ..... " TO FIRSTNAME
USE EMPLOYEE
LOCATE FOR FIRST_NAME=FIRSTNAME .AND. LAST_NAME=LASTNAME
CLEAR
* Activate the printer and go to a new page
SET DEVICE TO PRINT
EJECT
@5,7 SAY "EMPLOYEE'S PERSONAL DATA SHEET"
@7,5  SAY "Name (Last, First) : "+TRIM(LAST_NAME)+", "+TRIM(FIRST_NAME)
@9,5  SAY "Home Telephone No. : ("+AREA_CODE+") "+PHONE_NO
@11,5 SAY "         Birth Date : "+DTOC(BIRTH_DATE)
@13,5 SAY "       Annal Salary : "
@13,26 SAY ANNUAL_PAY PICTURE "$##,###.##"
SET DEVICE TO SCREEN
RETURN
```

Fig. 10.26. Program for printing hard copy.

When the ? command is entered, the output is displayed on the screen because the monitor is the default display medium used by dBASE III Plus. If the printer has been activated with the SET PRINT ON command, the output is printed as well.

The ? command displays the output elements from left to right on a new display line. The display position of an output element depends on the type of the element (see fig. 10.27). The output of the program is displayed in figure 10.28.

As you can see, the contents of the first alphanumeric string on the ? command line, *ABCDE*, are displayed on the far left position of the display line. The comma used to separate the alphanumeric strings causes a blank space to be inserted between the strings ABCDE and XYZ on the display line. The comma separating a date variable and a logical variable also inserts a blank space. However, the same spacing rules do not apply to numeric output. Figure 10.29 shows how numeric values are displayed with the ? command. When you execute the program, the results shown in figure 10.30 are displayed.

```
. TYPE PRINT1.PRG
*****    Program: PRINT1.PRG    *****
* A program to show the printing positions
SET TALK OFF
SET ECHO OFF
ASTRING="ABCDE"
BSTRING="XYZ"
VALUEX=-123.45
VALUEY=0.6789
VALUEZ=98765
DATE1=CTOD("03/08/85")
LOGIC=.T.
* Display a ruler
?"12345678901234567890123456789012345678901234567890"
?ASTRING,BSTRING
?VALUEX,VALUEY,VALUEZ
?DATE1,LOGIC
RETURN
```

Fig. 10.27. Program for demonstrating display positions.

```
. DO PRINT1
12345678901234567890123456789012345678901234567890
ABCDE XYZ
       -123.45              0.6789        98765
03/08/85 .T.
.
```

Fig. 10.28. Output of PRINT1.PRG.

```
. TYPE PRINT2.PRG
*****    Program: PRINT2.PRG    *****
* Show printing position of numeric variables
SET TALK OFF
SET ECHO OFF
VALUEX=-123.45
VALUEY=0.6789
VALUEZ=98765
* Display a ruler
?"12345678901234567890123456789012345678901234567890"
?VALUEX
?VALUEY
?VALUEZ
?VALUEX,VALUEY,VALUEZ
?VALUEY,VALUEX,VALUEZ
?VALUEZ,VALUEX,VALUEY
RETURN

.
```

Fig. 10.29. Positioning numeric variables.

```
.  DO PRINT2.PRG
12345678901234567890123456789012345678901234567890
       -123.45
            0.6789
       98765
       -123.45              0.6789         98765
            0.6789         -123.45         98765
       98765             -123.45           0.6789

  .
```

*Fig. 10.30. Results of PRINT2.PRG.*

The output of the program shows some interesting results. With a ?
command, the decimal point of the first numeric variable is always
displayed at the eleventh column. Commas do not provide the same
consistent spacing with the ? command, and, as a result, positioning
numeric values can be difficult. To solve the spacing problem, you
can convert the output elements to alphanumeric strings with the
STR function. For example, to convert the value of VALUEX
(–123.45) to an alphanumeric string, you enter

STR(VALUEX,7,2)

The result is a string of seven characters with two decimal places.
Figure 10.31 shows how to set equal lengths for numeric values and
how to position numeric output. The decimal points are aligned
vertically because the length of the return strings was set to 15
characters (see fig. 10.32).

```
.  TYPE PRINT3.PRG
*****    Program: PRINT3.PRG    *****
* Show effect of STR on printing position
SET TALK OFF
SET ECHO OFF
VALUEX=-123.45
VALUEY=0.6789
VALUEZ=98765
* Display a ruler
?"12345678901234567890123456789012345678901234567890"
?STR(VALUEX,15,4),STR(VALUEY,15,4),STR(VALUEZ,15,4)
?STR(VALUEY,15,4),STR(VALUEX,15,4),STR(VALUEZ,15,4)
?STR(VALUEZ,15,4),STR(VALUEX,15,4),STR(VALUEY,15,4)
RETURN



  .
```

*Fig. 10.31. Program using STR( ) function.*

```
. DO PRINT3
12345678901234567890123456789012345678901234567890123456789012345567890
       -123.4500              0.6789        98765.0000
          0.6789           -123.4500        98765.0000
       98765.0000          -123.4500            0.6789
.
```

*Fig. 10.32. Results of STR( ).*

As you have seen, a comma separating alphanumeric strings inserts blank space between elements. But what if you do not want a space between elements? To solve that problem, you can use arithmetic operators between elements and specify the string as an expression. For example, to display the contents of the strings ASTRING and BSTRING without a space between them, use a plus sign, as in

. ?ASTRING+BSTRING

Because of erratic spacing, you may wish to avoid placing commas in the ? command line. The following program converts data fields to alphanumeric strings, then displays the strings as alphanumeric expressions (see fig. 10.33). Commas are not used. The output produced by the program is shown in figure 10.34.

```
. TYPE PRINT4.PRG
*****    Program: PRINT4.PRG    *****
* A program to display an employee's record
USE EMPLOYEE
CLEAR
?"Employee's Name: "+TRIM(FIRST_NAME)+" "+LAST_NAME
?"Telephone No:    ("+AREA_CODE+") "+PHONE_NO
?"Birth Date:      "+DTOC(BIRTH_DATE)
?"Annual Salary:   "+STR(ANNUAL_PAY,8,2)
RETURN


.
```

*Fig. 10.33. Using ? without commas.*

```
Employee's Name: James C. Smith
Telephone No:    (206) 123-4567
Birth Date:      07/04/60
Annual Salary:   22000.00
.
```

*Fig. 10.34. Output of PRINT4.PRG.*

To print a copy of the program output, add the SET PRINT ON command to the beginning of the program. After printing the report, you can use SET PRINT OFF to deactivate the printer and return the display to the screen.

# The ?? Command

Because the ? command has a built-in line-feed instruction, output elements are always displayed on a new line. A line feed is about the same as a carriage return on a typewriter and generally works well for most output displays. However, in some cases you may need to display an element directly after the last element. To suppress line feeds, use the ?? command.

The only difference between the ? and ?? commands is that the ?? command does not begin a new display line. The ?? command displays the output after the last output element. Figure 10.35 shows an example of using the ?? command. As you can see, the print command ??STRINGB positions the string immediately after the output from the print command ?STRINGA.

```
. TYPE PRINT5.PRG
*****    Program: PRINT5.PRG    *****
* Show the effects of ??
STRINGA="This is the first string"
STRINGB="This is the second string"
?STRINGA
?STRINGB
?STRINGA
??STRINGB
RETURN

. DO PRINT5
This is the first string
This is the second string
This is the first stringThis is the second string
.
```

Fig. 10.35. Using ?? command.

# Chapter Summary

This chapter has introduced the ACCEPT, INPUT, and WAIT commands, which are used to assign a data element to a memory variable. Although all of these commands are input commands, ACCEPT, INPUT, and WAIT have different functions. ACCEPT assigns only alphanumeric strings to alphanumeric variables, whereas INPUT enters alphanumeric, numeric, date, or logical data to different kinds of variables. However, an alphanumeric string must be enclosed in quotation marks when used with the INPUT command. With the INPUT command, you can enter a date in a date variable by using the CTOD conversion function. Logical data items must include two periods (for example, .T. or .F.) when entered to the logical variable. The WAIT command assigns only one character to an alphanumeric variable.

The two basic output commands discussed in this chapter are the @. . . SAY and ? commands. With @ . . . SAY, you can position the output element at a specific location on the screen or printer. However, @ . . . SAY can display only one output element in the form of an alphanumeric or numeric expression. The ? command can display one or more different output elements separated by commas. The ?? command is similar to the ? command, except that ? positions the output on a new line, but ?? displays output wherever the last element ended. With proper use of the printing commands introduced in this chapter, you can design custom forms for editing, appending, and displaying data records.

# Conditional Branching and Program Loops

## An Overview

Up to this point, the program examples you have seen have been processed in logical sequence. That is, the processing started at the first instruction line and continued until the last command was executed.

This chapter shows how to change the normal processing sequence by using conditional branching and program loops. Conditional branching is one of dBASE III Plus's most powerful tools. The dBASE III Plus commands used in conditional branching are

```
IF . . . ENDIF
IF . . . ELSE . . . ENDIF
DO CASE . . . ENDCASE
DO CASE . . . OTHERWISE . . . ENDCASE
```

Another command discussed in this chapter, the WAIT TO command, enables you to select the processing path during program execution.

Program loops are also explained in this chapter. Instead of entering the same program lines to perform repetitive tasks at several places in a program, you can use a program loop to repeat the segment of the program efficiently. For example, a loop can be used to process each data record in a database file. The following dBASE III Plus commands are used in program loop operations:

DO WHILE . . . ENDDO
LOOP
EXIT

# Conditional Branching

Although sequential processing is adequate for simple data-processing tasks, more flexibility is needed in advanced data manipulations. In many data manipulations, you need to provide different processing "avenues" to meet varying types of computational conditions.

To calculate wages, for example, you multiply the total number of hours worked by the hourly wage. If overtime is involved, however, you must calculate the wage differently. For this reason, you need to provide a formula to calculate the wage in different ways, depending on whether overtime is involved. If 40 hours is a normal work week, and overtime is figured at 1 1/2 times the normal hourly rate, the computational logic is

*For a normal work week:*

Regular Pay = Hours × Wage Rate
Overtime Pay = 0

*For overtime:*

Regular Pay = 40 × Wage Rate
Overtime Pay = (Hours – 40) × Wage Rate × 1.5

If you were writing a program to calculate the weekly wage, you would create two different sections in your program; one for each condition. When the program is run, one of the two sections is executed, depending on whether there is overtime. This method is called *conditional branching*. Each branch represents a program section that is executed when a specific condition is met.

# IF . . . ENDIF

The IF . . . ENDIF command designates the program section to be executed when the condition is met. The condition is defined in a clause following the IF command, and the program section is enclosed between the IF command line and the ENDIF command:

IF <condition>

    <section executed when the condition is true>

ENDIF

An example of the IF . . . ENDIF command is

```
IF HOURS>40
   REGULARPAY=40*RATE
   OVERTIME=(HOURS−40)*RATE*1.5
ENDIF
```

If the condition is true (if HOURS > 40), the program section between IF and ENDIF is executed. If the condition is false, the section is skipped. The condition in the IF clause can be one of the following:

A logical variable or data field, as in

```
IF MALE
   ? "This is a male employee"
   . . .
   . . .
ENDIF
```

A simple numeric or alphanumeric relation, as in

```
IF ANNUAL_PAY>25000
   . . .
   . . .
ENDIF
IF AREACODE="216"
   . . .
   . . .
ENDIF
```

A compound relation, as in

IF LAST_NAME="Smith" .AND. FIRST_NAME="James"

. . .

. . .

ENDIF
IF MALE .AND. AREA_CODE="503"

. . .

. . .

ENDIF
IF SUBSTR(BIRTHDATE,7,2)="60" .OR.
SUBSTR(BIRTH_DATE,7,2)="62"

. . .

. . .

ENDIF
IF .NOT. MALE .AND. ANNUAL_PAY>=25000

. . .

. . .

ENDIF

To illustrate conditional branching, the hourly wage example has been converted to a program (see fig. 11.1). When you execute the program, you see the output shown in figure 11.2.

```
*****  Program: PAYROLL.PRG   *****
* A simplified payroll program
SET TALK OFF
SET ECHO OFF
* Get hours and rate
?
?
INPUT "          Enter Number of Hours Worked .... " TO HOURS
INPUT "                    Hourly Wage Rate .... " TO RATE
* Start computing wage
REGULARPAY=HOURS*RATE
OVERTIME=0
IF HOURS>40
   REGULARPAY=40*RATE
   OVERTIME=(HOURS-40)*RATE*1.5
ENDIF
?
?
? "          Regular Pay ......... "+STR(REGULARPAY,7,2)
? "          Overtime Pay ........ "+STR(OVERTIME,7,2)
? "          Total Gross Pay ..... "+STR(REGULARPAY+OVERTIME,7,2)
?
?
RETURN
```

Fig. 11.1. Program using IF . . . ENDIF.

```
.  DO PAYROLL


        Enter  Number  of  Hours  Worked  ....  38
                     Hourly  Wage  Rate  ....  7.50


            Regular  Pay  .........   285.00
            Overtime  Pay  ........     0.00
            Total  Gross  Pay  .....   285.00



.
```

*Fig. 11.2. Output from program using IF . . . ENDIF.*

The wage is calculated according to the numbers entered in the variables HOURS and RATE. The value stored in HOURS determines whether overtime pay is to be calculated.

Conditional branching can also be used to process data records. For illustration, a new database file, named WAGES.DBF, has been created. The structure of WAGES.DBF is shown in figure 11.3. Figure 11.4 displays the data records in WAGES.DBF.

Each data record contains the worker's name and wage information (hours worked, wage, and so on). A program similar to PAYROLL.PRG can be used to calculate the wage. PAYROLL.PRG can be modified so that it locates an employee's record according to the contents of a data field (see fig. 11.5). Figure 11.6 shows the output of PAYROLL1.PRG.

```
.  USE WAGES
.  DISPLAY STRUCTURE
Structure  for  database  :  B:WAGES.dbf
Number  of  data  records  :      16
Date  of  last  update      :  03/04/85
Field   Field  name   Type        Width      Dec
     1   FIRST_NAME   Character      10
     2   LAST_NAME    Character       8
     3   DEPT         Character       1
     4   HOURS        Numeric         2
     5   RATE         Numeric         5        2
     6   GROSS_PAY    Numeric         6        2
     7   DEDUCTIONS   Numeric         6        2
     8   NET_PAY      Numeric         6        2
** Total **                         45

.
```

*Fig. 11.3. Structure of WAGES.DBF.*

```
. USE WAGES
. LIST
Record#   FIRST_NAME  LAST_NAME  DEPT  HOURS   RATE  GROSS_PAY  DEDUCTIONS  NET_PAY
      1   Cindy T.    Baker.     B       38    7.50      0.00        0.00      0.00
      2   William B.  Davison    A       41   11.50      0.00        0.00      0.00
      3   Floyd C.    Fuller     C       40    7.50      0.00        0.00      0.00
      4   Bob R.      Hill       A       42    7.75      0.00        0.00      0.00
      5   Mike D.     James      B       38    6.50      0.00        0.00      0.00
      6   David F.    Larson     C       38   11.00      0.00        0.00      0.00
      7   Alice G.    Miller     A       45    8.50      0.00        0.00      0.00
      8   Peter A.    Morrison   A       48    8.25      0.00        0.00      0.00
      9   Ellen F.    Norton     B       58    7.50      0.00        0.00      0.00
     10   Charlie H.  Olson      A       36    9.25      0.00        0.00      0.00
     11   Tony W.     Palmer     A       37    7.25      0.00        0.00      0.00
     12   Grace S.    Porter     B       40   12.25      0.00        0.00      0.00
     13   Howard G.   Rosen      C       36    8.00      0.00        0.00      0.00
     14   Geroge D.   Stan       A       39   10.95      0.00        0.00      0.00
     15   Tamie K.    Tower      C       36    9.50      0.00        0.00      0.00
     16   Albert L.   Williams   B       43    8.50      0.00        0.00      0.00
.
```

Fig. 11.4. Data records in WAGES.DBF.

```
*****  Program: PAYROLL1.PRG   *****
* A payroll program for processing the WAGES.DBF
SET TALK OFF
SET ECHO OFF
* Get worker's name
?
ACCEPT "    Enter Worker's First Name .... " TO FIRSTNAME
ACCEPT "                  Last Name ..... " TO LASTNAME
USE WAGES
LOCATE FOR LAST_NAME=LASTNAME.AND.FIRST_NAME=FIRSTNAME
* Start computing wage
REGULARPAY=HOURS*RATE
OVERTIME=0
IF HOURS>40
   REGULARPAY=40*RATE
   OVERTIME=(HOURS-40)*RATE*1.5
ENDIF
?
? "    Worker's Name : "+TRIM(FIRST_NAME)+" "+TRIM(LAST_NAME)
?
? "         Regular Pay ......... "+STR(REGULARPAY,7,2)
? "         Overtime Pay ........ "+STR(OVERTIME,7,2)
? "         Total Gross Pay ..... "+STR(REGULARPAY+OVERTIME,7,2)
?
RETURN
```

Fig. 11.5. Program to process WAGES.DBF.

```
. DO PAYROLL1

      Enter Worker's First Name .... Cindy
                       Last Name ..... Baker

      Worker's Name : Cindy T. Baker

            Regular Pay ......... 285.00
            Overtime Pay ........   0.00
            Total Gross Pay .....  285.00

.
```

*Fig. 11.6. Output of PAYROLL1.PRG.*

You can see that the program has calculated the wages correctly. If you look closely, however, you see that the program is not efficient, because regular pay and overtime pay are computed twice when the number of hours is greater than 40. For example, when the condition HOURS > 40 is true, the regular pay is first computed by

REGULARPAY = HOURS*RATE

and then replaced by the result of

REGULARPAY = 40*RATE

To avoid repetition and increase execution speed, you can revise the computational logic:

If hours worked is less than or equal to 40,

Regular Pay = Hours × Wage Rate
Overtime Pay = 0

If hours worked is more than 40,

Regular Pay = 40 × Wage Rate
Overtime Pay = (Hours−40) × Wage Rate × 1.5

In this way, only one formula is used to calculate the wages, depending on the condition of the data. The new computational logic can be converted in a program by introducing the phrase ELSE in the IF . . . ENDIF command.

# IF . . . ELSE . . . ENDIF

The ELSE phrase in the IF . . . ENDIF command adds a second
condition that directs the computer to one section for a true
condition and to another section for a false condition. When
the condition in the IF clause is false, the program to be executed is
enclosed between ELSE and ENDIF:

IF <condition>

   <section executed when the condition is true>

ELSE

   <section executed when the condition is false>

ENDIF

An example of IF . . . ELSE . . . ENDIF is

```
IF HOURS<=40
   REGULARPAY=HOURS*RATE
   OVERTIME=0
ELSE
   REGULARPAY=40*RATE
   OVERTIME=(HOURS–40)*RATE*1.5
ENDIF
```

These program lines can be used in the program PAYROLL2.PRG
(see fig. 11.7) to accomplish the task performed by the program
PAYROLL1.PRG. The programs are identical, except that
PAYROLL2.PRG requires fewer steps than PAYROLL1.PRG.

In the examples, the instruction lines in the program section have
been indented. An instruction can begin anywhere on the program
line, so the indentation does not affect the execution of the
program. The indentation is used only to make the program more
readable; you may wish to adopt that format to make your programs
clearer.

In the PAYROLL2.PRG program, the wage is processed in two
different ways: one way when HOURS<=40, and the other when
HOURS>40. Many times, however, you need to handle more than
two conditions. For example, to calculate personal income taxes,
you need a formula for each income bracket. Calculating quantity

```
*****   Program: PAYROLL2.PRG    *****
* Another payroll program for processing the WAGES.DBF
SET TALK OFF
SET ECHO OFF
* Get worker's name
?
ACCEPT "    Enter Worker's First Name .... " TO FIRSTNAME
ACCEPT "                    Last Name ..... " TO LASTNAME
USE WAGES
LOCATE FOR LAST_NAME=LASTNAME.AND.FIRST_NAME=FIRSTNAME
* Start computing wage
IF HOURS<=40
  REGULARPAY=HOURS*RATE
  OVERTIME=0
ELSE
   REGULARPAY=40*RATE
   OVERTIME=(HOURS-40)*RATE*1.5
ENDIF
?
? "    Worker's Name : "+TRIM(FIRST_NAME)+" "+TRIM(LAST_NAME)
?
? "           Regular Pay ........ "+STR(REGULARPAY,7,2)
? "           Overtime Pay ....... "+STR(OVERTIME,7,2)
? "           Total Gross Pay ..... "+STR(REGULARPAY+OVERTIME,7,2)
?
RETURN
```

*Fig. 11.7. Program using IF . . . ENDIF.*

discount is another example, because you need a set of discount factors for different quantity levels. To manage these applications, you can use nested IF . . . ENDIF commands to check data ranges. To *nest* IF . . . ENDIF commands means to enclose one IF . . . ENDIF program segment within another, as in

    IF <condition>
      . . .
      . . .
       IF <condition>
        . . .
        . . .
         IF <condition>
          . . .
          . . .
        ENDIF
        . . .
        . . .
      ENDIF
      . . .
      . . .
    ENDIF

The following problem for calculating income tax illustrates the use of nested IF . . . ENDIF commands. Table 11.1 shows the withholding tax percentages for a single worker from June, 1983, through January, 1985.

**Table 10.1**
**Percentage Withholding Tax Table***
**For Wages Paid after June, 1983, and before January, 1985**
**For a Single Worker**

| If weekly wage is | Amount to withhold |
|---|---|
| Under $27 | $0 |
| $27 - not over  $79 | 12% of excess over   $27 |
| $79 - not over $183 | $6.24 + 15% of excess over   $79 |
| $183 - not over $277 | $21.84 + 19% of excess over $183 |
| $277 and over | $39.70 + 25% of excess over $277 |

* partially taken from 1984 Federal Income Tax Table

The program segment for calculating the amount of withholding tax (which is stored in the variable WITHHOLD) can be written with nested IF . . . ENDIF commands as follows (the variable GROSSWAGE contains the weekly gross pay):

```
IF GROSSWAGE >27
   WITHHOLD=.12*(GROSSWAGE-27)
     IF GROSSWAGE > 79
        WITHHOLD=6.24+.15*(GROSSWAGE-79)
          IF GROSSWAGE > 183
             WITHHOLD=21.84+.19*(GROSSWAGE-183)
               IF GROSSWAGE > 277
                  WITHHOLD=39.7+.25*(GROSSWAGE-277)
               ENDIF
          ENDIF
     ENDIF
ENDIF
```

Figure 11.8 shows a program that uses nested IF . . . ENDIF commands to calculate the weekly withholding tax for workers with records in WAGES.DBF. When NESTEDIF.PRG is executed, you see the output shown in figure 11.9.

```
*****   Program: NESTEDIF.PRG   *****
* Computing Withholding using nested IF commands
SET TALK OFF
SET ECHO OFF
* Get worker's name
?
ACCEPT "    Enter Worker's First Name .... " TO FIRSTNAME
ACCEPT "                    Last Name ..... " TO LASTNAME
USE WAGES
LOCATE FOR LAST_NAME=LASTNAME.AND.FIRST_NAME=FIRSTNAME
* Start computing wage
IF HOURS<=40
  REGULARPAY=HOURS*RATE
  OVERTIME=0
ELSE
    REGULARPAY=40*RATE
    OVERTIME=(HOURS-40)*RATE*1.5
ENDIF
GROSSWAGE=REGULARPAY+OVERTIME
* Determine withholding taxes
WITHHOLD=0
IF GROSSWAGE >27
    WITHHOLD=.12*(GROSSWAGE-27)
      IF GROSSWAGE > 79
        WITHHOLD=6.24+.15*(GROSSWAGE-79)
          IF GROSSWAGE > 183
            WITHHOLD=21.84+.19*(GROSSWAGE-183)
              IF GROSSWAGE > 277
                WITHHOLD=39.7+.25*(GROSSWAGE-277)
              ENDIF
          ENDIF
      ENDIF
ENDIF
NETWAGE=GROSSWAGE-WITHHOLD
?
? "    Worker's Name : "+TRIM(FIRST_NAME)+" "+TRIM(LAST_NAME)
?
? "        Regular Pay ......... "+STR(REGULARPAY,7,2)
? "        Overtime Pay ........ "+STR(OVERTIME,7,2)
? "        Total Gross Pay ..... "+STR(REGULARPAY+OVERTIME,7,2)
? "        Tax Withheld ........ "+STR(WITHHOLD,7,2)
? "        Net Pay ............. "+STR(NETWAGE,7,2)
RETURN
```

*Fig. 11.8. Program using nested IF . . . ENDIF commands.*

If the gross wage is greater than 277, the amount of withholding tax (WITHHOLD) is repeatedly calculated and replaced. Because the two-branch IF . . . ENDIF command is inefficient for this type of problem, you may wish to use the multiple-branch DO CASE. . . ENDCASE command.

```
. DO NESTEDIF

    Enter Worker's First Name .... Albert
                     Last Name ..... Williams

    Worker's Name : Albert L. Williams

            Regular Pay ......... 340.00
            Overtime Pay ........  38.25
            Total Gross Pay .....  378.25
            Tax Withheld ........   65.01
            Net Pay .............  313.24

.
```

Fig. 11.9. Output from NESTEDIF.PRG.

```
DO CASE
   CASE GROSSWAGE<27
      WITHHOLD=0
   CASE GROSSWAGE>=27 .AND. GROSSWAGE <79
      WITHHOLD=.12*(GROSSWAGE-27)
   CASE GROSSWAGE>=79 .AND. GROSSWAGE <183
      WITHHOLD=6.24+.15*(GROSSWAGE-79)
   CASE GROSSWAGE>=183 .AND. GROSSWAGE <277
      WITHHOLD=21.84+.19*(GROSSWAGE-183)
   CASE GROSSWAGE>=277
      WITHHOLD=39.7+.25*(GROSSWAGE-277)
ENDCASE
```

To understand the power of the multiple-branch commands, you can convert the nested IF . . . ENDIF commands in the NESTEDIF.PRG program to CASE conditions (see fig. 11.10). The output from the program is shown in figure 11.11.

In some database applications, it is not possible to anticipate all possible conditions. For this reason, you need to prepare the program to accommodate situations not included in CASE clauses. The OTHERWISE phrase can be used to include the situations not defined in the CASE clauses, as in

```
DO CASE
   CASE <condition 1>
       <program section for condition 1 being true>
```

```
*****   Program: DOCASES.PRG    *****
* Computing Withholding using DOCASE commands
SET TALK OFF
SET ECHO OFF
* Get worker's name
?
ACCEPT "     Enter Worker's First Name .... " TO FIRSTNAME
ACCEPT "                      Last Name ..... " TO LASTNAME
USE WAGES
LOCATE FOR LAST_NAME=LASTNAME.AND.FIRST_NAME=FIRSTNAME
* Computing gross wage
DO CASE
   CASE HOURS<=40
      REGULARPAY=HOURS*RATE
      OVERTIME=0
   CASE HOURS>40
      REGULARPAY=40*RATE
      OVERTIME=(HOURS-40)*RATE*1.5
ENDCASE
GROSSWAGE=REGULARPAY+OVERTIME
* Determine amount of tax withholding
DO CASE
   CASE GROSSWAGE<27
      WITHHOLD=0
   CASE GROSSWAGE>=27 .AND. GROSSWAGE <79
      WITHHOLD=.12*(GROSSWAGE-27)
   CASE GROSSWAGE>=79 .AND. GROSSWAGE <183
      WITHHOLD=6.24+.15*(GROSSWAGE-79)
   CASE GROSSWAGE>=183 .AND. GROSSWAGE <277
       WITHHOLD=21.84+.19*(GROSSWAGE-183)
   CASE GROSSWAGE>=277
       WITHHOLD=39.7+.25*(GROSSWAGE-277)
ENDCASE
NETWAGE=GROSSWAGE-WITHHOLD
?
? "    Worker's Name : "+TRIM(FIRST_NAME)+" "+TRIM(LAST_NAME)
?
? "          Regular Pay ........ "+STR(REGULARPAY,7,2)
? "          Overtime Pay ........ "+STR(OVERTIME,7,2)
? "          Total Gross Pay ..... "+STR(REGULARPAY+OVERTIME,7,2)
? "          Tax Withheld ........ "+STR(WITHHOLD,7,2)
? "          Net Pay ............. "+STR(NETWAGE,7,2)
RETURN
```

*Fig. 11.10. Replacing IF . . . ENDIF with CASE conditions.*

```
. DO DOCASES

    Enter Worker's First Name .... Albert
                 Last Name ..... Williams

    Worker's Name : Albert L. Williams

            Regular Pay ......... 340.00
            Overtime Pay ........  38.25
            Total Gross Pay .....  378.25
            Tax Withheld ........   65.01
            Net Pay .............  313.24

.
```

*Fig. 11.11. Results of DO CASE program.*

```
            CASE <condition 2>
                <program section for condition 2 being true>
            CASE <condition 3>
                <program section for condition 3 being true>
            . . .
            . . .
            OTHERWISE
                <program section when all above conditions are false>
            . . .
        ENDCASE
```

DOCASES.PRG can be modified as follows to make the first CASE clause (GROSSWAGE<27) an OTHERWISE clause:

```
    DO CASE
        CASE GROSSWAGE>=27 .AND. GROSSWAGE <79
            WITHHOLD=.12*(GROSSWAGE-27)
        CASE GROSSWAGE>=79 .AND. GROSSWAGE <183
            WITHHOLD=6.24+.15*(GROSSWAGE-79)
        CASE GROSSWAGE>=183 .AND. GROSSWAGE <277
            WITHHOLD=21.84+.19*(GROSSWAGE-183)
        CASE GROSSWAGE>=277
            WITHHOLD=39.7+.25*(GROSSWAGE-277)
        OTHERWISE
            WITHHOLD=0
    ENDCASE
```

# DO CASE . . . ENDCASE

The DO CASE . . . ENDCASE command defines multiple conditions and multiple program sections. When one of the conditions is met, the corresponding program section is executed. A CASE clause is used to define each condition. You can use as many conditions as necessary to define the conditional branchings. The phrases DO CASE and ENDCASE enclose all the CASE clauses used, as in

```
DO CASE
   CASE <condition 1>
      <program section for condition 1 being true>
   CASE <condition 2>
      <program section for condition 2 being true>
   CASE <condition 3>
      <program section for condition 3 being true>
   . . .
   . . .
ENDCASE
```

If the condition in the first CASE clause is true, the program section following that clause is executed. If the condition is not true, the section is "ignored." In the same way, if the second condition is true, the corresponding program section is processed.

# Program Loops

The conditional branching commands are powerful tools for data manipulation; however, they can process only one record at a time. The programs presented so far in this chapter return to the dot prompt after processing one data record. To process another data record, you must execute the program again. This can be time-consuming if you have a large set of data records. To calculate the weekly wage of all employees with records in the WAGES.DBF file, you need the program to repeat the section of wage calculation for each data record. You can use program loops to accomplish that task.

# DO WHILE . . . ENDDO

A *loop* is a section of a program that is to be repeated. The loop is enclosed between the DO WHILE and ENDDO commands:

DO WHILE <a condition>
    . . . <the program section to be repeated>
ENDDO

The condition following DO WHILE determines whether the program section in the loop is executed. If the condition is true, the program section is executed; otherwise, the program section is skipped, and execution proceeds from the program line following ENDDO. After the ENDDO command is encountered, execution returns to the DO WHILE statement, and the condition is evaluated again. If you are familiar with BASIC programming, you will see similarities between the DO WHILE . . . ENDDO loop and the FOR . . . NEXT loop. The conditional expression in the DO WHILE phrase can be one of the following:

A logical variable, such as

    DO WHILE MALE

The contents of a logical variable, such as

    DO WHILE .T.

An alphanumeric qualifier, such as

    DO WHILE ANSWER<>"QUIT"
    DO WHILE AREA_CODE="216"
    DO WHILE AREA_CODE="216" .OR. AREA_CODE="503"
    DO WHILE SUBSTR(MODEL,1,3)> "RCA" .AND. SUBSTR(DTOC(DATE),7,2)="84"

A numeric qualifier, such as

    DO WHILE KOUNT<=5
    DO WHILE ANNUAL_PAY>20000
    DO WHILE UNITS_SOLD<=3 .OR. UNITS_SOLD>=10
    DO WHILE UNITS_SOLD*UNITPRICE >= 10000

The end-of-file mark EOF( ), as in

    DO WHILE .NOT. EOF( )

# An Infinite Program Loop

The condition in the DO WHILE phrase determines whether the loop is repeated. The condition *.T.* creates an infinite program loop:

DO WHILE .T.

   . . .

   . . .

ENDDO

Because the condition must always be true, the loop will be repeat indefinitely unless you include a way to terminate the process. INFLOOPS.PRG shows an example of an infinite loop (see fig. 11.12).

```
*****    Program: INFLOOPS.PRG    *****
* An infinite program loop
SET TALK OFF
SET ECHO OFF
DO WHILE .T.
    ? "Hello !"
ENDDO
RETURN
```

*Fig. 11.12. Infinite program loop.*

When the program is executed, the phrase *Hello !* is displayed repeatedly. If you press Esc to stop the infinite loop, the following message is displayed:

```
Called from - B:INFLOOPS.prg
Terminate command file? (Y/N)
```

By answering *Y* to the question, you can exit the infinite loop and terminate the program. The output from the program is shown in figure 11.13.

A conditional branching operation can also be used to terminate an infinite loop. For example, LOOPEXIT.PRG shows how to use the contents of the memory variable ANSWER, which is entered with a WAIT command, to exit the loop (see fig. 11.14).

```
. DO INFLOOPS
Hello !
Hello !
Hello !
Hello !
Hello !
Hello !
Hello !
Hello !
Hello !
Hello !
Hello !
Hello !
Hello !
Hello !
Hello !
Hello !
Hello !
Called from - B:INFLOOPS.prg
Terminate command file? (Y/N) Yes
Do cancelled
.
```

Fig. 11.13. Output of infinite-loop program.

```
*****    Program: LOOPEXIT.PRG    *****
* An exit from the infinite program loop
SET TALK OFF
SET ECHO OFF
DO WHILE .T.
    ?
    ACCEPT "What is your name ? " TO NAME
    ?
    ? "Good morning! "+NAME
    ?
    WAIT "Do you want to continue (Y/N) ? " TO ANSWER
    IF UPPER(ANSWER)="Y"
       RETURN
    ENDIF
ENDDO
RETURN
```

Fig. 11.14. Using WAIT TO to exit infinite loop.

# WAIT TO

The WAIT TO command assigns a character string to a memory
variable. The form of the command is

. WAIT "<prompt>" TO <an alphanumeric variable>

This command stops the program until a key is pressed. The value of the character string is entered in the specified memory variable, as in

. WAIT "Do you want to continue (Y/N) ?" TO ANSWER

In LOOPEXIT.PRG, the variable ANSWER is used to determine whether the program loop is to continue. If the answer to the question is Y, then the conditional expression IF UPPER(ANSWER)=Y is true, and the RETURN command is executed. Otherwise, the program loop repeats until the value in ANSWER is Y. The results of the LOOPEXIT.PRG are shown in figure 11.15.

```
. DO LOOPEXIT

What is your name ? George

Good morning! George

Do you want to continue (Y/N) ? n

What is your name ? Jane

Good morning! Jane

Do you want to continue (Y/N) ? Y
```

*Fig. 11.15. Results of LOOPEXIT.PRG.*

# A Program Loop Counter

Another program loop can be designed so that it is repeated a specified number of times. A counter variable is used to record the number of passes through the loop the program makes. When the specified number is reached, the loop is exited. A program loop counter is shown in the program KLOOPS.PRG (see fig. 11.16). The counter variable used in the program is KOUNT (the word COUNT cannot be used as a variable name).

The counter variable KOUNT is initially set to 1. Because the condition in the DO WHILE phrase (KOUNT<=5) is true, the commands in the loop are processed:

?"Value of the Counter is ", KOUNT

```
*****  Program: KLOOPS.PRG   *****
* Control program loops with a counter variable
SET TALK OFF
SET ECHO OFF
* Initialize the counter, KCOUNT
* (Do not use "COUNT" as variable name, it is a reserved word)
KOUNT=1
DO WHILE KOUNT<=5
  ?"Value of the Counter is ", KOUNT
  * Increase the counter by 1
  KOUNT=KOUNT+1
ENDDO
RETURN
```

Fig. 11.16. Program using counter to control loops.

Each time the program section within the program loop is processed, the value in the counter variable is increased by 1:

KOUNT=KOUNT+1

As long as the value of KOUNT is less than or equal to 5, the program loop is repeated. When the value of KOUNT exceeds 5 and the condition in DO WHILE is no longer true, the program is terminated. As you can see, the program repeats the loop five times (see fig. 11.17).

```
. DO KLOOPS
Value of the Counter is        1
Value of the Counter is        2
Value of the Counter is        3
Value of the Counter is        4
Value of the Counter is        5
.
```

Fig. 11.17. Result of KLOOPS.PRG.

The following commands affect the number of passes made through the loop:

KOUNT=1
DO WHILE KOUNT <= 5
KOUNT=KOUNT+1

To alter the number of passes through the program loop, you can change one or more of these commands.

# EOF( )

A loop is an efficient way to process data records in a database file. The loop can be used to examine one data record at a time until the end of the file is reached. The program can be terminated when all the data records have been processed, using the system function EOF() as the condition in the DO WHILE phrase:

DO WHILE .NOT. EOF()

. . .

. . . <the program section to be repeated>

. . .

ENDDO

Like a logical variable, the EOF() function returns an .F. (false) logical state if the end-of-file mark has not been encountered in the database file. When the end-of-file mark is reached, EOF() returns a .T. logical state.

With a check for end of file in the DO WHILE phrase, the loop is repeated only if the end-of-file mark has not been found. Figure 11.18 illustrates how to use the EOF() function, using EMPLOYEE.DBF to create a phone list. (The SKIP command instructs the computer to go to the next data record after one record is processed.) The output produced by PHONLIST.PRG is shown in figure 11.19.

```
*****    Program: PHONLIST.PRG    *****
* Producing a phone list with a program loop
SET TALK OFF
SET ECHO OFF
* Select the database file
USE EMPLOYEE
?
? " Employee' Name          Telephone Number"
?
* The program loop ends when end of file is reached
DO WHILE .NOT. EOF()
  ?LAST_NAME,FIRST_NAME,AREA_CODE,PHONE_NO
  * Skip to next data record
  SKIP
ENDDO
RETURN
```

*Fig. 11.18. Program using EOF().*

```
. DO PHONLIST

Employee's Name               Telephone Number

Smith          James C.         206 123-4567
Zeller         Albert K.        212 457-9801
Gregory        Doris A.         503 204-8567
Nelson         Harry M.         315 576-0235
Baker          Tina B.          415 567-8967
Chapman        Kirk D.          618 625-7845
Thompson       Mary W.          213 432-6782
Duff           Charles N.       206 456-9873
Lee            Winston E.       503 365-8512
Hanson         Thomas T.        206 573-5085
.
```

Fig. 11.19. Output of PHONLIST.PRG.

The program PHONLIST.PRG displays all phone numbers in the
EMPLOYEE.DBF database file. The IF . . . ENDIF command can be
used to display a subset of the phone numbers. The program
LIST206.PRG in figure 11.20 shows an example, and the output
from the program is shown in figure 11.21.

```
***** Program: LIST206.PRG *****
* Listing phone numbers with area code of 206
SET TALK OFF
SET ECHO OFF
* Select the database file
USE EMPLOYEE
?
?
GO TOP
DO WHILE .NOT. EOF()
     IF AREA_CODE="206"
        ?LAST_NAME,FIRST_NAME,AREA_CODE,PHONE_NO
     ENDIF
     SKIP
ENDDO
RETURN
```

Fig. 11.20. Using IF . . . ENDIF with EOF().

```
.DO LIST206

Smith      James C.       206 123-4567
Duff       Charles N.     206 456-9873
Hanson     Thomas T.      206 573-5085
.
```

Fig. 11.21. Output from LIST206.PRG.

LIST206.PRG displays only the phone numbers with an area code of 206, but you can make the program more versatile by using a memory variable. The program BYARCODE.PRG shows how to enter the area code with an ACCEPT TO command (see fig. 11.22).

```
*****   Program: BYARCODE.PRG   *****
* Listing phone numbers by a given area code
SET TALK OFF
SET ECHO OFF
USE EMPLOYEE
* Get the area code to be searched
?
ACCEPT "Enter the area code to be searched:  " TO AREACODE
?
GO TOP
DO WHILE .NOT. EOF()
    IF AREA_CODE=AREACODE
        ?LAST_NAME,FIRST_NAME,AREA_CODE,PHONE_NO
    ENDIF
    SKIP
ENDDO
?
RETURN
```

*Fig. 11.22. Program using memory variable.*

In figure 11.23, BYARCODE.PRG is executed three times. A different searching area code is entered each time.

```
. DO BYARCODE

Enter the area code to be searched: 206

Smith     James C.        206 123-4567
Duff      Charles N.      206 456-9873
Hanson    Thomas T.       206 573-5085

. DO BYARCODE

Enter the area code to be searched: 503

Gregory   Doris A.        503 204-8567
Lee       Winston E.      503 365-8512

. DO BYARCODE

Enter the area code to be searched: 415

Baker     Tina B.         415 567-8967

.
```

*Fig. 11.23. Using BYARCODE with different variables.*

LIST216.PRG and BYARCODE.PRG search every data record and select only those that satisfy the IF condition. The approach is acceptable, but searching each data record can use valuable time when a large set of data records is involved. If you index your database file before using the search operation, you will save a considerable amount of time.

The program in figure 11.24 first indexes the data records by area code so that records with the same area codes are grouped together. To display all phone numbers with a given area code, such as 216, you simply place the record pointer at the beginning of the group. Then the data records in that group are displayed until a different area code is encountered. The SEEK command places the record pointer at the beginning of the 216 group. The results of SORTFONE.PRG are shown in figure 11.25.

```
***** Program: SORTFONE.PRG *****
* Sort and list phone numbers with area code of 206
SET TALK OFF
SET ECHO OFF
USE EMPLOYEE
* Sort by area code
INDEX ON AREA_CODE TO SORTFONE
* Find the first "206" area code
SEEK "206"
DO WHILE AREA_CODE="206"
   ?LAST_NAME,FIRST_NAME,AREA_CODE,PHONE_NO
   * Skip to next data record
   SKIP
ENDDO
RETURN
```

*Fig. 11.24. Program using SEEK.*

```
. DO SORTFONE
Smith      James C.      206 123-4567
Duff       Charles N.    206 456-9873
Hanson     Thomas T.     206 573-5085
.
```

*Fig. 11.25. Results of SORTFONE.*

The file SORTFONE.PRG is a target file for the indexing operation. The file will be created whenever you invoke the index command, as in

. INDEX ON AREA_CODE TO SORTFONE

If a file named SORTFONE.NDX has been created by a previous run of the program, the following warning message is displayed when the command is executed:

`SORTFONE. NDX already exists, overwrite it? (Y/N)`

When this happens, enter *Y*. To avoid a warning message, you can erase the old SORTFONE.NDX before you start the indexing operation. You can add the following command line to the program before the INDEX command line:

```
. . .
ERASE SORTFONE.NDX
INDEX ON AREA_CODE TO SORTFONE
. . .
```

However, if your program contains the ERASE SORTFONE.NDX command, the first time you execute the program, you may get another warning message:

`File does not exist`

The message is only a warning that the index file SORTFONE.NDX has not been created.

# Skipping Part of a Program Loop

An IF condition can be used to exit the loop in LOOPEXIT.PRG (refer to fig. 11.14):

```
DO WHILE .T.
    . . .
    . . .
   IF UPPER(ANSWER)="Y"
       RETURN
   ENDIF
ENDDO
```

When the condition in the IF command is true, the program loop is exited.

At times, you need to skip part of a program loop and "jump back" to the beginning. Suppose that you want to display all the phone numbers with an area code of 216, except for the employee with the last name of Smith. You can do this with a LOOP command.

# LOOP

The LOOP command transfers execution to the beginning of the DO WHILE . . . ENDDO structure. When the command is encountered within a program loop section, execution returns to the beginning of the DO WHILE . . . ENDDO structure; the rest of the program loop commands are ignored. For example, when the following LOOP command is executed, processing skips to the next data record and begins another pass through the program loop:

```
DO WHILE AREA_CODE="216"
    IF LAST_NAME="Smith"
        SKIP
        LOOP
    ELSE
        ?LAST_NAME,FIRST_NAME,AREA_CODE,PHONE_NO
    ENDIF
ENDDO
```

The SKIPLOOP.PRG program is shown in figure 11.26. The output from the program is displayed in figure 11.27.

```
***** Program: SKIPLOOP.PRG *****
* Sort and list phone numbers with area code of 206
SET TALK OFF
SET ECHO OFF
USE EMPLOYEE
* Sort by area code
INDEX ON AREA_CODE TO SORTFONE
* Find the first "206" area code
SEEK "206"
DO WHILE AREA_CODE="206"
    IF LAST_NAME="Smith"
        SKIP
        LOOP
    ELSE
        ?LAST_NAME,FIRST_NAME,AREA_CODE,PHONE_NO
        SKIP
    ENDIF
ENDDO
RETURN
```

Fig. 11.26. Program using SKIP.

```
.DO SKIPLOOP
SOFTFONE.ndx already exists, overwrite it? (Y/N) Yes
Duff        Charles N.     206 456-9873
Hanson      Thomas T.      206 573-5085
.
```

*Fig. 11.27. Results of SKIPLOOP.PRG.*

# EXIT

The EXIT command is used to abort the looping process; execution continues with the command line following the ENDDO line. The BYELOOP.PRG program is an example of the EXIT command (see fig. 11.28). The results of BYELOOP.PRG can be seen in figure 11.29. The output shows that EXIT stops the loop, but not the program.

```
*****    Program: BYELOOP.PRG    *****
* An exit from the infinite program loop
SET TALK OFF
SET ECHO OFF
DO WHILE .T.
    ?
    ACCEPT "What is your name ? " TO NAME
    ?
    ? "Good morninig ! "+NAME
    ?
    WAIT "Do you want to continue (Y/N) ? " TO ANSWER
    IF UPPER(ANSWER)="Y"
        EXIT
    ENDIF
ENDDO
?
? "Goodbye, "+NAME+" !"
RETURN
```

*Fig. 11.28. Using EXIT to end program loop.*

```
. DO BYELOOP

What is your name ? George

Good morninig ! George

Do you want to continue (Y/N) ? y

Goodbye, George !

.
```

*Fig. 11.29. Results of BYELOOP.PRG.*

# Nested Loops

The BYARCODE.PRG program lists phone numbers by area code, processing only one record at a time. The program is inefficient because it has to be executed again whenever you need to process a new area code. To repeat the program several times, you can put the original program segment in a loop. The original program already has a DO WHILE. . . ENDDO loop, so the extended program will have two program loops, one within the other. The diagram in figure 11.30 shows this structure, which is called a *nested loop*.

```
DO WHILE <condition 1>
   ...
   ...
   DO WHILE <condition 2>
     ...
     ...
     ...
   ENDDO
   ...
   ...
ENDDO
```

*Fig. 11.30. Nested loop design.*

To understand how nested loops work, you can modify the program by adding an outside program loop (see fig. 11.31).

The output of the program is shown in figure 11.32. As you can see, the program will process area codes until the word *END* (not *End* or *end*) is entered. END is used as the terminator for the outside program loop. When END is entered in the variable AREACODE, the program exits the program loop.

The example in NESTLOOP.PRG shows the simplest form of a nested loop. For more sophisticated applications, you may need nested loops several levels deep. The maximum number of levels allowed by dBASE III Plus is not stated in the manual, but you should be able to use four or five levels of nested loops without any problem. Five levels of nested loops would be sufficient to handle most database management applications. Figure 11.33 shows the structure of multiple-level nested loops.

```
*****    Program: NESTLOOP.PRG    *****
* An example of a nested loop
SET TALK OFF
SET ECHO OFF
USE EMPLOYEE
* This is the outer loop
DO WHILE .T.
    ?
    ?
    ACCEPT "Enter the area code to be searched (END to quit): " TO AREACODE
    IF AREACODE="END"
      EXIT
    ENDIF
    ?
    GO TOP
    * This is the inner loop
    DO WHILE .NOT. EOF()
      IF AREA_CODE=AREACODE
         ?LAST_NAME,FIRST_NAME,AREA_CODE,PHONE_NO
      ENDIF
      SKIP
    ENDDO
ENDDO
RETURN
```

Fig. 11.31. Program using nested loops.

```
. DO NESTLOOP

Enter the area code to be searched (END to quit): 206

Smith       James C.      206 123-4567
Duff        Charles N.    206 456-9873
Hanson      Thomas T.     206 573-5985

Enter the area code to be searched (END to quit): 503

Gregory     Doris A.      503 204-8567
Lee         Winston E.    503 365-8512

Enter the area code to be searched (END to quit): END
.
```

Fig. 11.32. Output of NESTLOOP.PRG.

Each loop must be enclosed between DO WHILE and ENDDO commands, and an ENDDO phrase must terminate each DO WHILE phrase. If a phrase is missing, the loops do not work correctly and produce erroneous results.

```
DO WHILE <condition 1>
   ...
   ...
   DO WHILE <condition 2>
      ...
      ...
      DO WHILE <condition 3>
         ...
         ...
      ENDDO
      ...
      ...
      DO WHILE <condition 4>
         ...
         ...
         DO WHILE <condition 5>
            ...
            ...
         ENDDO
         ...
      ENDDO
      ...
   ENDDO
   ...
   ...
   DO WHILE <condition 6>
      ...
   ENDDO
   ...
ENDDO
```

*Fig. 11.33. Multiple-level nested loops.*

# Chapter Summary

This chapter has introduced two of the most powerful programming features of dBASE III. With conditional branching, you can change the normal processing path according to specified conditions. Conditional branching operations use the IF . . . ENDIF and DO CASE . . . ENDCASE procedures. With the ELSE and OTHERWISE options, you can meet any data condition and direct the program any way you choose.

Program loops repeat a portion of a program until an EXIT condition is met. By setting up a counter variable within a program loop, you can control the number of passes the program makes. This chapter also introduced the nested loop structure for repetitive processing that is required by many database management applications.

The next chapter explains the important role that conditional branching and program loops play in modular programming and menu design.

# 12

Modular Programming

## An Overview

Modular programming entails designing your database management program around several small subprograms or procedures. Modules are generally small and easy to create. After being tested, the modules can be linked together to form a complete system. When a new application arises, you can reorganize the appropriate program modules to create another database management system.

Because this program structure uses various modules to perform data management tasks, you will learn different ways to pass information between modules. Memory variables often are used for that purpose. The dBASE III Plus commands used to control memory variables, PUBLIC and PRIVATE, are explained in this chapter. This chapter explains also how to maintain several database files at the same time and how to join the files together with the SELECT, UPDATE, and APPEND FROM commands. With a few simple dBASE III Plus commands, you can even design a graphics program to display diagrams.

# Designing Program Modules

As you have seen, using dBASE III Plus is not difficult. The small example programs presented in previous chapters can form the base of a more sophisticated database management system. Although a real database management program may be large and complicated, you will see the advantages in structuring the system in simple program modules.

A small program module is easy to create. After each module is designed, you can test it for errors in syntax and logic before linking the modules together to form a complete system.

With modular programming, you can easily reorganize the program modules whenever necessary. Reorganizing a modular system involves modifying only some of the program modules and is often a simple task. Because a program file cannot exceed 4,096 characters (4K bytes), modular programming often is necessary to keep your file size within memory limitations.

Figure 12.1 shows a program with three modules. Each program module is an individual procedure or program file (.PRG), such as PROGA.PRG, PROGB.PRG, and PROGC.PRG.

```
*****    Program: MAINPROG.PRG    *****
* This the main program
...
...
* Go do module A
   DO PROGA
   * Return from module A
...
...
* Go do module B
   DO PROGB
   * Return from module B
...
...
* Go do module C
   DO PROGC
   * Return from module C
...
...

RETURN
```

*Fig. 12.1. Modular program structure.*

Each module is a program file that ends with a RETURN command, which transfers execution back to the main program:

\*\*\*\*\*     Program: PROGA.PRG    \*\*\*\*\*
\* A program module

   . . .

   . . .

   . . .

RETURN

When MAINPROG.PRG is executed and the command DO PROGA is encountered, execution transfers to the module PROGA. After PROGA.PRG is processed, the RETURN command in the module returns program control to the main program. Then execution continues with the command line following DO PROGA in the main program.

To understand how execution passes from the main program to the program module, you can examine program MAINPROG.PRG (see fig. 12.2). The program modules PROGA.PRG (fig. 12.3) and PROGB.PRG (fig. 12.4) are also shown.

```
*****     Program: MAINPROG.PRG    *****
* The main program
?"***   We are now in the Main Program !"
* Go to PROGA.PRG
  DO PROGA
  ?
  ?"We have returned from PROGA.PRG !"
?
* Go to PROGB.PRG
  DO PROGB
  ?
  ?"We have returned from PROGB.PRG !"
RETURN
```

Fig. 12.2. Main program module.

```
*****   Program: PROGA.PRG    *****
* Program Module A
SET TALK OFF
SET ECHO OFF
?
?"             We have entered PROGA.PRG !"
* Return to main program
RETURN
```

Fig. 12.3. Program module A.

```
*****    Program: PROGB.PRG    *****
* Program Module B
?
?"            We have entered PROGB.PRG !"
* Return to main program
RETURN
```

*Fig. 12.4. Program module B.*

The output of MAINPROG.PRG (fig. 12.5) shows that execution passes from the main program to the modules and back again. When the command DO PROGA is encountered, execution transfers to the module PROGA.PRG. At RETURN, the execution returns to the main program, proceeding with the line immediately following the DO PROGA command line.

```
. DO MAINPROG
***  We are now in the Main Program !

        We have entered PROGA.PRG !

We have returned from PROGA.PRG !


        We have entered PROGB.PRG !

We have returned from PROGB.PRG !
.
```

*Fig. 12.5. Output of modular program.*

The structures you have seen are two-level modular designs. In other words, you saw execution change from the first level (main program) to the second level (PROGA.PRG or PROGB.PRG) and then back to the main program. If necessary, you can increase the number of levels to accommodate more sophisticated database management applications. For example, the structure in figure 12.6 shows a three-level module design.

In a multilevel modular design, the first level (main program) is the highest level. The program modules are numbered sequentially from the upper to lower levels. When execution transfers to a lower-level module from a higher-level module, the execution starts at the first program line of the lower-level module. (Transferring execution to a lower-level module is sometimes termed *calling* the module.) When the RETURN command is executed, control returns to the higher-level module. Figure 12.6 shows that when RETURN is

```
* Structure of main program (This is not an actual program)
...
...
DO PROGX
   <-----------     * Module PROGX.PRG
...                 ...
...                 ...
...                 DO PROGY
...                    <-----------     * Module PROGY.PRG
...                 ...                 ...
RETURN              ...                 ...
                    ...                 RETURN
                    RETURN
```

Fig. 12.6. Linking multiple program modules.

encountered in PROGZ.PRG, execution returns to PROGY.PRG, from which PROGZ.PRG was called.

# Passing Memory Variables between Program Modules

As you have seen, you can pass program control easily, using DO and RETURN. However, special instructions are required to pass memory-variable data from one program module to another. With dBASE III Plus, you can pass only higher-level module data to lower-level modules. The programs in figures 12.7 through 12.9 show how variable data elements are transferred among different program modules.

```
*****     Program: MAIN.PRG*****
* The main program
SET TALK OFF
SET ECHO OFF
?
INPUT "Enter Value of A ...   " TO A
INPUT "       Value of B ...   " TO B
?
? "In Main Program:"
? "A=",A
? "B=",B
* Go to ADDAB.PRG
DO SUMA&B
?
? "We have returned to MAIN.PRG from SUMA&B.prg !"
RETURN
```

Fig. 12.7. Main program using memory variables.

```
*****     Program: SUMA&B.PRG     *****
* Program module to add A and B
?
?"          We have entered SUMA&B.PRG !"
* Do not use the reserved word SUM for the variable name!
SUMAB=A+B
? "                         A = ",A
? "                         B = ",B
? "               SUM OF A, B = ",SUMAB
* Go to PRINTA&B.prg
DO PRINTA&B
?
?"          We have returned to SUMA&B.prg from PRINTA&B.prg !"
* Return to main program
RETURN
```

Fig. 12.8. Module using memory variable data.

```
*****   Program: PRINTA&B.PRG   *****
* Module to print results from SUMA&B.prg
?
? "                              We have entered PRINTA&B.PRG !"
? "                                               A = ",A
? "                                               B = ",B
? "                                     SUM OF A, B = ",SUMAB
* Return to SUMA&B.prg
RETURN
```

Fig. 12.9. Module to print data.

```
. DO MAIN

Enter Value of A ...   123
      Value of B ...   456

In Main Program:
A=        123
B=        456

          We have entered SUMA&B.PRG !
                         A =         123
                         B =         456
               SUM OF A, B =         579

                              We have entered PRINTA&B.PRG !
                                               A =         123
                                               B =         456
                                     SUM OF A, B =         579

          We have returned to SUMA&B.prg from PRINTA&B.prg !

We have returned to MAIN.PRG from SUMA&B.prg !

.
```

Fig. 12.10. Output of main program.

When you execute the main program in figure 12.7, you see the output shown in figure 12.10.

Variables A and B are created in the main program and then passed to the second-level module SUMA&B.PRG. The variable SUMAB is created in the second level and passed to the third-level module PRINTA&B.PRG. This passing of variables occurs automatically, and the values in the variables are available to the lower-level modules.

However, data elements created in lower-level modules are not automatically passed to higher-level modules. The problem is illustrated in the main program MAINPAY.PRG (fig. 12.11) and in the program module CALCWAGE.PRG (fig. 12.12). The output of MAINPAY.PRG is shown in figure 12.13.

```
*****    Program: MAINPAY.PRG    *****
* Main program to compute weekly gross pay
SET TALK OFF
SET ECHO OFF
* Get worker's name
?
ACCEPT "     Enter Worker's First Name .... " TO FIRSTNAME
ACCEPT "                   Last Name ..... " TO LASTNAME
USE WAGES
LOCATE FOR LAST_NAME=LASTNAME .AND. FIRST_NAME=FIRSTNAME
* Call out CALWAGE.prg for computing wage
DO CALWAGE
* Display results returned from CALWAGE.prg
?
? "     Worker's Name : "+TRIM(FIRST_NAME)+" "+TRIM(LAST_NAME)
?
? "          Hours Worked ........ "+STR(HOURS,7,0)
? "          Hourly Wage Rate .... "+STR(RATE,7,2)
? "          Regular Pay ......... "+STR(REGULARPAY,7,2)
? "          Overtime Pay ........ "+STR(OVERTIME,7,2)
? "          Total Gross Pay ..... "+STR(REGULARPAY+OVERTIME,7,2)
?
RETURN
```

Fig. 12.11. Program module MAINPAY.PRG.

```
*****    Program: CALWAGE.PRG    *****
* Module calculate GROSSWAGE with given HOURS, PAYRATE
IF HOURS<=40
  REGULARPAY=HOURS*RATE
  OVERTIME=0
ELSE
  REGULARPAY=40*RATE
  OVERTIME=(HOURS-40)*RATE*1.5
ENDIF
RETURN
```

Fig. 12.12. Program module CALWAGE.PRG.

```
. DO MAINPAY

    Enter Worker's First Name .... Albert
                  Last Name ..... Williams


    Worker's Name : Albert L. Williams

            Hours Worked ........        43
            Hourly Wage Rate ....     8.50
Variable not found
                                                        ?
? "              Regular Pay ......... "+STR(REGULARPAY,7,2)
Called from - B:MAINPAY.prg
Terminate command file? (Y/N)
```

Fig. 12.13. Output of MAINPAY.PRG.

The value in the variable REGULARPAY is not available to the main program, and an error message is displayed:

**Variable not found**

REGULARPAY is available only to CALWAGE.PRG, the module in which the variable was created. To ensure that higher-level modules can share data created in lower-level modules, you declare the variables PUBLIC.

# PUBLIC

The PUBLIC command controls which memory variables can be accessed from any program module at any level. The names of the memory variables are entered in the PUBLIC command line, as in

PUBLIC <memory variable list>

To solve the problem demonstrated in figure 12.13, for example, you can add the following command line to pass the variables back and forth between the main program and the lower-level module:

PUBLIC REGULARPAY,OVERTIME

This line has been entered in PUBLIC.PRG (fig. 12.14), which otherwise is the same as MAINPAY.PRG.

When you run PUBLIC.PRG, you see the results shown in figure 12.15. The contents of the public variables REGULARPAY and OVERTIME have been returned to the main program.

```
*****    PROGRAM: PUBLIC.PRG    *****
* Main program to compute weekly gross pay
SET TALK OFF
SET ECHO OFF
* Declare all public variables
PUBLIC REGULARPAY,OVERTIME
* Get worker's name
?
ACCEPT "    Enter Worker's First Name .... " TO FIRSTNAME
ACCEPT "                   Last Name ..... " TO LASTNAME
USE WAGES
LOCATE FOR LAST_NAME=LASTNAME.AND.FIRST_NAME=FIRSTNAME
* Call out CALWAGE.prg for computing wage
DO CALWAGE
* Display results returned from CALWAGE.prg
?
? "    Worker's Name : "+TRIM(FIRST_NAME)+" "+TRIM(LAST_NAME)
?
? "         Hours Worked ........ "+STR(HOURS,7,0)
? "         Hourly Wage Rate .... "+STR(RATE,7,2)
? "         Regular Pay ......... "+STR(REGULARPAY,7,2)
? "         Overtime Pay ........ "+STR(OVERTIME,7,2)
? "         Total Gross Pay ..... "+STR(REGULARPAY+OVERTIME,7,2)
?
RETURN
```

Fig. 12.14. Program using PUBLIC variables.

```
. DO PUBLIC

    Enter Worker's First Name .... Albert
                   Last Name ..... Williams

    Worker's Name : Albert L. Williams

             Hours Worked ........      43
             Hourly Wage Rate ....    8.50
             Regular Pay .........  340.00
             Overtime Pay ........   38.25
             Total Gross Pay .....  378.25

    .
```

Fig. 12.15. Results of PUBLIC.PRG.

PUBLIC memory variables can be created at any level and can be used throughout the whole program structure. Memory variables can also be designated as PRIVATE so that the variables are recognized only within the module that creates them.

# PRIVATE

With the PRIVATE command, you can use memory variables with
the same names as variables in other levels. But when execution
passes from a program module using a PRIVATE variable to a higher-
level module using a variable with the same name, the variable
assumes the value that it has within the higher-level module. A
PRIVATE command can be written as

    PRIVATE ALL
    PRIVATE <memory variable list>
    PRIVATE ALL LIKE <memory variable description>
    PRIVATE ALL EXCEPT <memory variable description>

Examples of PRIVATE are

    PRIVATE ALL
    PRIVATE REGULARPAY,OVERTIME
    PRIVATE ALL LIKE *NET
    PRIVATE ALL EXCEPT NET?????

In a PRIVATE command, you can use an asterisk (*) or a question
mark (?) to mask the "skeleton" for describing private variables. (To
review masking a memory variable, see Chapter 7.)

Private variables are illustrated in the programs FIRST.PRG (fig.
12.16) and SUBPROG.PRG (fig. 12.17). The results of these
programs are shown in figure 12.18.

The variables A and STRING, created by FIRST.PRG, are declared
PRIVATE in the module SUBPROG.PRG. The variables are then
used as new variables in the program module SUBPROG.PRG, and
different values are assigned to each. However, when you leave the

```
*****    Program: FIRST.PRG    *****
A=123
STRING="A Test String"
?
?" Before entering SUBPROG.prg: "
?"           A = ",A
?"      STRING = ",STRING
DO SUBPROG
?
?" After returning from SUBPROG.prg"
?"           A = ",A
?"      STRING = ",STRING
RETURN
```

Fig. 12.16. Program demonstrating PRIVATE variables.

```
******      Program: SUBPROG.PRG    *****
* Hide those variables created by FIRST.PRG
PRIVATE A,STRING
?
?"                    We have entered SUBPROG.PRG !"
A=999
STRING="We have changed!"
?"                            A = ",A
?"                       STRING = ",STRING
RETURN
```

*Fig. 12.17. Module with PRIVATE variables.*

```
. DO FIRST

  Before entering SUBPROG.prg:
          A =           123
     STRING =   A Test String

              We have entered SUBPROG.PRG !
                        A =            999
                   STRING =   We have changed!

  After returning from SUBPROG.prg
          A =           123
     STRING =   A Test String
  .
```

*Fig. 12.18. Results of FIRST.PRG.*

program module and return to the main program, the variables lose
their PRIVATE status and resume their previous values.

The status of a memory variable can be changed at any time. If you
wish to change a public variable to a private variable, or a private
variable to a public variable, you need only to use the appropriate
commands.

# Passing Data Records between Program Modules

Unlike memory variables, data records are considered public and can
be shared by every module in the program structure. You can USE a
database file in a program module and retain the data-record position
throughout the program structure.

In the program MAINGET.PRG (fig. 12.19), the module
GETFILE.PRG (fig. 12.20) accesses the database file
EMPLOYEE.DBF. That module calls another module,
GETRECRD.PRG (fig. 12.21), which positions the record pointer at
the fifth data record. The output of these program modules is shown
in figure 12.22.

```
*****    Program: MAINGET.PRG    *****
* The main program to get records
SET TALK OFF
SET ECHO OFF
* Go to get a file from GETFILE.prg module
DO GETFILE
* Display the record returned from GETRECRD.prg
?
? "Data record retrieved from GETFILE.Prg and GETRECRD.prg"
?
DISPLAY
* Look at the next data record
SKIP
?
? "Returned from GETFILE.prg!"
?
DISPLAY
RETURN
```

Fig. 12.19. Main program using modules.

```
*****    Program: GETFILE.PRG    *****
* Open a database file
USE EMPLOYEE
RECORDNO=5
* Go to get No.5 data record
DO GETRECRD
* Return to main program
RETURN
```

Fig. 12.20. Program module GETFILE.PRG.

```
*****    Program: GETRECRD.PRG    *****
* Set the record pointer at record no. RECORDNO set by GETFILE.prg
GOTO RECORDNO
RETURN
```

Fig. 12.21. Program module GETRECRD.PRG.

```
. DO MAINGET

Data record retrieved via GETFILE.Prg and GETRECRD.prg

Record#   FIRST_NAME    LAST_NAME    AREA_CODE  PHONE_NO  MALE  BIRTH_DATE  ANNUAL_PAY
      5   Kirk D.       Chapman      618        625-7845  .T.   08/04/61      20737.50

Returned from GETFILE.prg!

Record#   FIRST_NAME    LAST_NAME    AREA_CODE  PHONE_NO  MALE  BIRTH_DATE  ANNUAL_PAY
      6   Mary W.       Thompson     213        432-6782  .F.   06/18/55      25725.00
.
```

*Fig. 12.22. Output of MAINGET.PRG.*

When execution returns to the main program after the modules GETFILE.PRG and GETRECRD.PRG are called, the record pointer is still positioned at data record 5. The fields of the data record can be accessed by any module or the main program.

# A Graphics Program Module

The programming tools of dBASE III Plus can also be used to generate graphics output. To develop a program module to produce a bar chart, you need to set up a database file containing the necessary data elements. Figure 12.23 shows the structure of the database file BARCHART.DBF.

```
. USE BARCHART
. DISPLAY STRUCTURE
Structure for database : B:BARCHART.dbf
Number of data records :      5
Date of last update    : 03/25/85
Field   Field name   Type        Width     Dec
    1    CLASSCOUNT   Numeric        2
    2    CLASSLABEL   Character     20
** Total **                        23

. LIST ALL
Record#   CLASSCOUNT  CLASSLABEL
      1         30    GROUP A
      2         25    GROUP B
      3         55    GROUP C
      4         45    GROUP D
      5         20    GROUP E
.
```

*Fig. 12.23. Structure and contents of BARCHART.DBF.*

The database file contains five data records, each of which contains the class frequency (CLASSCOUNT) and a class description (CLASSLABEL). A bar chart of the class frequencies might look like the diagram shown in figure 12.24.

```
I
IXXXXXXXXXXXXXXXXXXXXXXXXXXXXXX
IXXXXXXXXXXXXXXXXXXXXXXXXXXXXXX     GROUP A (30)
IXXXXXXXXXXXXXXXXXXXXXXXXXXXXXX
I
IXXXXXXXXXXXXXXXXXXXXXXXXX
IXXXXXXXXXXXXXXXXXXXXXXXXX       GROUP B (25)
IXXXXXXXXXXXXXXXXXXXXXXXXX
I
IXXXXXXXXXXXXXXXXXXXXXXXXXXXXXXXXXXXXXXXXXXXXXXXXXXXXXXXX
IXXXXXXXXXXXXXXXXXXXXXXXXXXXXXXXXXXXXXXXXXXXXXXXXXXXXXXXX     GROUP C (55)
IXXXXXXXXXXXXXXXXXXXXXXXXXXXXXXXXXXXXXXXXXXXXXXXXXXXXXXXX
I
IXXXXXXXXXXXXXXXXXXXXXXXXXXXXXXXXXXXXXXXXXXXXXXX
IXXXXXXXXXXXXXXXXXXXXXXXXXXXXXXXXXXXXXXXXXXXXXXX     GROUP D (45)
IXXXXXXXXXXXXXXXXXXXXXXXXXXXXXXXXXXXXXXXXXXXXXXX
I
IXXXXXXXXXXXXXXXXXXXX
IXXXXXXXXXXXXXXXXXXXX       GROUP E (20)
IXXXXXXXXXXXXXXXXXXXX

                    THIS IS A SAMPLE BAR CHART
```

Fig. 12.24. Sample bar chart.

Each wide bar in the diagram represents a frequency class. The width of a horizontal bar is determined by the class frequency. The bar is formed from the character *X*, which is used as a graphics symbol. The module PRINTBAR.PRG displays a horizontal bar whose length is controlled by the value of the variable NCHARS (see fig. 12.25).

The length of the horizontal bar is determined by the class frequency. A DO WHILE . . . ENDDO loop is used to build the bar by assigning a variable (NCHARS) number of graphics symbols to BAR. After the value has been assigned to BAR, the bar is displayed three times to form a wider diagram. A class description or label, such as *GROUP A(30)*, also is displayed.

Each time the module PRINTBAR.PRG is called, a wide horizontal bar is displayed. You can set up a loop in the program BARCHART.PRG to retrieve the data records from BARCHART.DBF and use the PRINTBAR.PRG module to produce a horizontal bar (see fig. 12.26). The values in the variables NCHARS and ALABEL are passed to the module.

```
*****    Program: PRINTBAR.PRG    *****
* Module to print a bar with NCHARS characters long
KOUNT=1
* Use a given ASCII character for a graphic symbol
GRAFSYMBOL="X"
* Set the first character of BAR to the graphic symbol
BAR=GRAFSYMBOL
* Build the bar with graphic symbols
DO WHILE KOUNT<=(NCHARS-1)
BAR=BAR+GRAFSYMBOL
KOUNT=KOUNT+1
ENDDO
* Display the bar
?SPACE(3)+"I"
?SPACE(3)+"I"+BAR
?SPACE(3)+"I"+BAR+SPACE(3)+TRIM(ALABEL)+"  ("+STR(KOUNT,2,0)+")"
?SPACE(3)+"I"+BAR
RETURN
```

Fig. 12.25. Module for creating bars.

```
*****    Program: BARCHART.PRG    *****
* A program to show a bar chart by using data from BARCHART.DBF
SET TALK OFF
SET ECHO OFF
CLEAR
USE BARCHART.DBF
DO WHILE .NOT. EOF()
* Get class count and class description
NCHARS=CLASSCOUNT
ALABEL=CLASSLABEL
DO PRINTBAR
SKIP
ENDDO
?
?"                        THIS IS A SAMPLE BAR CHART"
RETURN
```

Fig. 12.26. Program using BARCHART.DBF to display a bar chart.

To print the bar chart, insert the command SET PRINT ON in BARCHART.PRG before the call to PRINTBAR.PRG. After printing, you can deactivate the printer by inserting the SET PRINT OFF command before the RETURN line.

In figure 12.24, X was used as the graphics symbol to form the horizontal bar. You can use other characters to produce different horizontal bars (see fig. 12.27).

The bar chart was produced by printing repeatedly one of the ASCII graphics characters available on the IBM PC. Some other ASCII

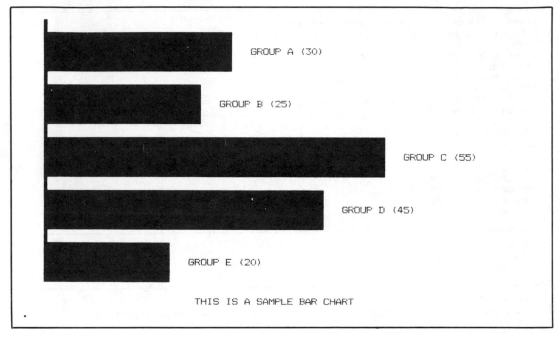

*Fig. 12.27. Bar chart using graphics characters.*

graphics characters used by the IBM PC are shown in figure 12.28. For a listing of the ASCII characters, see Appendix A.

To produce the bar chart shown in figure 12.27, use ASCII character 219 in place of *X* and ASCII character 222 in place of I (the vertical axis). Figure 12.29 shows the FANCYBAR.PRG program module. The main program DOFANCY.PRG, which calls the FANCYBAR.PRG module, is shown in figure 12.30.

Using ASCII character 222 as both the graphics symbol and the vertical axis results in a different bar design (see fig. 12.31).

If you enter the graphics programs, you can reproduce the results on your IBM monochrome or "generic" graphics monitor. However, to print these bar charts, your printer must have special graphics capabilities. (If you are unsure whether your printer has these capabilities, check your printer manual.) Figures 12.29 and 12.30 were generated on an Epson printer by means of special screen-print software.

```
. TYPE GRAFCHAR.PRG
*****   Program: GRAFCHAR.PRG   *****
* Display some ASCII graphic characters
SET TALK OFF
SET ECHO OFF
?
?
?"     Some Useful ASCII Graphic Characters Supported by an IBM PC"
CHARNO=219
?
?
DO WHILE CHARNO<=223
?"           ASCII Character No. "+STR(CHARNO,3,0)+": "+CHR(CHARNO)
?
CHARNO=CHARNO+1
ENDDO
RETURN

.



. DO GRAFCHAR


     Some Useful ASCII Graphic Characters Supported by an IBM PC


               ASCII Character No. 219: █

               ASCII Character No. 220: ▄

               ASCII Character No. 221: ▌

               ASCII Character No. 222: ▐

               ASCII Character No. 223: ▀

.
```

Fig. 12.28. ASCII graphics characters.

```
*****     Program: FANCYBAR.PRG     *****
* Module to print a bar with NCHARS characters long
KOUNT=1
* Use a given ASCII character for a graphic symbol
GRAFSYMBOL=CHR(219)
* Set the first character of BAR to the graphic symbol
BAR=GRAFSYMBOL
* Build the bar with graphic symbols
DO WHILE KOUNT<=(NCHARS-1)
BAR=BAR+GRAFSYMBOL
KOUNT=KOUNT+1
ENDDO
* Display the bar
?SPACE(3)+CHR(222)
?SPACE(3)+CHR(222)+BAR
?SPACE(3)+CHR(222)+BAR+SPACE(3)+TRIM(ALABEL)+" ("+STR(KOUNT,2,0)+")"
?SPACE(3)+CHR(222)+BAR
RETURN
```

Fig. 12.29. Program module FANCYBAR.PRG.

```
*****     Program: DOFANCY.PRG     *****
* A program to show a bar chart by using data from BARCHART.DBF
SET TALK OFF
SET ECHO OFF
CLEAR
USE BARCHART.DBF
DO WHILE .NOT. EOF()
* Get class count and class description
NCHARS=CLASSCOUNT
ALABEL=CLASSLABEL
DO FANCYBAR
SKIP
ENDDO
?
?"                         THIS IS A SAMPLE BAR CHART"
RETURN
```

Fig. 12.30. Main program DOFANCY.PRG.

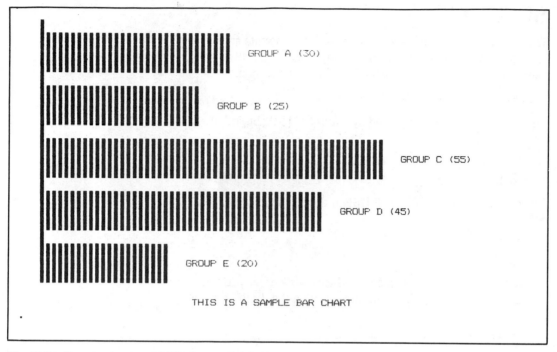

*Fig. 12.31. Bar chart using ASCII character 222.*

# Accessing Multiple Database Files

Up to this point, you have used only one database file at a time, and the record pointer has been positioned at the current active record. You have been able to access the current data record at any time, in any program module, and at any level.

However, if you open another database file with the USE command, the current active database file is replaced, and the data record pointer is repositioned. As a result, you cannot return to a data record of the original database file. This can be a serious problem if you need to access more than one database file at one time. To solve this problem, use the SELECT command.

# SELECT

The SELECT command is used to choose a database file and store it in an active work area. dBASE III Plus supports the use of up to 10 different work areas. The format of the SELECT command is

. SELECT <work area>

The work area can be designated by a number (1 through 10), or a letter (A through J), such as

. SELECT 1
. SELECT A

For instance, to put EMPLOYEE.DBF in the first work area, you enter

. SELECT 1
. USE EMPLOYEE

When a database file has been assigned to a work area, you can activate the file with SELECT without entering the database name, as in

. SELECT 1

Although you can use 10 different work areas, only one database file is active at a time. The last database file you used with the SELECT command is the active file, and the other files remain in the background work area. You can bring another file to the foreground by again using SELECT. When you call up another file, the record pointer of the previous database file marks the current data record location in that file. When the previous file is brought back to the foreground, the data record marked is still the active data record for that database file. In figure 12.32, the program GETFILES.PRG alternates between the EMPLOYEE.DBF and QTYSOLD.DBF databases.

The output from the program is shown in figure 12.33. As you can see, the record pointers have remained intact.

```
*****    Program: GETFILES.PRG    *****
* Accessing different database files in the same program
SET TALK OFF
SET ECHO OFF
* Put EMPLOYEE.dbf in work area 1
SELECT 1
USE EMPLOYEE
GOTO 5
DISPLAY
* Put QTYSOLD.dbf in work area 2
SELECT 2
USE QTYSOLD
DISPLAY
* Switch back to EMPLOYEE.dbf
SELECT 1
* Go to the next data record
SKIP
DISPLAY
RETURN
```

Fig. 12.32. Accessing different database files.

```
. DO GETFILES
Record#  FIRST_NAME    LAST_NAME    AREA_CODE PHONE_NO MALE BIRTH_DATE ANNUAL_PAY
     5   Kirk D.       Chapman      618       625-7845 .T.  08/04/61     20737.50
Record#  DATE      MODEL       UNITS_SOLD
     1   12/07/84 RCA-XA100          2
Record#  FIRST_NAME    LAST_NAME    AREA_CODE PHONE_NO MALE BIRTH_DATE ANNUAL_PAY
     6   Mary W.       Thompson     213       432-6782 .F.  06/18/55     25725.00
.
```

Fig. 12.33. Output of GETFILES.PRG.

You can also use the database file name as an alias:

```
. SELECT 1 ALIAS
. USE EMPLOYEE

      . . .

      . . .
. SELECT 2
. USE  . . .

      . . .

      . . .
. SELECT EMPLOYEE
```

By adding ALIAS to the phrase *SELECT 1*, you name the work area EMPLOYEE. Whenever you want to bring that database file to the foreground, you can enter *SELECT EMPLOYEE* instead of *SELECT 1*.

You cannot use the database file name for the work area designation without the ALIAS command. If you try to access a file by the file name, and if the file has been assigned to a SELECT number, the error message **ALIAS name already in use** appears (see fig. 12.34). When this happens, you can solve the problem by using the CLOSE DATABASE command.

```
. SELECT 1
. USE EMPLOYEE
. SELECT 2
. USE QTYSOLD
. USE EMPLOYEE
ALIAS name already in use
                ?
USE EMPLOYEE
Do you want some help? (Y/N) No
.
```

Fig. 12.34. Error message with SELECT.

# An Example of Multiple Database File Processing

An inventory evaluation program can demonstrate the use of SELECT to switch between the two database files. The database file structures and data are shown in figures 12.35 through 12.38. The database STOCKS.DBF stores the inventory items. Each data record contains the description of an inventory item and the quantities on hand and on order. The costs of the inventory items are stored in the database file COSTS.DBF.

The program in figure 12.39 calculates the value of each inventory item. To calculate the inventory value, the DO WHILE . . . ENDDO loop accesses records for each of the items in STOCKS.DBF. Then the corresponding costs and stock numbers of the items are located in COSTS.DBF. The output of VALUES.PRG is shown in figure 12.40.

```
Structure for database : B:STOCKS.DBF
Number of data records :       11
Date of last update     : 03/20/85
Field  Field name  Type        Width    Dec
    1  STOCK_NO    Character      12
    2  MODEL_NO    Character      10
    3  MFG         Character       9
    4  OPTIONS     Character      25
    5  ON_HAND     Numeric         3
    6  ON_ORDER    Numeric         3
** Total **                      63
```

Fig. 12.35. *Structure of database file STOCKS.DBF.*

```
Record# STOCK_NO      MODEL_NO   MFG       OPTIONS                     ON_HAND ON_ORDER
     1  ST-01-19P-01  RCA-XA100  RCA       Standard                         5        2
     2  ST-01-25C-02  RCA-XA200  RCA       Stereo, Wireless Remote         10        5
     3  ST-02-19P-01  ZENITH-19P ZENITH    Standard, Portable               7        3
     4  ST-02-21C-02  ZENITH-21C ZENITH    Standard, Wire Remote            3        2
     5  ST-02-25C-03  ZENITH-25C ZENITH    Stereo, Wireless Romote          5        5
     6  ST-03-17P-01  SONY1700P  SONY      Standard                         4        4
     7  ST-03-26C-02  SONY2600XT SONY      Stereo, Wireless Remote          5        5
     8  ST-03-19P-01  PANAV019PT PANASONIC Monitor, Wireless Remote         3        2
     9  ST-03-25C-02  PANAV25CTX PANASONIC Monitor, Wireless Remote         4        5
    10  ST-04-19P-01  SANYO-19-P SANYO     Standard                         3        2
    11  ST-04-21C-02  SANYO-21-C SANYO     Table Model, Wire Remote         5        4
```

Fig. 12.36. *Data for inventory evaluation.*

```
Structure for database : B:COSTS.dbf
Number of data records :       11
Date of last update     : 03/20/85
Field  Field name  Type        Width    Dec
    1  STOCK_NO    Character      12
    2  MODEL_NO    Character      10
    3  LIST_PRICE  Numeric         7       2
    4  OUR_COST    Numeric         7       2
    5  DLR_COST    Numeric         7       2
** Total **                      44
```

Fig. 12.37. *Structure of database COSTS.DBF.*

```
Record#   STOCK_NO      MODEL_NO     LIST_PRICE  OUR_COST  DLR_COST
      1   ST-01-19P-01  RCA-XA100        349.95    229.50    259.95
      2   ST-01-25C-02  RCA-XA200        595.00    389.00    459.00
      3   ST-02-19P-01  ZENITH-19P       385.00    255.00    325.00
      4   ST-02-21C-02  ZENITH-21C       449.95    339.00    389.50
      5   ST-02-25C-03  ZENITH-25C       759.95    589.00    669.50
      6   ST-03-17P-01  SONY1700P        450.95    330.00    380.50
      7   ST-03-26C-02  SONY2600XT      1390.95    850.00   1095.00
      8   ST-03-19P-01  PANAVO19PT       579.95    395.00    425.00
      9   ST-03-25C-02  PANAV25CTX      1095.95    795.00    885.00
     10   ST-04-19P-01  SANYO-19-P       369.00    249.00    319.00
     11   ST-04-21C-02  SANYO-21-C       525.95    365.50    425.50
```

Fig. 12.38. Contents of COSTS.DBF.

```
*****    Program : VALUES.PRG    *****
* A program to compute value of each stock item
SET TALK OFF
SET ECHO OFF
?
?"                     Value of Stock Items"
?
?" Stock No.       Model      Quantity    Unit Cost    Total Value"
* Put database files to work areas
SELECT 1
USE STOCKS
SELECT 2
USE COSTS
* Get stock items sequentially from STOCKS.dbf
DO WHILE .NOT. EOF()
SELECT 1
STOCKNO=STOCK_NO
* Get its cost from COSTS.dbf
SELECT 2
LOCATE FOR STOCK_NO=STOCKNO
* Store cost in memory variable
COST=OUR_COST
* Return toSTOCKS.dbf
SELECT 1
VALUE=COST*ON_HAND
? STOCK_NO+"  "+MODEL_NO+"   "+STR(ON_HAND,5,0)+STR(COST,14,2)+STR(VALUE,13,2)
* Process next stock item
SKIP
ENDDO
```

Fig. 12.39. Program to calculate value of inventory items.

```
. DO VALUES

                     Value of Stock Items

   Stock No.        Model      Quantity   Unit Cost    Total Value
   ST-01-19P-01   RCA-XA100        5        229.50       1147.50
   ST-01-25C-02   RCA-XA200       10        389.00       3890.00
   ST-02-19P-01   ZENITH-19P       7        255.00       1785.00
   ST-02-21C-02   ZENITH-21C       3        339.00       1017.00
   ST-02-25C-03   ZENITH-25C       5        589.00       2945.00
   ST-03-17P-01   SONY1700P        4        330.00       1320.00
   ST-03-26C-02   SONY2600XT       5        895.00       4475.00
   ST-03-19P-01   PANAVO19PT       3        395.00       1185.00
   ST-03-25C-02   PANAV25CTX       4        795.00       3180.00
   ST-04-19P-01   SANYO-19-P       3        249.00        747.00
   ST-04-21C-02   SANYO-21-C       5        365.50       1827.50
.
```

*Fig. 12.40. Output of VALUES.PRG.*

VALUES.PRG stores the stock number (STOCK_NO) from the records in STOCKS.DBF in a memory variable named STOCKNO. Then the contents of the memory variable are used as a search key to find the cost in COSTS.DBF, as in

. LOCATE FOR STOCK_NO=STOCKNO

# Joining Database Files

The UPDATE command is used to change the data records in the active file, using data from another database file.

# UPDATE

UPDATE uses data from a source file to change records in the active database file. To UPDATE a file, you match the records in two databases on a specified key field. The format of the command is

. UPDATE ON <key field> FROM <source file> REPLACE <existing field> WITH <expression>

When you use UPDATE, you can update only the active file, and the source file must be in a background work area. Make sure that both the source file and the file to be updated have been sorted or indexed. If you have not sorted the files, you must add the word RANDOM to the end of the command.

Suppose that the database file NEWCOSTS.DBF contains new cost information on the stock items. The contents of the database file are shown in figure 12.41.

```
. USE NEWCOSTS
. DISPLAY STRUCTURE
Structure for database : B:NEWCOSTS.dbf
Number of data records :        3
Date of last update     : 03/26/85
Field  Field name  Type        Width     Dec
    1  STOCK_NO    Character      12
    2  MODEL_NO    Character      10
    3  OUR_COST    Numeric         7        2
** Total **                      30

. LIST
Record#   STOCK_NO      MODEL_NO    OUR_COST
      1  ST-03-26C-02  SONY2600XT   850.00
      2  ST-01-25C-02  RCA-XA200    369.00
      3  ST-02-21C-02  ZENITH-25C   559.00
.
```

Fig. 12.41. Structure and contents of NEWCOSTS.DBF.

The structure of NEWCOSTS.DBF was defined by copying the structure from the file COSTS.DBF:

. USE COSTS
. COPY STRUCTURE TO NEWCOSTS.DBF

The unnecessary data fields were deleted after the structure was copied to the new file.

The data records in NEWCOSTS.DBF contain the revised costs for the stock items. Instead of returning to COSTS.DBF to update each of the new cost items, you can use an UPDATE command. UPDACOST.PRG, the program used for the updating operation, is shown in figure 12.42.

```
*****   Program: UPDACOST.prg   *****
* Use data in NEWCOSTS.dbf to update COSTS.dbf
SET TALK OFF
SET ECHO OFF
SELECT B
USE NEWCOSTS
INDEX ON STOCK_NO TO SORT1
SELECT A
USE COSTS
INDEX ON STOCK_NO TO SORT2
UPDATE ON STOCK_NO FROM NEWCOSTS REPLACE OUR_COST WITH B->OUR_COST
RETURN
```

Fig. 12.42. Program using UPDATE command.

The UPDATE command used in the UPDACOST.PRG is

. UPDATE ON STOCK_NO FROM NEWCOSTS REPLACE
OUR_COST WITH B->OUR_COST

The symbol *B->* designates the work area in which the data field is found. When UPDACOST.PRG is executed, the costs of the items in COSTS.DBF are updated. For example, the cost of ST-03-26C-02 is now $850.00 instead of the original $895.00 (see fig. 12.43).

```
. DO UPDACOST
. USE COSTS
. LIST
Record#    STOCK_NO      MODEL_NO      LIST_PRICE  OUR_COST  DLR_COST
       1   ST-01-19P-01  RCA-XA100         349.95    229.50    259.95
       2   ST-01-25C-02  RCA-XA200         595.00    369.00    459.00
       3   ST-02-19P-01  ZENITH-19P        385.00    255.00    325.00
       4   ST-02-21C-02  ZENITH-21C        449.95    559.00    389.50
       5   ST-02-25C-03  ZENITH-25C        759.95    589.00    669.50
       6   ST-03-17P-01  SONY1700P         450.95    330.00    380.50
       7   ST-03-26C-02  SONY2600XT       1390.95    850.00   1095.00
       8   ST-03-19P-01  PANAVO19PT        579.95    395.00    425.00
       9   ST-03-25C-02  PANAV25CTX       1095.95    795.00    885.00
      10   ST-04-19P-01  SANYO-19-P        369.00    249.00    319.00
      11   ST-04-21C-02  SANYO-21-C        525.95    365.50    425.50
.
```

Fig. 12.43. Results of UPDACOST.PRG.

You can also use the UPDATE command to add the contents of the records in a source file to the corresponding records in the master file. For example, RESTOCK.PRG updates the items in the master file STOCKS.DBF, using the data records in the source file RECEIVED.DBF (see fig. 12.44).

```
*****    Program: RESTOCK.PRG    *****
* Use data in NEWITEMS.dbf to update STOCKS.dbf
SET TALK OFF
SET ECHO OFF
SELECT B
USE RECEIVED
INDEX ON STOCK_NO TO SORT1
SELECT A
USE STOCKS
INDEX ON STOCK_NO TO SORT2
UPDATE ON STOCK_NO FROM RECEIVED REPLACE ON_HAND WITH ON_HAND+B->ON_HAND
RETURN
```

Fig. 12.44. Using new data to update STOCKS.DBF.

Figure 12.45 shows the contents of the master file STOCKS.DBF before the updating operation is performed. The structure and the contents of the source file RECEIVED.DBF are displayed in figure 12.46. After RESTOCK.PRG is executed, you can see in figure 12.47 that the on-hand quantities are updated.

```
. USE STOCKS
. LIST STOCK_NO,MODEL_NO,ON_HAND,ON_ORDER
Record#  STOCK_NO      MODEL_NO     ON_HAND ON_ORDER
      1  ST-01-19P-01  RCA-XA100         5        2
      2  ST-01-25C-02  RCA-XA200        10        5
      3  ST-02-19P-01  ZENITH-19P        7        3
      4  ST-02-21C-02  ZENITH-21C        3        2
      5  ST-02-25C-03  ZENITH-25C        5        5
      6  ST-03-17P-01  SONY1700P         4        4
      7  ST-03-26C-02  SONY2600XT        5        5
      8  ST-03-19P-01  PANAVO19PT        3        2
      9  ST-03-25C-02  PANAV25CTX        4        5
     10  ST-04-19P-01  SANYO-19-P        3        2
     11  ST-04-21C-02  SANYO-21-C        5        4
.
```

Fig. 12.45. STOCKS.DBF before updating.

```
. USE RECEIVED
. DISPLAY STRUCTURE
Structure for database : e:RECEIVED.dbf
Number of data records :       3
Date of last update    : 07/30/85
Field  Field name  Type       Width    Dec
    1  STOCK_NO    Character      12
    2  MODEL_NO    Character      10
    3  ON_HAND     Numeric         3
** Total **                       26

. LIST
Record#  STOCK_NO      MODEL_NO     ON_HAND
      1  ST-03-26C-02  SONY2600XT        2
      2  ST-01-25C-02  RCA-XA200         1
      3  ST-02-21C-02  ZENITH-21C        2
.
```

Fig. 12.46. Structure and contents of RECEIVED.DBF.

```
. DO RESTOCK
SORT1.ndx already exists, overwrite it? (Y/N) Yes
SORT2.ndx already exists, overwrite it? (Y/N) Yes
. USE STOCKS
. LIST STOCK_NO,MODEL_NO,ON_HAND,ON_ORDER
Record#    STOCK_NO       MODEL_NO      ON_HAND ON_ORDER
        1  ST-01-19P-01   RCA-XA100          5        2
        2  ST-01-25C-02   RCA-XA200         11        5
        3  ST-02-19P-01   ZENITH-19P         7        3
        4  ST-02-21C-02   ZENITH-21C         5        2
        5  ST-02-25C-03   ZENITH-25C         5        5
        6  ST-03-17P-01   SONY1700P          4        4
        7  ST-03-26C-02   SONY2600XT         7        5
        8  ST-03-19P-01   PANAVO19PT         3        2
        9  ST-03-25C-02   PANAV25CTX         4        5
       10  ST-04-19P-01   SANYO-19-P         3        2
       11  ST-04-21C-02   SANYO-21-C         5        4
.
```

*Fig. 12.47. Results of RESTOCK.DBF.*

# APPEND FROM

The APPEND FROM command joins files. With APPEND FROM, you can take data records from the source file and append the files to the active database file, with or without a qualifier. The form of the command is

. APPEND FROM <name of source file> <a qualifier, if needed>

The source file may or may not have the same data structure as the active database file. The APPEND FROM command appends only the data fields common to both files. To append NEWITEMS.DBF to STOCKS.DBF, you enter

. USE STOCKS
. APPEND FROM NEWITEMS

To append only selected records (those with model number RCA-200XA, for example), you can add a qualifier to APPEND FROM:

. APPEND FROM NEWITEMS FOR MODEL_NO="RCA-200XA"

A program to append the records of NEWITEMS.DBF to the STOCKS.DBF database is shown in figure 12.48.

The structure and contents of the source file NEWITEMS.DBF are displayed in figure 12.49.

```
*****    Program: ADDITEMS.prg    *****
* Append data records of NEWITEMS.dbf to STOCKS.dbf
SET TALK OFF
SET ECHO OFF
USE STOCKS
APPEND FROM NEWITEMS
RETURN
```

Fig. 12.48. Program to append records to STOCKS.DBF.

```
Structure for database : B:NEWITEMS.dbf
Number of data records :        2
Date of last update      : 03/26/85
Field  Field name  Type        Width    Dec
    1   STOCK_NO    Character     12
    2   MODEL_NO    Character     10
    3   MFG         Character      9
    4   OPTIONS     Character     25
    5   ON_HAND     Numeric        3
    6   ON_ORDER    Numeric        3
** Total **                      63


Record# STOCK_NO    MODEL_NO   MFG    OPTIONS                    ON_HAND ON_ORDER
      1 ST-05-19P-01 PHILCO-19X PHILCO Standard                        5        0
      2 ST-05-25C-01 GE-2500-ST GE     Stereo, Wireless Remote         3        1
```

Fig. 12.49. Structure and contents of NEWITEMS.DBF.

After the appending operation, you see the contents of
STOCKS.DBF, as shown in figure 12.50.

# Using the Macro Function

Up to this point, you have used a fixed field name in the conditional
qualifier of a LOCATE command, such as *FOR STOCK_NO=*. You
have also specified a fixed database file name in a USE command,
such as USE EMPLOYEE or USE QTYSOLD. A program with fixed
field names and database file names can be used only to process
those fields and files. If you want the program to process a different
database file, you must change the database file name in the USE
command line.

With a more flexible program, you could process different data items
by simply entering their names. The macro function of dBASE III
Plus was created for that purpose. By placing the & symbol before a

```
Record#  STOCK_NO      MODEL_NO    MFG       OPTIONS                    ON_HAND ON_ORDER
    1  ST-01-19P-01 RCA-XA200   RCA       Standard                        5       2
    2  ST-01-25C-02 RCA-XA200   RCA       Stereo, Wireless Remote        11       5
    3  ST-02-19P-01 ZENITH-19P  ZENITH    Standard, Portable              7       3
    4  ST-02-21C-02 ZENITH-21C  ZENITH    Standard, Wire Remote           5       2
    5  ST-02-25C-03 ZENITH-25C  ZENITH    Stereo, Wireless Romote         5       5
    6  ST-03-17P-01 SONY1700P   SONY      Standard                        4       4
    7  ST-03-26C-02 SONY2600XT  SONY      Stereo, Wireless Remote         7       5
    8  ST-03-19P-01 PANAV019PT  PANASONIC Monitor, Wireless Remote        3       2
    9  ST-03-25C-02 PANAV25CTX  PANASONIC Monitor, Wireless Remote        4       5
   10  ST-04-19P-01 SANYO-17-P  SANYO     Standard                        3       2
   11  ST-04-21C-02 SANYO-21-C  SANYO     Table Model, Wire Remote        5       4
   12  ST-05-19P-01 PHILCO-19X  PHILCO    Standard                        5       0
   13  ST-05-25C-01 GE-2500-ST  GE        Stereo, Wireless Remote         3       1
```

Fig. 12.50. Results of appending new records.

memory variable name, you can use the contents of the variable as a data field or database file name. For example, if you use the command

. STORE "EMPLOYEE" TO FILENAME

or

FILENAME="EMPLOYEE"

to store the string EMPLOYEE in a memory variable FILENAME, you can then activate the database file by entering

. USE &FILENAME

By changing the contents of the variable FILENAME, you can activate different database files without changing the USE command in the program. The program GETDATA.PRG (fig. 12.51) shows how to find the data record containing a given key data item (KEYITEM) in a key field (KEYFIELD) of a key database file (KEYFILE). The results of the program are shown in figure 12.52.

# Chapter Summary

This chapter has introduced modular programming. The examples have shown different types of program structures. Some program structures involved two-level modules, and others used a multiple-level design.

A program module can be accessed from any other module in the program. The DO command transfers execution from one program

```
*****    Program: GETDATA.prg    *****
* Search a key data item in a key field of a key file
SET TALK OFF
SET ECHO OFF
?
ACCEPT "       Enter Name of Database File .... " TO KEYFILE
ACCEPT "                    Data Field ....... " TO KEYFIELD
ACCEPT "                    The Search Key ... " TO KEYITEM
* Activate the keyfile
USE &KEYFILE
* Locate the key item
LOCATE FOR &KEYFIELD=KEYITEM
* Display the data record found
?
? "The Data Record Found:"
DISPLAY
?
RETURN
```

Fig. 12.51. Program module GETDATA.PRG.

```
. DO GETDATA

        Enter Name of Database File .... EMPLOYEE
                    Data Field ....... LAST_NAME
                    The Search Key ... Nelson

The Data Record Found:
Record#  FIRST_NAME    LAST_NAME    AREA_CODE PHONE_NO MALE BIRTH_DATE ANNUAL_PAY
      3  Harry M.      Nelson          315    576-0235 .T.  02/15/58    30450.00

. DO GETDATA

        Enter Name of Database File .... COSTS
                    Data Field ....... STOCK_NO
                    The Search Key ... ST-03-26C-02

The Data Record Found:
Record#  STOCK_NO     MODEL_NO    LIST_PRICE OUR_COST DLR_COST
      7  ST-03-26C-02 SONY2600XT    1390.95   850.00  1095.00

.
```

Fig. 12.52. Results of GETDATA.PRG.

module to another. Execution begins with the first command line of the called module. After the called module is executed, execution continues with the line following the DO command.

In dBASE III Plus, memory variables created in a higher-level module can be passed to a lower-level module, but the reverse is not true. PUBLIC variables can be shared within a whole program, whereas PRIVATE variables can be used only in a particular program module.

Program modules simplify the designing of powerful programs to perform sophisticated data management functions, such as joining and updating files. The next chapter explains linking the modules with a menu to form an integrated database management system.

# 13

## An Integrated Database System

## An Overview

The introduction to this book stated that dBASE III's programming capability is one of its most powerful features. No other database management program has programming tools that match those of dBASE III Plus. If you use this programming feature in batch-processing mode, you can create well-designed, menu-driven programs that make database management functions simple enough for nonprogrammers to use effectively.

In Chapters 9 through 11, you saw how a program can be written to perform a specific database management task. Chapter 12 introduced the concept of modular programming, in which a complex database management system is designed around several small, simple, functional program modules. This chapter shows you how to integrate these program modules with a menu-driven structure.

The chapter presents for illustration a multiple-level, menu-driven database management program. The program consists of program modules for performing such functions as billing, controlling inventory, and maintaining customers' accounts. These modules are deliberately kept simple so that they can be easily understood.

Note that this database management program by no means represents a complete, practical system. Instead, this program is only a simple example to show how a database program can be designed to perform various data management functions. Nevertheless, even though the example itself is not adequate for handling complex data of a large corporation, the program does provide valuable insights on how to design a sophisticated database management system.

# An Integrated Database Management Program

You will recall that modular programming divides a complex database management system into simple program modules. Each module performs a specific task. Using modular programming, you can design a large database management system by creating several small program modules. After you design and test them, you can use menus to link them in a complete program.

A simple database management system for Super Stereo and Television Distributors, Inc., a television wholesaler, is shown as an example. The company currently performs five basic data management functions:

Maintaining business accounts for each retailer

Billing customers for purchases made during a specified period

Maintaining stock information, including descriptions and costs

Monitoring and controlling inventory level

Maintaining personnel files

# Main Menu Design

A main menu presents the five basic database management functions. When you invoke the main program MAINMENU.PRG, using the dot command

. DO MAINMENU

the menu shown in figure 13.1 is displayed. The program that produces the main menu is shown in figure 13.2.

```
**********************************
***           MAIN MENU        ***
**********************************


    Task Code              Task

      [A]         ACCOUNT Maintenance

      [B]         Prepare BILLING

      [C]         COST Maintenance

      [I]         INVENTORY Control

      [P]         PERSONNEL File Maintenance

      [Q]         Quit


Enter your choice (type in task code)
```

*Fig. 13.1. The main menu.*

You can select a task from the main menu by entering the task code A, B, C, etc., after the prompt:

Enter your choice (type in task code)

When you select task code A, D, E, or M, control passes to one of the program modules: ADDACCT.PRG, DELTACCT.PRG, EDITACCT.PRG, or MAILLIST.PRG. If you select Q, control passes back to the main program, MAINMENU.PRG. The logical links between ACCTMENU.PRG and the submodules are shown in figure 13.8.

```
*****  Program: MAINMENU.PRG   *****
* The Main Program, Display Main Menu
SET TALK OFF
SET ECHO OFF
STORE " " TO CHOICE
DO WHILE .T.
   CLEAR
   ?"                       **********************************"
   ?"                       ***          MAIN MENU        ***"
   ?"                       **********************************"
   ?
   ?
   ?"                  Task Code           Task"
   ?
   ?"                     [A]         ACCOUNT Maintenance"
   ?
   ?"                     [B]         Prepare BILLING"
   ?
   ?"                     [C]         COST Maintenance"
   ?
   ?"                     [I]         INVENTORY Control"
   ?
   ?"                     [P]         PERSONNEL File Maintenance"
   ?
   ?"                     [Q]         Quit"
   ?
   ?
   WAIT "                Enter your choice (type in task code) " TO CHOICE
   DO CASE
      CASE UPPER(CHOICE)="A"
           DO ACCTMENU
      CASE UPPER(CHOICE)="B"
           DO BILLING
      CASE UPPER(CHOICE)="C"
           DO COSTMENU
      CASE UPPER(CHOICE)="I"
           DO INVNMENU
      CASE UPPER(CHOICE)="P"
           DO EMPLMENU
   CASE UPPER(CHOICE)="Q"
          RETURN
      OTHERWISE
          LOOP
   ENDCASE
ENDDO
```

Fig. 13.2. Program module MAINMENU.PRG

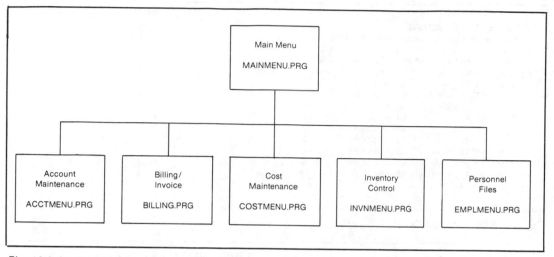

*Fig. 13.3. Logical links of main menu system.*

# The Account Maintenance Submenu: ACCTMENU.PRG

Each program module represents a data management function that consists of a number of subtasks. They are defined with a second-level submenu, such as ACCTMENU.PRG. The program module ACCTMENU.PRG defines the tasks required to maintain accounts. The tasks include:

   Adding a new retailer's account

   Deleting an existing account

   Examining or modifying the contents of an existing account

   Preparing and printing a mailing list of all existing accounts

The database file ACCOUNTS.DBF contains information about the existing accounts. The structure of the file can be seen in figure 13.4. The file contains data records for ten retailers. These records are shown in figure 13.5.

The submenu for selecting account maintenance tasks is shown in figure 13.6. The program module ACCTMENU.PRG is presented in figure 13.7.

```
. USE ACCOUNTS
. DISPLAY STRUCTURE
Structure for database : B:ACCOUNTS.dbf
Number of data records :      10
Date of last update   : 04/10/85
Field  Field name  Type        Width    Dec
    1   ACCT_NO     Character       5
    2   ACCT_NAME   Character      20
    3   ADDRESS     Character      20
    4   CITY        Character      12
    5   STATE       Character       2
    6   ZIP         Character       5
    7   AREA_CODE   Character       3
    8   PHONE_NO    Character       8
    9   MAX_CREDIT  Numeric         8
** Total **                       84
```

Fig. 13.4. Structure of ACCOUNTS.DBF.

| Record# | ACCT_NO | ACCT_NAME | ADDRESS | CITY | STATE | ZIP | AREA_CODE | PHONE_NO | MAX_CREDIT |
|---|---|---|---|---|---|---|---|---|---|
| 1 | 10001 | SUPER SOUNDS | 123 Main Street | Portland | OR | 97201 | 503 | 224-6890 | 25000 |
| 2 | 10002 | ABC T.V. STORE | 3459 Fifth Avenue | Portland | OR | 97203 | 503 | 246-5687 | 20000 |
| 3 | 10003 | ACE SUPERVISION | 2345 Columbia St. | Vacouver | WA | 98664 | 206 | 892-4569 | 12000 |
| 4 | 10004 | DYNAVISION T.V. SHOP | 13560 S.W. Division | Portland | OR | 97201 | 503 | 287-8754 | 22000 |
| 5 | 10005 | Tower Stereo & TV | 7865 Highway 99 | Vancouver | WA | 98665 | 206 | 574-7892 | 10000 |
| 6 | 10006 | REDDING SUPER TV | 1245 Lakeview Drive | Redding | CA | 94313 | 432 | 877-6543 | 20000 |
| 7 | 10007 | National TV & Stereo | 4567 Oak Street | Portland | OR | 97204 | 503 | 289-6832 | 25000 |
| 8 | 10008 | Superior TV & Sound | 5789 S.W. Broadway | Portland | OR | 97202 | 503 | 224-6541 | 5000 |
| 9 | 10009 | Electronic Mart | 2568 Evergreen Blvd. | Vancouver | WA | 98662 | 503 | 256-4578 | 15000 |
| 10 | 10010 | Stereo Super Store | 12008 S. Division | Portland | OR | 97206 | 503 | 224-7275 | 20000 |

Fig. 13.5. Data records in ACCOUNTS.DBF.

```
=========================================
===    ACCOUNT MAINTENANCE SUBMENU    ===
=========================================


Task Code          Task

   [A]     ADD a new account

   [D]     DELETE an existing account

   [E]     EXAMINE/EDIT an account

   [M]     Print MAILING LIST

   [Q]     QUIT, return to mainmenu


Enter your choice (type in task code)
```

Fig. 13.6. Account maintenance submenu.

```
*****  Program: ACCTMENU.PRG    *****
* Display Account Maintenance Submenu
SET TALK OFF
SET ECHO OFF
STORE " " TO CHOICE
DO WHILE .T.
   CLEAR
   ?
   ?
   ?"                       =========================================="
   ?"                       ===    ACCOUNT MAINTENANCE SUBMENU    ==="
   ?"                       =========================================="
   ?
   ?
   ?"                  Task Code              Task"
   ?
   ?"                    [A]      ADD a new account"
   ?
   ?"                    [D]      DELETE an existing account"
   ?
   ?"                    [E]      EXAMINE/EDIT an account"
   ?
   ?"                    [M]      Print MAILING LIST"
   ?
   ?"                    [Q]      QUIT, return to mainmenu"
   ?
   ?
   WAIT "                   Enter your choice (type in task code) " TO CHOICE
   DO CASE
      CASE UPPER(CHOICE)="A"
           DO ADDACCT
      CASE UPPER(CHOICE)="D"
           DO DELTACCT
      CASE UPPER(CHOICE)="E"
           DO EDITACCT
      CASE UPPER(CHOICE)="M"
           DO MAILLIST
      CASE UPPER(CHOICE)="Q"
           RETURN
   ENDCASE
ENDDO
RETURN
```

*Fig. 13.7. Program module ACCTMENU.PRG.*

When you select task code A, D, E, or M, control passes to one of
the program modules: ADDACCT.PRG, DELTACCT.PRG,
EDITACCT.PRG, or MAILLIST.PRG. If you select Q, control passes
back to the main program, MAINMENU.PRG. The logical links
between ACCTMENU.PRG and the submodules are shown in
figure 13.8.

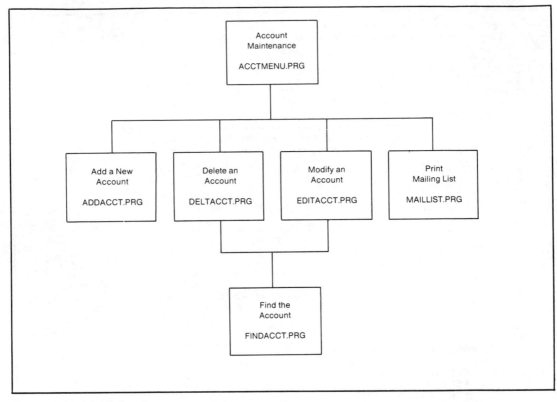

Fig. 13.8. Logical links of account maintenance submenu.

# ADDACCT.PRG

The program module ADDACCT.PRG is called from
ACCTMENU.PRG. This module, shown in figure 13.9, appends a

```
*****   Program: ADDACCT.PRG   *****
* Add a new account to ACCOUNTS.DBF
SET TALK OFF
SET ECHO OFF
USE ACCOUNTS
* Use custom format ACCOUNT.FMT
SET FORMAT TO ACCOUNT.FMT
APPEND BLANK
READ
RETURN
```

Fig. 13.9. Program module ADDACCT.PRG.

new data record to the database file ACCOUNTS.DBF. This program uses the custom format file ACCOUNT.FMT to label the record fields (see fig. 13.10).

```
*****   A Format File: ACCOUNT.FMT   *****
* Format file for editing or appending an account
@3,10 SAY "      Account Number: " GET ACCT_NO
@5,10 SAY "        Account Name: " GET ACCT_NAME
@7,10 SAY "             Address: " GET ADDRESS
@9,10 SAY "                City: " GET CITY
@11,10 SAY "               State: " GET STATE
@13,10 SAY "            ZIP Code: " GET ZIP
@15,10 SAY "           Area Code: " GET AREA_CODE
@17,10 SAY "        Phone Number: " GET PHONE_NO
@19,10 SAY "        Credit Limit: " GET MAX_CREDIT
```

Fig. 13.10. Format file ACCOUNT.FMT.

When you invoke ADDACCT.PRG, you see the custom form used to append a record (see fig. 13.11). When you have entered the contents of the data fields, press Ctrl-End to append the data to the database file and exit the program module.

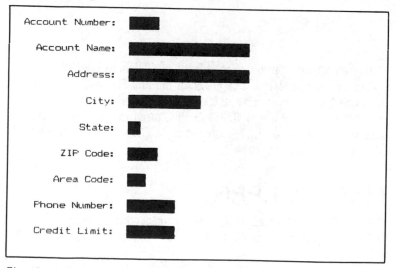

Fig. 13.11. Custom form in ADDACCT.PRG.

# DELTACCT.PRG

The DELTACCT.PRG program module removes a data record from the database file ACCOUNTS.DBF. DELTACCT.PRG is shown in figure 13.12.

```
*****    Program: DELTACCT.PRG    *****
* Delete an existing account
SET TALK OFF
SET ECHO OFF
* Find the account by its account number
DO FINDACCT
IF .NOT. ACCTFOUND
   * No such account found
   RETURN
ELSE
* Delete the account found
DELETE
PACK
@10,1 SAY "                    The account has been deleted !"
RETURN
ENDIF
RETURN
```

Fig. 13.12. Program module DELTACCT.PRG.

Before an account can be deleted from ACCOUNTS.DBF, the account must be located. The program module FINDACCT.PRG accomplishes that task. The logical memory variable ACCTFOUND stores the results of the FINDACCT.PRG program module. If the account has been found, .T. is stored in ACCTFOUND. Otherwise, .F. is assigned to the variable.

# FINDACCT.PRG

FINDACCT.PRG locates an account by the account number (ACCT_NO). A listing of FINDACCT.PRG is shown in figure 13.13.

```
*****    Program: FINDACCT.PRG    *****
* Find an accoung by its account number
PUBLIC ACCTFOUND
SET TALK OFF
SET ECHO OFF
ACCTFOUND=.T.
CLEAR
?
?
?
?
ACCEPT "                Enter  account  number : " TO ACCTNO
* Find the account
USE ACCOUNTS
LOCATE FOR ACCT_NO=ACCTNO
IF EOF()
   * No such account
   ACCTFOUND=.F.
   RETURN
ENDIF
RETURN
```

Fig. 13.13. Program module FINDACCT.PRG.

When FINDACCT.PRG is called, you see the prompt

**Enter Account No.**

The number you enter is assigned to the memory variable
ACCTNO. Then the content of ACCTNO is used to locate the data
record with that account number in the ACCT_NO data field. If the
account number is not found before the end of the file, the content
of the variable ACCTFOUND is .F. Otherwise, the content of the
variable is .T.

# EDITACCT.PRG

The program module EDITACCT.PRG,shown in figure 13.14, calls
the program module FINDACCT.PRG, which finds the record that
is to be edited by EDITACCT.PRG. (Notice that FINDACCT.PRG is
called both by EDITACCT.PRG and by DELTACCT.PRG.) When the
account is found, the format file ACCOUNT.FMT is used to display
the data fields. For example, after you enter *10005* in response to
the FINDACCT.PRG prompt, the contents of the record for account
number 10005 are displayed with the custom labels specified in the
ACCOUNT.FMT file (see fig. 13.15).

```
*****    Program: EDITACCT.PRG    *****
* Edit an existing account
SET TALK OFF
SET ECHO OFF
* Find the account by its account number
DO FINDACCT
IF .NOT. ACCTFOUND
   * No such account found, Return to account submenu
   RETURN
ENDIF
* Use custom format ACCOUNT.FMT
SET FORMAT TO ACCOUNT.FMT
READ
RETURN
```

*Fig. 13.14. Program module EDITACCT.PRG.*

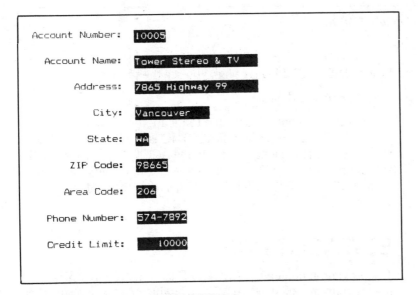

*Fig. 13.15. Entry form for EDITACCT.PRG.*

If you do not need to modify the record, press Esc to return to the
ACCTMENU.PRG program module. To modify the record, use the
editing keystrokes described in earlier chapters. When you finish
editing, press Ctrl-End to return to the ACCTMENU.PRG program
module.

# MAILLIST.PRG

The MAILLIST.PRG program module prints a mailing list of all
addresses in ACCOUNTS.DBF. The mailing list can be constructed
and ordered by one of the three search keys shown in the screen
display of figure 13.16.

```
    Choose one of the following search keys:


         [A]    By ACCOUNT NUMBER

         [S]    By STATE

         [Z]    By Zip Code

         [Q]    Quit, return to mainmenu




  Enter your choice (type in the search key)
```

*Fig. 13.16. Menu produced by MAILLIST.PRG.*

After you choose a search key, MAILLIST.PRG requests the range of
accounts to be included in the mailing list. For example, if you select
option A, the screen display shown in figure 13.17 appears.

```
   Enter:   Beginning account number ... 10003

            Ending account number ...... 10006






    Beginning account number must belong to an existing account!



Turn on and align the printer, strike any key to begin printing!
```

*Fig. 13.17. Searching by account number.*

After entering the account numbers, you are prompted to turn on the printer. When you press a key to indicate that the printer is ready, a mailing list of the specified accounts is printed (see fig. 13.18).

```
ACE SUPERVISION
2345 Columbia St.
Vacouver,  WA  98664


DYNAVISION T.V. SHOP
13560 S.W. Division
Portland,  OR  97201


Tower Stereo & TV
7865 Highway 99
Vancouver,  WA  98665


REDDING SUPER TV
1245 Lakeview Drive
Redding,  CA  94313
```

Fig. 13.18. Results of MAILLIST.PRG.

The logic for producing a mailing list entails indexing the database file ACCOUNT.DBF according to the search key (by account number, by state, or by ZIP code). When the database file is indexed, it supplies the names and addresses of the accounts between the beginning key code (stored in the memory variable BCODE) and the ending key code (stored in ECODE).

Depending on the search key you choose, the key codes can contain account numbers, state codes, or ZIP codes. The beginning key code (BCODE) is used to position the record pointer at the first account in the selected range. The beginning code must be an existing key code, or no accounts will be located. A listing of MAILLIST.PRG is shown in figure 13.19.

# The Billing Submenu: BILLING.PRG

The second major data management function is billing, which includes preparing and printing invoices for sales made within a

```
*****   Program: MAILLIST.PRG   *****
* Print mailing list of accounts in ACCOUNTS.DBF
SET ECHO OFF
SET TALK OFF
CLEAR
@3,1SAY " "
?"                    Choose one of the following search keys:"
?
?
?"                        [A]   By ACCOUNT NUMBER"
?
?"                        [S]   By STATE"
?
?"                        [Z]   By Zip Code"
?
?"                        [Q]   Quit, return to mainmenu"
@20,1SAY " "
WAIT "            Enter your choice (type in the search key) " TO CHOICE
DO CASE
    CASE UPPER(CHOICE)="A"
      CLEAR
      @15,10 SAY "Beginning account number must belong to an existing account!"
      @3,10SAY " "
      ACCEPT "            Enter:  Beginning account number ... " TO BCODE
      ?
      ACCEPT "                      Ending account number ...... " TO ECODE
      @20,1SAY " "
      WAIT " Turn on and align the printer, strike any key to begin printing!"
      USE ACCOUNTS
      INDEX ON ACCT_NO TO KEYCODE
      SEEK BCODE
      SET PRINT ON
      DO WHILE ACCT_NO>=BCODE.AND.ACCT_NO<=ECODE
          ?SPACE(5)+ACCT_NAME
          ?SPACE(5)+ADDRESS
          ?SPACE(5)+TRIM(CITY)+",  "+STATE+"  "+ZIP
          ?
          ?
          SKIP
      ENDDO
    CASE UPPER(CHOICE)="Z"
      CLEAR
      @15,10 SAY "Beginning zip code must be an existing zip code !"

      @3,10SAY " "
      ACCEPT "            Enter:  Beginning zip code ....... " TO BCODE
      ?
      ACCEPT "                      Ending zip code .. ....... " TO ECODE
      @20,1SAY " "
      WAIT " Turn on and align the printer, strike any key to begin printing!"
      USE ACCOUNTS
      INDEX ON ZIP TO KEYCODE
      SEEK BCODE
      SET PRINT ON
```

*(Continued on next page)*

```
      DO WHILE ZIP>=BCODE .AND. ZIP<=ECODE
        ?SPACE(5)+ACCT_NAME
        ?SPACE(5)+ADDRESS
        ?SPACE(5)+TRIM(CITY)+",   "+STATE+" "+ZIP
        ?
        ?
        SKIP
      ENDDO
    CASE UPPER(CHOICE)="S"
      CLEAR
      @15,10 SAY "Beginning state code must belong to an existing account!"
      @3,10SAY " "
      ACCEPT "                    Enter:  Beginning state code ....... " TO BCODE
      ?
      ACCEPT "                         Ending state code ......... " TO ECODE
      @20,1SAY " "
      WAIT " Turn on and align the printer, strike any key to begin printing!"
      INDEX ON STATE TO KEYCODE
      SEEK BCODE
      SET PRINT ON
      DO WHILE STATE>=BCODE .AND. STATE<=ECODE
        ?SPACE(5)+ACCT_NAME
        ?SPACE(5)+ADDRESS
        ?SPACE(5)+TRIM(CITY)+",   "+STATE+"   "+ZIP
        ?
        ?
        SKIP
      ENDDO
    CASE UPPER(CHOICE)="Q"
      RETURN
  ENDCASE
SET PRINT OFF
* Clean up working file, KEYCODE.NDX
CLOSE INDEX
ERASE KEYCODE.NDX
RETURN
```

Fig. 13.19. Program module MAILLIST.PRG.

specific time period. Billing programs can be complex, depending on the type of business involved. The billing example in this section has been kept simple so that you can easily understand the program logic.

Two program modules are used in billing: BILLING.PRG and PRINTINV.PRG. BILLING.PRG gathers information about the invoice items, and PRINTINV.PRG displays and prints the invoice. The logical link between these two program modules is shown in figure 13.20.

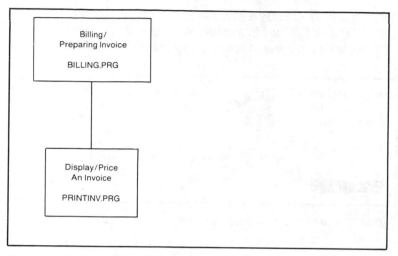

Fig. 13.20. Logical links of BILLING.PRG.

The BILLING.PRG program can be described as a series of five steps.

1. The program prompts you to enter the following information:

Invoice number

Invoice date (set by default to the current date)

Account number

The form requesting the information is shown in figure 13.21.

Fig. 13.21. Information requested on quantities.

2. The validity of the account number you enter is checked against the ACCOUNT.DBF database file. If the account in valid, the customer's name and address are displayed (see fig.

13.22). The items are saved in a temporary database file
INVOICE.DBF and in memory variables that can later be
passed on to the next program module, PRINTINV.PRG.

*Fig. 13.22. Valid account number entered.*

3.  The program then requests information on the items sold.
    For each item, the requested information includes:

    Stock number

    Quantity ordered

    Quantity shipped

    Quantity back-ordered (automatically computed as
    quantity ordered minus quantity shipped)

    Figure 13.23 is an example of the screen display.

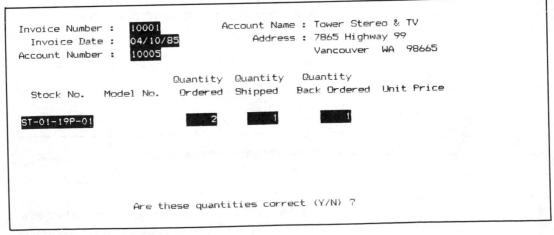

*Fig. 13.23. Screen display of requested information.*

4. After you enter the stock number, quantity ordered, quantity shipped, and quantity back-ordered, the program verifies the stock number against COSTS.DBF. If the stock number is valid, the model number and the unit price are displayed (see fig. 13.24). The items are then saved in the temporary file SALE.DBF and in memory variables that will be passed to another module. When the item is saved, the program requests information on the next item.

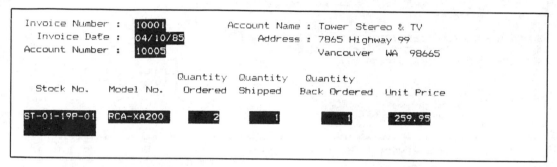

Fig. 13.24. Display with valid stock number.

After you have entered all the items sold, press Enter at the stock number field (see fig. 13.25). This keystroke causes PRINTINV.PRG to be activated and displays the invoice on the screen.

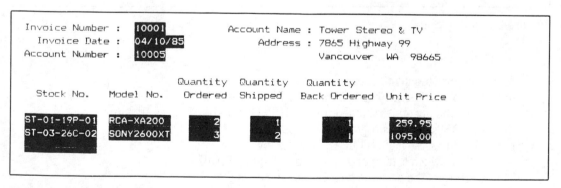

Fig. 13.25. Screen with all information entered.

5. When you select PRINTINV.PRG, the program retrieves the information from the memory variables that contain the account number, invoice number, invoice date, account

address, and so on. Information including stock numbers, order quantities, unit prices, etc., is obtained from the temporary database file SALE.DBF. These items are then organized and displayed as an invoice (see fig. 13.26). You can then print the invoice by selecting P in response to the prompt at the bottom of the screen.

```
            >>>>>>>>>>>   INVOICE   <<<<<<<<<<

SUPER STEREO AND TELEVISION DISTRIBUTORS, INC.
         12345 Main Avenue
         Portland, Oregon 97201
                                    Invoice No.    10001
                                    Invoice Date : 04/10/85

      Sold to:  Tower Stereo & TV
                7865 Highway 99
                Vancouver, WA  98665

==================================================================
  Stock Number       Model    Ordered   Shipped  B.Ordered    Unit Price    Total
------------------------------------------------------------------
  ST-01-19P-01     RCA-XA200      2         1         1          259.95       259.95
  ST-03-26C-02     SONY2600XT     3         2         1         1095.00      2190.00
                                                                            -----------
                                            Total Sale                       2449.95
                                                                            ===========

      [S] Display invoice on screen    [P] Print it    [Q] Return to mainmenu
```

Fig. 13.26. Sample invoice.

After you print the invoice, the program updates the inventory of stock items in the STOCKS.DBF database file by subtracting the quantities shipped (QTY_SHIPED) stored in the SALE.DBF file. The program then appends to the permanent database file INVOICES.DBF the invoice information, which is temporarily stored in INVOICE.DBF. The structure of the database files INVOICE.DBF and INVOICES.DBF is the same. Figure 13.27 shows the structure and content of INVOICE.DBF after the processing of Invoice No. 10001.

```
. USE INVOICE
. DISPLAY STRUCTURE
Structure for database : B:INVOICE.dbf
Number of data records :        1
Date of last update     : 04/10/85
Field  Field name   Type        Width    Dec
    1   INV_NO       Character       5
    2   INV_DATE     Date           8
    3   ACCT_NO      Character       5
** Total **                        19

. LIST
Record#   INV_NO INV_DATE ACCT_NO
      1   10001  04/10/85 10005
.
```

*Fig. 13.27. Structure of INVOICE.DBF.*

The structure and content of SALE.DBF after the processing of Invoice No. 10001 are shown in figure 13.28.

```
. USE SALE
. DISPLAY STRUCTURE
Structure for database : B:SALE.dbf
Number of data records :       3
Date of last update     : 04/10/85
Field  Field name   Type       Width    Dec
    1   INV_NO       Character      5
    2   STOCK_NO     Character     12
    3   MODEL_NO     Character     10
    4   QTY_ORDERD   Numeric        5
    5   QTY_SHIPED   Numeric        5
    6   QTY_BO       Numeric        5
    7   UNIT_PRICE   Numeric        7        2
** Total **                       50

. LIST
Record#   INV_NO STOCK_NO      MODEL_NO    QTY_ORDERD QTY_SHIPED QTY_BO UNIT_PRICE
      1   10001  ST-01-19P-01  RCA-XA200        2          1        1     259.95
      2   10001  ST-03-26C-02  SONY2600XT       3          2        1    1095.00
      3
```

*Fig. 13.28. Structure of SALE.DBF.*

STOCKS.DBF contains all items currently on hand or on order. The structure and content of STOCKS.DBF after printing Invoice No. 10001 are shown in figure 13.29.

```
Structure for database : B:STOCKS.dbf
Number of data records :      11
Date of last update    : 03/10/85
Field  Field name   Type         Width    Dec
    1  STOCK_NO     Character      12
    2  MODEL_NO     Character      10
    3  MFG          Character       9
    4  OPTIONS      Character      25
    5  ON_HAND      Numeric         3
    6  ON_ORDER     Numeric         3
** Total **                       63


Record# STOCK_NO    MODEL_NO   MFG       OPTIONS                ON_HAND ON_ORDER
     1  ST-01-19P-01 RCA-XA100 RCA       Standard                  5       2
     2  ST-01-25C-02 RCA-XA200 RCA       Stereo, Wireless Remote  11       5
     3  ST-02-19P-01 ZENITH-19P ZENITH   Standard, Portable        7       3
     4  ST-02-21C-02 ZENITH-21C ZENITH   Standard, Wire Remote     5       2
     5  ST-02-25C-03 ZENITH-25C ZENITH   Stereo, Wireless Romote   5       5
     6  ST-03-17P-01 SONY1700P SONY      Standard                  4       4
     7  ST-03-26C-02 SONY2600XT SONY     Stereo, Wireless Remote   7       5
     8  ST-03-19P-01 PANAV019PT PANASONIC Monitor, Wireless Remote 3       2
     9  ST-03-25C-02 PANAV25CTX PANASONIC Monitor, Wireless Remote 4       5
    10  ST-04-19P-01 SANYO-19-P SANYO    Standard                  3       2
    11  ST-04-21C-02 SANYO-21-C SANYO    Table Model, Wire Remote  5       4
```

*Fig. 13.29. Structure of STOCKS.DBF.*

The structure and content of COSTS.DBF are shown in figure 13.30. This file contains cost information on the stock items.

The program module BILLING.PRG is listed in figure 13.31.

# Printing Invoices: PRINTINV.PRG

BILLING.PRG calls the program module PRINTINV.PRG, which displays and prints the invoice. The ? and ?? output commands are used to display the invoice. You can use the commands with the @ . . . SAY PICTURE commands to generate a different output format. A listing of PRINTINV.PRG is shown in figure 13.32.

```
Structure for database : B:COSTS.dbf
Number of data records :      11
Date of last update    : 03/10/85
Field  Field name  Type        Width    Dec
    1   STOCK_NO    Character    12
    2   MODEL_NO    Character    10
    3   LIST_PRICE  Numeric       7       2
    4   OUR_COST    Numeric       7       2
    5   DLR_COST    Numeric       7       2
** Total **                     44

Record#   STOCK_NO      MODEL_NO    LIST_PRICE  OUR_COST  DLR_COST
      1   ST-01-19P-01  RCA-XA100      349.95    229.50    259.95
      2   ST-01-25C-02  RCA-XA200      595.00    369.00    459.00
      3   ST-02-19P-01  ZENITH-19P     385.00    255.00    325.00
      4   ST-02-21C-02  ZENITH-21C     449.95    559.00    389.50
      5   ST-02-25C-03  ZENITH-25C     759.95    589.00    669.50
      6   ST-03-17P-01  SONY1700P      450.95    330.00    380.50
      7   ST-03-26C-02  SONY2600XT    1390.95    850.00   1095.00
      8   ST-03-19P-01  PANAVO19PT     579.95    395.00    425.00
      9   ST-03-25C-02  PANAV25CTX    1095.95    795.00    885.00
     10   ST-04-19P-01  SANYO-19-P     369.00    249.00    319.00
     11   ST-04-21C-02  SANYO-21-C     525.95    365.50    425.50
```

Fig. 13.30. Structure of COSTS.DBF.

```
*****    Program: BILLING.PRG   *****
* A Billing Program
SET TALK OFF
SET ECHO OFF
PUBLIC INVNO,INVDATE,ACCTNO,ACCTNAME,MADDRESS,CITYSTZIP
* Enter Invoice Number, Date, Account Number via keyboard
CLEAR
DO WHILE .T.
   * Clean up working file, INVOICE.DBF
   USE INVOICE
   DELETE ALL
   PACK
   APPEND BLANK
   * Set invoice date to today's date
   REPLACE INV_DATE WITH DATE()
   @3,1 SAY "   Invoice Number : " GET INV_NO
   @4,1 SAY "     Invoice Date : " GET INV_DATE
   @5,1 SAY "   Account Number : " GET ACCT_NO
   READ
   INVNO=INV_NO
   INVDATE=INV_DATE
   ACCTNO=ACCT_NO
   * Get account name, address, etc. from ACCOUNTS.DBF
   USE ACCOUNTS
   LOCATE FOR ACCT_NO=ACCTNO
   IF EOF()
      CLEAR
      ?"  Invalid Account Number, Reenter !"
      LOOP
```

*(Continued on next page)*

```
    ELSE
        @1,1 SAY "                                              "
        EXIT
    ENDIF
ENDDO
@3,35 SAY " Account Name : " +ACCT_NAME
@4,35 SAY "       Address : " +ADDRESS
@5,51 SAY TRIM(CITY)+"  "+STATE+"   "+ZIP
ACCTNAME=ACCT_NAME
MADDRESS=ADDRESS
CITYSTZIP=TRIM(CITY)+", "+STATE+"   "+ZIP
* Enter sale information
@7,5 SAY "                            Quantity   Quantity    Quantity"
@8,5 SAY "Stock No.    Model No.   Ordered   Shipped   Back Ordered   Unit Price"
SELECT 1
USE SALE
SELECT 2
USE COSTS
SELECT 1
DELETE ALL
PACK
ITEMNO=1
APPEND BLANK
DO WHILE .T.
    @9+ITEMNO,1 SAY " " GET STOCK_NO
    READ
    IF STOCK_NO=" "
        EXIT
    ENDIF
    STOCKNO=STOCK_NO
    @9+ITEMNO,28 SAY " " GET QTY_ORDERD
    @9+ITEMNO,38 SAY " " GET QTY_SHIPED
    READ
    REPLACE QTY_BO WITH QTY_ORDERD-QTY_SHIPED
    @9+ITEMNO,50 SAY " " GET QTY_BO
    READ
    @21,1 SAY " "
    WAIT "                           Are these quantities correct (Y/N) ? " TO ANSWER
    IF UPPER(ANSWER)="Y"
        * Erase the prompt
        @22,15 SAY "                                                      "
        * Get model no and unit price from COSTS.DBF
        SELECT 2
        LOCATE FOR STOCK_NO=STOCKNO
        IF EOF()
            * No such stock item
            SELECT 1
            LOOP
        ENDIF
        * The stock item has been found
        @9+ITEMNO,15 SAY " " GET MODEL_NO
        @9+ITEMNO,61 SAY " " GET DLR_COST
        CLEAR GET
        MODELNO=MODEL_NO
        UNITPRICE=DLR_COST
        SELECT 1
        * Save model no and unit price to SALE.DBF
        REPLACE INV_NO WITH INVNO
        REPLACE MODEL_NO WITH MODELNO
        REPLACE UNIT_PRICE WITH UNITPRICE
```

(Continued on next page)

```
         * Go to get next stock item sold
         ITEMNO=ITEMNO+1
         APPEND BLANK
         LOOP
      ELSE
         LOOP
      ENDIF
ENDDO
CLOSE DATABASE
DO PRINTINV
RETURN
```

*Fig. 13.31. Listing of BILLING.PRG.*

```
*****    Program: PRINTINV.PRG    *****
* Display and Print Invoice
* Clear totals
ANSWER="S"
DO WHILE .T.
   ITEMTOTAL=0
   GRANDTOTAL=0
   CLEAR
   ?"                         >>>>>>>>>>  INVOICE   <<<<<<<<<<"
   ?
   ?
   ?"SUPER STEREO AND TELEVISION DISTRIBUTORS, INC."
   ?"            12345 Main Avenue"
   ?"          Portland, Oregon 97201"
   ? SPACE(50)+"Invoice No.      "+INVNO
   ? SPACE(50)+"Invoice Date : "+DTOC(INVDATE)
   ? SPACE(5)+"Sold to:   "+ACCTNAME
   ? SPACE(10)+MADDRESS
   ? SPACE(10)+CITYSTZIP
   ?
   ?"=================================================================="
   ??"==============="
   ?"  Stock Number       Model   Ordered   Shipped  B.Ordered   Unit Price "
   ??"  Total"
   ?"------------------------------------------------------------------"
   ??"---------------"
   * Display stock items sold in SALE.DBF
   SELECT A
   USE SALE
   DO WHILE INV_NO<>" " .AND. .NOT. EOF()
      ITEMTOTAL=UNIT_PRICE*QTY_SHIPED
      GRANDTOTAL=GRANDTOTAL+ITEMTOTAL
      ? "  "+STOCK_NO+"    "+MODEL_NO+ "    "+STR(QTY_ORDERD,3,0)+"       "
      ??STR(QTY_SHIPED,3,0)+"         "+STR(QTY_BO,3,0)+"        "
      ??STR(UNIT_PRICE,10,2)+STR(ITEMTOTAL,12,2)
      SKIP
   ENDDO
   ?SPACE(68)+"-----------"
   ?SPACE(40)+" Total Sale "+SPACE(15)+STR(GRANDTOTAL,12,2)
   ?SPACE(68)+"==========="
   ?
   ?
```

*(Continued on next page)*

```
    IF UPPER(ANSWER)="P"
        * Invoice has been printed, update inventory level
        SELECT A
        INDEX ON STOCK_NO TO SORT1
        SELECT B
        USE STOCKS
        INDEX ON STOCK_NO TO SORT2
        UPDATE ON STOCK_NO FROM SALE REPLACE ON_HAND WITH ON_HAND-A->QTY_SHIPED
        ERASE SORT1.NDX
        ERASE SORT2.NDX
        * Save records in INVOICE.dbf to permanent file INVOICES.dbf
        USE INVOICES
        APPEND FROM INVOICE
        RETURN
    ENDIF
    ?"    [S] Display invoice on screen    [P] Print it    "
    ??" [Q] Return to mainmenu "
    WAIT " " TO ANSWER
    DO CASE
        CASE UPPER(ANSWER)="S"
            LOOP
        CASE UPPER(ANSWER)="P"
            SET PRINT ON
            LOOP
        CASE UPPER(ANSWER)="Q"
            RETURN
    ENDCASE
ENDDO
RETURN
```

Fig. 13.32. Listing of PRINTINV.PRG.

# The Cost Maintenance Submenu: COSTMENU.PRG

The program module COSTMENU.PRG selects the tasks necessary for maintaining the price and cost information for each item in stock. The functions include:

Adding a new cost item to COSTS.DBF

Deleting a cost item

Examining and editing the contents of a cost item

When you select COSTMENU.PRG, the functions appear as tasks in the cost maintenance submenu (see fig. 13.33). A listing of COSTMENU.PRG is shown in figure 13.34.

```
==========================================
===        COST MAINTENANCE SUBMENU      ===
==========================================


Task Code              Task

    [A]       ADD a new cost item

    [D]       DELETE an existing cost item

    [E]       EXAMINE/EDIT an cost item

    [Q]       QUIT, return to mainmenu


Enter your choice (type in task code)
```

Fig. 13.33. COSTMENU.PRG submenu.

```
****   Program: COSTMENU.PRG    *****
  Display COST Maintenance Submenu
SET TALK OFF
SET ECHO OFF
STORE " " TO CHOICE
DO WHILE .T.
   CLEAR
   ?
   ?
   ?"                        =========================================="
   ?"                        ===        COST MAINTENANCE SUBMENU      ==="
   ?"                        =========================================="
   ?
   ?
   ?"                        Task Code              Task"
   ?
   ?"                            [A]       ADD a new cost item"
   ?
   ?"                            [D]       DELETE an existing cost item"
   ?
   ?"                            [E]       EXAMINE/EDIT an cost item"
   ?
   ?"                            [Q]       QUIT, return to mainmenu"
   ?
   ?
   WAIT "                   Enter your choice (type in task code) " TO CHOICE
   DO CASE
      CASE UPPER(CHOICE)="A"
         DO ADDCOST
      CASE UPPER(CHOICE)="D"
         DO DELTCOST
      CASE UPPER(CHOICE)="E"
         DO EDITCOST
      CASE UPPER(CHOICE)="Q"
         RETURN
   ENDCASE
ENDDO
RETURN
```

Fig. 13.34. Listing of COSTMENU.PRG.

The modules ADDACCT.PRG, DELTACCT.PRG, and
EDITACCT.PRG are used to perform the cost maintenance function.
Before a cost item is edited or deleted, it is searched by stock
number and located with FINDITEM.PRG. Figure 13.35 shows how
the modules are linked.

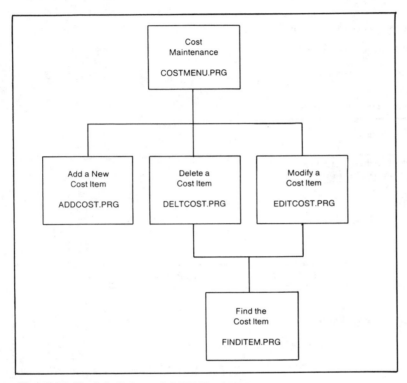

*Fig. 13.35. Module links of COSTMENU.PRG.*

# ADDCOST.PRG

COSTMENU.PRG calls the program module ADDCOST.PRG,
which appends a new data record to COSTS.DBF. A listing of the
program is given in figure 13.36.

ADDCOST.PRG displays an entry form, using the custom field labels
in the COST.FMT format file. The entry form is shown in figure
13.37. COST.FMT is listed in figure 13.38.

```
*****    Program: ADDCOST.PRG    *****
* Add a new cost item to COSTS.DBF
SET TALK OFF
SET ECHO OFF
USE COSTS
* Use custom format COST.FMT
SET FORMAT TO COST.FMT
APPEND BLANK
READ
RETURN
```

*Fig. 13.36. Listing of ADDCOST.PRG.*

*Fig. 13.37. ADDCOST.PRG entry form.*

```
*****   A Format File: COST.FMT    *****
* Format file for editing or appending a cost item
@3,10 SAY "    Stock Number: " GET STOCK_NO
@5,10 SAY "    Model Number: " GET MODEL_NO
@7,10 SAY "      List Price: " GET LIST_PRICE
@9,10 SAY "        Our Cost: " GET OUR_COST
@11,10 SAY "      Dealer Cost: " GET DLR_COST
```

*Fig. 13.38. Listing of COST.FMT.*

# DELTCOST.PRG

DELTCOST.PRG calls the FINDITEM.PRG program module, which finds a cost item by stock number. Similar to ACCTFOUND, the logical variable ITEMFOUND indicates whether the item is found. DELTCOST.PRG is listed in figure 13.39.

```
*****    Program: DELTCOST.PRG    *****
* Delete an existing cost item
SET TALK OFF
SET ECHO OFF
* Find the stock item by its stock number
USE COSTS
DO FINDITEM
IF .NOT. ITEMFOUND
   * No such stock item found
   RETURN
ELSE
* Delete the cost item found
DELETE
PACK
@10,1 SAY "                    The cost item has been deleted !"
RETURN
ENDIF
RETURN
```

Fig. 13.39. Listing of DELTCOST.PRG.

# FINDITEM.PRG

Similar to FINDACCT.PRG, the program module FINDITEM.PRG
locates a data record in COSTS.DBF by the contents of the data field
STOCK_NO. When the record is found, the content of
ITEMFOUND is .T. Figure 13.40 lists FINDITEM.PRG.

```
*****    Program: FINDITEM.PRG    *****
* Find a stock item by its stock number
PUBLIC ITEMFOUND
SET TALK OFF
SET ECHO OFF
ITEMFOUND=.T.
CLEAR
?
?
?
?
ACCEPT "                Enter stock number: " TO STOCKNO
* Find the account
LOCATE FOR STOCK_NO=STOCKNO
IF EOF()
   * No such account
   ITEMFOUND=.F.
   RETURN
ENDIF
RETURN
```

Fig. 13.40. Listing of FINDITEM.PRG.

# EDITCOST.PRG

EDITCOST.PRG calls FINDITEM.PRG to find the record to be edited. The stock number is used as the search key, and the data record is then displayed, using the format defined in COST.FMT. If you do not wish to edit the record, press Esc to return to COSTMENU.PRG. After you have modified the record, press Ctrl-End to exit the program module. EDITCOST.PRG is shown in figure 13.41.

```
*****    Program: EDITCOST.PRG    *****
* Edit an existing cost item
SET TALK OFF
SET ECHO OFF
* Find the cost item by its stock number
USE COSTS
DO FINDITEM
IF .NOT. ITEMFOUND
   * No such stock item found
   RETURN
ENDIF
* Use custom format COST.FMT
SET FORMAT TO COST.FMT
READ
RETURN
```

*Fig. 13.41. Listing of EDITCOST.PRG.*

# The Inventory Control Submenu: INVNMENU.PRG

The program module INVNMENU.PRG defines the tasks needed for inventory control. These tasks include the following functions:

Adding a new stock item to the inventory database file STOCKS.DBF

Deleting a stock item in the inventory database file

Examining and editing the contents of a data record

Adjusting the inventory level of a stock item

Evaluating the total inventory value for each stock item on hand

The submenu used to perform these inventory control functions is shown in figure 13.42. The program module INVNMENU.PRG is listed in figure 13.43.

```
========================================
===     INVENTORY CONTROL SUBMENU    ===
========================================


Task Code              Task

   [A]      ADD a new stock item

   [D]      Delete an existing item

   [E]      EXAMINE/EDIT a stock item

   [J]      ADJUSTING inventory level

   [V]      Evaluation of inventory

   [Q]      QUIT, return to mainmenu


Enter your choice (type in task code)
```

Fig. 13.42. Inventory control submenu.

```
*****  Program: INVNMENU.PRG    *****
* Display Inventory Control Submenu
SET TALK OFF
SET ECHO OFF
STORE " " TO CHOICE
DO WHILE .T.
   CLEAR
   ?
   ?
   ?"                       ========================================"
   ?"                       ===     INVENTORY CONTROL SUBMENU    ==="
   ?"                       ========================================"
   ?
   ?
   ?"               Task Code              Task"
   ?
   ?"                  [A]      ADD a new stock item"
   ?
   ?"                  [D]      Delete an existing item"
   ?
   ?"                  [E]      EXAMINE/EDIT a stock item"
   ?
   ?"                  [J]      ADJUSTING inventory level"
   ?
   ?"                  [V]      Evaluation of inventory"
   ?
   ?"                  [Q]      QUIT, return to mainmenu"
   ?
   ?
   WAIT "                 Enter your choice (type in task code) " TO CHOICE
   DO CASE
      CASE UPPER(CHOICE)="A"
         DO ADDITEM
```

```
        CASE UPPER(CHOICE)="D"
            DO DELTITEM
        CASE UPPER(CHOICE)="E"
            DO EDITITEM
        CASE UPPER(CHOICE)="J"
            DO ADJSTOCK
        CASE UPPER(CHOICE)="V"
            DO VALUES
        CASE UPPER(CHOICE)="Q"
            RETURN
    ENDCASE
ENDDO
RETURN
```

*Fig. 13.43. Listing of INVNMENU.PRG.*

When you select A, D, E, J, or V, the program calls one of the corresponding program modules: ADDITEM.PRG, DELTITEM.PRG, EDITITEM.PRG, ADJSTOCK.PRG, and VALUES.PRG. FINDITEM.PRG is used to locate the stock item. Figure 13.44 shows how the modules are linked.

# ADDITEM.PRG

ADDITEM.PRG appends a new data record to the database file STOCKS.DBF, using the entry form defined in STOCK.FMT. A listing of the program is given in figure 13.45.

When ADDITEM.PRG is called from INVNMENU.PRG, an entry form is displayed (see fig. 13.46). The STOCK.FMT format file that produces the entry form is shown in figure 13.47.

# DELTITEM.PRG

After DELTITEM.PRG locates the stock item by stock number, the module deletes the record from STOCKS.DBF. DELTITEM.PRG calls FINDITEM.PRG to locate the stock item. As in the other modules, ITEMFOUND is the memory variable that indicates whether the item has been found. The DELTITEM.PRG program module is listed in figure 13.48.

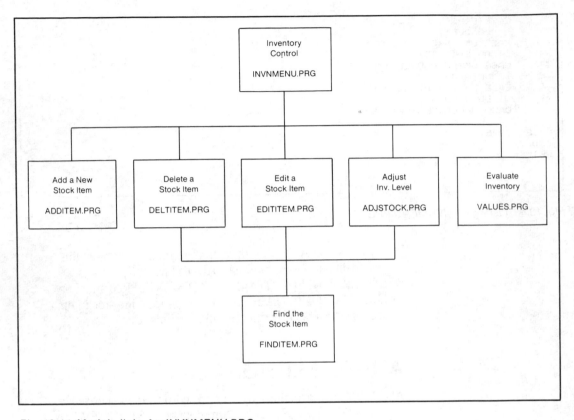

Fig. 13.44. Module links for INVNMENU.PRG.

```
*****   Program: ADDITEM.PRG   *****
* Add a new stock item to STOCKS.DBF
SET TALK OFF
SET ECHO OFF
USE STOCKS
* Use custom format STOCK.FMT
SET FORMAT TO STOCK.FMT
APPEND BLANK
READ
RETURN
```

Fig. 13.45. Listing of ADDITEM.PRG.

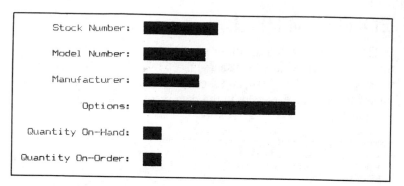

*Fig. 13.46. The ADDITEM.PRG entry form.*

```
*****   A Format File: STOCK.FMT    *****
* Format file for editing or appending a stock item
@3,10 SAY "          Stock Number: " GET STOCK_NO
@5,10 SAY "          Model Number: " GET MODEL_NO
@7,10 SAY "          Manufacturer: " GET MFG
@9,10 SAY "               Options: " GET OPTIONS
@11,10 SAY "     Quantity On-Hand: " GET ON_HAND
@13,10 SAY "    Quantity On-Order: " GET ON_ORDER
```

*Fig. 13.47. Listing of STOCK.FMT.*

```
*****     Program: DELTITEM.PRG     *****
* Delete an existing stock item
SET TALK OFF
SET ECHO OFF
* Find the stock item by its stock number
USE STOCKS
DO FINDITEM
IF .NOT. ITEMFOUND
   * No such stock item found
   RETURN
ELSE
* Delete the stock item found
DELETE
PACK
@10,1 SAY "                    The stock item has been deleted !"
RETURN
ENDIF
RETURN
```

*Fig. 13.48. Listing of DELTITEM.PRG.*

# EDITITEM.PRG

EDITITEM.PRG is used to edit or modify the contents of a data record in the STOCKS.DBF database file. FINDITEM.PRG locates the stock item to be edited, and the custom format file STOCK.FMT is used to label the data fields in the data record. EDITITEM.PRG is listed in figure 13.49.

```
*****     Program: EDITITEM.PRG     *****
* Edit an existing stock item
SET TALK OFF
SET ECHO OFF
* Find the stock item by its stock number
USE STOCKS
DO FINDITEM
IF .NOT. ITEMFOUND
    * No such stock item found
    RETURN
ENDIF
* Use custom format STOCK.FMT
SET FORMAT TO STOCK.FMT
READ
RETURN
```

*Fig. 13.49. Listing of EDITITEM.PRG.*

# ADJSTOCK.PRG

The inventory level, represented in STOCKS.DBF by the quantities on hand and on order, must be adjusted in one of the following situations:

When the inventory level is reduced because of sales

When the quantity on order is received

When adjustments must be made to avoid a discrepancy between the database file and the warehouse record

Inventory adjustments as a result of sales were discussed earlier in this chapter. After an invoice is printed with PRINTINV.PRG, the on-hand quantity of the item is adjusted to reflect the quantity shipped. The program module ADJSTOCK.PRG is used to adjust the current inventory level (quantities on hand and on order) for the other two situations. After FINDITEM.PRG locates the stock item, ADJSTOCK.PRG displays the current inventory level (see fig. 13.50).

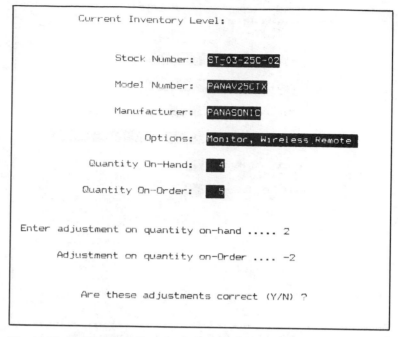

```
                    Current Inventory Level:


                    Stock Number:  ST-03-25C-02

                    Model Number:  PANAV25CTX

                    Manufacturer:  PANASONIC

                         Options:  Monitor, Wireless Remote

                 Quantity On-Hand:     4

                Quantity On-Order:     5


    Enter adjustment on quantity on-hand ..... 2

         Adjustment on quantity on-Order .... -2


              Are these adjustments correct (Y/N) ?
```

*Fig. 13.50. ADJSTOCK.PRG entry form.*

Below the inventory information, you see the request for
adjustments. You can enter them from the keyboard, using negative
or positive values.

For example, if two units of item number ST-03-25C-02 have
arrived, you can enter the adjustments as shown in figure 13.50
(that is, add two units to quantity on hand and subtract two units
from quantity on order). As you can see from the prompt at the
bottom of the screen, you can reenter adjustments if you enter them
incorrectly. After the adjustments are complete, the program
changes the data fields accordingly and displays the inventory level
(see fig. 13.51).

ADJSTOCK.PRG is listed in figure 13.52.

# VALUES.PRG

INVNMENU.PRG calls the program module VALUES.PRG to
calculate and display the total value of each item in stock. The

```
     Inventory Level After Adjustments:


              Stock Number:  ST-03-250-02

              Model Number:  PANAV25CIX

              Manufacturer:  PANASONIC

                   Options:  Monitor, wireless Remote

           Quantity On-Hand:     6

          Quantity On-Order:     3







     [A] Adjust inventory again   [Q] Return to mainmenu
```

Fig. 13.51. ADJSTOCK.PRG entry form after adjustments.

```
*****    Program: ADJSTOCK.PRG    *****
* Adjusting level of inventory of an existing stock item
SET TALK OFF
SET ECHO OFF
* Get the stock item
USE STOCKS
DO FINDITEM
IF .NOT. ITEMFOUND
   * No such stock item found
   RETURN
ENDIF
* Display current inventory level
DO WHILE .T.
   CLEAR
   ?
   ?"            Current Inventory Level:"
   ?
   @5,10 SAY "          Stock Number: " GET STOCK_NO
   @7,10 SAY "          Model Number: " GET MODEL_NO
   @9,10 SAY "          Manufacturer: " GET MFG
   @11,10 SAY "               Options: " GET OPTIONS
   @13,10 SAY "     Quantity On-Hand: " GET ON_HAND
   @15,10 SAY "    Quantity On-Order: " GET ON_ORDER
   CLEAR GET
   DO WHILE .T.
      @17,1 SAY " "
      INPUT "    Enter adjustment on quantity on-hand ..... " TO ADJONHAND
      @19,1 SAY " "
```

(Continued on next page)

```
         INPUT "            Adjustment on quantity on-Order .... " TO ADJONORDER
         @22,1 SAY " "
         WAIT "             Are these adjustments correct (Y/N) ?" TO ANSWER
         IF  UPPER(ANSWER)="Y"
            EXIT
         ELSE
            LOOP
         ENDIF
      ENDDO
      * Adjust the inventory level
      REPLACE ON_HAND WITH ON_HAND+ADJONHAND
      REPLACE ON_ORDER WITH ON_ORDER+ADJONORDER
      * Display inventory level after adjustements
      CLEAR
      ?
      ?"            Inventory Level After Adjustments:"
      @5,10 SAY "          Stock Number: " GET STOCK_NO
      @7,10 SAY "          Model Number: " GET MODEL_NO
      @9,10 SAY "          Manufacturer: " GET MFG
      @11,10 SAY "              Options: " GET OPTIONS
      @13,10 SAY "      Quantity On-Hand: " GET ON_HAND
      @15,10 SAY "     Quantity On-Order: " GET ON_ORDER
      CLEAR GET
      DO WHILE .T.
         @22,10 SAY " "
         WAIT "     [A] Adjust inventory again  [Q] Return to mainmenu " TO CHOICE
         DO CASE
            CASE UPPER(CHOICE)="Q"
               RETURN
            CASE UPPER(CHOICE)="A"
               EXIT
            OTHERWISE
               LOOP
         ENDCASE
      ENDDO
   ENDDO
ENDDO
RETURN
```

Fig. 13.52. Listing of ADJSTOCK.PRG.

inventory value of a stock item is calculated by multiplying its on-hand quantity (STOCKS.DBF) by the cost (OUR_COST) in the COSTS.DBF database file. Figure 13.53 shows a sample inventory evaluation report produced with VALUES.PRG. A listing of VALUES.PRG is shown in figure 13.54.

# The Personnel File Maintenance Submenu: EMPLMENU.PRG

The EMPLMENU.PRG program module maintains the personnel files of the employees. The data management tasks include:

```
                        Value of Stock Items


    Stock No.        Model      Quantity    Unit Cost    Total Value
 -----------     -----------   ---------   ----------   -----------
 ST-01-19P-01    RCA-XA100         5         229.50        1147.50
 ST-01-25C-02    RCA-XA200        11         369.00        4059.00
 ST-02-19P-01    ZENITH-19P        7         255.00        1785.00
 ST-02-21C-02    ZENITH-21C        5         559.00        2795.00
 ST-02-25C-03    ZENITH-25C        5         589.00        2945.00
 ST-03-17P-01    SONY1700P         4         330.00        1320.00
 ST-03-26C-02    SONY2600XT        7         850.00        5950.00
 ST-03-19P-01    PANAVO19PT        3         395.00        1185.00
 ST-03-25C-02    PANAV25CTX        6         795.00        4770.00
 ST-04-19P-01    SANYO-19-P        3         249.00         747.00
 ST-04-21C-02    SANYO-21-C        5         365.50        1827.50
                                 ---                     ---------
           Total                  61                     28531.00
                                 ===                     ========


    [P] Print reports               [Q] Return to mainmenu
```

Fig. 13.53. Sample inventory report with VALUES.PRG.

```
*****    Program : VALUES.PRG    *****
* A program to compute value of each stock item
SET TALK OFF
SET ECHO OFF
DO WHILE .T.
CLEAR
?
?SPACE(32)+"Value of Stock Items"
?
?
?SPACE(10)+" Stock No.        Model      Quantity    Unit Cost    Total Value"
?SPACE(10)+"-----------    -----------   --------    ----------   -----------"
* Put database files to work areas
SELECT 1
USE STOCKS
SELECT 2
USE COSTS
* Clear counter and accumulator
TOTALUNITS=0
TOTALVALUE=0
* Get stock items sequentially from STOCKS.dbf
DO WHILE .NOT. EOF()
SELECT 1
STOCKNO=STOCK_NO
* Get its cost from COSTS.dbf
SELECT 2
LOCATE FOR STOCK_NO=STOCKNO
* Store cost in memory variable
COST=OUR_COST
* Return toSTOCKS.dbf
SELECT 1
VALUE=COST*ON_HAND
?SPACE(10)+ STOCK_NO+"   "+MODEL_NO+"    "+STR(ON_HAND,5,0)+STR(COST,14,2)
```

```
??STR(VALUE,13,2)
* Increase counter and accumulator
TOTALUNITS=TOTALUNITS+ON_HAND
TOTALVALUE=TOTALVALUE+VALUE
* Process next stock item
SKIP
ENDDO
?SPACE(38)+"---"+SPACE(19)+"--------"
?SPACE(21)+"Total "+SPACE(10)+STR(TOTALUNITS,5,0)+SPACE(14)
??STR(TOTALVALUE,13,2)
?SPACE(38)+"==="+SPACE(19)+"========"
?
?
SET PRINT OFF
?"            [P] Print reports                [Q] Return to mainmenu"
WAIT " " TO CHOICE
DO CASE
   CASE UPPER(CHOICE)="P"
      SET PRINT ON
      LOOP
   CASE UPPER(CHOICE)="Q"
      RETURN
   OTHERWISE
      LOOP
ENDCASE
ENDDO
RETURN
```

Fig. 13.54. Listing of VALUES.PRG.

Adding a new employee's record to EMPLOYEE.DBF

Deleting an employee's record

Examining or modifying the contents of a record

Sorting records by different data fields and producing an employee roster

The structure and content of EMPLOYEE.DBF are shown in figure 13.55

The submenu used to select the personnel file maintenance tasks is shown in figure 13.56. The program that produces the submenu, EMPLMENU.PRG, is listed in figure 13.57.

When you select A, D, E, or S, control passes to the corresponding module: ADDEMPL.PRG, DELTEMPL.PRG, EDITEMPL.PRG, and SORTEMPL.PRG, respectively. If you choose Q, control returns to the main program MAINMENU.PRG. Figure 13.58 shows the links between the modules.

```
Structure for database : B:EMPLOYEE.dbf
Number of data records :        9
Date of last update     : 03/15/85
Field    Field name    Type        Width      Dec
    1    FIRST_NAME    Character     12
    2    LAST_NAME     Character     10
    3    AREA_CODE     Character      3
    4    PHONE_NO      Character      8
    5    MALE          Logical        1
    6    BIRTH_DATE    Date           8
    7    ANNUAL_PAY    Numeric        8         2
** Total **                         51


Record# FIRST_NAME  LAST_NAME  AREA_CODE PHONE_NO MALE BIRTH_DATE ANNUAL_PAY
     1  James C.    Smith      216       123-4567 .T.  07/04/60   23100.00
     2  Albert K.   Zeller     212       457-9801 .T.  10/10/59   29347.50
     3  Harry M.    Nelson     315       576-0235 .T.  02/15/58   30450.00
     4  Tina B.     Baker      415       567-7777 .F.  10/12/56   27195.00
     5  Kirk D.     Chapman    618       625-7845 .T.  08/04/61   20737.50
     6  Mary W.     Thompson   213       432-6782 .F.  06/18/55   25725.00
     7  Charles N.  Duff       216       456-9873 .T.  07/22/64   14175.00
     8  Winston E.  Lee        513       365-8512 .T.  05/14/39   36645.00
     9  Thomas T.   Hanson     216       573-5085 .T.  12/24/45   30397.50
```

Fig. 13.55. The EMPLOYEE.DBF file.

```
========================================
===     PERSONNEL FILE  SUBMENU     ===
========================================


Task Code           Task

   [A]      ADD a new employee record

   [D]      Delete an existing employee record

   [E]      EXAMINE/EDIT an employee record

   [S]      SORT employee records

   [Q]      QUIT, return to mainmenu


Enter your choice (type in task code)
```

Fig. 13.56. The EMPLMENU.PRG submenu.

```
*****  Program: EMPLMENU.PRG   *****
* Display personnel file sub-menu
SET TALK OFF
SET ECHO OFF
STORE " " TO CHOICE
DO WHILE .T.
   CLEAR
   ?
   ?
   ?"                     ======================================="
   ?"                     ===      PERSONNEL FILE  SUBMENU    ==="
   ?"                     ======================================="
   ?
   ?
   ?"                  Task Code             Task"
   ?
   ?"                      [A]     ADD a new employee record"
   ?
   ?"                      [D]     Delete an existing employee record"
   ?
   ?"                      [E]     EXAMINE/EDIT an employee record"
   ?
   ?"                      [S]     SORT employee records"
   ?
   ?"                      [Q]     QUIT, return to mainmenu"
   ?
   ?
   WAIT "                Enter your choice (type in task code) " TO CHOICE
   DO CASE
      CASE UPPER(CHOICE)="A"
         DO ADDEMPL
      CASE UPPER(CHOICE)="D"
         DO DELTEMPL
      CASE UPPER(CHOICE)="E"
         DO EDITEMPL
      CASE UPPER(CHOICE)="S"
         DO SORTEMPL
      CASE UPPER(CHOICE)="Q"
         RETURN
   ENDCASE
ENDDO
RETURN
```

Fig. 13.57. Listing of EMPLMENU.PRG.

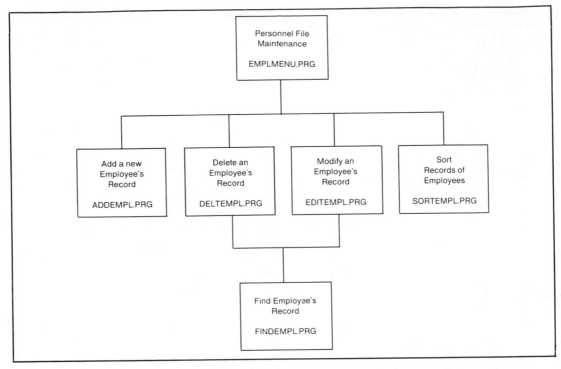

*Fig. 13.58. Module links for personnel file maintenance.*

# ADDEMPL.PRG

ADDEMPL.PRG appends a new data record to the database file
EMPLMENU.PRG, using the format file EMPLOYEE.FMT. The
format file is shown in figure 13.59, and a listing of ADDEMPL.PRG
is shown in figure 13.60.

```
*****  A Format File: EMPLOYEE.FMT   *****
* Format file for editing or appending the record of an employee
@3,10 SAY " Employee's First Name : " GET FIRST_NAME
@5,10 SAY "              Last Name : " GET LAST_NAME
@7,10 SAY "              Area Code : " GET AREA_CODE
@9,10 SAY "      Home Phone Number : " GET PHONE_NO
@11,10 SAY "          Male? (T/F) : " GET MALE
@13,10 SAY "            Birth Date : " GET BIRTH_DATE
@15,10 SAY "          Annual Salary : " GET ANNUAL_PAY PICTURE "$###,###"
```

*Fig. 13.59. Listing of EMPLOYEE.FMT.*

```
*****    Program: ADDEMPL.PRG    *****
* Add a new employee record to EMPLOYEE.dbf
SET TALK OFF
SET ECHO OFF
USE EMPLOYEE
* Use custom format EMPLOYEE.FMT
SET FORMAT TO EMPLOYEE.FMT
APPEND BLANK
READ
RETURN
```

*Fig. 13.60. Listing of ADDEMPL.PRG.*

# DELTEMPL.PRG

As in other modules, FINDEMPL.PRG is used to locate the record; the memory variable EMPLFOUND is used to indicate whether the employee record is found. Then DELTEMPL.PRG deletes the record. Figure 13.61 shows the program module DELTEMPL.PRG. A listing of FINDEMPL.PRG is shown in figure 13.62.

```
*****    Program: DELTEMPL.PRG    *****
* Delete an existing employee record
SET TALK OFF
SET ECHO OFF
* Find the employee by first & last name
DO FINDEMPL
IF .NOT. EMPLFOUND
    * No such employee record found
    RETURN
ELSE
* Delete the employee record found
DELETE
PACK
@10,1 SAY "            The employee record has been deleted !"
RETURN
ENDIF
RETURN
```

*Fig. 13.61. Listing of DELTEMPL.PRG.*

```
*****    Program: FINDEMPL.PRG    *****
* Find an employee record by first name and last name
PUBLIC EMPLFOUND
SET TALK OFF
SET ECHO OFF
EMPLFOUND=.T.
CLEAR
?
?
?
?
ACCEPT "                 Enter employee's first name : " TO FIRSTNAME
?
ACCEPT "                               Last name : " TO LASTNAME
* Find the employee record
USE EMPLOYEE
LOCATE FOR UPPER(FIRST_NAME)=UPPER(FIRSTNAME).AND.;
  UPPER(LAST_NAME)=UPPER(LASTNAME)
IF EOF()
   * No such employee record
   ACCTFOUND=.F.
   RETURN
ENDIF
RETURN
```

Fig. 13.62. Listing of FINDEMPL.PRG.

# EDITEMPL.PRG

EDITEMPL.PRG uses FINDEMPL.PRG to locate and display an employee's record so that you can edit it. The format file EMPLOYEE.FMT is used for editing. If you do not need to edit the record, press Esc, and the program returns to the submenu EMPLMENU.PRG. After you have entered any necessary changes, press Ctrl-End to return to the submenu. EDITEMPL.PRG is shown in figure 13.63.

```
*****    Program: EDITEMPL.PRG    *****
* Edit an existing employee record
SET TALK OFF
SET ECHO OFF
* Find the employee record by first name and last name
DO FINDEMPL
IF .NOT. EMPLFOUND
   * No such employee record found
   RETURN
ENDIF
* Use custom format EMPLOYEE.FMT
SET FORMAT TO EMPLOYEE.FMT
READ
RETURN
```

Fig. 13.63. Listing of EDITEMPL.PRG.

# SORTEMPL.PRG

SORTEMPL.PRG can sort the database file EMPLOYEE.DBF on any of the sorting keys shown in figure 13.64.

```
          Choose one of the following sorting keys:


              [B]    By employee BIRTH DATE

              [F]    By employee FIRST NAME

              [L]    By employee LAST NAME

              [P]    By employee home PHONE NUMBER

              [S]    By employee annual SALARY

              [Q]    Quit, return to mainmenu



     Enter your choice (type in the sorting key)
```

*Fig. 13.64. Sorting keys for SORTEMPL.PRG.*

After the sort is complete, the data records of the sorted file are displayed on the screen. For example, if you select B (BIRTH_DATE), the data records in EMPLOYEE.DBF are ordered by birth dates and displayed (see fig. 13.65).

```
  Sorted Employee Records:


Name of Employee           Phone Number       Birth Date    Annual Salary

Winston E. Lee            (513) 365-8512       05/14/39         36645
Thomas T. Hanson          (216) 573-5085       12/24/45         30398
Mary W. Thompson          (213) 432-6782       06/18/55         25725
Tina B. Baker             (415) 567-7777       10/12/56         27195
Harry M. Nelson           (315) 576-0235       02/15/58         30450
Albert K. Zeller          (212) 457-9801       10/10/59         29348
James C. Smith            (216) 123-4567       07/04/60         23100
Kirk D. Chapman           (618) 625-7845       08/04/61         20738
Charles N. Duff           (216) 456-9873       07/22/64         14175


     [P] Print sorted records on printer;  [Q] Quit
```

*Fig. 13.65. EMPLOYEE.DBF sorted by BIRTH_DATE.*

The program module SORTEMPL.PRG represents the last link in the integrated data management system (see fig. 13.66). A diagram showing all the components of the integrated data management system is shown in figure 13.67.

```
*****   Program: SORTEMPL.PRG   *****
* Sort employee records by a given key field
SET TALK OFF
SET ECHO OFF
* Display selection of sorting keys
DO WHILE .T.
   CLEAR
   @3,1 SAY " "
   ?"                Choose one of the following sorting keys:"
   ?
    ?
   ?"                     [B]    By employee BIRTH DATE"
   ?
   ?"                     [F]    By employee FIRST NAME"
   ?
   ?"                     [L]    By employee LAST NAME"
   ?
   ?"                     [P]    By employee home PHONE NUMBER"
   ?
   ?"                     [S]    By employee annual SALARY"
   ?
   ?"                     [Q]    Quit, return to mainmenu"
   @20,1SAY " "
   WAIT "           Enter your choice (type in the sorting key) " TO CHOICE
   USE EMPLOYEE
   DO CASE
      CASE UPPER(CHOICE)="B"
         INDEX ON BIRTH_DATE TO SORTED
      CASE UPPER(CHOICE)="F"
         INDEX ON FIRST_NAME TO SORTED
      CASE UPPER(CHOICE)="L"
         INDEX ON LAST_NAME TO SORTED
      CASE UPPER(CHOICE)="P"
         INDEX ON AREA_CODE+PHONE_NO TO SORTED
      CASE UPPER(CHOICE)="S"
         INDEX ON ANNUAL_PAY TO SORTED
      CASE UPPER(CHOICE)="Q"
         RETURN
      OTHERWISE
         LOOP
   ENDCASE
   EXIT
ENDDO
* Display sorted employee record
DO WHILE .T.
   CLEAR
   ? "     Sorted Employee Records: "
   ?
   ?
   ?"   Name of Employee               Phone Number      Birth Date;
   Annual Salary"
   ?
   GO TOP
   DO WHILE .NOT. EOF()
```

```
         * Insert blank space to align employee name
         BLANKS=25-LEN(TRIM(FIRST_NAME)+" "+LAST_NAME)
         ?"    "+TRIM(FIRST_NAME)+" "+LAST_NAME+SPACE(BLANKS)+" ("+AREA_CODE+;
           ") "+PHONE_NO+"        "+DTOC(BIRTH_DATE)+"        "+STR(ANNUAL_PAY,7,0)
         SKIP


      ENDDO
      SET PRINT OFF
      ?
      ?
      ?
      WAIT "              [P] Print sorted records on printer;  [Q] Quit " TO CHOICE
      DO CASE
         CASE UPPER(CHOICE)="P"
            SET PRINT ON
         CASE UPPER(CHOICE)="Q"
            EXIT
         OTHERWISE
            LOOP
      ENDCASE
ENDDO
* Clean up working index file
CLOSE INDEX
ERASE SORTED.NDX
RETURN
```

*Fig. 13.66. Listing of SORTEMPL.PRG.*

# Chapter Summary

This final chapter has presented an integrated database management
system. This simple example includes only five major data
management functions. The program modules presented in this
chapter are not necessarily the most efficient means of accomplishing
data management tasks. The modules were designed to show you
how to construct and execute a menu-driven data management
system. Because programming is an art rather than a science, you
should apply your talent to design a system more suitable to your
needs. I wish you the best of luck in using the powerful tools of
dBASE III Plus.

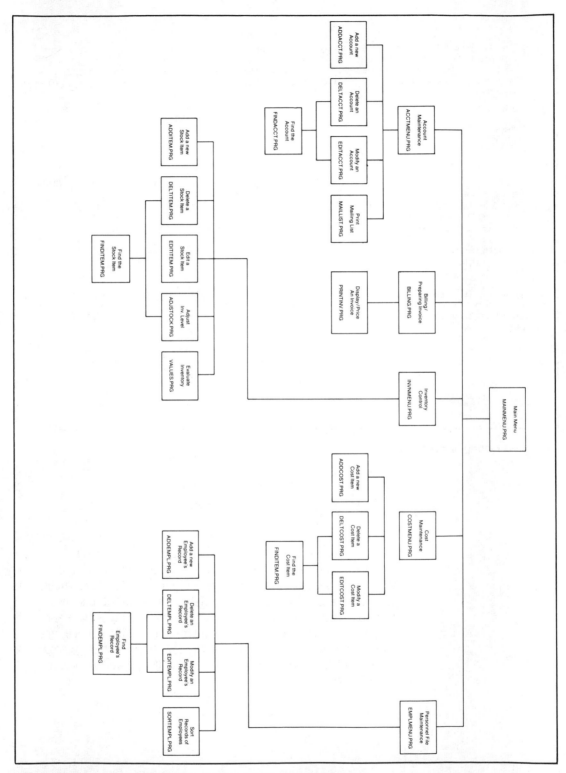

*Fig. 13.67. Flowchart of complete database management system.*

# A
# ASCII Character Set

The table lists the ASCII characters and their codes in decimal notation. Characters can be displayed with

? CHR(n)

where *n* is the ASCII value. Characters not appearing on the keyboard can be entered by holding down the Alt key while you enter the ASCII value, using the numeric keypad. The standard interpretations of ASCII codes 0 to 31 are presented in the Control Character column.

| ASCII Value | Character | Control Character | ASCII Value | Character | Control Character |
|---|---|---|---|---|---|
| 000 | (null) | NUL | 016 | ► | DLE |
| 001 | ☺ | SOH | 017 | ◄ | DC1 |
| 002 | ● | STX | 018 | ↕ | DC2 |
| 003 | ♥ | ETX | 019 | !! | DC3 |
| 004 | ♦ | EOT | 020 | ¶ | DC4 |
| 005 | ♣ | ENQ | 021 | § | NAK |
| 006 | ♠ | ACK | 022 | ▬ | SYN |
| 007 | (beep) | BEL | 023 | ↨ | ETB |
| 008 | ■ | BS | 024 | ↑ | CAN |
| 009 | (tab) | HT | 025 | ↓ | EM |
| 010 | (line feed) | LF | 026 | → | SUB |
| 011 | (home) | VT | 027 | ← | ESC |
| 012 | (form feed) | FF | 028 | (cursor right) | FS |
| 013 | (carriage return) | CR | 029 | (cursor left) | GS |
| 014 | ♫ | SO | 030 | (cursor up) | RS |
| 015 | ☼ | SI | 031 | (cursor down) | US |

| ASCII Value | Character | ASCII Value | Character |
|---|---|---|---|
| 032 | (space) | 069 | E |
| 033 | ! | 070 | F |
| 034 | '' | 071 | G |
| 035 | # | 072 | H |
| 036 | $ | 073 | I |
| 037 | % | 074 | J |
| 038 | & | 075 | K |
| 039 | ' | 076 | L |
| 040 | ( | 077 | M |
| 041 | ) | 078 | N |
| 042 | * | 079 | O |
| 043 | + | 080 | P |
| 044 | , | 081 | Q |
| 045 | - | 082 | R |
| 046 | . | 083 | S |
| 047 | / | 084 | T |
| 048 | 0 | 085 | U |
| 049 | 1 | 086 | V |
| 050 | 2 | 087 | W |
| 051 | 3 | 088 | X |
| 052 | 4 | 089 | Y |
| 053 | 5 | 090 | Z |
| 054 | 6 | 091 | [ |
| 055 | 7 | 092 | \ |
| 056 | 8 | 093 | ] |
| 057 | 9 | 094 | ∧ |
| 058 | : | 095 | — |
| 059 | ; | 096 | ' |
| 060 | < | 097 | a |
| 061 | = | 098 | b |
| 062 | > | 099 | c |
| 063 | ? | 100 | d |
| 064 | @ | 101 | e |
| 065 | A | 102 | f |
| 066 | B | 103 | g |
| 067 | C | 104 | h |
| 068 | D | 105 | i |

| ASCII Value | Character | ASCII Value | Character |
|---|---|---|---|
| 106 | j | 143 | Å |
| 107 | k | 144 | É |
| 108 | l | 145 | æ |
| 109 | m | 146 | Æ |
| 110 | n | 147 | ô |
| 111 | o | 148 | ö |
| 112 | p | 149 | ò |
| 113 | q | 150 | û |
| 114 | r | 151 | ù |
| 115 | s | 152 | ÿ |
| 116 | t | 153 | Ö |
| 117 | u | 154 | Ü |
| 118 | v | 155 | ¢ |
| 119 | w | 156 | £ |
| 120 | x | 157 | ¥ |
| 121 | y | 158 | Pt |
| 122 | z | 159 | ƒ |
| 123 | { | 160 | á |
| 124 | \| | 161 | í |
| 125 | } | 162 | ó |
| 126 | ~ | 163 | ú |
| 127 | ⌂ | 164 | ñ |
| 128 | Ç | 165 | Ñ |
| 129 | ü | 166 | ª |
| 130 | é | 167 | º |
| 131 | â | 168 | ¿ |
| 132 | ä | 169 | ⌐ |
| 133 | à | 170 | ¬ |
| 134 | å | 171 | ½ |
| 135 | ç | 172 | ¼ |
| 136 | ê | 173 | ¡ |
| 137 | ë | 174 | « |
| 138 | è | 175 | » |
| 139 | ï | 176 | |
| 140 | î | 177 | ░ |
| 141 | ì | 178 | ▒ |
| 142 | Ä | 179 | │ |

| ASCII Value | Character |
|---|---|
| 180 | ┤ |
| 181 | ╡ |
| 182 | ╢ |
| 183 | ╖ |
| 184 | ╕ |
| 185 | ╣ |
| 186 | ║ |
| 187 | ╗ |
| 188 | ╝ |
| 189 | ╜ |
| 190 | ╛ |
| 191 | ┐ |
| 192 | └ |
| 193 | ┴ |
| 194 | ┬ |
| 195 | ├ |
| 196 | ─ |
| 197 | ┼ |
| 198 | ╞ |
| 199 | ╟ |
| 200 | ╚ |
| 201 | ╔ |
| 202 | ╩ |
| 203 | ╦ |
| 204 | ╠ |
| 205 | ═ |
| 206 | ╬ |
| 207 | ╧ |
| 208 | ╨ |
| 209 | ╤ |
| 210 | ╥ |
| 211 | ╙ |
| 212 | ╘ |
| 213 | ╒ |
| 214 | ╓ |
| 215 | ╫ |
| 216 | ╪ |
| 217 | ┘ |

| ASCII Value | Character |
|---|---|
| 218 | ┌ |
| 219 | █ |
| 220 | ▄ |
| 221 | ▌ |
| 222 | ▐ |
| 223 | ▀ |
| 224 | $\alpha$ |
| 225 | $\beta$ |
| 226 | $\Gamma$ |
| 227 | $\pi$ |
| 228 | $\Sigma$ |
| 229 | $\sigma$ |
| 230 | $\mu$ |
| 231 | $\tau$ |
| 232 | $\Phi$ |
| 233 | $\theta$ |
| 234 | $\Omega$ |
| 235 | $\delta$ |
| 236 | $\infty$ |
| 237 | $\emptyset$ |
| 238 | $\epsilon$ |
| 239 | $\cap$ |
| 240 | $\equiv$ |
| 241 | $\pm$ |
| 242 | $\geq$ |
| 243 | $\leq$ |
| 244 | $\lceil$ |
| 245 | $\rfloor$ |
| 246 | $\div$ |
| 247 | $\approx$ |
| 248 | $\circ$ |
| 249 | $\bullet$ |
| 250 | $\cdot$ |
| 251 | $\sqrt{}$ |
| 252 | $\eta$ |
| 253 | $^2$ |
| 254 | ■ |
| 255 | (blank 'FF') |

# B

# Differences between dBASE II, dBASE III, and dBASE III Plus

## I. Operating Differences

|  | dBASE II | dBASE III and dBASE III Plus |
|---|---|---|
| Microprocessors | 8080/8085/Z80 8088/8086 | 8088/8086/80286 |
| Disk Operating System | CP/M-80, CP/M-86, Z-DOS, MS-DOS, IBM PC DOS | PC DOS, MS-DOS |

# II. Capacity Differences

|  | dBASE II | dBASE III and dBASE III Plus |
|---|---|---|
| Open data files allowed | 2 | 10 |
| Records per data file | 65,535 | 1 billion |
| Characters per record | 1,000 | 4,000 |
| Data fields per record | 32 | 128 |
| Memory variables allowed | 64 | 256 |
| Digits allowed | 10 | 15.9 |

# III. File-Type Differences

File types available in dBASE III and dBASE III Plus that are not available in dBASE II are

> Label (.LBL) files
> Memory (.DBT) files

PLUS   File types available only in dBASE III Plus are

> Catalog (.CAT) files
> Query (.QRY) files
> Screen (.SCR) files
> View (.VUE) files

# IV. Built-In Function Differences

A.  The dBASE III functions that are not available in dBASE II are

| | | | | | |
|---|---|---|---|---|---|
| ASC | BOF | CDOW | CMONTH | COL | CTOD |
| DAY | DOW | DTOC | EXP | LOG | LOWER |
| MONTH | PCOL | PROW | ROUND | ROW | SPACE |
| SQRT | TIME | TYPE | YEAR | | |

PLUS   B.  Functions available only in dBASE III Plus are

| | | | | | |
|---|---|---|---|---|---|
| ABS | DBF | DISKSPACE | ERROR | FIELD | FKLABEL |
| FKMAX | FOUND | GETENV | IIF | ISALPHA | ISCOLOR |
| ISLOWER | ISUPPER | LEFT | LTRIM | LUPDATE | MAX |
| MESSAGE | MIN | MOD | NDX | OS | RECCOUNT |
| RECSIZE | RIGHT | RTRIM | STUFF | VERSION | |

C. Differences in Function Names:

| | dBASE II | dBASE III and dBASE III Plus |
|---|---|---|
| Converting to uppercase | ! | UPPER |
| Number of active record | # | RECNO |
| Substring | $ | SUBSTR |
| Searching for Substring | @ | AT |
| End-of-file mark | EOF | EOF |

# V. Processing Command Differences

A. The dBASE III commands that are not available in dBASE II are

| | | |
|---|---|---|
| ASSIST | AVERAGE | CLOSE |
| COPY FILE TO | CREATE LABEL | EXIT |
| LABEL FORM | MODIFY LABEL | PARAMETERS |
| PRIVATE | PROCEDURE | PUBLIC |
| SEEK | SET DECIMALS | SET DELIMITER |
| SET DEVICE TO | SET FILTER TO | SET FIXED ON/OFF |
| SET FUNCTION TO | SET HELP ON/OFF | SET MENUS ON/OFF |
| SET PROCEDURE TO | SET RELATION TO | SET SAFETY ON/OFF |
| SET UNIQUE ON/OFF | | |

B. Commands that are available in dBASE III Plus only are

PLUS

| | | |
|---|---|---|
| CREATE QUERY | CREATE SCREEN | CREATE VIEW |
| EXPORT TO | IMPORT FROM | MODIFY QUERY |
| MODIFY SCREEN | MODIFY VIEW | RESUME |
| SET CATALOG | SET DATE | SET FIELDS |
| SET HISTORY | SET MEMOWIDTH | SET ORDER |
| SET STATUS | SET TITLE | SET TYPEAHEAD |
| SUSPEND | | |

C. Differences in Command Names

|  | dBASE II | dBASE III and dBASE III Plus |
|---|---|---|
| Clear the screen | ERASE | CLEAR |
| Delete a file | DELETE FILE | ERASE |
| Deletes all records | DELETE ALL, PACK | ZAP |
| Display file directory | DISPLAY FILES | DIR |
| Execute DOS file | QUIT TO | RUN |
| Exit to DOS | QUIT TO | QUIT |
| Return to the highest program module | None | RETURN TO MASTER |

# VI. Other Major Differences

A. Variable Names

dBASE II accepts a colon (:) as part of a data field or variable name, such as LAST:NAME. In dBASE III and dBASE III Plus, the underscore (_) is used, as in LAST_NAME.

B. Contents of Logical Variables

In dBASE II, T or F is assigned to a logical variable, whereas dBASE III and dBASE III Plus store .T. or .F. in the variable.

C. Sending Output to the Printer

In dBASE III and dBASE III Plus, you can send output to the printer by adding TO PRINT to the end of DISPLAY, DISPLAY MEMORY, DISPLAY STATUS, DISPLAY STRUCTURE, LIST, or TYPE.

D. Defining Data Format

dBASE II uses the USING clause to define a data format, whereas dBASE III and dBASE III Plus use the PICTURE clause.

PLUS E. Processing Method

dBASE III Plus uses an interactive pull-down menu for many commands.

F.  Networking Capabilities

    dBASE III Plus can be used in a networking environment.

G.  Processing Speed

    In most applications, the processing speed of dBASE III Plus is greater than that of dBASE III and dBASE II.

# C
# Summary of Function and Control Keys

## I. Default Settings for the Function Keys

| Key | Command* |
|-----|----------|
| F1 | HELP |
| F2 | ASSIST |
| F3 | LIST |
| F4 | DIR |
| F5 | DISPLAY STRUCTURE |
| F6 | DISPLAY STATUS |

| F7 | DISPLAY MEMORY |
|---|---|
| F8 | DISPLAY |
| F9 | APPEND |
| F10 | EDIT |

*Different commands can be assigned to these keys with the SET FUNCTION commands.

# II. Control Keystrokes for Screen Editing

| Keystroke | Function |
|---|---|
| Enter (↵) | Moves the cursor to the next data field or line |
| | In APPEND: exits and saves the contents of a file when issued from the first character of a blank data record |
| | In EDIT: exits and saves the file contents when issued from the last field of the last data record |
| | In text editor: inserts a new line in insert mode |
| Up arrow (↑) | Moves the cursor up one line or one data field |
| Down arrow (↓) | Moves the cursor down one line or one data field |
| Left arrow (←) | Moves the cursor left one space |
| Right arrow (→) | Moves the cursor right one space |
| Ctrl-left arrow (^←) | In BROWSE: pans one data field to the left |
| | In MODIFY STRUCTURE: scrolls down the file structure display |
| | In MODIFY COMMAND: moves the cursor to the beginning of the line |

| | |
|---|---|
| Ctrl-right arrow (^→) | In BROWSE: pans one data field to the right |
| | In MODIFY REPORT: scrolls up the file structure display |
| | In MODIFY COMMAND: moves the cursor to the end of the line |
| Backspace (←) | Erases the character to the left of the cursor |
| Delete (Del) | Erases the character above the cursor |
| End | Moves the cursor right one word |
| Home | Moves the cursor left one word |
| Insert (Ins) | Toggles INSERT mode on and off |
| Page Up (PgUp) | Moves back to previous data record |
| Page Down (PgDn) | Moves to next data record |
| Ctrl-End (^End) | Exits and saves modified data items |
| Escape (Esc) | Exits without saving modified data items |
| Ctrl-KW (^KW) | In text editor: writes the file to another file |
| Ctrl-KR (^KR) | In text editor: reads another file into the current text at the cursor position |
| Ctrl-N (^N) | In MODIFY STRUCTURE: inserts a new line or data field |
| Ctrl-T (^T) | Erases one word to the right of the cursor |
| Ctrl-U (^U) | In BROWSE or EDIT: marks a record for deletion |
| | In MODIFY REPORT or MODIFY STRUCTURE: deletes a data field |
| Ctrl-Y (^Y) | Erases the entire line at the cursor |

# III. Keystrokes for Control Processing

| Keystroke | Function |
|-----------|----------|
| Ctrl-P (^P) | Toggles printer on and off |
| Ctrl-S (^S) | Starts and stops the screen scroll |
| Ctrl-X (^X) | Erases the command line in interactive processing mode |

# D
# Summary of dBASE III Plus Commands

The commands used in interactive-processing and batch-processing are summarized in this appendix. Although most of these commands have been discussed in this book, you may find a few commands that have not been introduced. In many cases, several different commands can be used to perform the same task. This book has introduced the easiest commands that yield the best results. Feel free to explore any unfamiliar commands, using the information in this appendix.

## I. Definition of Terms

The following special terms are used in this appendix. When entering the commands, enter only the file name or other element; do not enter the angle brackets (<>).

# &lt;file name&gt;

A string of up to 8 characters, including the underscore, with a file extension (for example, .DBF, .DBT, .FMT, .FRM, .LBL, .MEM, .NDX, .PRG, and .TXT). A sample file name is EMPLOYEE.DBF.

# &lt;data field name&gt;

A string of up to 8 characters, including the underscore, such as

LAST_NAME

# &lt;data field list&gt;

A series of data field names separated by commas, such as

LAST_NAME, FIRST_NAME, AREA_CODE, PHONE_NO

# &lt;variable name&gt;

A string of up to 10 characters, including underscores, such as

TOTALPRICE

# &lt;variable list&gt;

A series of variable names separated by commas, such as

HOURS, PAYRATE, GROSSWAGE, TOTALSALE

# &lt;expression&gt;

An alphanumeric or numeric expression.

# &lt;alphanumeric expression&gt;

A collection of alphanumeric data joined with plus signs, such as

"Employee's Name: "+TRIM(LAST_NAME)+
FIRST_NAME+MIDDLENAME

# <numeric expression>

A collection of numeric data joined with arithmetic operators (+, −, *, /, ^), such as

40*PAYRATE+(HOURS−40)*PAYRATE*1.5

# <expression list>

A series of expressions separated by commas, such as

<expression 1>, <expression 2>, <expression 3>, . . .

# <qualifier>

A clause that begins with FOR, followed by one or more conditions.

FOR AREA_CODE="206"
FOR ANNUAL_PAY>=25000
FOR LAST_NAME="Smith" .AND. FIRST_NAME="James C."

# II. Listing of dBASE III Commands by Function

## To Create, Modify, and Manipulate Files

APPEND FROM
CLOSE ALTERNATE
CLOSE DATABASES
CLOSE FORMAT
CLOSE INDEX
CLOSE PROCEDURE
COPY TO
COPY FILE
COPY STRUCTURE TO
CREATE
CREATE LABEL
CREATE QUERY
CREATE REPORT
CREATE SCREEN
CREATE VIEW

EXPORT
IMPORT
INDEX ON
JOIN
MODIFY COMMAND
MODIFY LABEL
MODIFY QUERY
MODIFY REPORT
MODIFY SCREEN
MODIFY STRUCTURE
MODIFY VIEW
REINDEX
RENAME
SAVE TO
SELECT
SORT
TOTAL
USE

# To Add Data Records to a Database File

APPEND
BROWSE
INSERT

# To Edit Data in a Database File

BROWSE
CHANGE
DELETE
EDIT
PACK
READ
RECALL
REPLACE
UPDATE

# To Display Data

@ . . . SAY
?
??
AVERAGE
BROWSE
COUNT
DISPLAY
LIST
REPORT
SUM
TEXT

# To Control the Record Pointer

CONTINUE
FIND
GO BOTTOM
GOTO
GO TOP
LOCATE
SEEK
SKIP

# To Use Memory Variables

ACCEPT
AVERAGE
CLEAR ALL
CLEAR MEMORY
COUNT
DISPLAY MEMORY
INPUT
READ
RELEASE
RESTORE FROM
SAVE TO
STORE
SUM
WAIT

# To Program

ACCEPT TO
CANCEL
CASE
DO
DO WHILE . . . ENDDO
DO CASE . . . ENDCASE
EXIT
IF . . . ENDIF
IF . . . ELSE . . . ENDIF
INPUT
LOOP
MODIFY COMMAND
PARAMETERS
PRIVATE
PROCEDURE
PUBLIC
QUIT
RETRY
RETURN
TEXT
WAIT TO

# To Control Media Display*

CLEAR
EJECT
SET COLOR TO
SET CONFIRM on/OFF
SET CONSOLE ON/off
SET INTENSITY ON/off
SET PRINT on/OFF
SET DEVICE TO PRINT
SET DEVICE TO SCREEN
SET MARGIN TO

*Uppercase indicates default settings.

# To Specify Control Parameters*

SET ALTERNATE TO
SET ALTERNATE on/OFF
SET BELL ON/off
SET CARRY on/OFF
SET CATALOG ON/off
SET CATALOG TO
SET DATE
SET DEBUG
SET DECIMALS TO
SET DEFAULT TO
SET DELETED on/OFF
SET DELIMITERS on/OFF
SET DOHISTORY on/OFF
SET DOHISTORY TO
SET ECHO on/OFF
SET ESCAPE ON/off
SET EXACT on/OFF
SET FIELDS on/OFF
SET FIELDS TO
SET FILTER TO
SET FIXED on/OFF
SET FORMAT TO
SET FUNCTION TO
SET HEADING ON/off
SET HELP ON/off
SET HISTORY ON/off
SET INDEX TO
SET MARGIN TO
SET MENUS ON/off
SET MESSAGE TO
SET ORDER TO
SET PATH TO
SET PROCEDURE TO
SET RELATION TO
SET SAFETY ON/off
SET SCOREBOARD ON/off
SET STATUS ON/off
SET STEP on/OFF
SET TALK ON/off

SET TITLE ON/off
SET TYPEAHEAD TO
SET UNIQUE on/OFF

*Uppercase indicates default settings.

# III. Summary of Commands

## ?

Displays the contents of an alphanumeric or numeric expression on a
new display line, such as

> ? "Employee's name . . . "+FIRST_NAME+LAST_NAME
> ? HOURS*PAYRATE
> ? "Gross Pay . . . "+STR(GROSSPAY,7,2)

## ??

Displays output on the same display line, such as

> ?? "Invoice number: "+INVNO

## @<row,column> GET

Displays user-formatted data at the screen location specified by
<row,column>, as in

> @5,10 GET LAST_NAME
> @8,10 GET SC_NO PICTURE "###-##-####"

## @<row,column> SAY

Displays user-formatted data on the screen or printer at the location
specified by <row,column>, as in

@5,10 SAY LAST_NAME
@5,10 SAY "Last name . . . " LAST_NAME
@10,5 SAY "Annual salary:" ANNUAL_PAY PICTURE "$##,###.##"

# @<row,column> SAY . . . GET

Displays user-formatted data on screen at the location specified by <row,column>; used for appending or editing a data field.

@5,10 SAY "Last name : " GET LAST_NAME

# ACCEPT

Assigns an alphanumeric string to a memory variable, with or without a prompt.

ACCEPT "Enter your last name . . . " TO LASTNAME
ACCEPT TO LASTNAME

# APPEND

Adds a data record to the end of the active database file. The data fields are the field labels on the entry form.

USE EMPLOYEE
APPEND

# APPEND BLANK

Same as APPEND but does not display an entry form.

USE EMPLOYEE
APPEND BLANK

# APPEND FROM

Adds data records from one database file (FILE1.DBF) to another database file (FILE2.DBF), with or without a qualifier.

USE FILE2
APPEND FROM FILE1

USE FILE2
APPEND FROM FILE1 FOR ACCT_NO<="10123"

# ASSIST

Activates The Assistant.

# AVERAGE

Computes the average of a numeric expression and assigns the value
to a memory variable, with or without a condition.

```
AVERAGE ANNUAL_PAY TO AVERAGEPAY
AVERAGE QTY_SOLD TO AVG_SALE FOR MODEL_NO="XYZ"
AVERAGE HOURS*PAYRATE TO AVERAGEPAY FOR .NOT. MALE
```

# BROWSE

Displays for review or modification up to 17 records from the active
database file.

```
USE EMPLOYEE
GO TOP
BROWSE
```

# BROWSE FIELDS

Browses selected data fields in the current database file.

```
USE EMPLOYEE
GO TOP
BROWSE FIELDS FIRST_NAME, LAST_NAME, PHONE_NO
```

# CANCEL

Terminates the processing of a program file and returns the program
to the dot prompt.

```
IF EOF()
   CANCEL
ENDIF
```

# CHANGE

Displays the data records in an active database file sequentially, with
or without a qualifier.

```
USE EMPLOYEE
CHANGE
```

```
USE EMPLOYEE
CHANGE FOR AREA_CODE="206"
```

# CHANGE FIELDS

Displays selected data fields sequentially, with or without a qualifier.

    USE EMPLOYEE
    CHANGE FIELDS ANNUAL_PAY

    USE EMPLOYEE
    CHANGE FIELDS AREA_CODE,PHONE_NO FOR AREA_CODE="206"

# CLEAR

Clears the screen.

# CLEAR ALL

Closes all open database files (including .DBF, .NDX, .FMT, and .DBT files) and releases all memory variables.

# CLEAR FIELDS

Releases the data fields that have been created by the SET FIELDS TO command.

# CLEAR GETS

Causes the subsequent READ command to be ignored for the @. . . SAY . . . GET commands issued before the command, such as

    @5,10 SAY "Account number : " GET ACCT_NO
    CLEAR GETS
    @7,10 Say "Account name : " GET ACCT_NAME
    READ

# CLEAR MEMORY

Releases or erases all memory variables.

# CLEAR TYPEAHEAD

Empties the type-ahead buffer.

# CLOSE

Closes various types of files:

> CLOSE ALL
> CLOSE ALTERNATIVE
> CLOSE DATABASES
> CLOSE FORMAT
> CLOSE INDEX
> CLOSE PROCEDURE

# CONTINUE

Resumes the search started with the LOCATE command.

> USE EMPLOYEE
> LOCATE FOR AREA_CODE="206"
> DISPLAY
> CONTINUE
> DISPLAY

# COPY TO

Copies selected fields of a source database file to a new file, with or without a qualifier.

> USE EMPLOYEE
> COPY TO ROSTER.DBF FIELDS FIRST_NAME, LAST_NAME
> COPY TO SALARY.DBF FIELDS LAST_NAME, ANNUAL_PAY FOR MALE

# COPY FILE

Duplicates an existing dBASE III file of any type.

> COPY FILE MAINPROG.PRG TO MAIN.PRG
> COPY FILE COST.FMT TO NEWCOST.FMT
> COPY FILE ROSTER.FRM TO NAMELIST.FRM

# COPY STRUCTURE

Copies the data structure to another database file.

    USE COST
    COPY STRUCTURE TO NEWCOST.DBF

# COUNT

Counts the number of records in the active database file and assigns the number to a memory variable.

    USE EMPLOYEE
    COUNT TO NRECORDS
    COUNT FOR ANNUAL_PAY>="50000" .AND. MALE TO RICHMEN

# CREATE

Sets up a new file structure and adds data records, if desired.

    CREATE EMPLOYEE

# CREATE LABEL

Displays a design form to set up a label file (.LBL).

    CREATE LABEL MAILLIST

# CREATE QUERY

Creates a new query file (.QRY).

    USE EMPLOYEE
    CREATE QUERY FINDEMPL.QRY

`PLUS`

# CREATE REPORT

Displays a design form to set up a report-form file (.FRM).

    CREATE REPORT WEEKLY

# CREATE SCREEN

Creates a new screen file (.SCR).

    USE EMPLOYEE
    CREATE SCREEN SHOWEMPL.SCR

`PLUS`

| PLUS |

# CREATE VIEW

Creates a new view file (.VUE).

```
USE EMPLOYEE
CREATE VIEW SAMPLE.VUE
```

# DELETE

Marks the records in the active database file with a deletion symbol (*).

```
USE EMPLOYEE
DELETE
DELETE RECORD 5
DELETE NEXT 3
DELETE FOR AREA_CODE="503"
```

# DIR

Displays the file directory:

| | |
|---|---|
| DIR | *(Displays .DBF files)* |
| DIR *.* | *(Displays all files)* |
| DIR *.PRG | *(Displays program files)* |
| DIR *.NDX | *(Displays index files)* |
| DIR X*.DBF | *(Displays .DBF file names beginning with X)* |
| DIR ??X???.PRG | *(Displays .PRG file names having six letters and X as the third character)* |
| DIR ???.* | *(Displays all file names that are three characters long)* |

# DISPLAY

Shows the contents of the data records.

```
USE EMPLOYEE
DISPLAY
DISPLAY RECORD 3
DISPLAY NEXT 2
DISPLAY LAST_NAME,FIRST_NAME
DISPLAY AREA_CODE,PHONE_NO FOR AREA_CODE="206"
```

# DISPLAY MEMORY

Shows the contents of active memory variables.

# DISPLAY STATUS

Shows the current processing situation, including the names of active files, the work area number, etc.

# DISPLAY STRUCTURE

Shows the data structure of an active database file.

    USE EMPLOYEE
    DISPLAY STRUCTURE

# DO

Executes a program file.

    DO MAINPROG

# DO CASE . . . ENDCASE

A multiple-avenue branching command, such as

    DO CASE
        CASE ANSWER="Y"
            . . .
        CASE ANSWER="N"
            . . .
        OTHERWISE
            RETURN
    ENDCASE


# DO WHILE . . . ENDDO

A program loop command, such as

    DO WHILE .NOT. EOF()
      . . .
      . . .
    ENDDO

# EDIT

Displays a data record for editing, such as

```
USE EMPLOYEE
GOTO 5
EDIT

USE EMPLOYEE
EDIT RECORD 5
```

# EJECT

Advances the printer paper to the top of the next page.

# ERASE

Removes a file from the directory. The file to be erased must be closed.

```
ERASE SALE.DBF
ERASE SAMPLE.PRG
```

# EXIT

Exits from a program loop, such as one created with DO WHILE . . . ENDDO.

```
DO WHILE .T.
   . . .
   . . .
   IF EOF()
      EXIT
   ENDIF
   . . .
ENDDO
```

# PLUS EXPORT TO

Converts a dBASE III Plus file to a PFS file.

```
EXPORT TO <name of the PFS file> TYPE PFS
```

# FIND

Searches for the first data record in an indexed file with a specified search key, such as

    USE EMPLOYEE
    INDEX ON AREA_CODE TO AREAS
    FIND "206"
    DISPLAY

# GO BOTTOM

Positions the record pointer at the last record in the database file.

    USE EMPLOYEE
    GO BOTTOM

# GO TOP

Positions the record pointer at the first record in the database file.

    USE EMPLOYEE
    GO TOP

# GOTO

Positions the record pointer at a specified record.

    USE EMPLOYEE
    GOTO 4

# HELP

Calls up the help screens. Can be used with a key word to specify the subject, such as

    HELP
    HELP CREATE
    HELP STR

# IF

A conditional branching command, such as

```
WAIT "Enter your choice ([Q] to quit) " TO CHOICE
IF CHOICE="Q"
        RETURN
ELSE
    . . .
    . . .
ENDIF
```

PLUS # IMPORT FROM

Converts a PFS file to a dBASE III Plus file.

```
IMPORT FROM <name of the PFS file> TYPE PFS
```

# INDEX

Creates a key file in which all records are ordered according to the contents of the specified key field. The records can be arranged in alphabetical, chronological, or numerical order.

```
INDEX ON AREA_CODE TO AREACODE
INDEX ON AREA_CODE+PHONE_NO TO PHONES
```

# INPUT

Assigns a data element to a memory variable, using information entered from the keyboard.

```
INPUT PAYRATE
INPUT "Enter units sold :" TO UNITSSOLD
```

# INSERT

Adds a new record to the database file at the current record location.

    USE EMPLOYEE
    GOTO 4
    INSERT
    GOTO 6
    INSERT BEFORE
    GOTO 5
    INSERT BLANK

# JOIN

Creates a new database file by merging specified data records from two open database files.

    SELECT A
    USE NEWSTOCKS
    SELECT B
    USE STOCKS
    JOIN WITH NEWSTOCKS TO ALLSTOCK FOR
    STOCK_NO=A–>STOCK_NO

    JOIN WITH NEWSTOCKS TO ALLSTOCK FOR
    STOCK_NO=A–>STOCK_NO;
    FIELDS MODEL_NO, ON_HAND, ON_ORDER

# LABEL FORM

Displays data records with labels specified in a label file.

    USE EMPLOYEE
    LABEL FORM ROSTER
    LABEL FORM ROSTER TO PRINT
    LABEL FORM ROSTER TO AFILE.TXT
    LABEL FORM ROSTER FOR AREA_CODE="206" .AND. MALE

# LIST

Shows the contents of selected data records in the active database
file.

    USE EMPLOYEE
    LIST
    LIST RECORD 5
    LIST LAST_NAME,FIRST_NAME
    LIST LAST_NAME,FIRST_NAME FOR AREA_CODE="206" .OR. MALE

# LIST MEMORY

Shows name, type, and size of each active memory variable.

# LIST STATUS

Lists current processing situation, including the names of active files,
work area number, etc.

    LIST STATUS
    LIST STATUS TO PRINT

# LIST STRUCTURE

Displays the data structure of the active database file, such as

    USE EMPLOYEE
    LIST STRUCTURE
    LIST STRUCTURE TO PRINT

# LOCATE

Sequentially searches data records of the active database file for a
record that satisfies a specified condition, such as

    USE EMPLOYEE
    LOCATE FOR LAST_NAME="Smith"
    LOCATE FOR UPPER(FIRST_NAME)="JAMES"
    LOCATE FOR FIRST_NAME="J" .AND. LAST_NAME="S"

# LOOP

Transfers execution from the middle of a program loop to the beginning of the loop:

        DO WHILE .T.
            . . .
            . . .
            IF . . .
                LOOP
            ENDIF
            . . .
        ENDDO

# MODIFY COMMAND

Invokes the text editor to create or edit a program file (.PRG), a format file (.FMT), or a text file (.TXT). The default file extension is .PRG.

        MODIFY COMMAND MAINPROG
        MODIFY COMMAND BILLING.PRG
        MODIFY COMMAND EMPLOYEE.FMT
        MODIFY COMMAND TEXTFILE.TXT

# MODIFY LABEL

Creates or edits a label file (.LBL) for the active database file.

        USE EMPLOYEE
        MODIFY LABEL MAILLIST

# MODIFY QUERY

Creates or edits a query file (.QRY).

        USE EMPLOYEE
        MODIFY QUERY FINDEMPL.QRY

PLUS

# MODIFY REPORT

Create or edits a report file (.FRM) for the active database file.

        USE QTYSOLD
        MODIFY REPORT WEEKLY

## PLUS MODIFY SCREEN

Creates or edits a screen file (.SCR).

    USE EMPLOYEE
    MODIFY SCREEN SHOWEMPL.SCR

## MODIFY STRUCTURE

Displays for modification the structure of the active database file.

    USE EMPLOYEE
    MODIFY STRUCTURE

## PLUS MODIFY VIEW

Creates or edits a view file (.VUE).

    USE EMPLOYEE
    MODIFY VIEW SAMPLE.VUE

## NOTE

Marks the beginning of a remark line in a program.

    SET TALK OFF*
    SET ECHO OFF
    NOTE Enter hours worked and payrate from the keyboard
    INPUT "Enter hours worked . . . " TO HOURS
    INPUT " hourly rate . . . " TO PAYRATE

    . . .
    . . .

    *This is a simplified payroll program.

## PACK

Removes data records marked for deletion by the DELETE command.

    USE EMPLOYEE
    DELETE RECORD 5
    PACK

# PARAMETERS

Assigns local variable names to data items that are to be passed from a calling program module.

***** Program: MULTIPLY.PRG *****
* A program to multiply variable A by variable B
PARAMETERS A,B,C
C=A*B
RETURN

The preceding program is called from the main program:

* The main program
HOURS=38
PAYRATE=8.5
DO MULTIPLY WITH HOURS,PAYRATE,GROSSPAY
?"Gross Wage =",GROSSPAY
RETURN

# PRIVATE

Declares private variables in a program module, for example

PRIVATE VARIABLEA, VARIABLEB, VARIABLEC

# PROCEDURE

Identifies the beginning of each procedure in a procedure file.

# PUBLIC

Declares public variables to be shared by all program modules.

PUBLIC VARIABLEA, VARIABLEB, VARIABLEC

# QUIT

Closes all open files, terminates dBASE III processing, and exits to DOS.

# READ

Activates all the @ . . . SAY . . . GET commands issued since the
last CLEAR GETS was issued.

```
USE EMPLOYEE
@5,10 SAY "Last name : " GET LAST_NAME
@6,10 SAY "First name : " GET FIRST_NAME
READ
```

# RECALL

Recovers all data records marked for deletion.

```
RECALL
RECALL ALL
RECALL RECORD 5
```

# REINDEX

Rebuilds all active index (.NDX) files.

```
USE EMPLOYEE
SET INDEX TO AREACODE
REINDEX
```

# RELEASE

Deletes all or selected memory variables, such as

```
RELEASE ALL
RELEASE ALL LIKE NET*
RELEASE ALL EXCEPT ???COST
```

# RENAME

Changes the name of a disk file, such as

```
RENAME XYZ.DBF TO ABC.DBF
RENAME MAINPROG.PRG TO MAIN.PRG
RENAME MAILIST.LBL TO MAILLIST.LBL
```

# REPLACE

Changes the contents of specified data fields in an active database file.

```
USE EMPLOYEE
REPLACE ALL ANNUAL_PAY WITH ANNUAL_PAY*1.05
REPLACE FIRST_NAME WITH "James K." FOR FIRST_NAME="James C."
REPLACE ALL AREA_CODE WITH "206" FOR AREA_CODE="216"
```

# REPORT FORM

Displays information from the active database file with the custom form specified in the report form (.FRM) file.

```
USE QTYSOLD
REPORT FORM WEEKLY                    (Sends output to screen)
REPORT FORM WEEKLY TO PRINT           (Sends output to printer)
REPORT FORM WEEKLY TO TEXTFILE.TXT    (Sends output to text file)
```

# RESTORE FROM

Retrieves memory variables from a memory (.MEM) file.

```
RESTORE FROM MEMLIST.MEM
RESTORE FROM MEMLIST ADDITIVE
```

# RESUME

PLUS

Resumes execution of a program or procedure after it has been stopped by the SUSPEND command.

# RETURN

Terminates a program and either returns to dot prompt or transfers execution to the calling program module.

# RUN

Executes an .EXE, .COM or .BAT DOS disk file from within dBASE III.

```
RUN B:XYZ        (Where XYZ.EXE, XYZ.COM or XYZ.BAT is an
                 executable disk file in a DOS directory)
```

# SAVE TO

Stores all or selected memory variables to a memory (.MEM) file.

    SAVE TO ALLVARS
    SAVE TO VARLIST ALL EXCEPT NET*
    SAVE TO VARLIST ALL LIKE COST????

# SEEK

Searches an indexed database file for the first data record containing the specified key expression.

    USE EMPLOYEE
    INDEX ON AREA_CODE TO AREACODE
    SEEK "206"

# SELECT

Places a database file in a specified work area.

    SELECT 1
    USE EMPLOYEE
    SELECT A
    USE COSTS

# SET

Sets control parameters for processing. The default settings (indicated by uppercase letters) are appropriate for most purposes.

## SET ALTERNATE on/OFF

Creates a text file, as designated by the SET ALTERNATE TO command, to record the processing activities.

## SET BELL ON/off

Turns on/off the warning bell.

## SET CARRY on/OFF

Carries the contents of the previous record into an APPENDed record.

## SET CATALOG ON/off

Adds files to open catalog.

## SET CATALOG TO

Create, opens and closes a catalog file.

## SET CENTURY on/OFF

Shows the century in date displays.

## SET COLOR ON/OFF

Sets output display to color/monochrome monitor. The default is the mode from which dBASE III Plus is started.

## SET COLOR TO

Sets color screen attributes. Available colors and their letter codes are

| Color | Letter |
|---|---|
| black | N |
| blue | B |
| green | G |
| cyan | BG |
| blank | X |
| red | R |
| magenta | RB |
| brown | GR |
| white | W |

An asterisk indicates blinking characters and a plus sign (+) indicates high intensity. Format of the command is

SET COLOR TO <standard>,<enhanced>,<border>,<background>

For example,

SET COLOR TO GR+/R,W/R,GR

sets standard video to yellow characters on a red background and enhanced video to white letters on a red background, with a yellow screen border.

## SET CONFIRM on/OFF

Controls the cursor movement from one variable to the next when the first variable is filled.

## SET CONSOLE ON/off

Turns the video display on/off.

PLUS ## SET DATE

Specifies the format for date expressions.

| | |
|---|---|
| SET DATE AMERICAN | (mm/dd/yy) |
| SET DATE ANSI | (yy.mm.dd) |
| SET DATE BRITISH | (dd/mm/yy) |
| SET DATE ITALIAN | (dd-mm-yy) |
| SET DATE FRENCH | (dd/mm/yy) |
| SET DATE GERMAN | (dd.mm.yy) |

## SET DEBUG on/OFF

Traces the command errors during processing. When DEBUG is ON, messages from SET ECHO ON are routed to the printer.

## SET DECIMALS TO

Set the number of decimal places for values, such as

SET DECIMALS TO 4

## SET DEFAULT TO

Designates the default disk drive, such as

SET DEFAULT TO B:

## SET DELETED on/OFF

Determines whether data records marked for deletion are to be ignored.

## SET DELIMITERS on/OFF

Marks field widths with the delimiter defined by means of the SET DELIMITERS TO command.

## SET DELIMITERS TO

Specifies the characters for marking a field.

SET DELIMITERS TO '[]'
SET DELIMITERS ON

## SET DEVICE TO SCREEN/print

Selects display medium.

## SET ECHO on/OFF

Displays instructions during execution.

## SET ESCAPE ON/off

Controls capability of aborting execution with the Esc key. When ESCAPE is ON, pressing Esc aborts execution of a program.

## SET EXACT on/OFF

Determines how two alphanumeric strings are compared.

## SET FIELDS on/OFF

Activates the selection of data fields named with the SET FIELDS TO command.

## SET FIELDS TO

PLUS

Selects a set of data fields to be used in one or more files.

```
USE EMPLOYEE
SET FIELDS TO LAST_NAME, FIRST_NAME
SET FIELDS ON
```

## SET FILTER TO

Defines the filter conditions.

```
USE EMPLOYEE
SET FILTER TO AREA_CODE="216"
```

## SET FIXED on/OFF

Sets all numeric output to the fixed number of decimal places defined by SET DECIMALS TO.

## SET FORMAT

Selects custom format defined in a format (.FMT) file.

## SET FUNCTION

Redefines a function key for a specific command, such as

    SET FUNCTION 10 TO "QUIT"

## SET HEADING ON/off

Uses field names as column titles for display of data records with the DISPLAY, LIST, SUM, and AVERAGE commands.

## SET HELP ON/off

Determines whether Help screen is displayed.

PLUS **SET HISTORY ON/off**

Turns on the history feature.

## SET HISTORY TO

Specifies the number of executed commands to be saved in the HISTORY.

    SET HISTORY TO 10

## SET INDEX

Opens the specified index files.

## SET INTENSITY ON/off

Displays data fields in reverse video with EDIT and APPEND commands.

## SET MARGIN

Adjusts the left margin for all printed output, such as

    SET MARGIN TO 10

PLUS **SET MEMOWIDTH TO**

Defines the width of memo field output (default width is 50).

    SET MEMOWIDTH TO 30

## SET MENUS ON/off

Displays a cursor-movement key menu.

## SET MESSAGE TO

Displays an alphanumeric string in the message window.

> SET MESSAGE TO "Hello!"

## SET ORDER TO

PLUS

Sets up an open index file as the controlling index file. The format is

> SET ORDER TO <n>

where <n> is the number of the file within the series of index files named with the INDEX command. The following commands cause AREACODE.NDX to be used:

> USE EMPLOYEE INDEX LASTNAME.NDX, PAYRANK.NDX,
> AREACODE.NDX
> SET ORDER TO 3

## SET PATH TO

Defines the search directory path.

> SET PATH TO C:\DBDATE\SALES

## SET PRINT on/OFF

Directs output generated with @ . . . SAY commands to the printer and the screen.

## SET PROCEDURE

Opens a specified procedure file.

## SET RELATION TO

Links two open database files according to a common key expression.

## SET SAFETY ON/off

Displays a warning message when overwriting an existing file.

## SET SCOREBOARD ON/off

Displays or hides dBASE messages on the status line.

## PLUS  SET STATUS ON/off

Displays or hides the status bar at the bottom of the screen.

## SET STEP on/OFF

Causes execution to pause after each command.

## SET TALK ON/off

Displays interactive messages during processing.

## PLUS  SET TITLE ON/off

Displays the catalog file title prompt.

## SET TYPEAHEAD TO

Specifies the size of the type-ahead buffer (possible values are 0 to 32,000 characters; default is 20 characters).

    SET TYPEAHEAD TO 30

## SET UNIQUE on/OFF

When on, prepares an ordered list with the INDEX command, allowing only the first record with identical keys to be displayed.

## SET VIEW TO

Selects the view file.

    SET VIEW TO EMPLOYEE.VUE

## SKIP

Moves the record pointer forward or backward through the records in the database file, such as

    USE EMPLOYEE
    GOTO 3
    DISPLAY
    SKIP 3
    DISPLAY
    SKIP -1
    DISPLAY

# SORT

Rearranges data records on one or more key fields in ascending or descending order. The default setting is ascending order.

```
USE EMPLOYEE
SORT ON AREA_CODE TO AREACODE
SORT ON ANNUAL_PAY/D TO RANKED
SORT ON AREA_CODE, LAST_NAME TO PHONLIST FOR
AREA_CODE="206"
```

# STORE

Assigns a data element to a memory variable

```
STORE 1 TO COUNTER
STORE "James" TO FIRSTNAME
```

# SUM

Totals the value of a numeric expression and stores the total in a memory variable, such as

```
USE EMPLOYEE
SUM ANNUAL_PAY TO TOTALPAY
SUM ANNUAL_PAY*0.1 TO DEDUCTIONS
```

# SUSPEND

PLUS

Suspends the execution of a program or procedure.

# TEXT

Displays a block of text on the screen or printer; used in a program.

```
***** Program: BULLETIN.PRG *****
SET PRINT ON
TEXT
This is a sample message to be displayed on the printer when
this program is executed.
ENDTEXT
```

# TOTAL

Sums the numeric values of the active database file on a key field and stores the results to another file.

```
USE STOCKS
TOTAL ON MODEL_NO TO BYMODEL
TOTAL ON STOCK_NO TO BYSTOCNO FOR ON_HAND>="2"
```

# TYPE

Displays the contents of a disk file to the screen or printer.

```
TYPE MAINPROG.PRG
TYPE EMPLOYEE.FMT TO PRINT
```

# UPDATE

Uses records in one database file to update records in another file, such as

```
SELECT A

USE RECEIVED

SELECT B

USE STOCKS

UPDATE ON STOCK_NO FROM RECEIVED REPLACE
ON_HAND WITH; ON_HAND+A->ON_HAND
```

# USE

Opens an existing database file.

```
USE EMPLOYEE
```

# WAIT

Causes execution to pause until a key is pressed, as in

```
WAIT
WAIT TO CHOICE
WAIT "Enter your answer (Y/N)? " TO ANSWER
```

# ZAP

Removes all data records from the database file without deleting the data structure, such as

    USE EMPLOYEE
    ZAP

# E
# Built-In Functions

## I. Built-In Functions Listed by Purpose

To manipulate time and date data:

CDOW()
CMONTH()
DATE()
DAY()
DOW()
MONTH()
TIME()
YEAR()

To convert contents of data fields or memory variables:

CTOD()
DTOC()
STR()
VAL()

To convert alphanumeric strings:

ASC()
CHR()
LOWER()
UPPER()

To manipulate alphanumeric strings:

AT()
LEFT()
LEN()
LTRIM()
REPLICATE()
RIGHT()
RTRIM()
SPACE()
STUFF()
SUBSTR()
TRANSFORM()
TRIM()

To perform mathematical operations:

ABS()
EXP()
INT()
LOG()
MAX()
MIN()
MOD()
ROUND()
SQRT()

To track the record pointer:

RECNO()
RECCOUNT()
RECSIZE()

To identify location of the cursor and the print head:

    COL()
    PCOL()
    ROW()
    PROW()

To check file attributes, error conditions, and data-element types:

    BOF()
    DELETED()
    DISKSPACE()
    EOF()
    ERROR()
    FILE()
    FOUND()
    IIF()
    ISALPHA()
    ISCOLOR()
    ISLOWER()
    ISUPPER()
    LUPDATE()
    MESSAGE()
    TYPE()

To use the macro function:

    &

To check keyboard input:

    INKEY()
    READKEY()

To identify attributes of database and DOS files:

    DBF()
    FIELD()
    FKLABEL()
    FKMAX()
    GETENV()
    NDX()
    OS()
    VERSION()

# II. Summary of Built-In Functions

## &

Causes the contents of an alphanumeric memory variable to be substituted for the variable name.

```
STORE "ACCOUNTS.DBF" TO FILENAME
STORE "ACCT_NO" TO FIELDNAME
USE &FILENAME
LOCATE FOR &FIELDNAME="10005"
```

PLUS
## ABS( )

Returns the absolute value of a numeric argument.

```
A=10
B=20
?ABS(A–B)
      10
```

## ASC( )

Returns the ASCII code for the leftmost character of the alphanumeric argument.

```
?ASC("Smith")
83
```

## AT( )

Returns the starting position of the first alphanumeric argument within the second alphanumeric argument.

```
?AT("ABC","XYZABC")
4
```

## BOF( )

Returns the logical value .T. if the record pointer is at the beginning of the file.

# CDOW( )

Returns the name of the day of the week from the date memory variable supplied as an argument. If today is Saturday, 6/01/85, the function returns results as follows:

```
?CDOW(DATE())
Saturday
```

# CHR( )

Returns the ASCII character corresponding to the numeric value supplied as an argument.

```
?CHR(85)
U
```

# CMONTH( )

Returns the name of the month from the date memory variable supplied as an argument. For example, if today is 6/01/85, the function returns results as follows:

```
?CMONTH(DATE())
June
```

# COL( )

Returns the current column location of the cursor.

```
?COL()
5
```

# CTOD( )

Converts an alphanumeric string to a date.

```
STORE CTOD("12/25/85") TO CHRISTMAS
```

# DATE( )

Returns the system date. Assuming that the system date is 6/01/85, the function returns results as follows:

```
?DATE()
06/01/85
```

# DAY( )

Returns the numeric value of the day of the month from a date memory variable supplied as an argument. For example, assume that the memory variable CHRISTMAS contains the date 12/25/85:

```
?DAY(CHRISTMAS)
25
```

PLUS  # DBF( )

Returns the name of the current database file.

```
USE EMPLOYEE
?DBF()
B:EMPLOYEE.dbf
```

# DELETED( )

Returns the logical value .T. if the current data record has been marked for deletion. Assuming that the current data record has been marked for deletion, the function returns results as follows:

```
?DELETED()
.T.
```

PLUS  # DISKSPACE( )

Returns an integer representing the number of bytes available on the default disk drive.

```
? DISKSPACE()
309248
```

# DOW( )

Returns the numeric code for the day of week from the date memory variable supplied as an argument. If the date is Saturday, June 6, the function returns

```
?DOW(DATE())
7
```

# DTOC( )

Converts a date to an alphanumeric string. If today's date is 6/25/85, the function returns results as follows:

    ?"Today's date is "+DTOC(DATE())
    Today's date is 6/25/85

# EOF( )

Returns the logical value .T. if the record pointer is at end of file.

# ERROR( )

PLUS

Used with the ON ERROR command for trapping errors in programming. When an error occurs in the program, this function returns the error number. The number can be used with a conditional command (such as IF or CASE) so that corrective action can be taken if recovery from the error is possible.

# EXP( )

Returns the exponential value of the numeric argument.

    ?EXP(1.00000000)
    2.71828183

# FIELD( )

PLUS

Returns name of the field whose position in the database file structure corresponds to the numeric argument. Assuming that LAST_NAME is the second field defined in EMPLOYEE.DBF, the function returns results as follows:

    USE EMPLOYEE
    ?FIELD(2)
    LAST_NAME

# FILE( )

Returns the logical value .T. if a file in the current directory has the name specified in the alphanumeric argument.

```
?FILE("EMPLOYEE.dbf")
.T.
```

# PLUS FKLABEL( )

Returns the name of the function key whose number correponds to the numeric argument.

```
?FKLABEL(3)
F4
```

# PLUS FKMAX( )

Returns an integer representing the maximum number of programmable function keys available.

```
?FKMAX()
9
```

# PLUS FOUND( )

Returns the logical value .T. if the previous FIND, SEEK, or CONTINUE command was successful. Otherwise, a logical .F. is returned.

```
USE EMPLOYEE
LOCATE FOR LAST_NAME="Smith"
Record = 1
?FOUND()
.T.
```

# PLUS GETENV( )

Returns a character string describing the contents of a specific DOS environmental variable. This function is used by advanced programmers.

# IIF( )

PLUS

Evaluates the condition specified in the first argument and returns the second argument if the condition is true. Otherwise, the third argument is returned.

    TITLE = IIF(MALE, "Mr. ", "Ms. ") + LAST_NAME

# INKEY( )

Returns the numeric code of the key most recently pressed. Consult the dBASE III PLUS manual for these key codes.

# INT( )

Converts a numeric value to an integer.

    ?INT(3.568)
    3

# ISALPHA( )

PLUS

Returns a logical .T. if the specified character expression begins with an alpha character. Otherwise, returns a logical .F.

    ?ISALPHA("ABC–123")
    .T.
    ?ISALPHA("123–abc")
    .F.

# ISCOLOR( )

PLUS

Returns the logical value .T. if the program is running in color mode. Otherwise, returns a logical .F.

    ?ISCOLOR()
    .T.

PLUS

# ISLOWER( )

Returns a logical .T. if the leftmost character of the alphanumeric argument is a lowercase letter. Otherwise, returns a logical .F.

```
?ISLOWER("aBC–234")
.T.
?ISLOWER("Abc–234")
.F.
```

PLUS

# ISUPPER( )

Returns a logical .T. if the leftmost character of the alphanumeric argument is an uppercase. Otherwise, returns a logical .F.

```
?ISUPPER("aBC–234")
.F.
?ISUPPER("Abc–234")
.T.
```

PLUS

# LEFT( )

Returns the specified number of characters from the left of the alphanumeric argument.

```
?LEFT("John J. Smith", 6)
John J.
?"Dear "+LEFT("John J. Smith",4)+":"
Dear John:
```

# LEN( )

Returns the number of characters in the alphanumeric argument.

```
?LEN("James Smith")
11
```

# LOG( )

Returns the natural logarithm of the numeric argument.

```
?LOG(2.71828183)
1.00000000
```

# LOWER( )

Converts to lowercase characters any uppercase characters in the alphanumeric argument.

?LOWER("James Smith")
james smith

# LTRIM( )

PLUS

Trims leading blanks from the alphanumeric argument. This function is useful for trimming a character string created with the STR function.

. ?STR(3.145,10,2)
     3.15
. ?LTRIM(STR(3.145,10,2))
3.15

# LUPDATE( )

PLUS

Returns the date of the last update of the current database file.

?LUPDATE()
06/27/86

# MAX( )

PLUS

Returns the larger value of the two numeric arguments.

A=3.45
B=6.78
?MAX(A,B)
6.78

# MESSAGE( )

PLUS

Returns error-message character strings. See dBASE III PLUS manual for error messages.

# MIN( )

Returns the smaller value of the two numeric arguments.

```
A=3.45
B=6.78
?MIN(A,B)
3.45
```

 # MOD( )

Returns the remainder that results from dividing the first numeric argument by the second numeric argument.

```
A=10
B=3
?MOD(A,B)
      1
```

# MONTH( )

Returns the numeric code for the month from the date memory variable supplied as an argument. Assuming that the the memory variable CHRISTMAS contains 12/25/85, the function returns results as follows:

```
?MONTH(CHRISTMAS)
12
```

# NDX( )

Returns the name of the current active index file in the selected work area.

```
USE EMPLOYEE
INDEX ON LAST_NAME TO LASTNAME.NDX

. . . .
?NDX(1)
B:LASTNAME.NDX
```

# OS( )

Returns the name of the version of DOS under which the program is running.

?OS()
DOS 2.00

# PCOL( )

Determines the current column position of the print head.

?PCOL()
10

# PROW( )

Determines the current row position of the print head.

?PROW()
5

# READKEY( )

Returns the numeric key code for the key pressed in order to exit from a full-screen command.

?READKEY()
271

# RECCOUNT( )

Returns the number of records in the current database file.

USE EMPLOYEE
?RECCOUNT()
10

# RECNO( )

Returns the number of the active data record.

?RECNO()
5

PLUS ## RECSIZE( )

Returns the total width of each record in the active database file.

```
USE EMPLOYEE
?RECSIZE()
      51
```

## REPLICATE( )

Repeats the first argument the number of times specified in the second argument.

```
?REPLICATE("Hello! ",3)
Hello! Hello! Hello!
```

PLUS ## RIGHT( )

Returns the number of characters specified in the second argument from the right of first argument.

```
?RIGHT("John J. Smith", 5)
Smith
?"Dear Mr. "+RIGHT("John J. Smith",5)+":"
Dear Mr. Smith:
```

## ROUND( )

Rounds the first numeric argument to the given number of decimal places specified in the second numeric argument.

```
?ROUND(3.71689,2)
3.72
```

## ROW( )

Returns the current row location of the cursor.

```
?ROW()
5
```

# RTRIM( )

Trims the trailing blanks from a character expression. The effect of this function is identical to that of the TRIM function.

    ?RTRIM(FIRST_NAME)+" "+RTRIM(LAST_NAME)

# SPACE( )

Creates an alphanumeric string of blanks.

    ?SPACE(10)+LAST_NAME+SPACE(5)+AREA_CODE+PHONE_NO

# SQRT( )

Returns the square root of the numeric argument.

    ?SQRT(9)
    3

# STR( )

Converts the numeric argument to an alphanumeric string.

    ANNUALPAY=25950.50
    ?"Annual salary = "+STR(ANNUALPAY,8,2)

# STUFF( )

Replaces a portion of the first alphanumeric argument with the second alphanumeric argument, beginning at the character position specified in the second argument and continuing for the number of characters specified in the third argument.

    STUFF(<1st string>,<beginning position>, <number of characters>,<2nd string>)

    ?STUFF("Mary Jane Smith",6,4,"Kay")
    Mary Kay Smith

# SUBSTR( )

Returns characters from the first alphanumeric argument. The second argument specifies the starting position, and the third argument specifies the number of characters to be returned.

```
?SUBSTR("ABCDEFG",4,3)
DEF
```

# TIME( )

Returns the system time. Assuming that the system time is 22:15:35, the results are as follows:

```
?TIME()
22:15:35
```

# TRANSFORM( )

Used with ?, ??, DISPLAY, LABEL, LIST, and REPORT to display a character expression with the specified picture format.

```
. USE EMPLOYEE
. GOTO 5
. DISPLAY TRANSFORM(LAST_NAME, "@R X X X X X X X X X X X X")
Record# TRANSFORM(LAST_NAME, "@R X X X X X X X X X X X X")
     5 B a k e r
```

# TRIM( )

Removes trailing blanks from an alphanumeric string.

```
?TRIM(FIRST_NAME)+" "+TRIM(LAST_NAME)
James Smith
```

# TYPE( )

Returns a single character representing the type of the specified expression:

```
?TYPE(BIRTH_DATE)
D
?TYPE(ASTRING)
C
```

# UPPER( )

Converts to uppercase letters any lowercase letters in the alphanumeric argument.

>?UPPER("James Smith")
>JAMES SMITH
>IF UPPER(ANSWER)="Y"
>
>. . .
>ENDIF

# VAL( )

Converts an alphanumeric string to a numeric value, based on the value of SET DECIMALS TO.

>?VAL("34.567")
>34.57
>?VAL("34.567")*1000
>34567

# VERSION( )

PLUS

Returns the version number of the dBASE III PLUS program.

>?VERSION()
>dBASE III PLUS version 1.0

# YEAR( )

Returns the numeric code of the year from a date memory variable supplied as an argument. Assuming that the system date is 06/01/85, the function returns results as follows:

>?YEAR(DATE())
>1985

# F
## Structure of the Assistant Menu

The chart on the following page shows the options of the main Assistant menu. The submenus for main-menu options (**Setup** and **Create**, for example) are shown on remaining pages.

The charts in this appendix have been condensed to conserve space and enhance readability. Whenever several options lead to the same set of suboptions, the suboptions are printed only once. On the **Update** submenu, for example, the **Replace**, **Delete**, and **Recall** options all lead to the suboptions **Execute the command**, **Specify scope**, etc. The converging lines under **Replace**, **Delete**, and **Recall** indicate that those options lead to the same suboptions.

PLUS

# The Main Assistant Menu

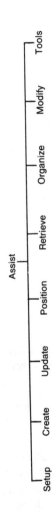

# The Setup Menu

PLUS

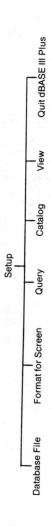

PLUS

# The Create Menu

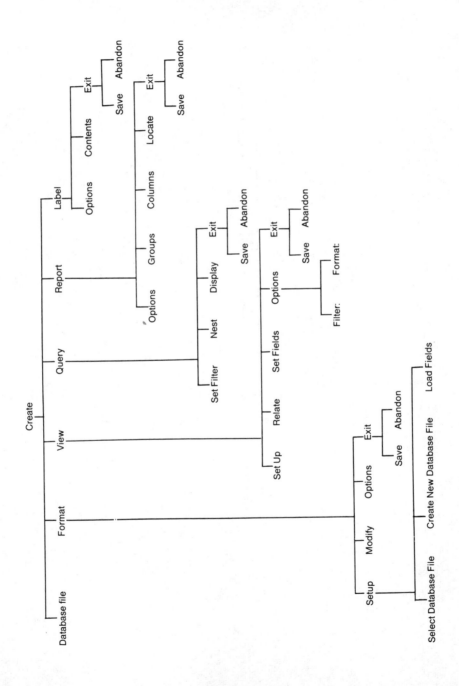

# The Update Menu

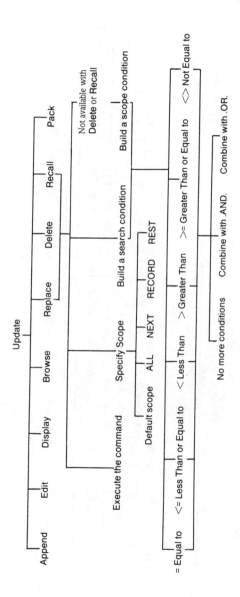

PLUS

# The Position Menu

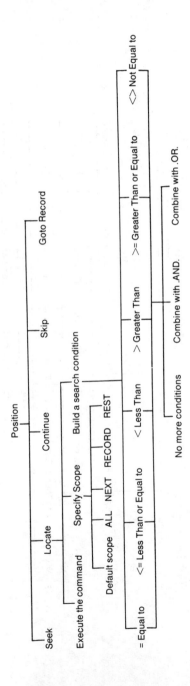

# The Retrieve Menu

PLUS

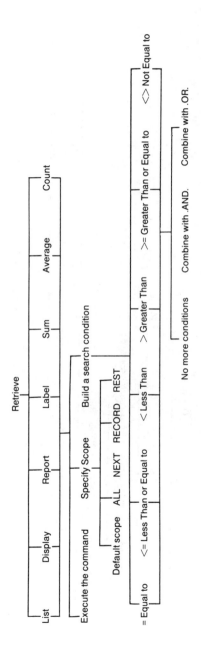

PLUS

# The Organize Menu

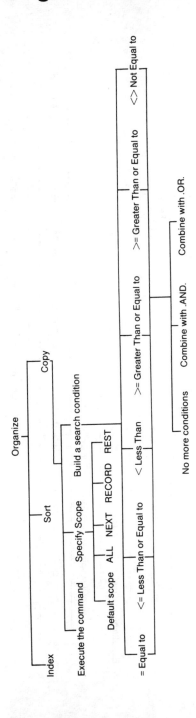

# The Modify Menu

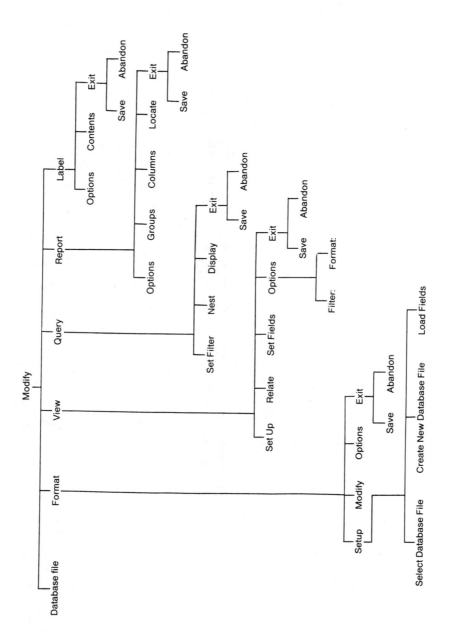

PLUS

# The Tools Menu

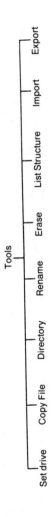

# Index

# More Computer Knowledge from Que

FOLD HERE

Place
Stamp
Here

Que Corporation
P.O. Box 90
Carmel, IN 46032

# REGISTRATION CARD

Register your copy of *dBASE III Plus Handbook*, 2nd Edition, and receive information about Que's newest products. Complete this registration card and return it to Que Corporation, P.O. Box 90, Carmel, IN 46032.

Name _____ Phone _____

Company _____ Title _____

Address _____

City _____ St _____ ZIP _____

*Please check the appropriate answers:*

Where did you buy *dBASE III Plus Handbook*, 2nd Edition?
- ☐ Bookstore (name: _____)
- ☐ Computer store (name: _____)
- ☐ Catalog (name: _____)
- ☐ Direct from Que
- ☐ Other: _____

How many computer books do you buy a year?
- ☐ 1 or less
- ☐ 2-5
- ☐ 6-10
- ☐ More than 10

How many Que books do you own?
- ☐ 1
- ☐ 2-5
- ☐ 6-10
- ☐ More than 10

How long have you been using dBASE software?
- ☐ Less than 6 months
- ☐ 6 months to 1 year
- ☐ 1 to 3 years
- ☐ Over 3 years

What influenced your purchase of *dBASE III Plus Handbook*, 2nd Edition?
- ☐ Personal recommendation
- ☐ Advertisement
- ☐ In-store display
- ☐ Price
- ☐ Que catalog
- ☐ Que postcard
- ☐ Que's reputation
- ☐ Other: _____

How would you rate the overall content of *dBASE III Plus Handbook*, 2nd Edition?
- ☐ Very good
- ☐ Good
- ☐ Not useful
- ☐ Poor

How would you rate *Chapter 13: An Integrated Database System*?
- ☐ Very good
- ☐ Good
- ☐ Satisfactory
- ☐ Poor

How would you rate *Chapter 9: Fundamentals of Command-File Programming*?
- ☐ Very good
- ☐ Good
- ☐ Satisfactory
- ☐ Poor

How would you rate *Appendix D: Summary of dBASE III Plus Commands*?
- ☐ Very good
- ☐ Good
- ☐ Satisfactory
- ☐ Poor

What do you like *best* about *dBASE III Plus Handbook*, 2nd Edition?

What do you like *least* about *dBASE III Plus Handbook*, 2nd Edition?

How do you use *dBASE III Plus Handbook*, 2nd Edition?

What other Que products do you own?

For what other programs would a Que book be helpful?

Please feel free to list any other comments you may have about *dBASE III Plus*, 2nd Edition.

_____

_____

_____

_____

_____

FOLD HERE

---

_____

_____

_____

_____

Que Corporation
P.O. Box 90
Carmel, IN 46032

# If you use 1-2-3 or Symphony more than two hours a day, please accept a FREE evaluation copy of *Absolute Reference.*

## Introducing the only journal for serious spreadsheet users. It's *guaranteed* to save you time and dramatically increase your capability.

**M**ost spreadsheet users tap only a fraction of the tremendous power lying dormant within 1-2-3 and Symphony. Unfortunately, the user's guidebooks—even Que's own—can only scratch the surface.

That's why if you work regularly with 1-2-3 or Symphony, you owe it to yourself to examine *Absolute Reference.*

### Save more than one week's time in the coming year.

**F**irst of all, *Absolute Reference* will save you time . . . and time is money. In fact, we guarantee that the techniques you gain in your monthly issues *will save you at least an hour a week* over the next year—that's 52 hours! Multiply 52 hours by a minimum of $25 per hour for your time—and you've increased your productivity *by $1,300.*

But that's the least of what *Absolute Reference* will do for you.

### How *Absolute Reference* helps you become a spreadsheet master.

**E**very month, with a passion for practicality, *Absolute Reference* articles tell you how to increase your capability with 1-2-3 and Symphony. Neat new macros, new applications, shortcuts, more professional printouts, more logical layout, avoiding pitfalls, outspoken product reviews, and reader tips—you'll get concise reports like these in every monthly issue. (See next page for sample articles.)

### Our 100% Moneyback Guarantee makes this offer risk free.

**U**se the subscription form below, but SEND NO MONEY. Examine your first issue with no obligation. If for any reason you are not satisfied, simply write cancel on your invoice. Even after you've paid, if you're not delighted with *Absolute Reference,* we'll refund your entire subscription fee.

---

# YES! Please send my FREE SAMPLE ISSUE with no obligation.

Please start my one-year, no-risk subscription and send my FREE SAMPLE ISSUE immediately. I'll receive 12 additional monthly issues at your discounted subscription rate of $59—a $25 savings off the normal $84 price. (Subscriptions payable in U.S. funds. Foreign orders add $20.) I NEED *NOT* SEND ANY MONEY NOW, and if I am *not satisfied* after evaluating my first issue for 30 days, I may write "CANCEL" on my invoice and owe nothing. I have signed below.

**Signature Required**_____

**Name**_____

**Title**_____

**Company**_____ **Phone (___)** _____

**Address**_____

**City, State, Zip**_____

**Country**_____

 **For even faster service, call toll free: 1-800-227-7999, ext. 552. (In Indiana: 1-317-573-2540)**

## ABSOLUTE REFERENCE
### THE JOURNAL FOR 1-2-3 AND SYMPHONY USERS

Que Corporation
11711 N. College Avenue
Carmel, Indiana 46032

# Here's a tiny sample of the kinds of articles you'll read in every issue of *Absolute Reference*:

**Discover the incredible power of macros— shortcuts for hundreds of applications and subroutines.**
- A macro for formatting text
- Monitoring preset database conditions with a macro
- Three ways to design macro menus
- Building macros with string formulas
- Having fun with the marching macro
- Using the ROWs macro
- Generating a macro for tracking elapsed time

**New applications and new solutions—every issue gives you novel ways to harness 1-2-3 and Symphony.**
- Creating customized menus for your spreadsheets
- How to use criteria to unlock your spreadsheet program's data management power
- Using spreadsheets to monitor investments
- Improving profits with more effective sales forecasts
- An easy way to calculate year-to-date performance
- Using /Data Fill to streamline counting and range filling

**Extend your uses—and your command— of spreadsheets.**
- Printing spreadsheets sideways can help sell your ideas
- How to add goal-seeking capabilities to your spreadsheet

- Hiding columns to create custom worksheet printouts
- Lay out your spreadsheet for optimum memory management
- Toward an "intelligent" spreadsheet
- A quick way to erase extraneous zeros

**Techniques for avoiding pitfalls and repairing the damage when disaster occurs.**
- Preventing and trapping errors in your worksheet
- How to create an auditable spreadsheet
- Pinpointing specific errors in your spreadsheets
- Ways to avoid failing formulas
- Catching common debugging and data-entry errors
- Detecting data-entry errors
- Protecting worksheets from accidental (or deliberate) destruction
- Avoiding disaster with the /System command

**Objective product reviews—we accept *no advertising*, so you can trust our editors' outspoken opinions.**
- Metro Desktop Manager
- Freelance Plus
- Informix
- 4Word, InWord, Write-in
- Spreadsheet Analyst
- 101 macros for 1-2-3

**Mail this card today for your free evaluation copy or call 1-800-277-7999.**

---

## BUSINESS REPLY MAIL
FIRST CLASS PERMIT NO. 278   CARMEL, IN

Postage will be paid by the addressee

NO POSTAGE
NECESSARY
IF MAILED
IN THE
UNITED STATES

ABSOLUTE REFERENCE — THE JOURNAL FOR 1 2 3 AND SYMPHONY USERS

Que Corporation
11711 N. College Avenue
Carmel, Indiana 46032-9903